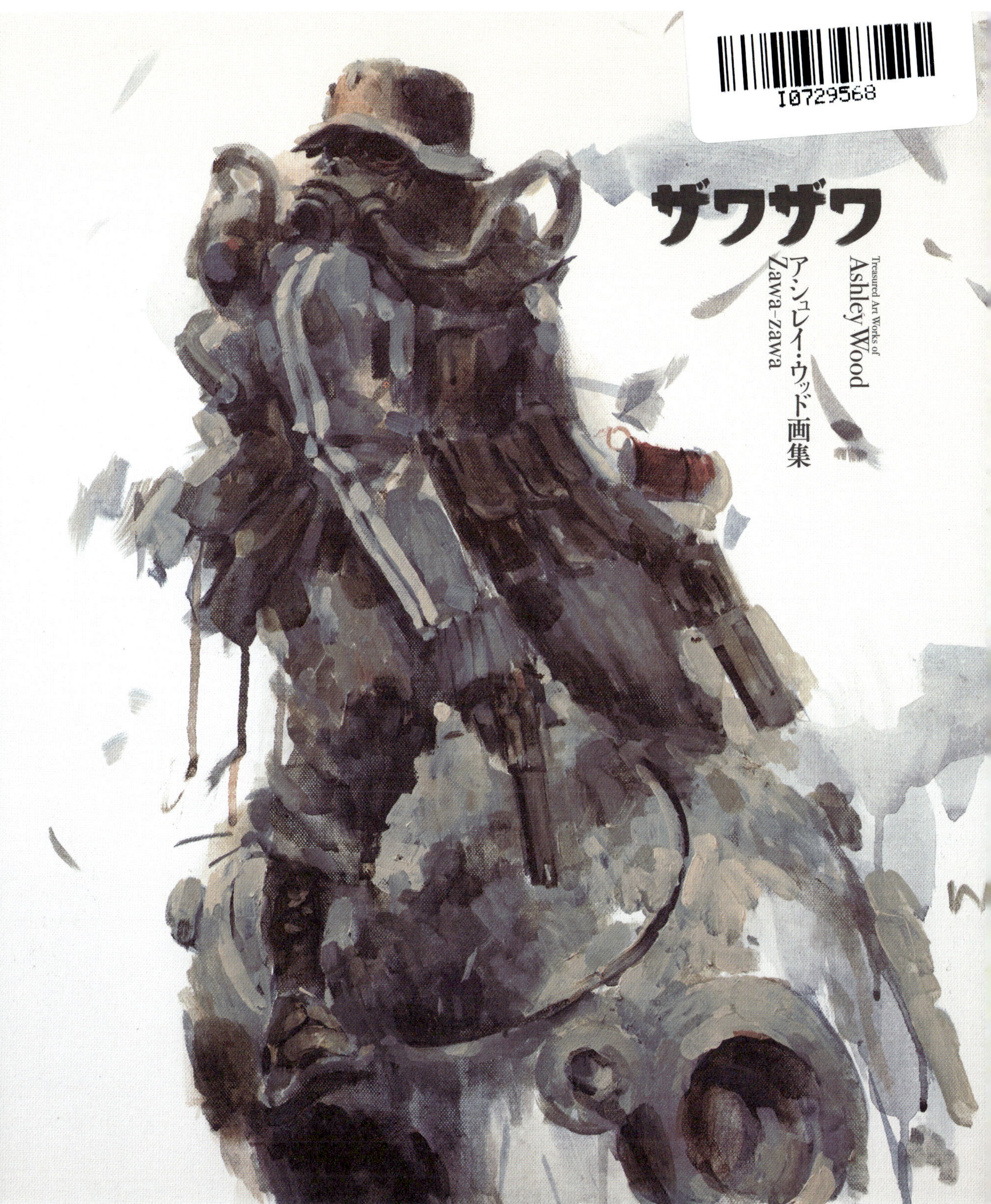

ザワザワ

Treasured Art Works of
Ashley Wood
アシュレイ・ウッド画集
Zawa-zawa

I have for many years enjoyed and been inspired by many Japanese artists, their history and work have defined and instructed the path of many artists outside of their home country, from the early influence of the woodcut prints to modern manga and anime. I'm no different, the visual culture of Japan has played a role in my artistic ideal from my first experience with Manga such as Mighty Atom by Osamu Tezuka to photographers such as Nobuyoshi Araki, inspiring and demanding to push harder and look deeper!

With this book, I feel a milestone has been reached, it's hard to explain, but it's special and it makes me feel closer to something I dearly love, the visual language of Japanese comics and art.

ZAWA-ZAWA

Ashley Wood

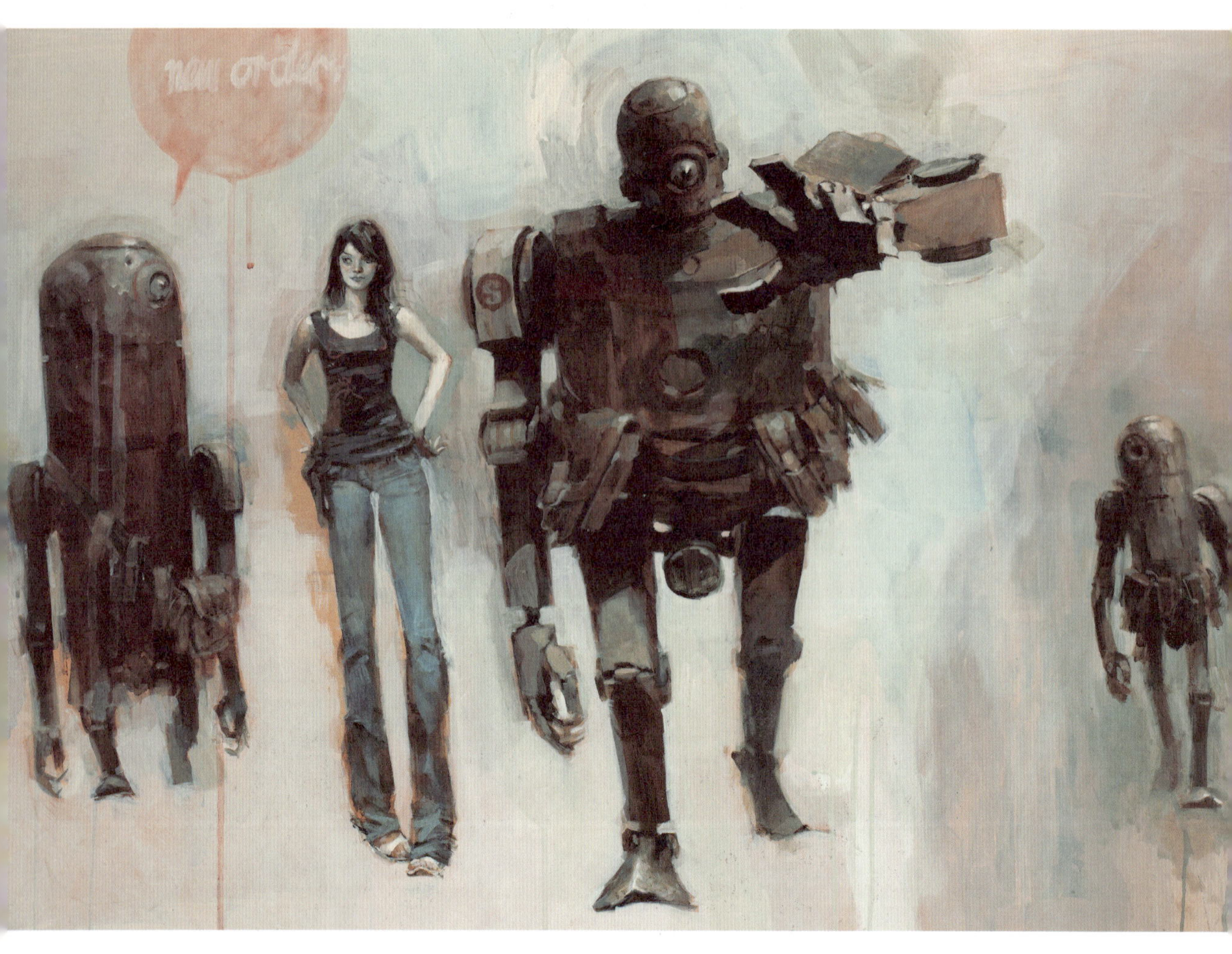

自分は昔から数多くの日本のアーティスト達の作品を楽しみ、そこからインスピレーションを得てきました。彼らの歴史と作品は国境を越え、古くは木版画から、そして現代のマンガやアニメに至るまで、世界中のアーティスト達に影響を与え、道を指し示してきました。それは自分にとっても例外ではありません。日本のビジュアル・カルチャーは、自分のアートの理想像を形成するのに重要な役割を果たしています。初めて読んだマンガである鉄腕アトムを描いた手塚治虫から、荒木経惟といった写真家まで、彼らにより常にインスパイアされ、そして更なる努力と追及が必要だということを思い知らされて来ました！

この本のリリースによって、ひとつのマイルストーンに到達できたと思っています。うまく説明できないのですが、これは自分にとってスペシャルなもので、自分が愛して止まないもの ——日本のコミックやアートと言ったビジュアル・ランゲージ—— に近づくことが出来たと感じています。

アシュレイ・ウッド　　ザワザワ

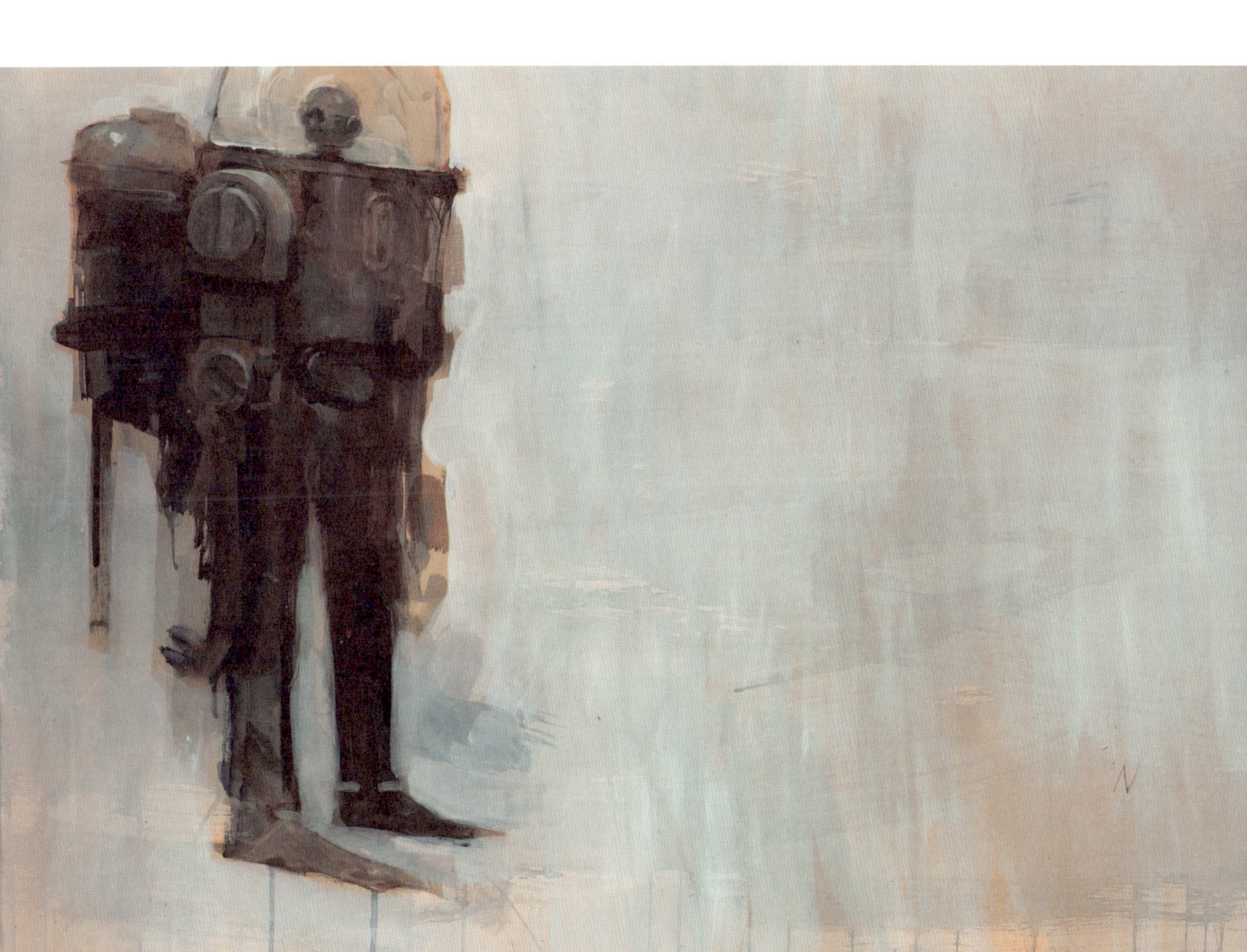

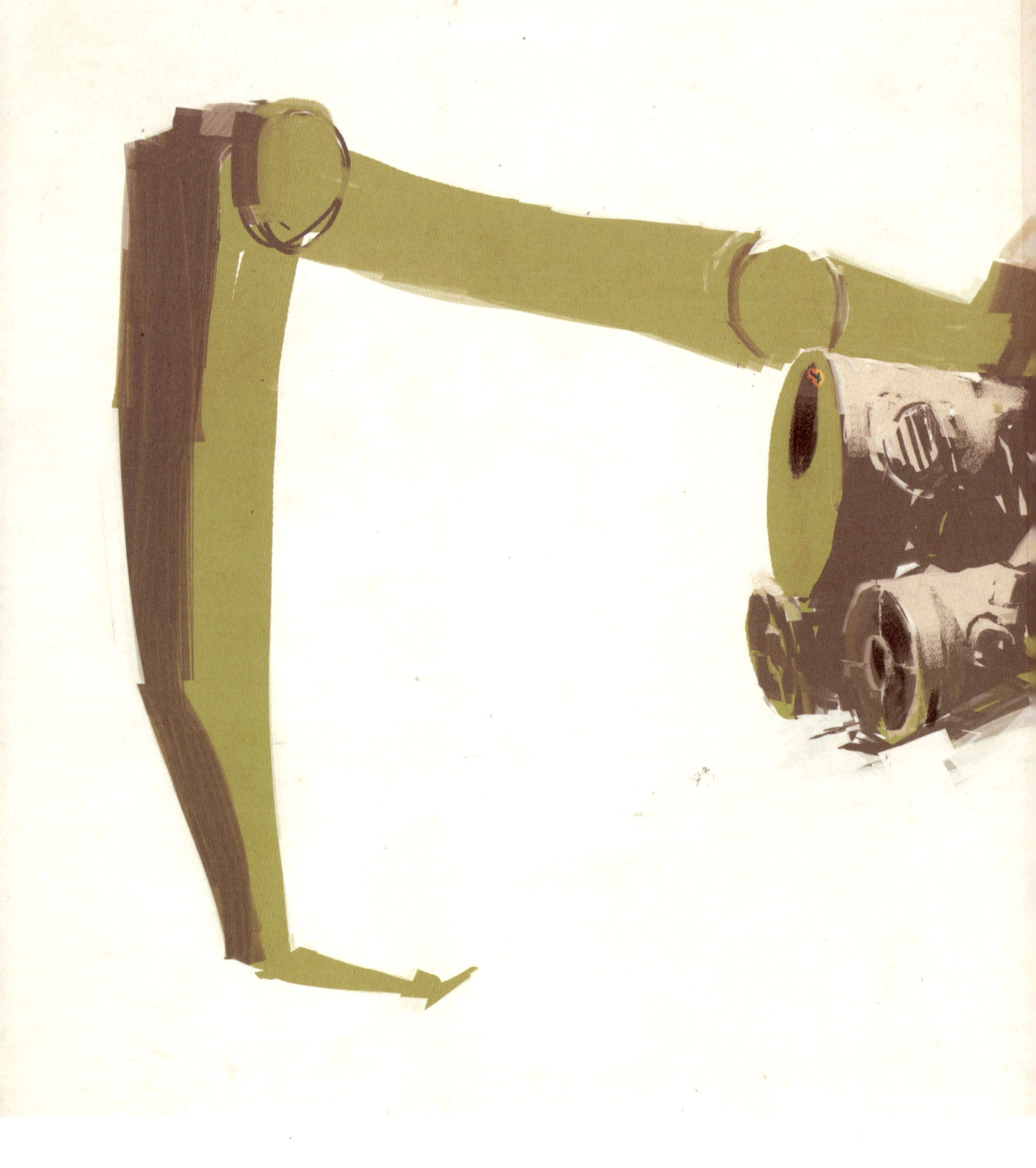

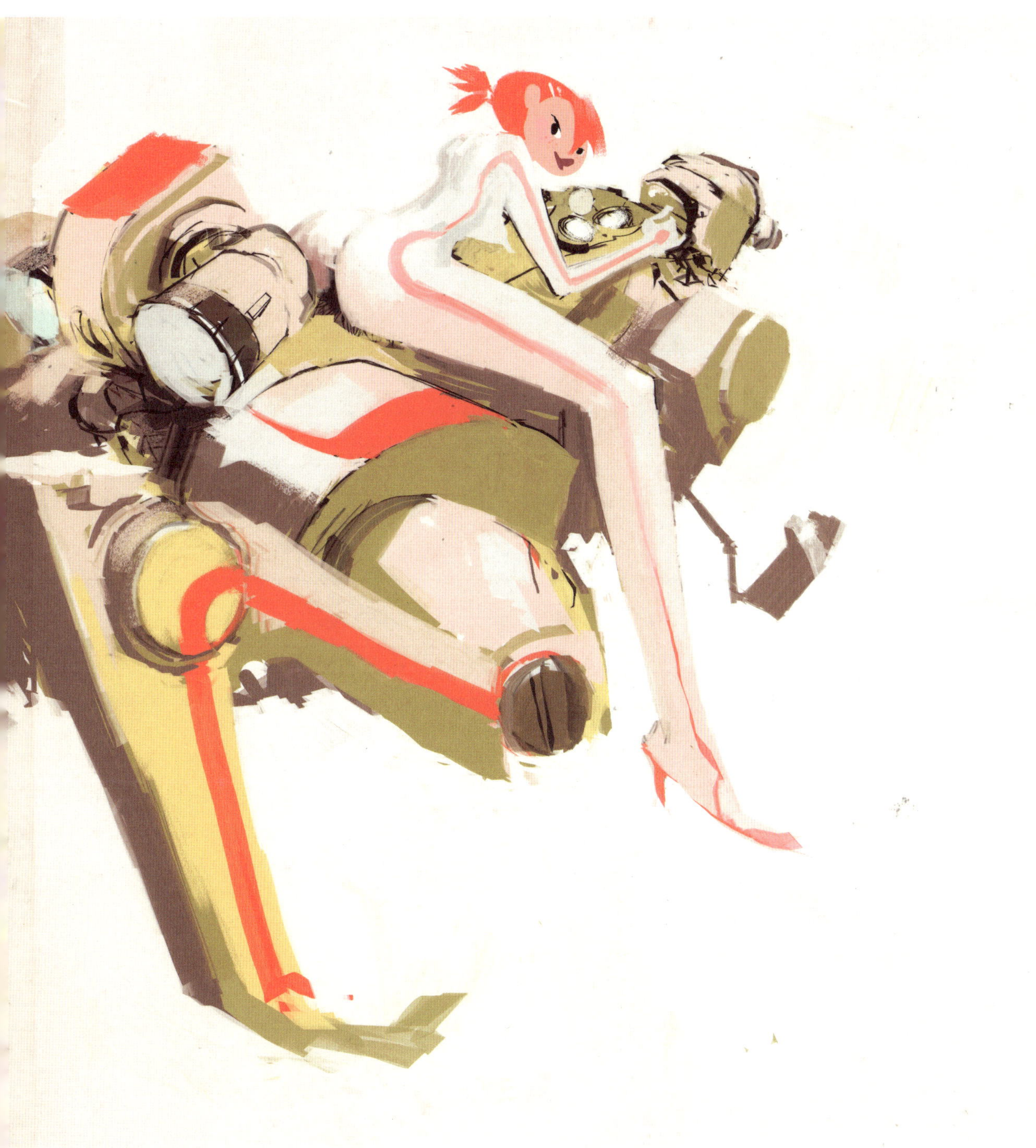

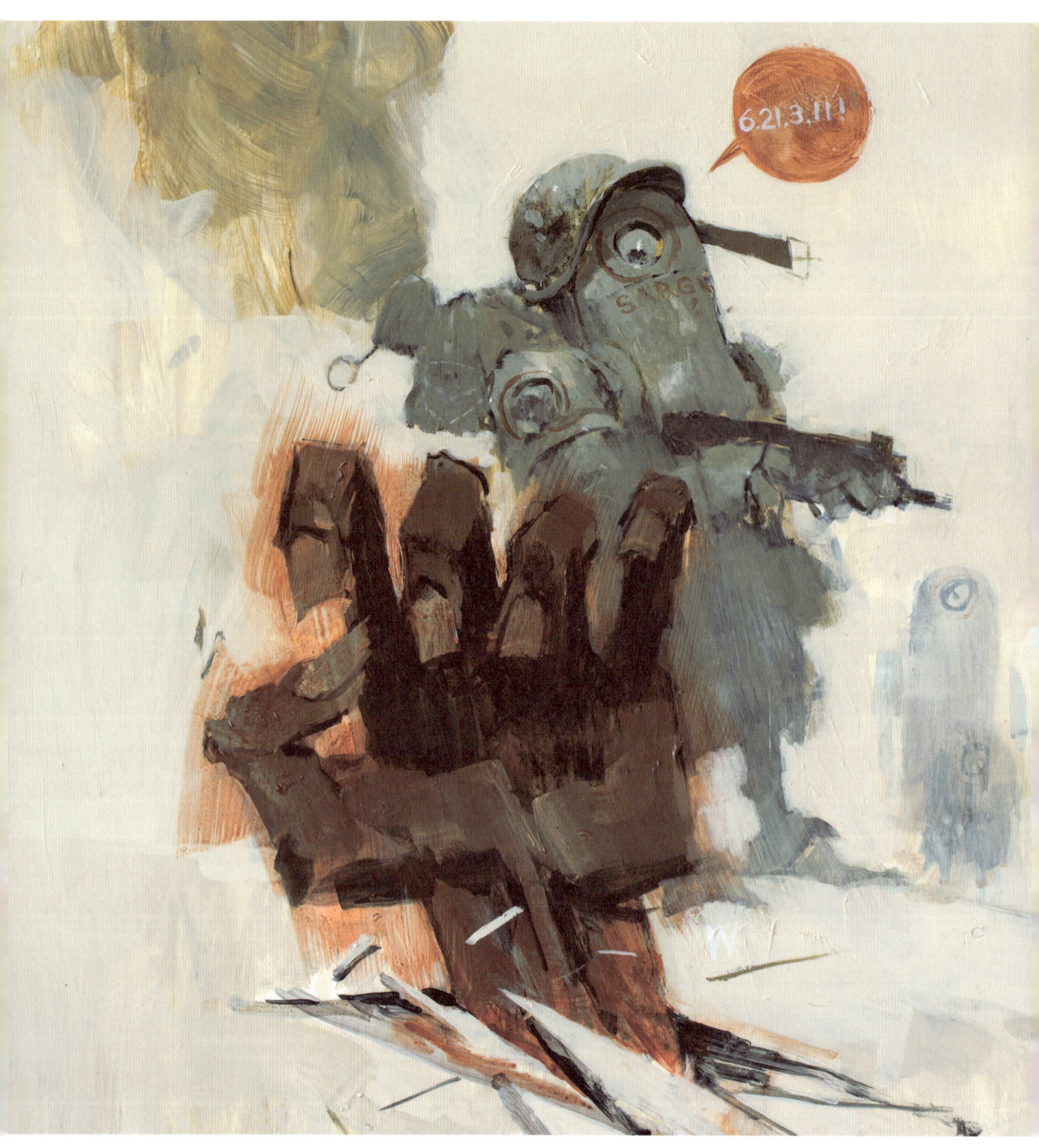

6.21.3.111

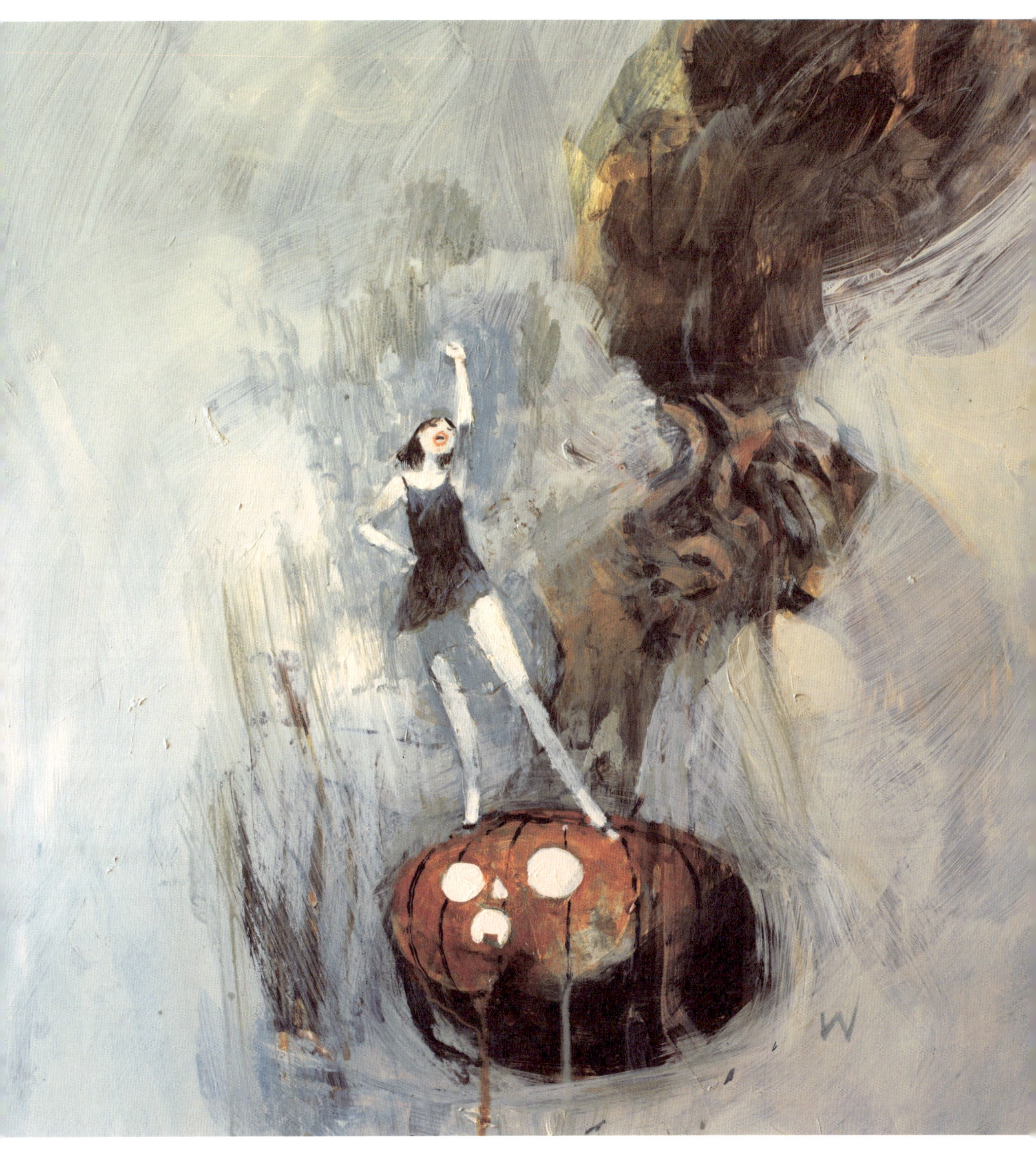

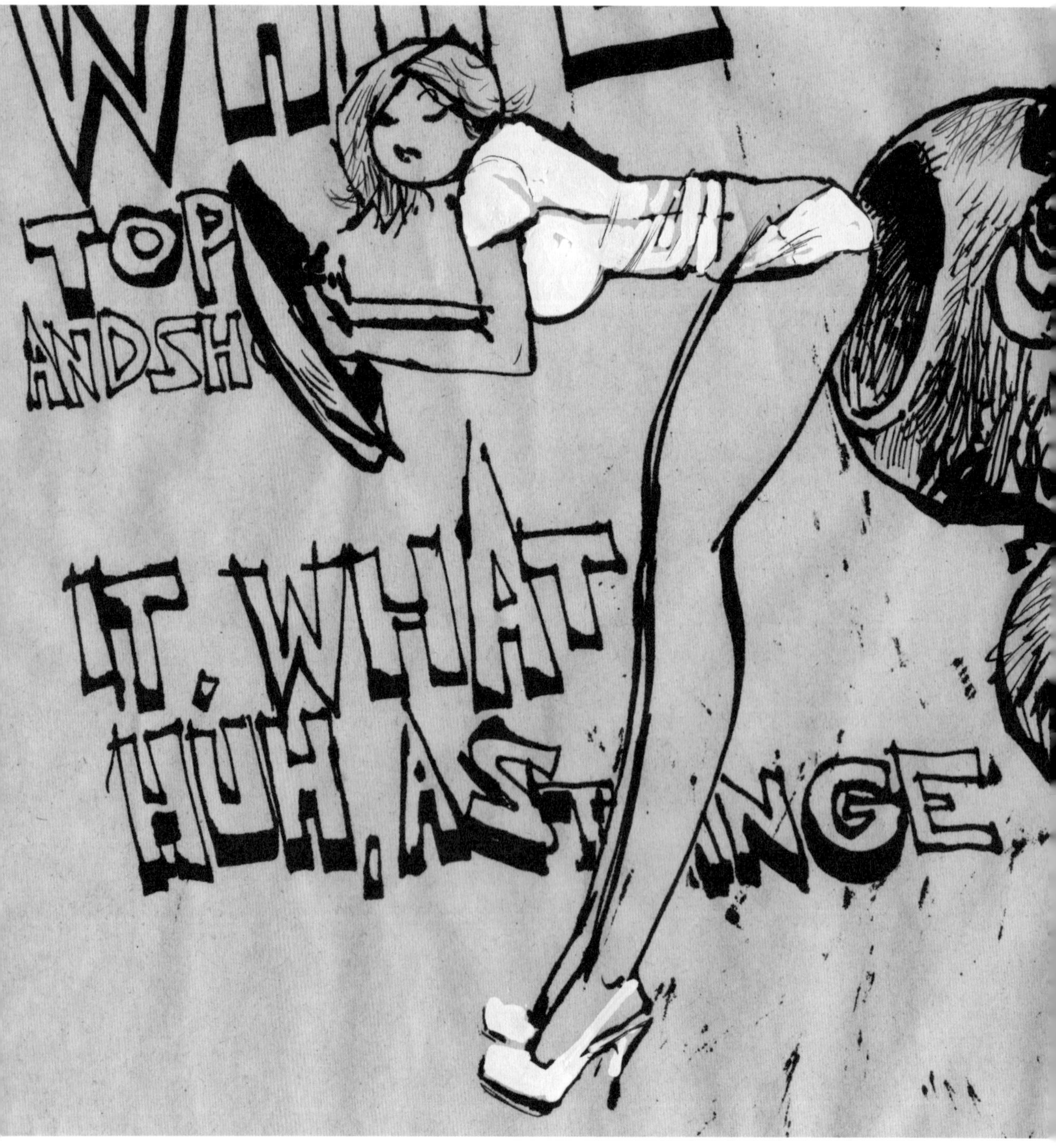
WHITE
TOP
ANDSH
T. WHAT
HUH, AS
NGE

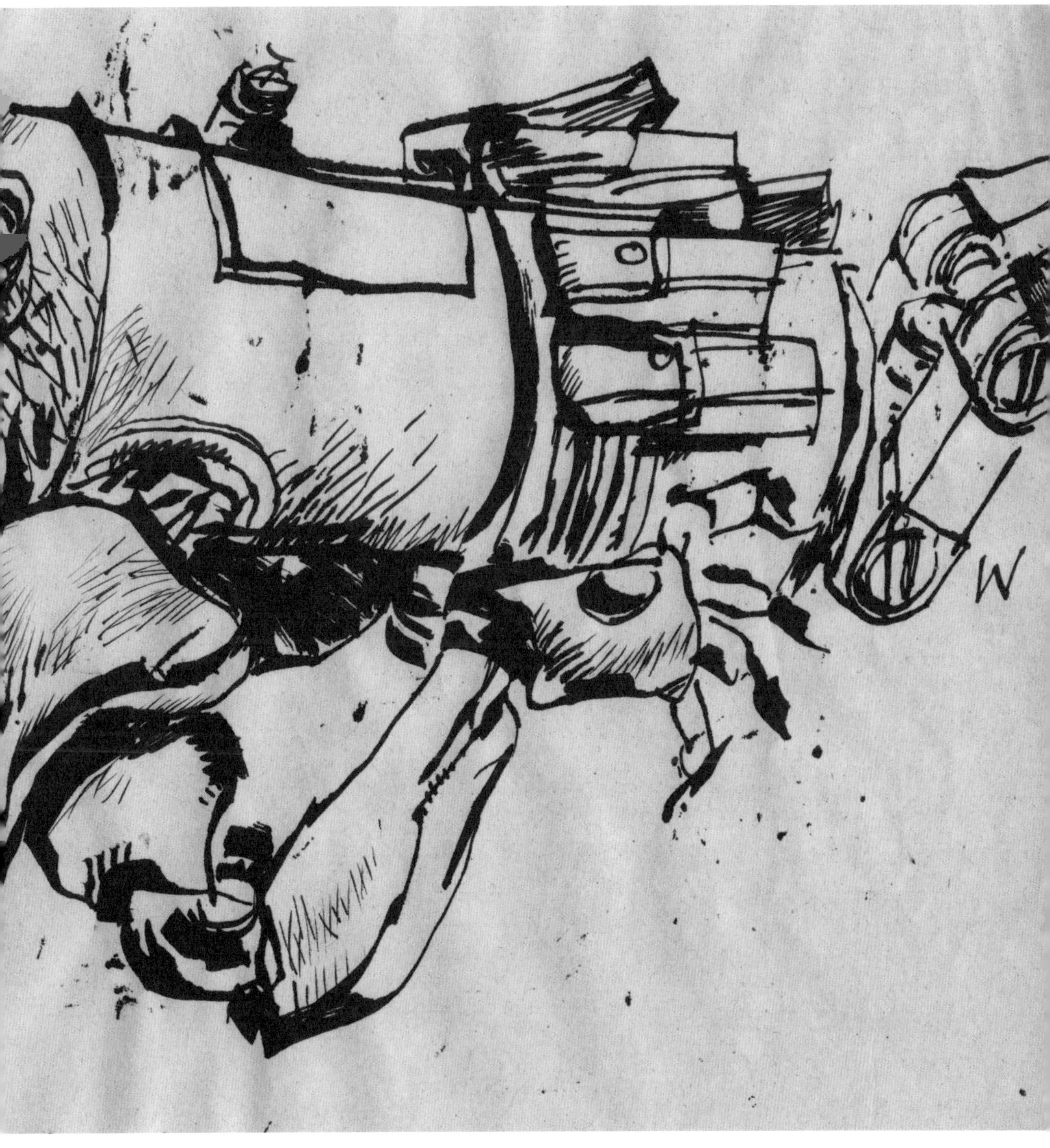

W

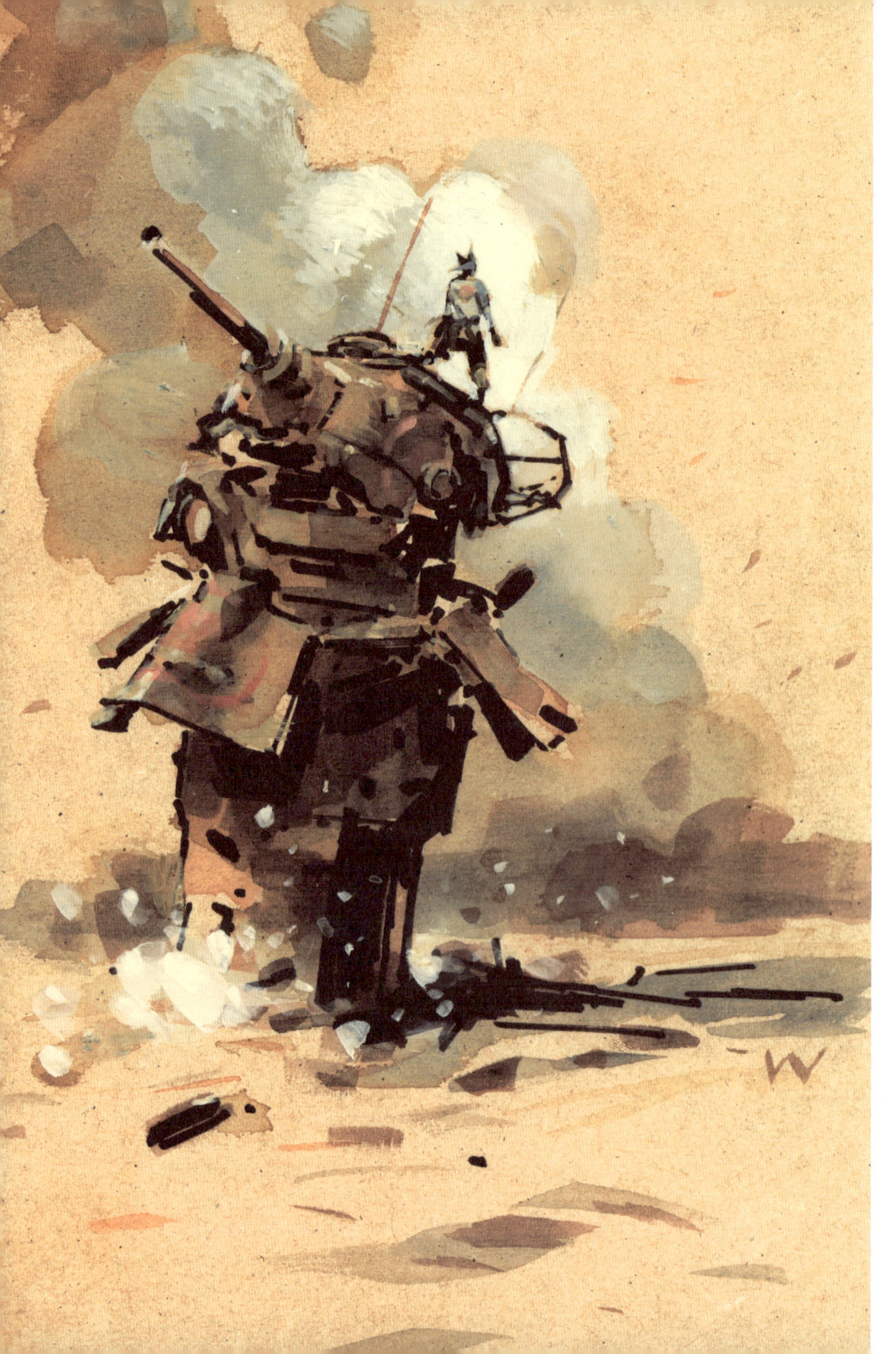

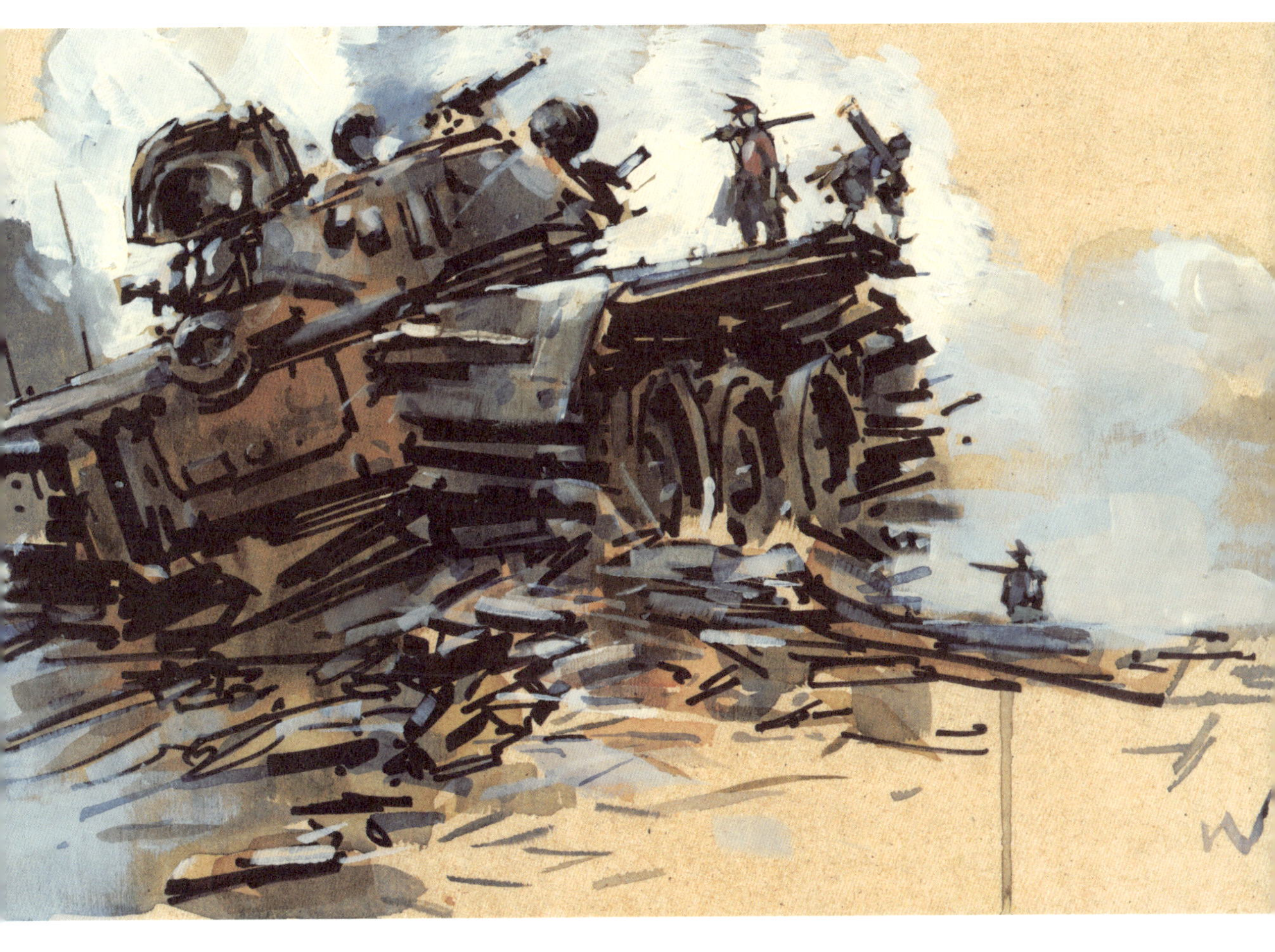

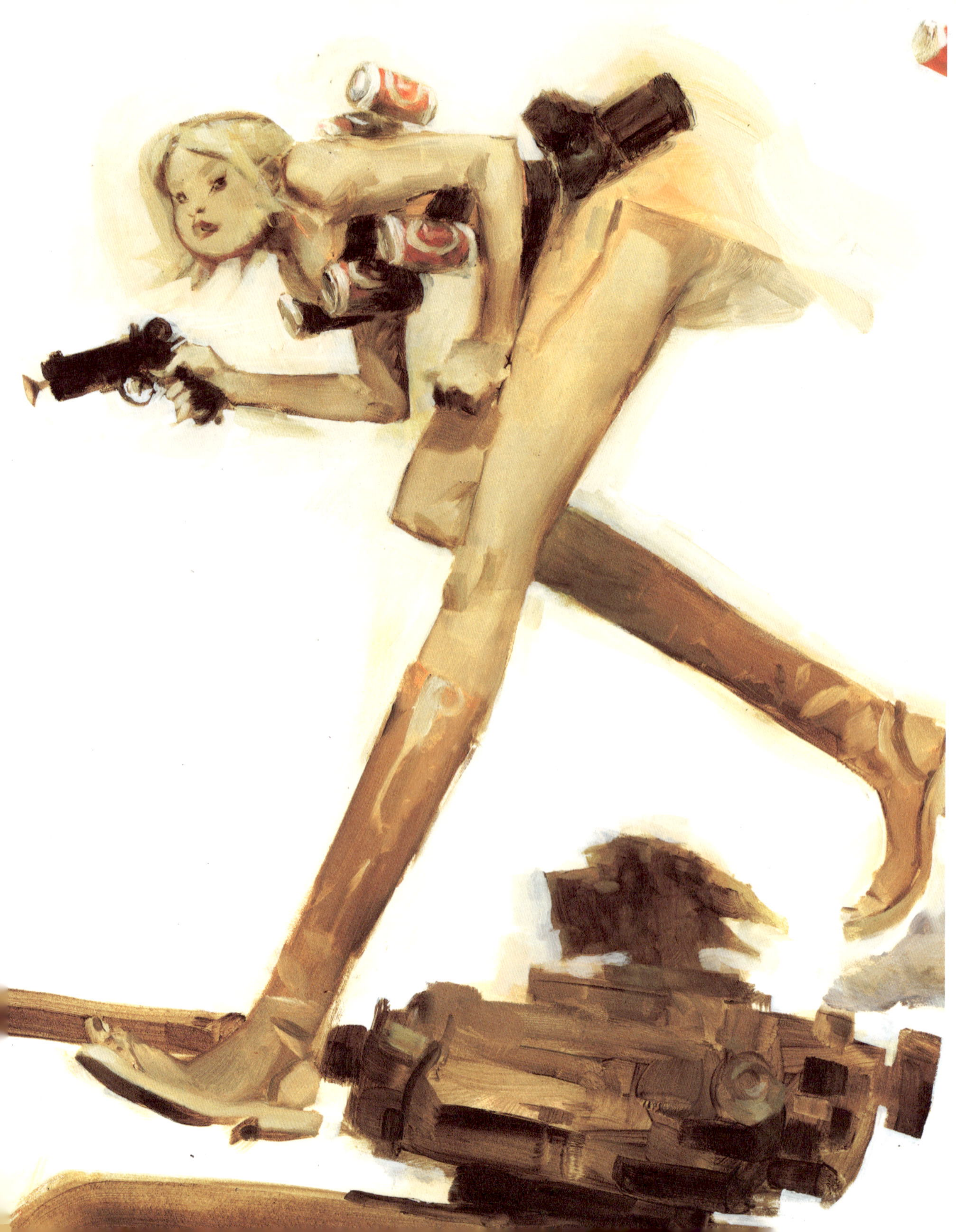

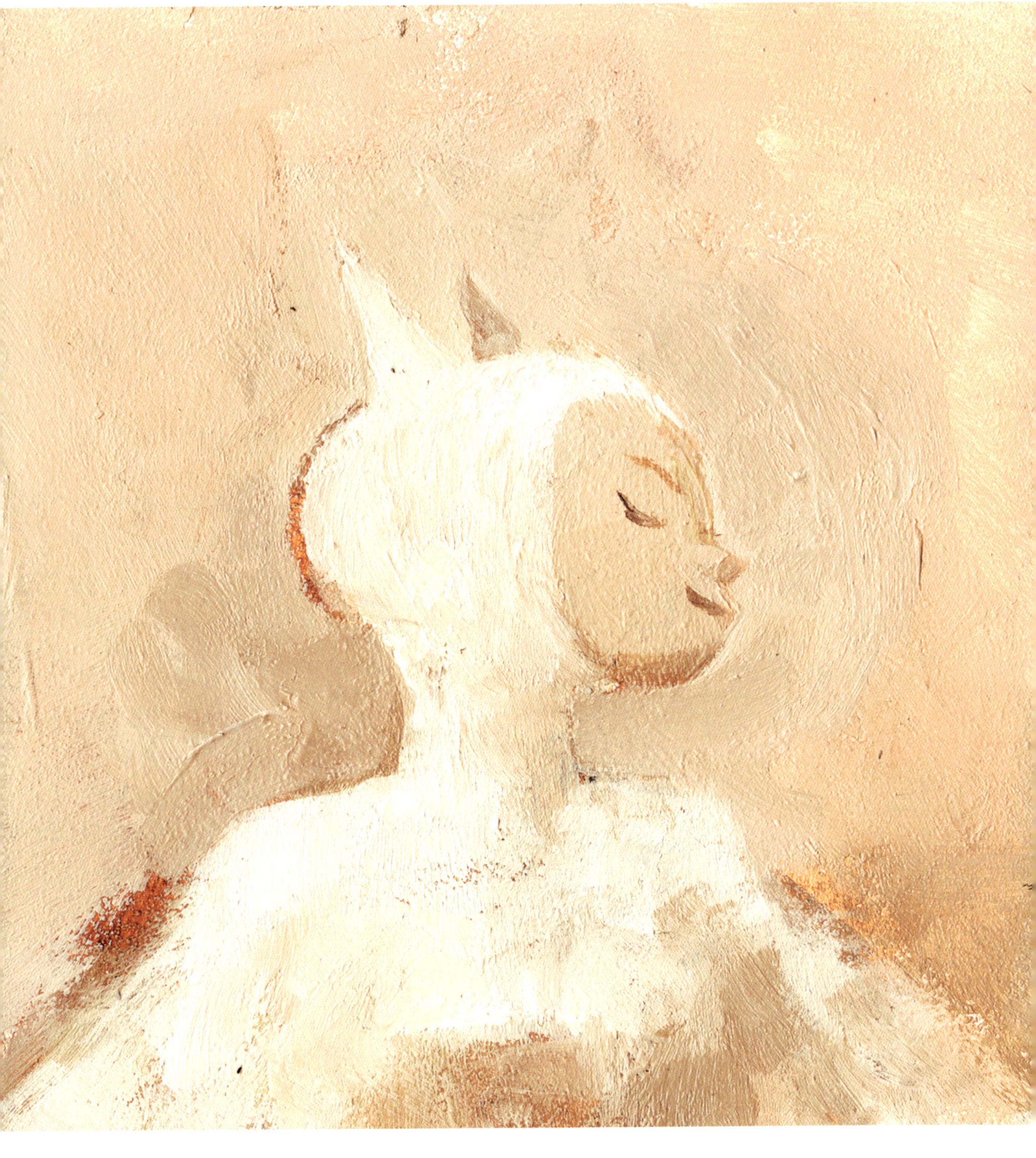

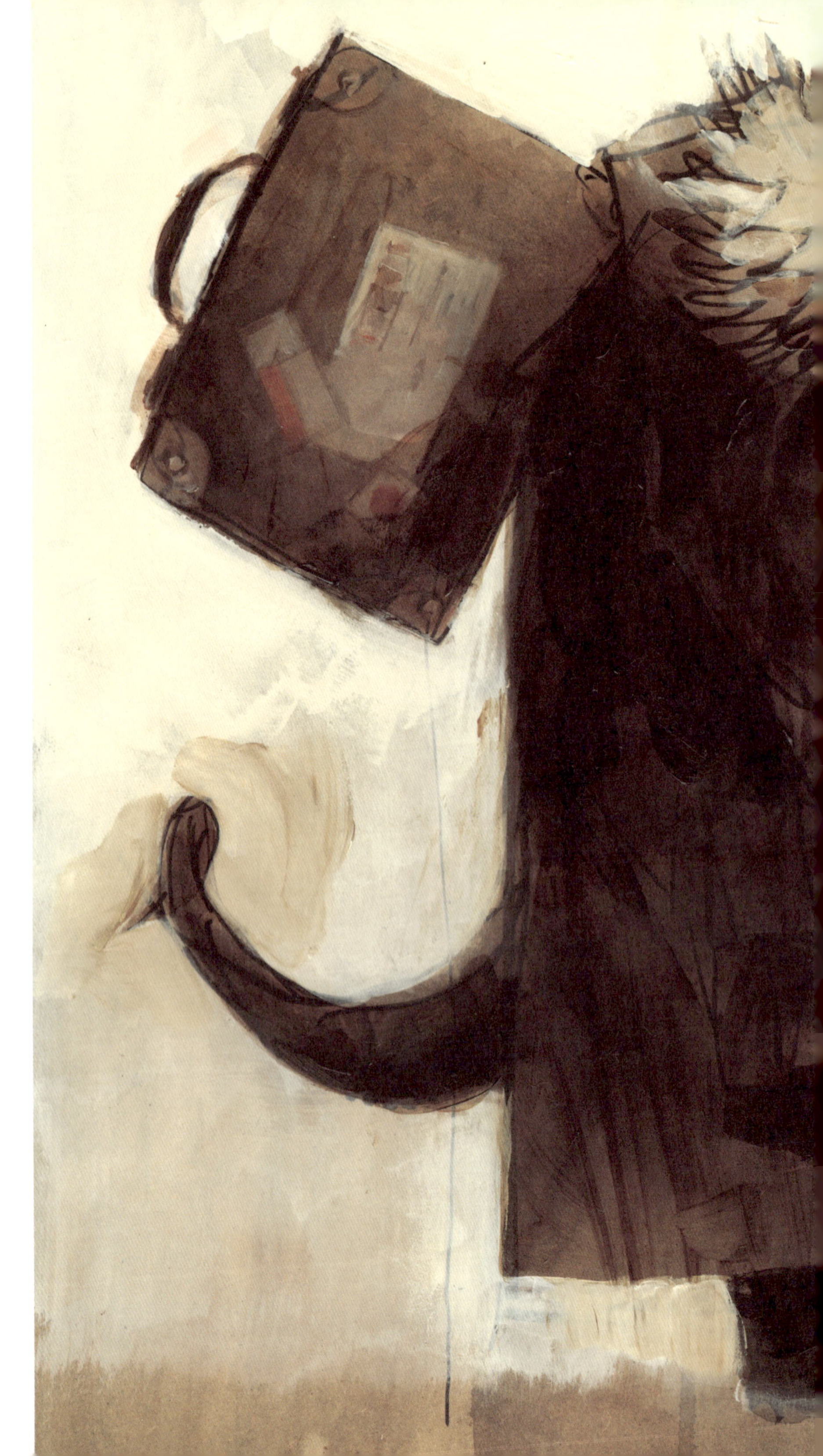

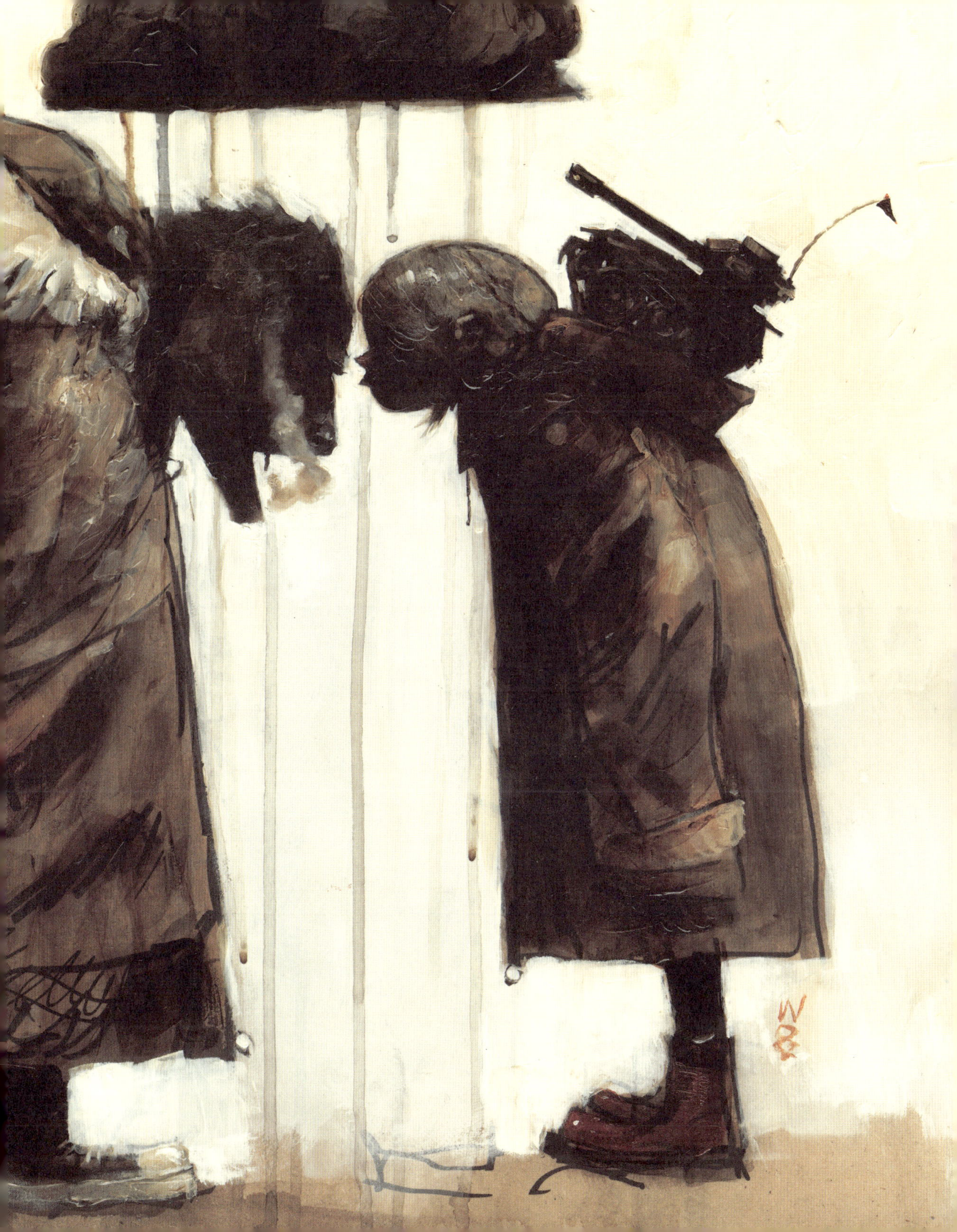

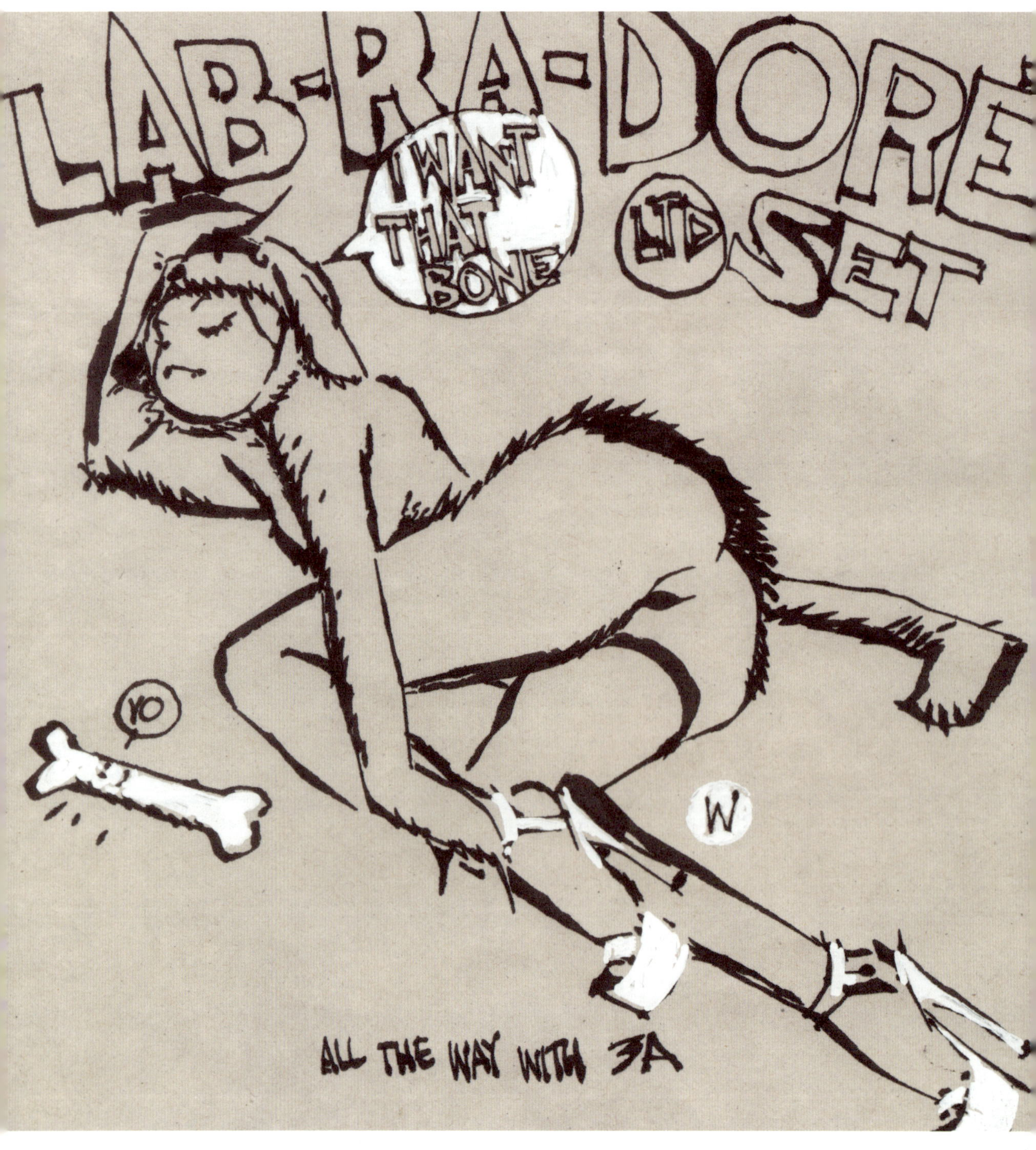

LAB-RA-DORE LTD SET
I WANT THAT BONE
ALL THE WAY WITH 3A

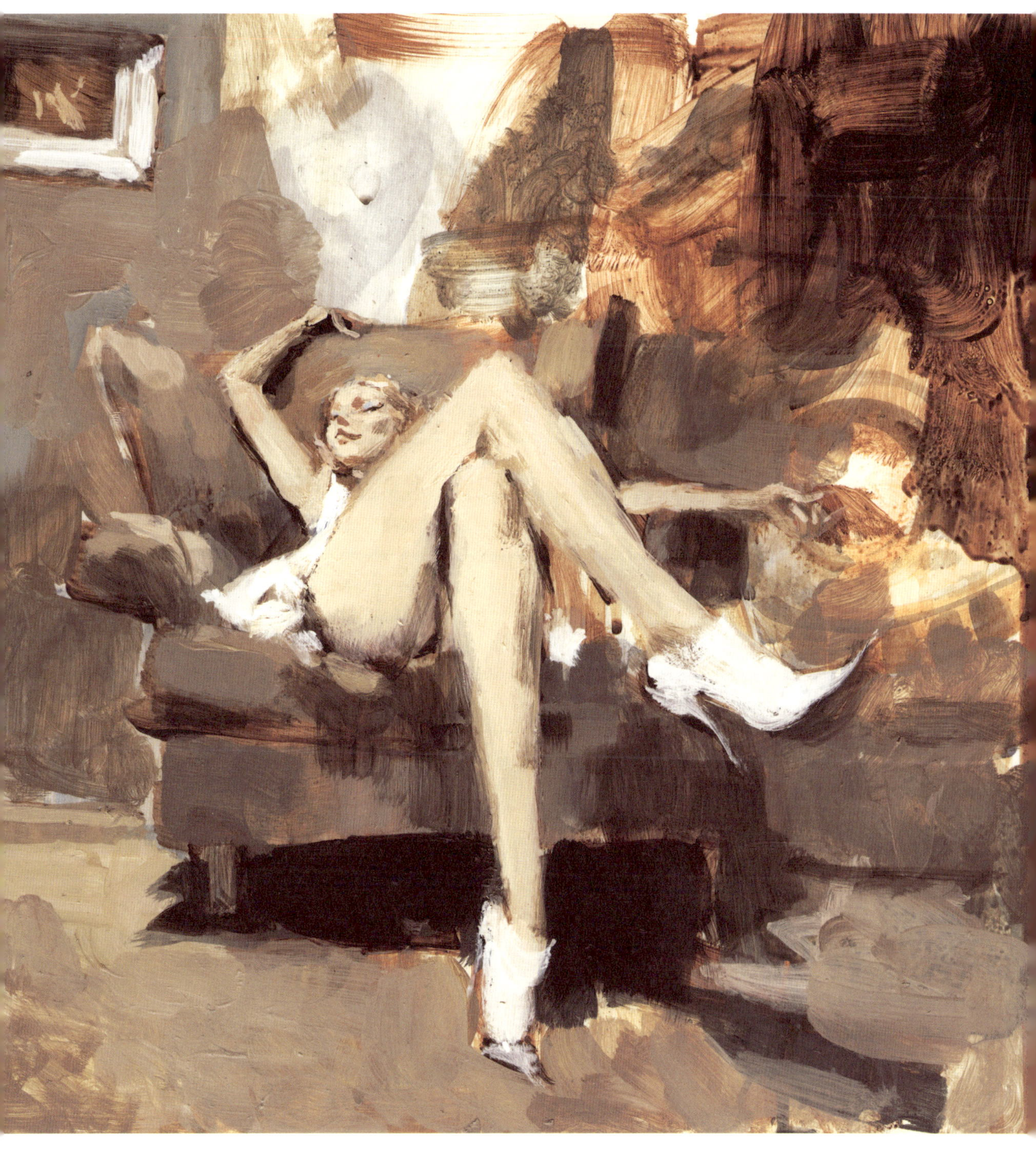

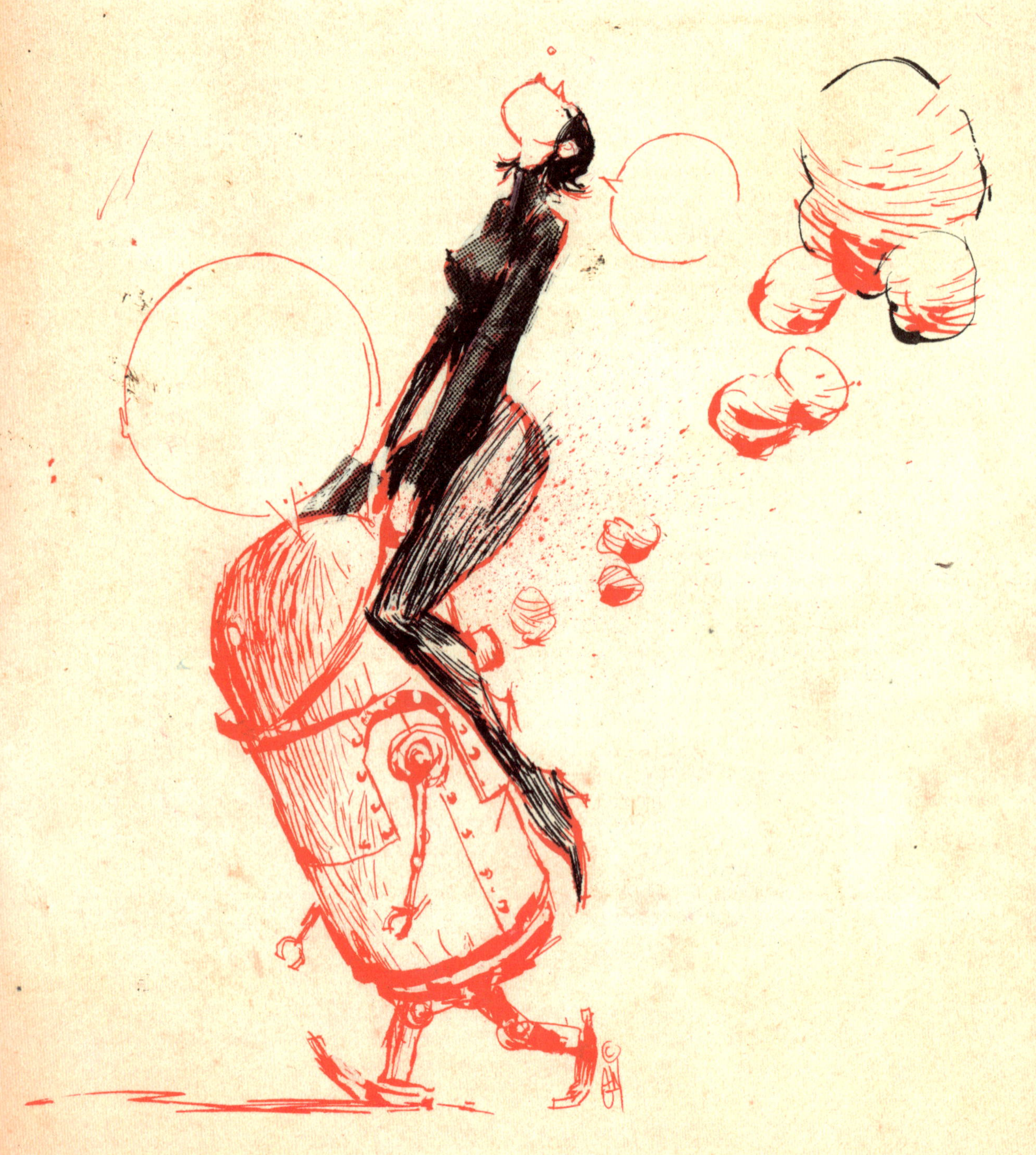

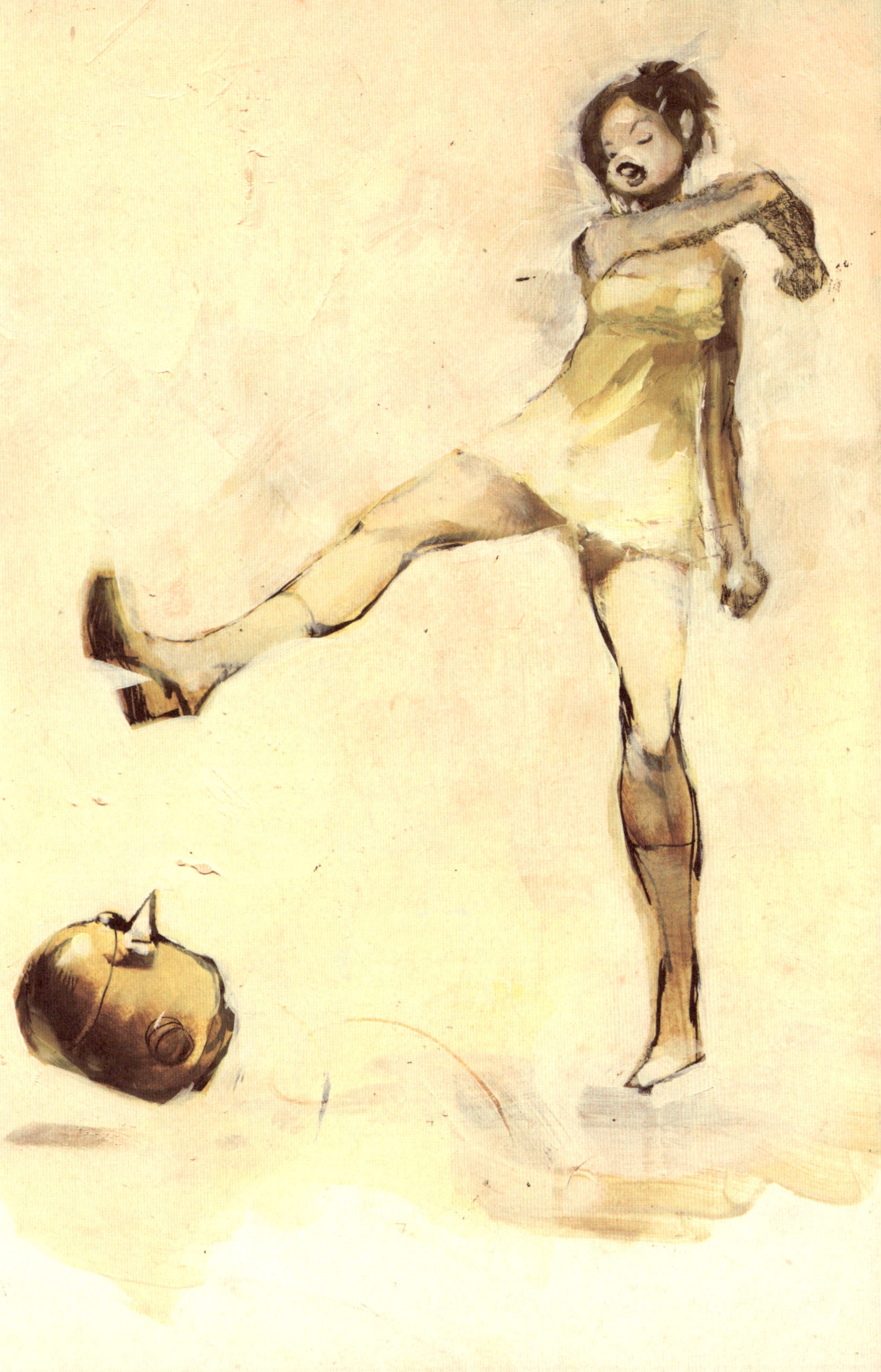

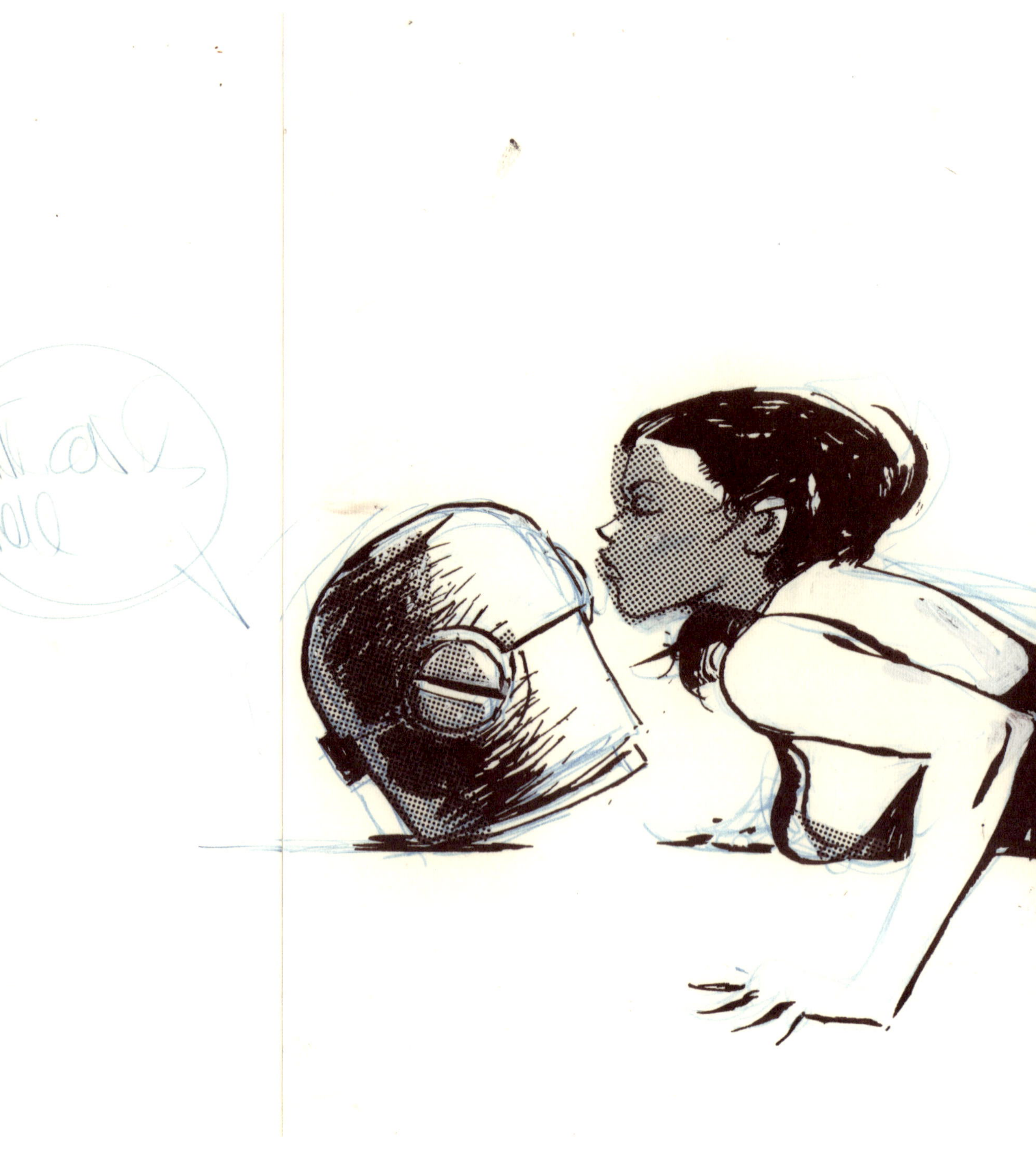

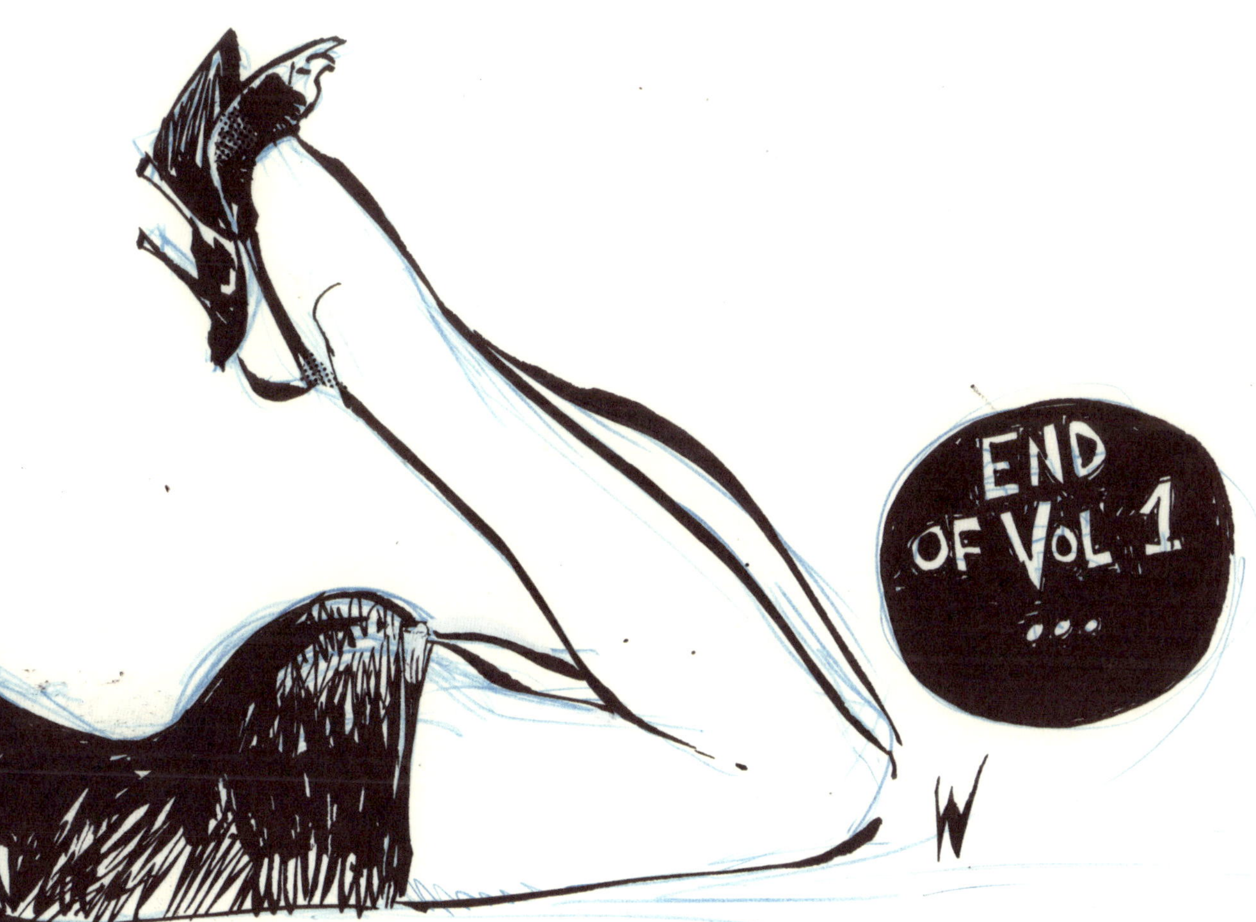
END
OF VOL 1
...

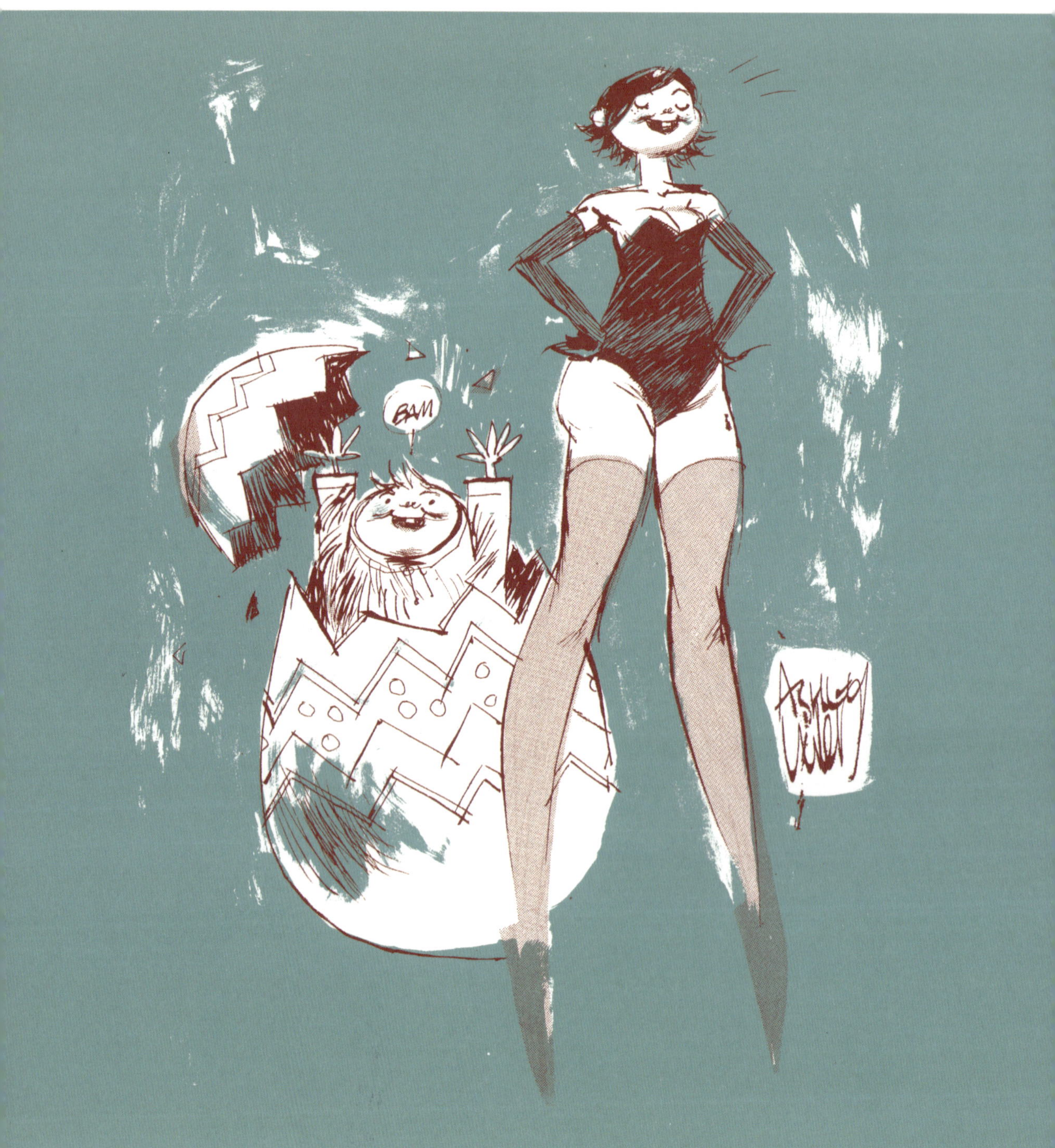
BAM

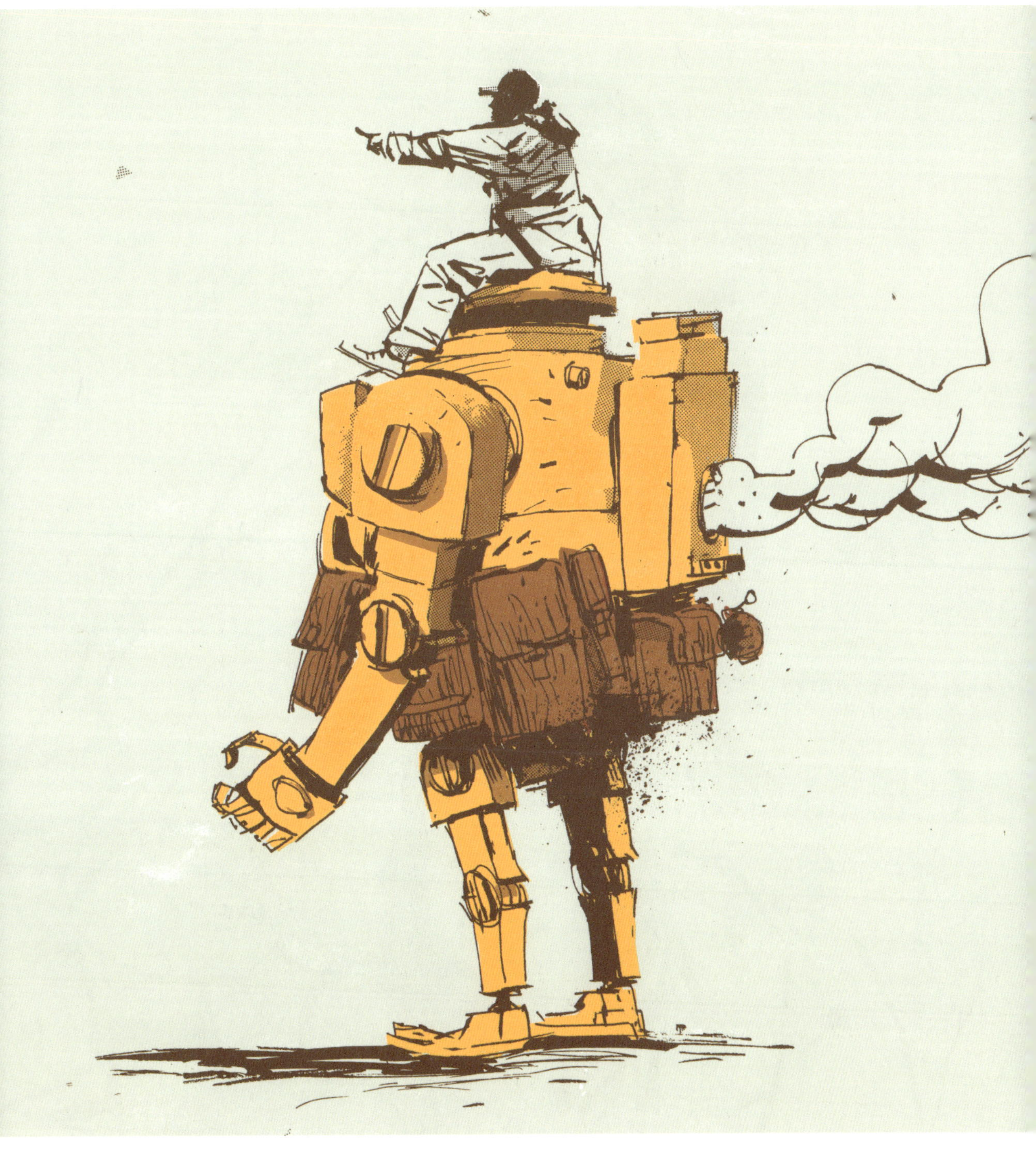

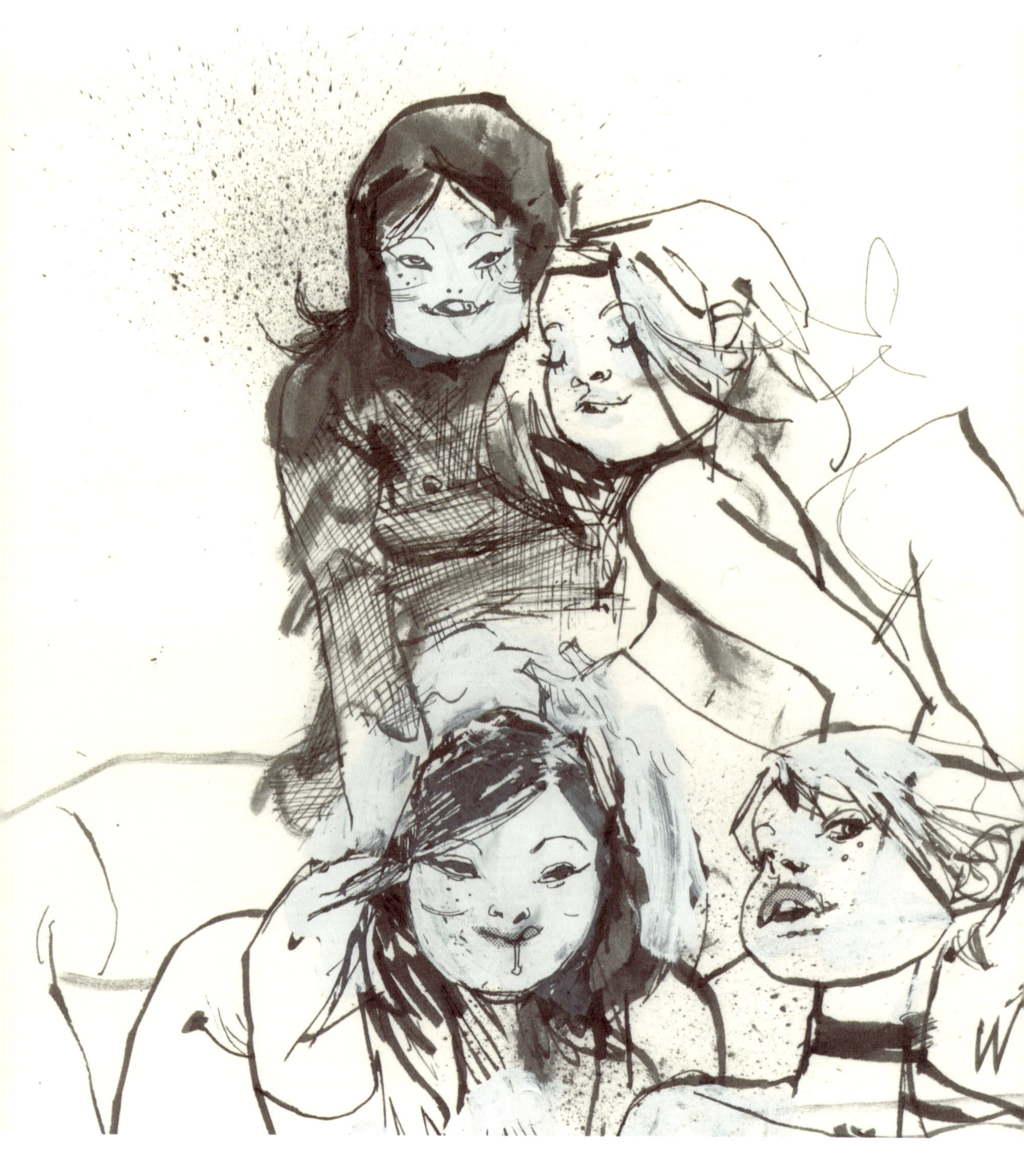

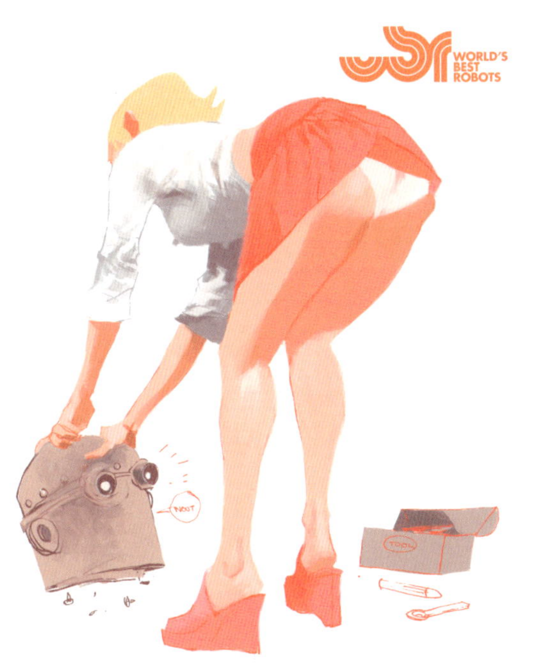

WORLD'S
BEST
ROBOTS
TOOT
TOOL

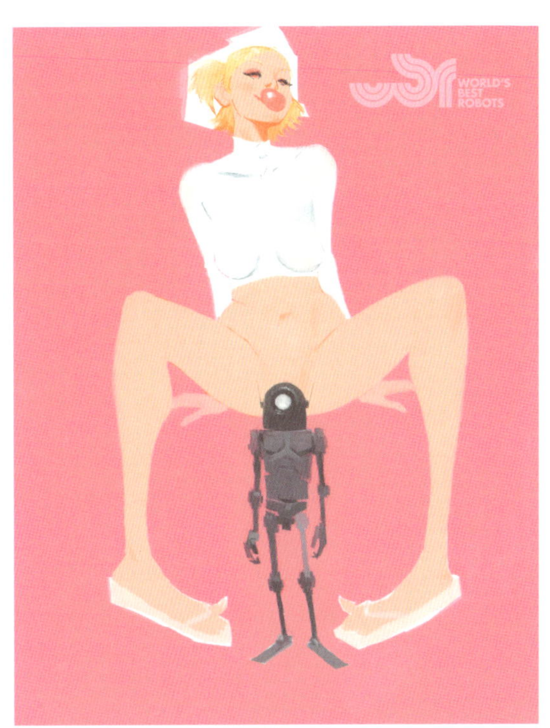

WORLD'S
BEST
ROBOTS

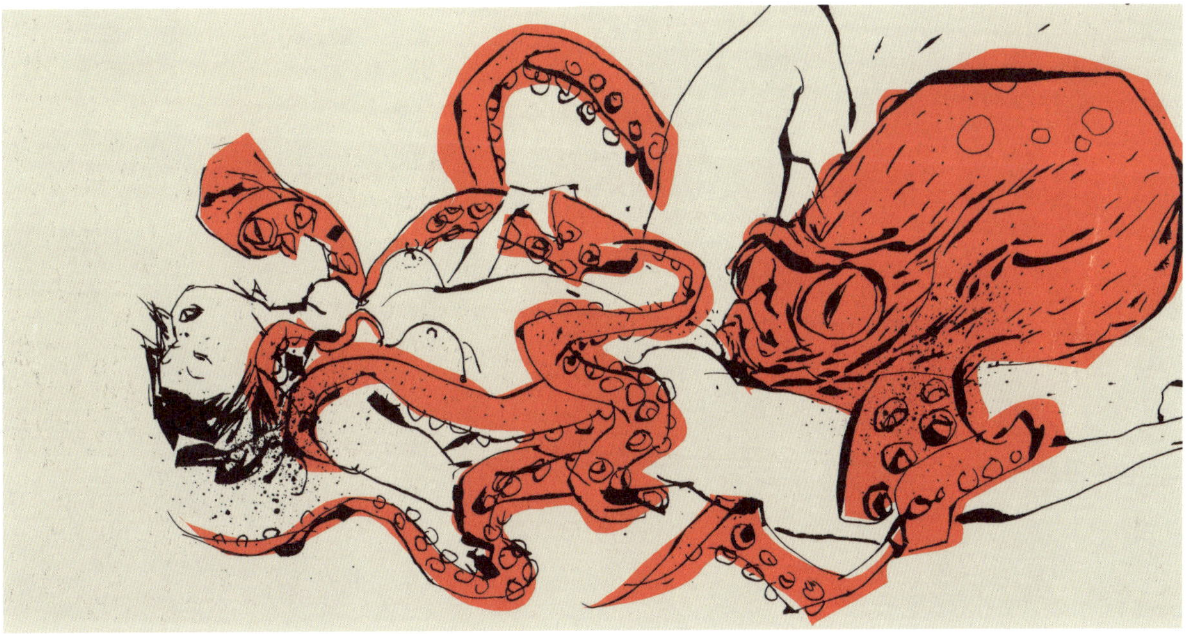

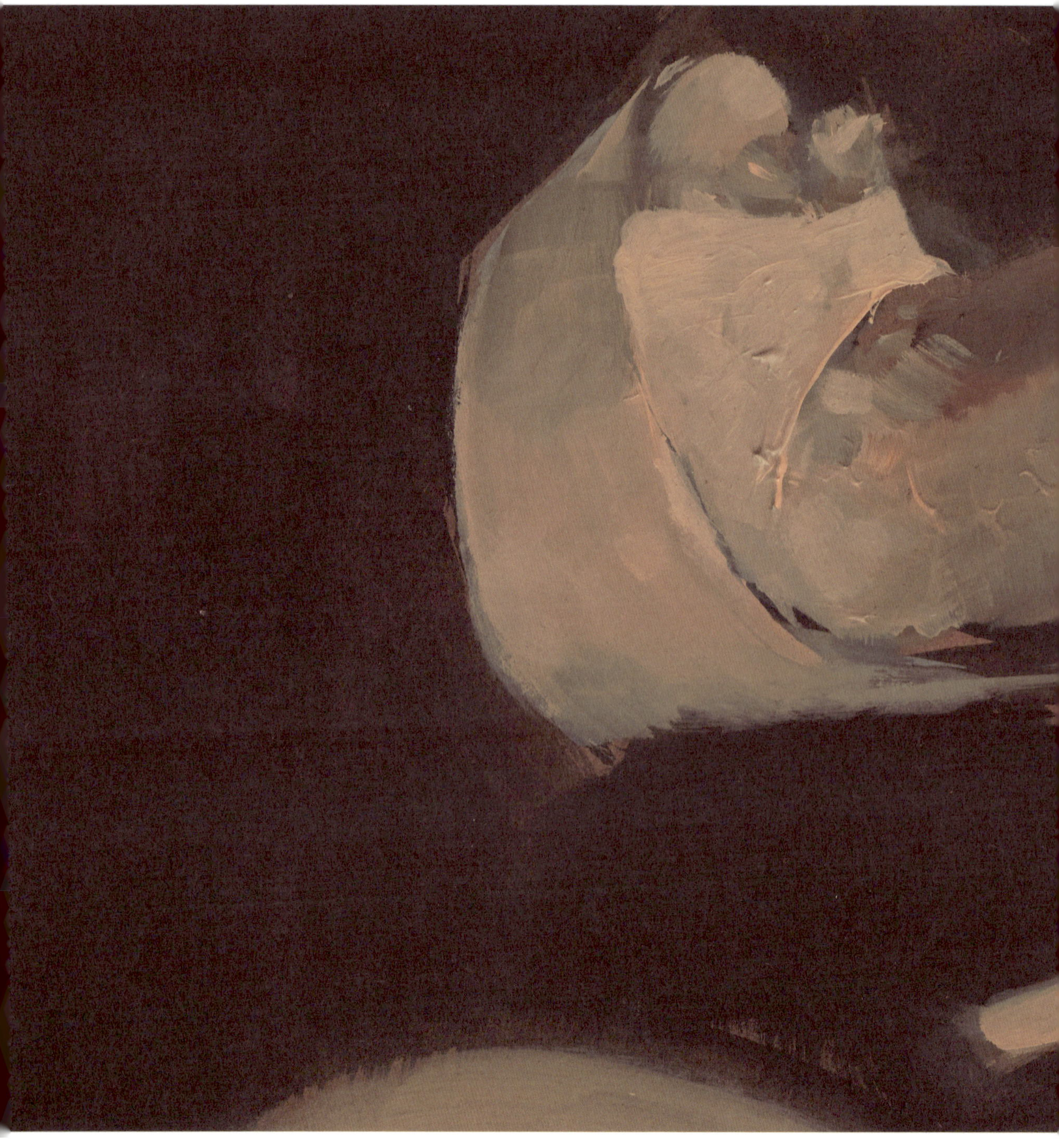

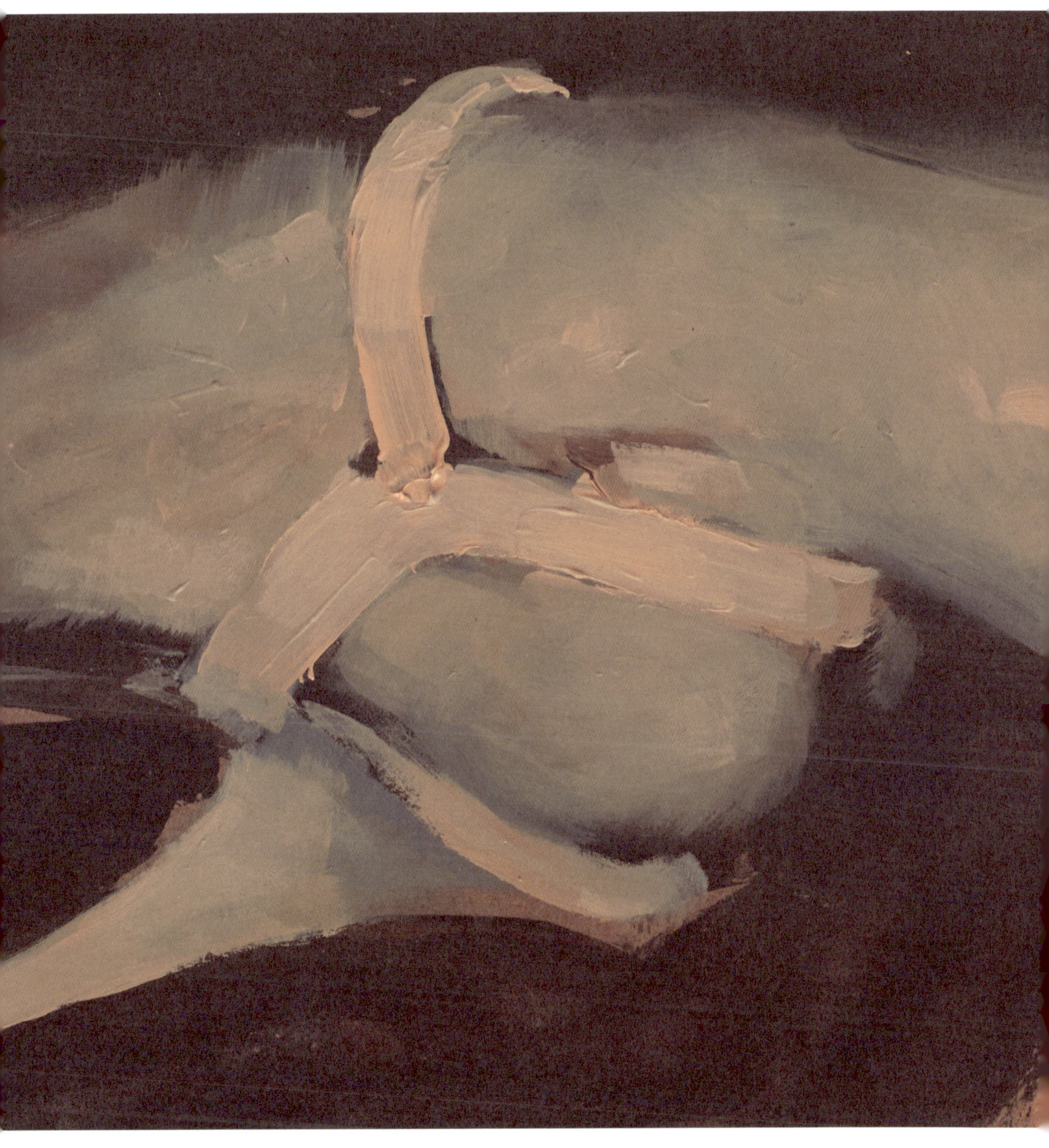

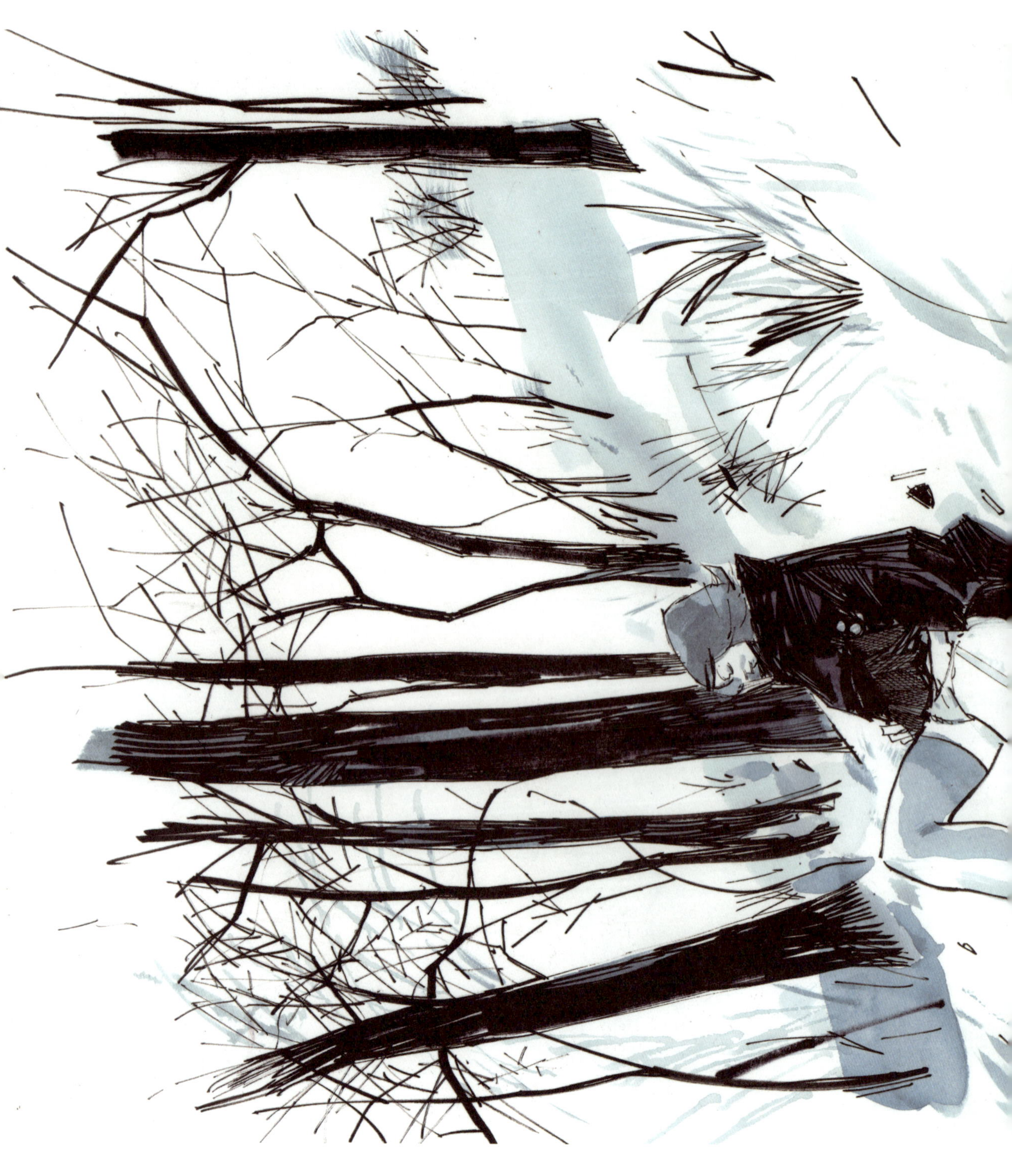

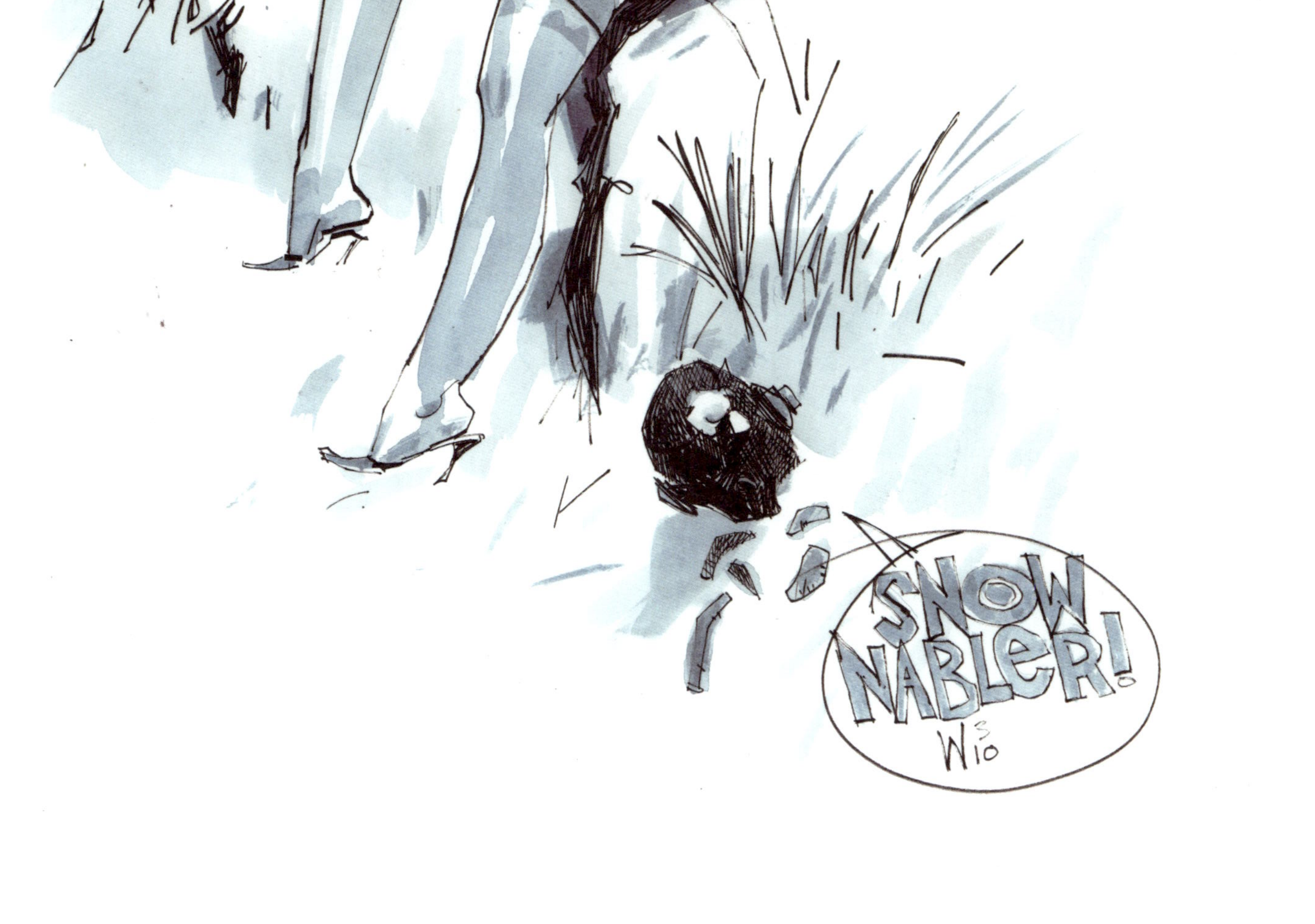

SNOW
NABLER!

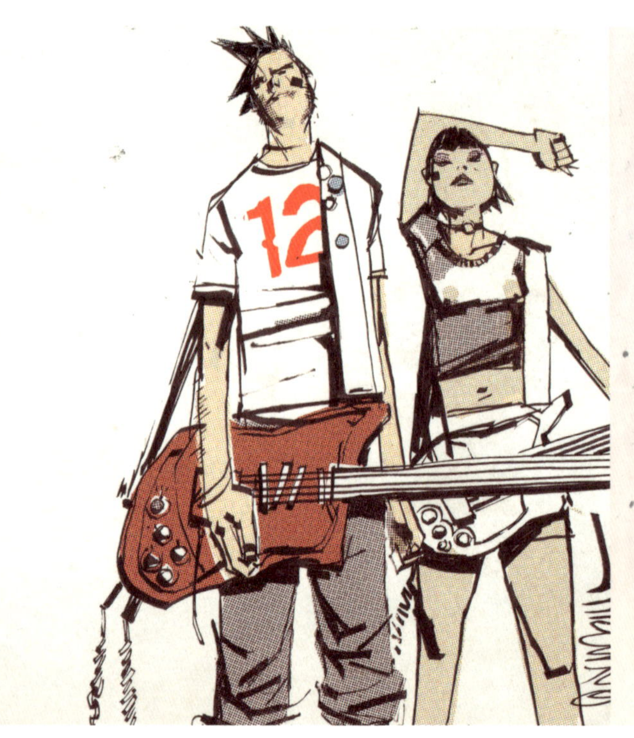

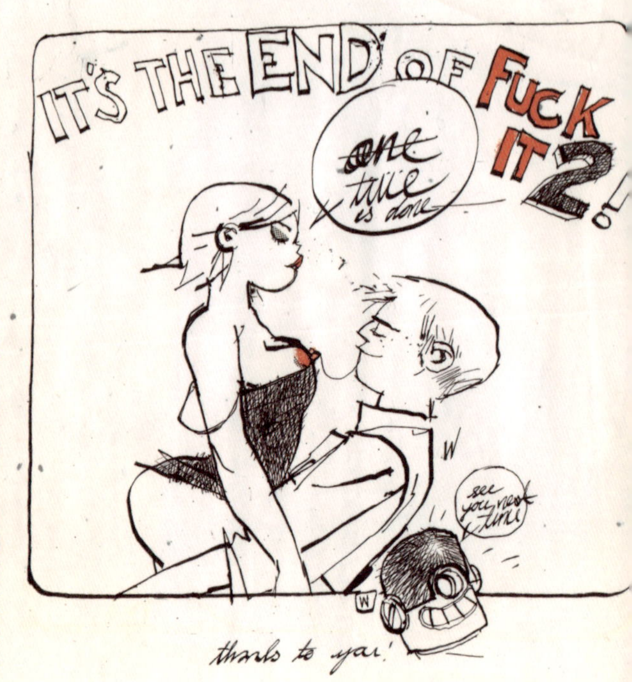
IT'S THE END OF FUCK IT 2!
one true is done
see you next time
thanks to you!

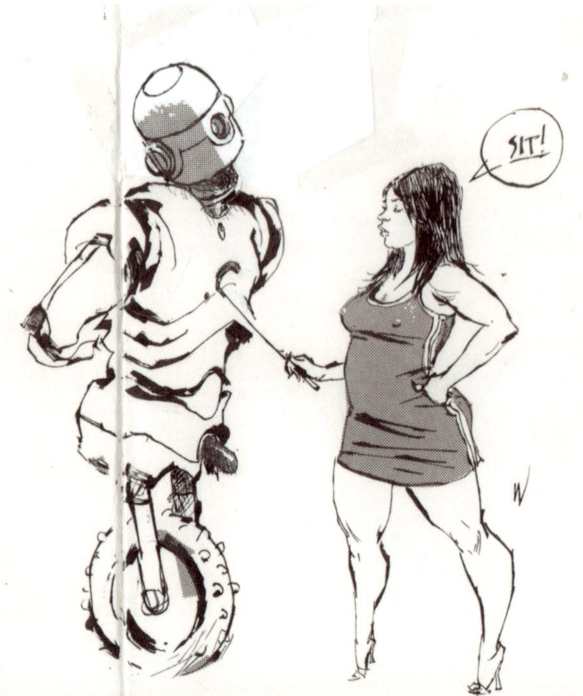
SIT!

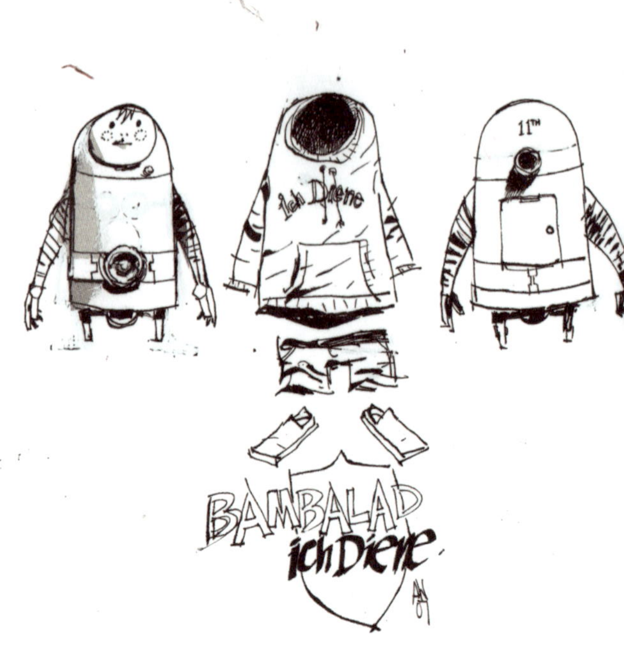
11TH
Ich Diene
BAMBALAD
ich Diene

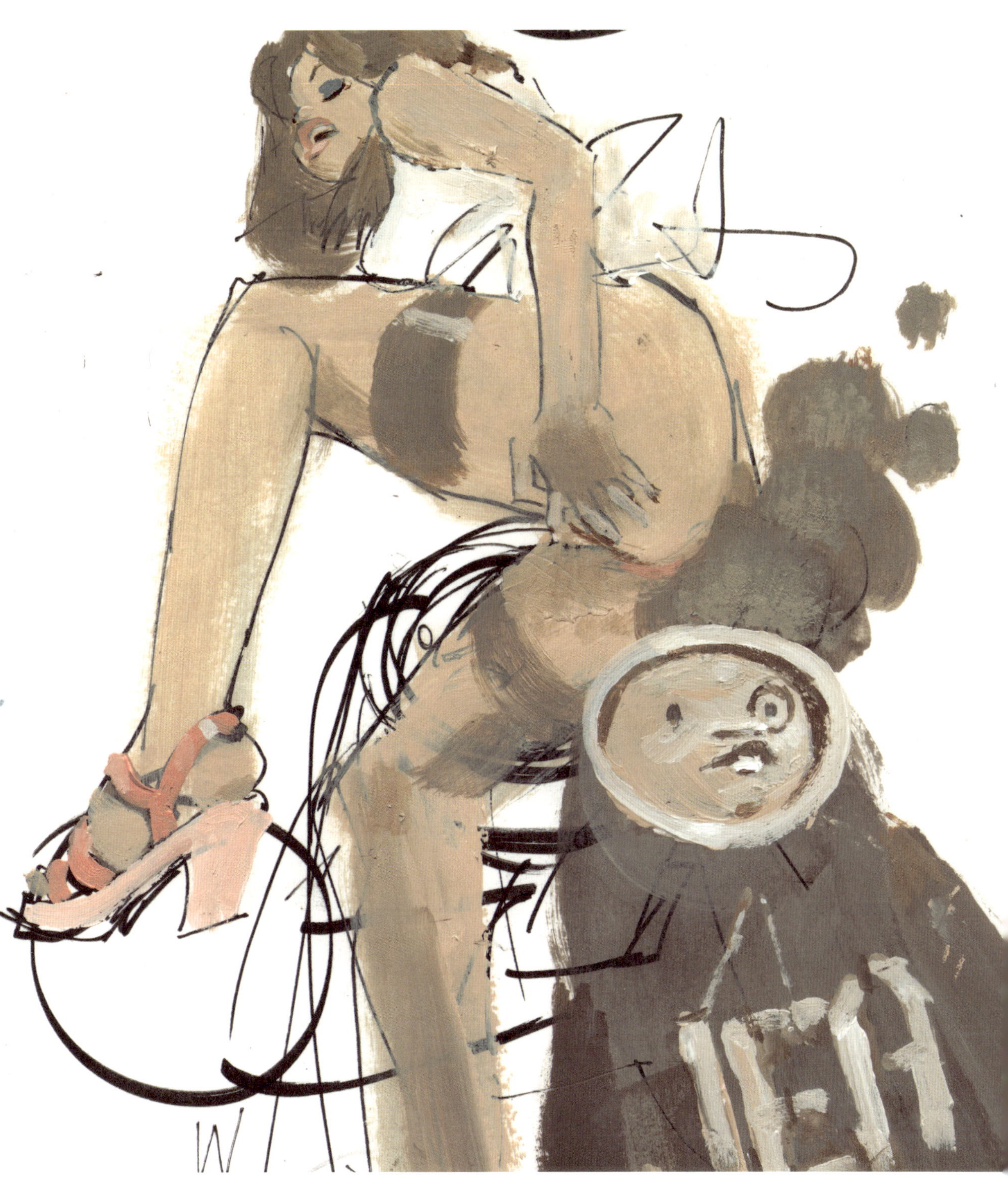

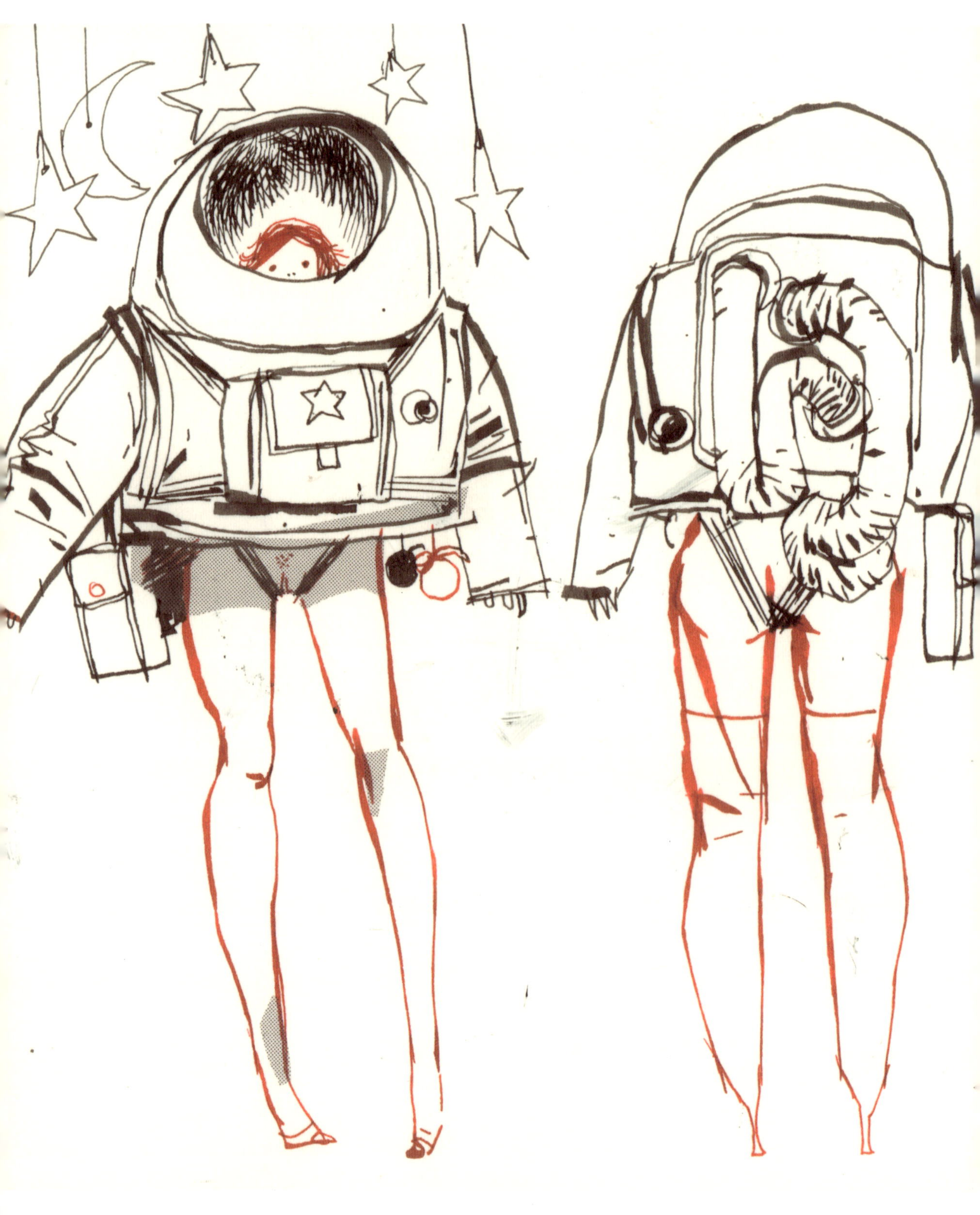

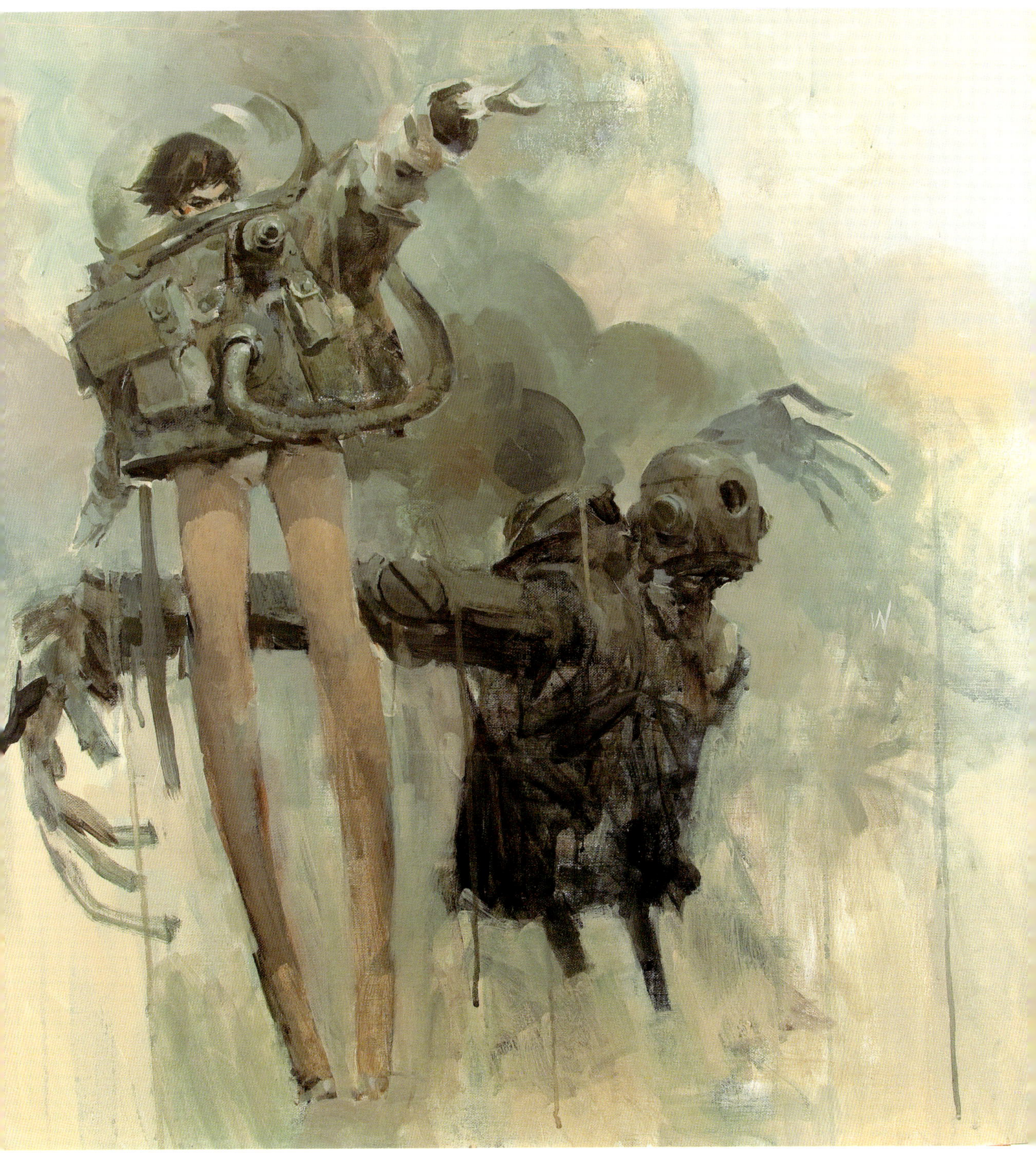

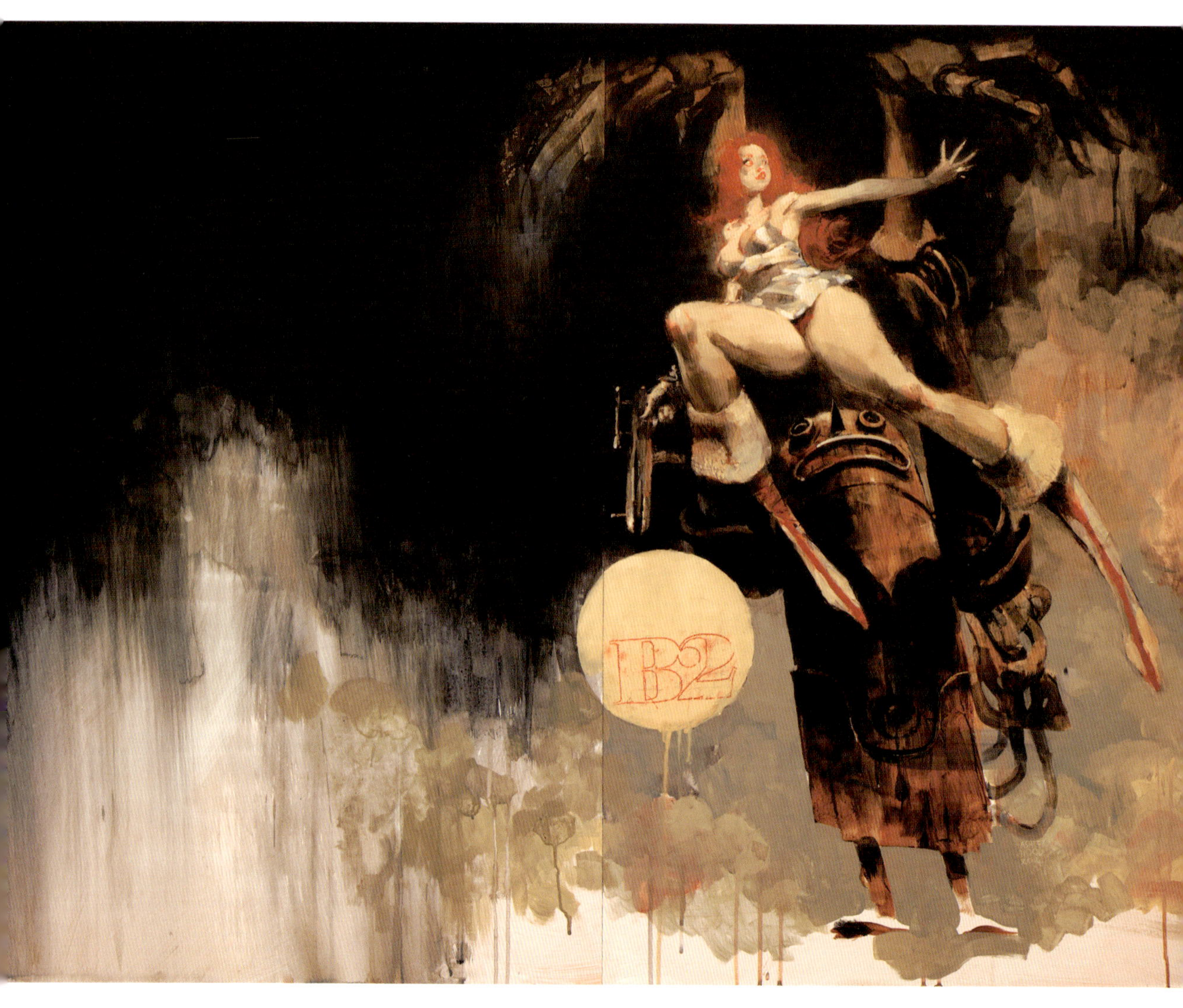
B2

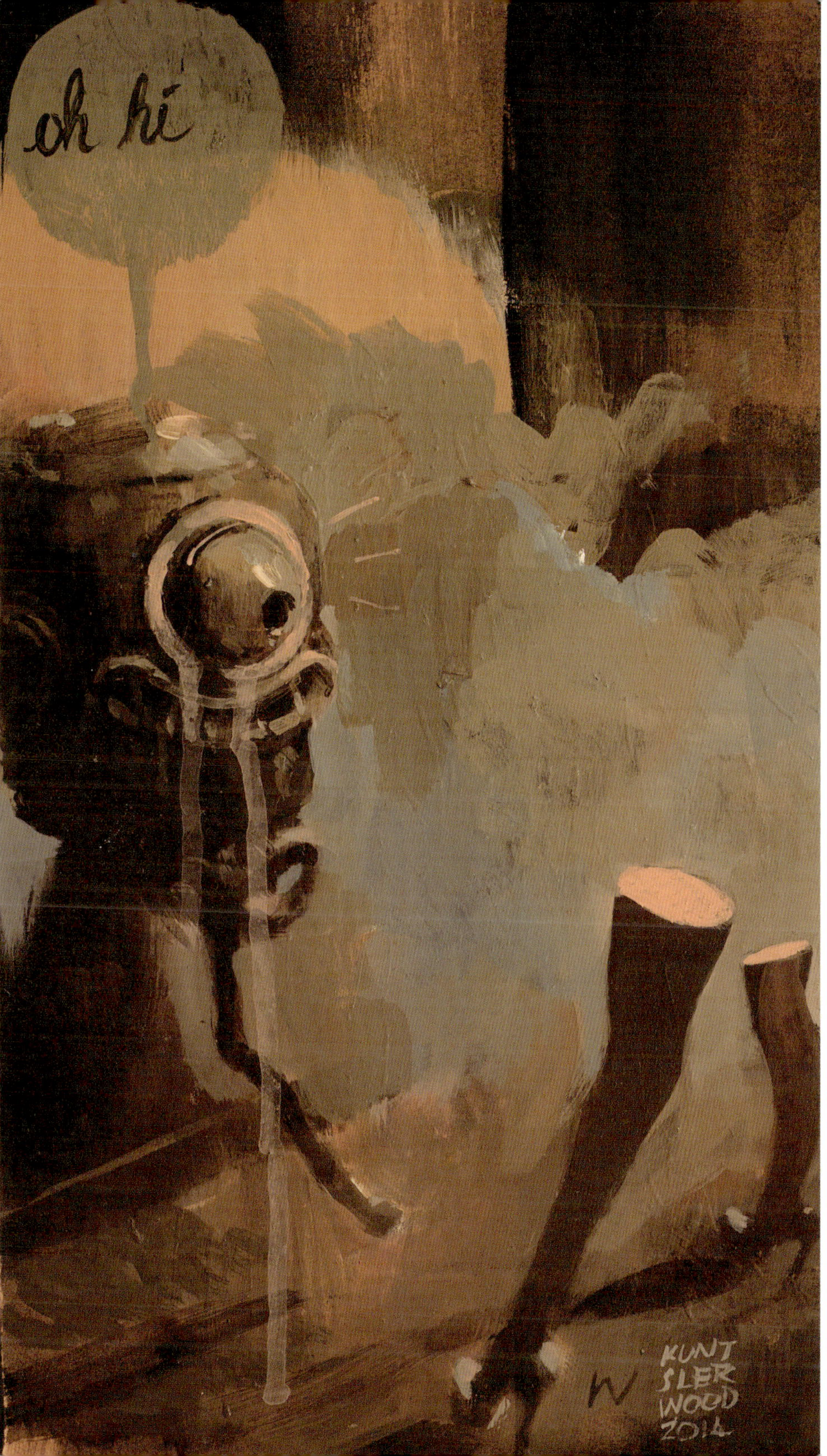
oh hi
KUNT
SLER
WOOD
2014

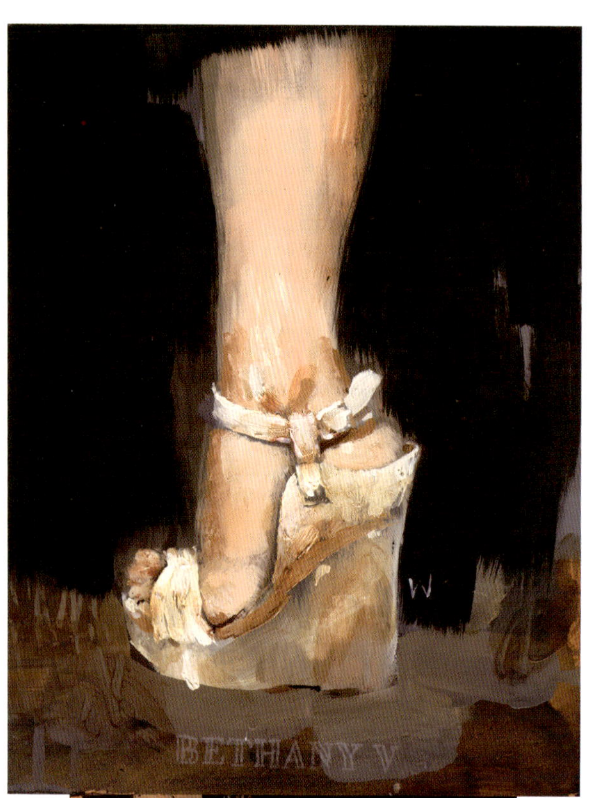
BETHANY V.

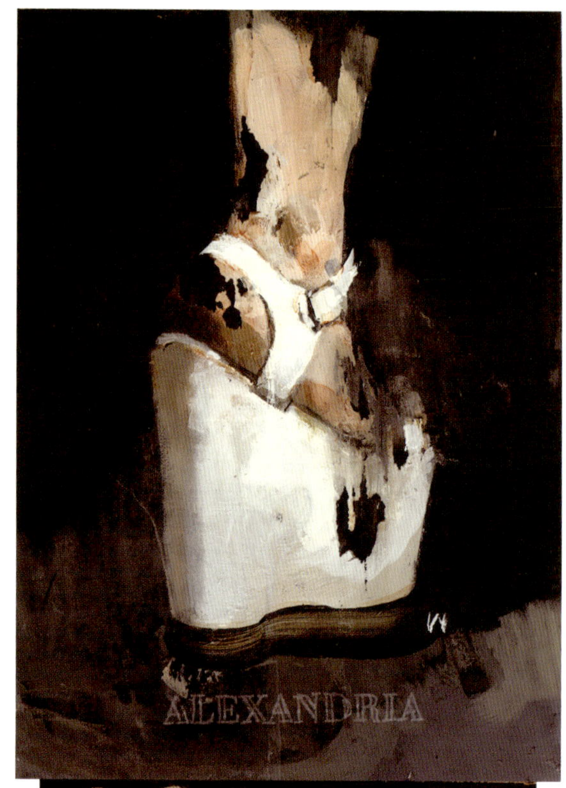
ALEXANDRIA

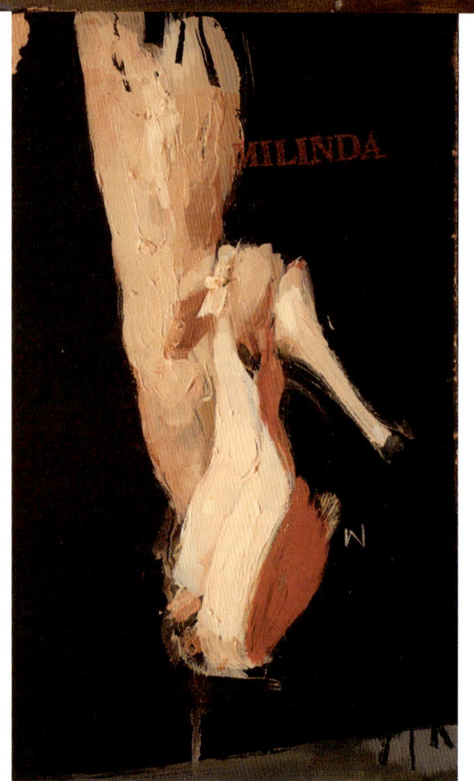
MILINDA

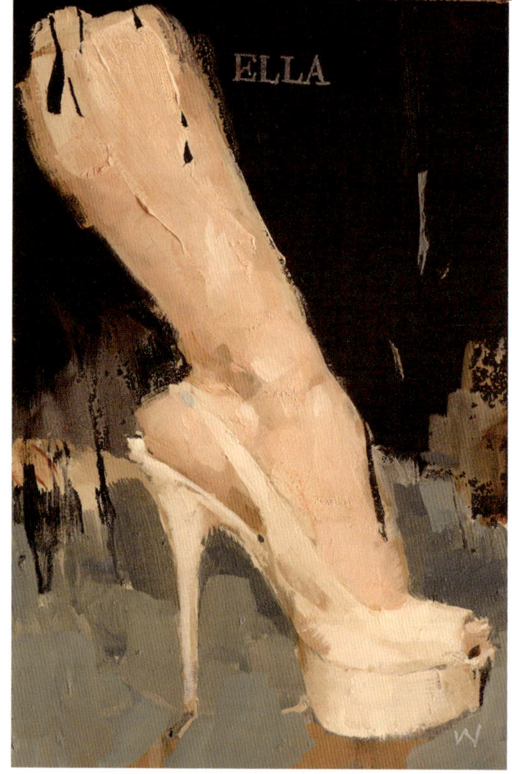
ELLA

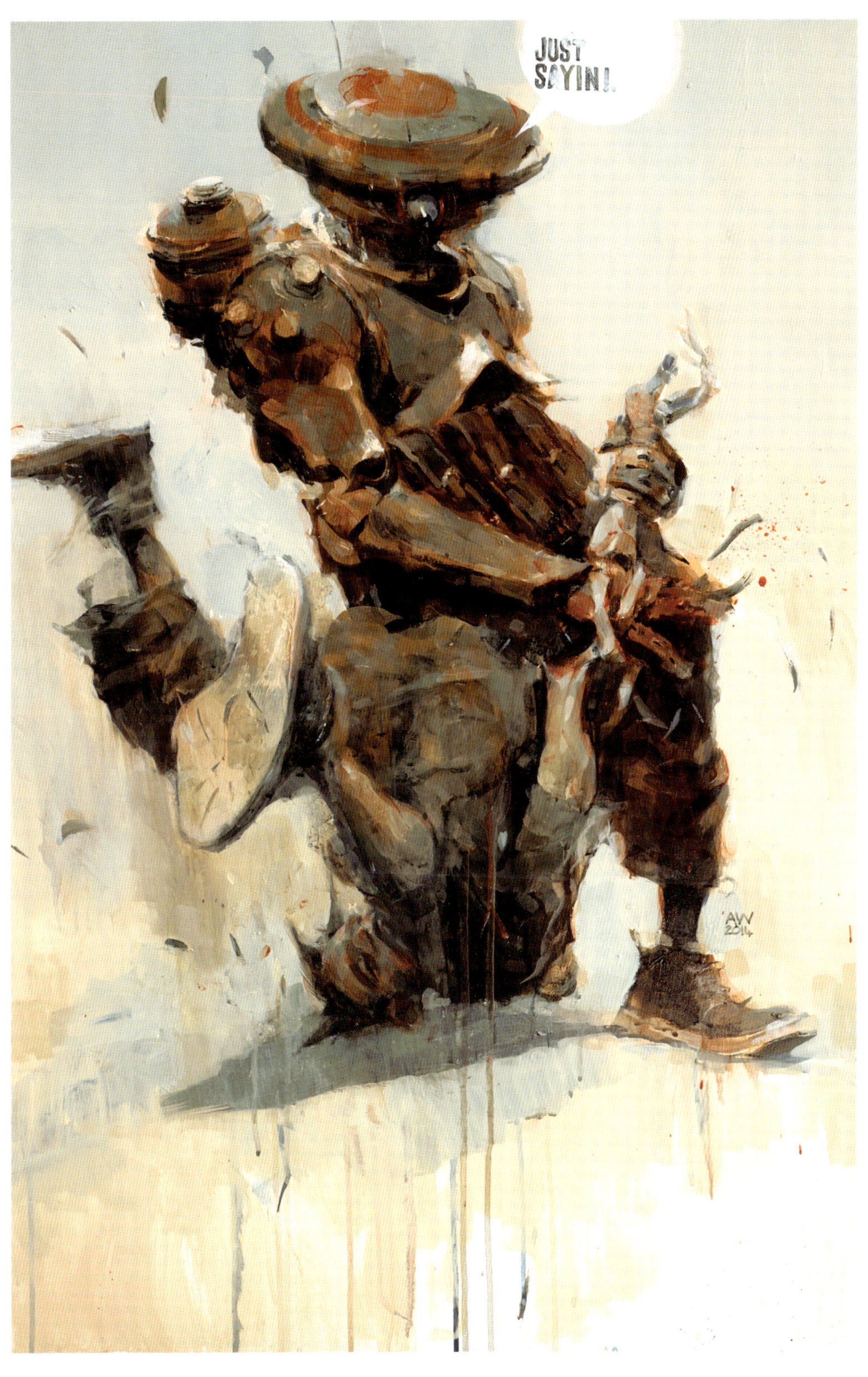
JUST
SAYIN'.

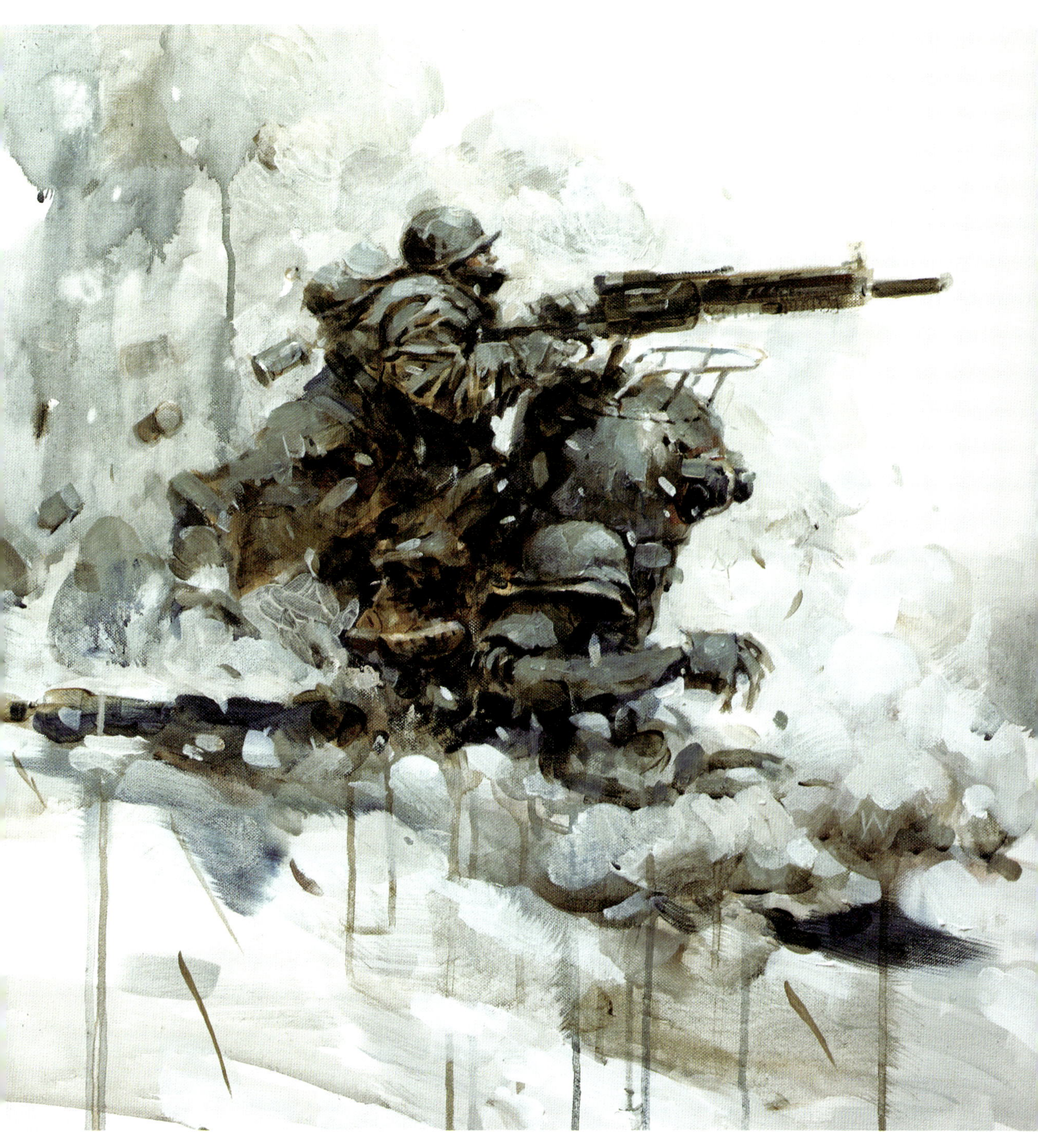

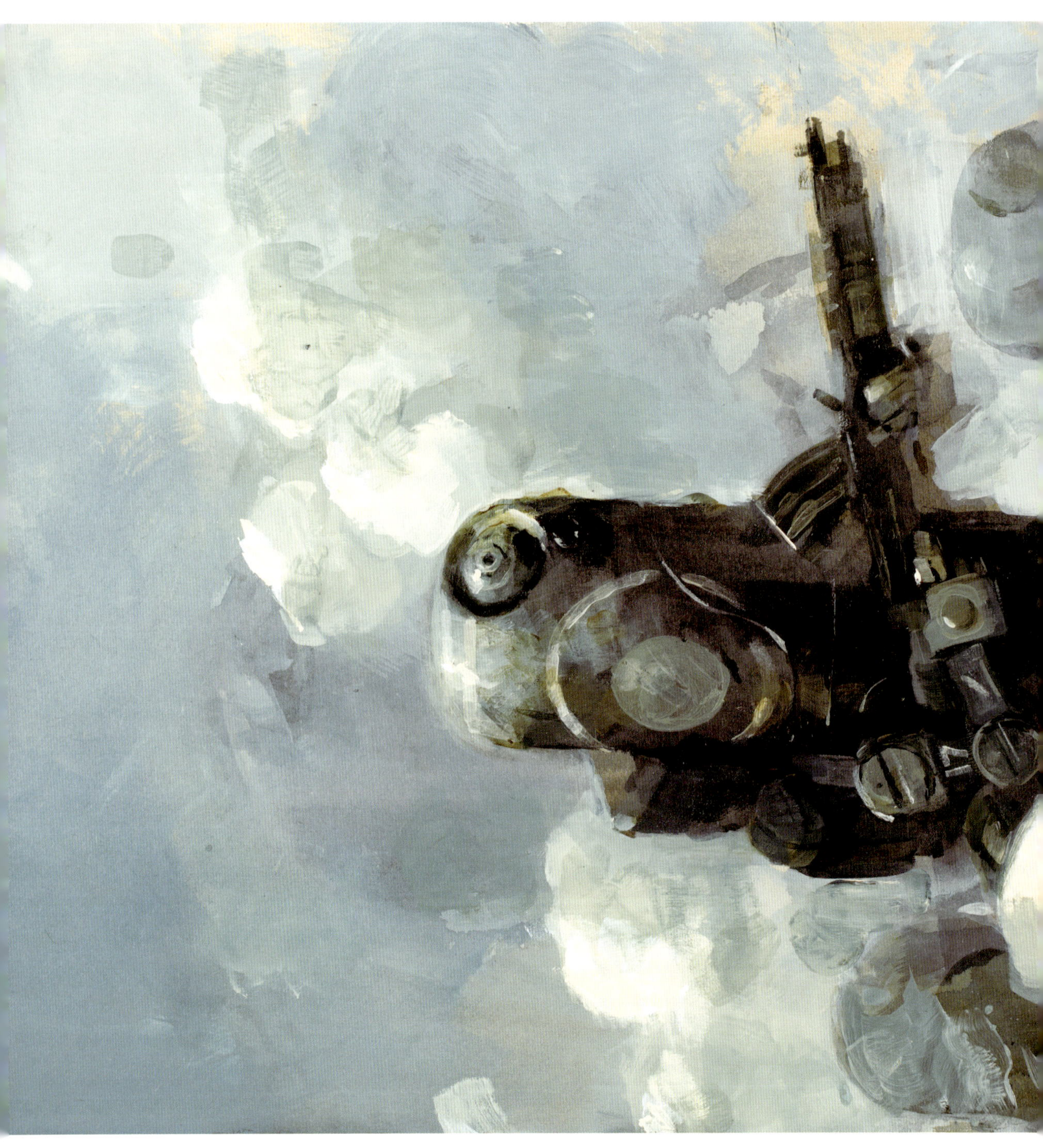

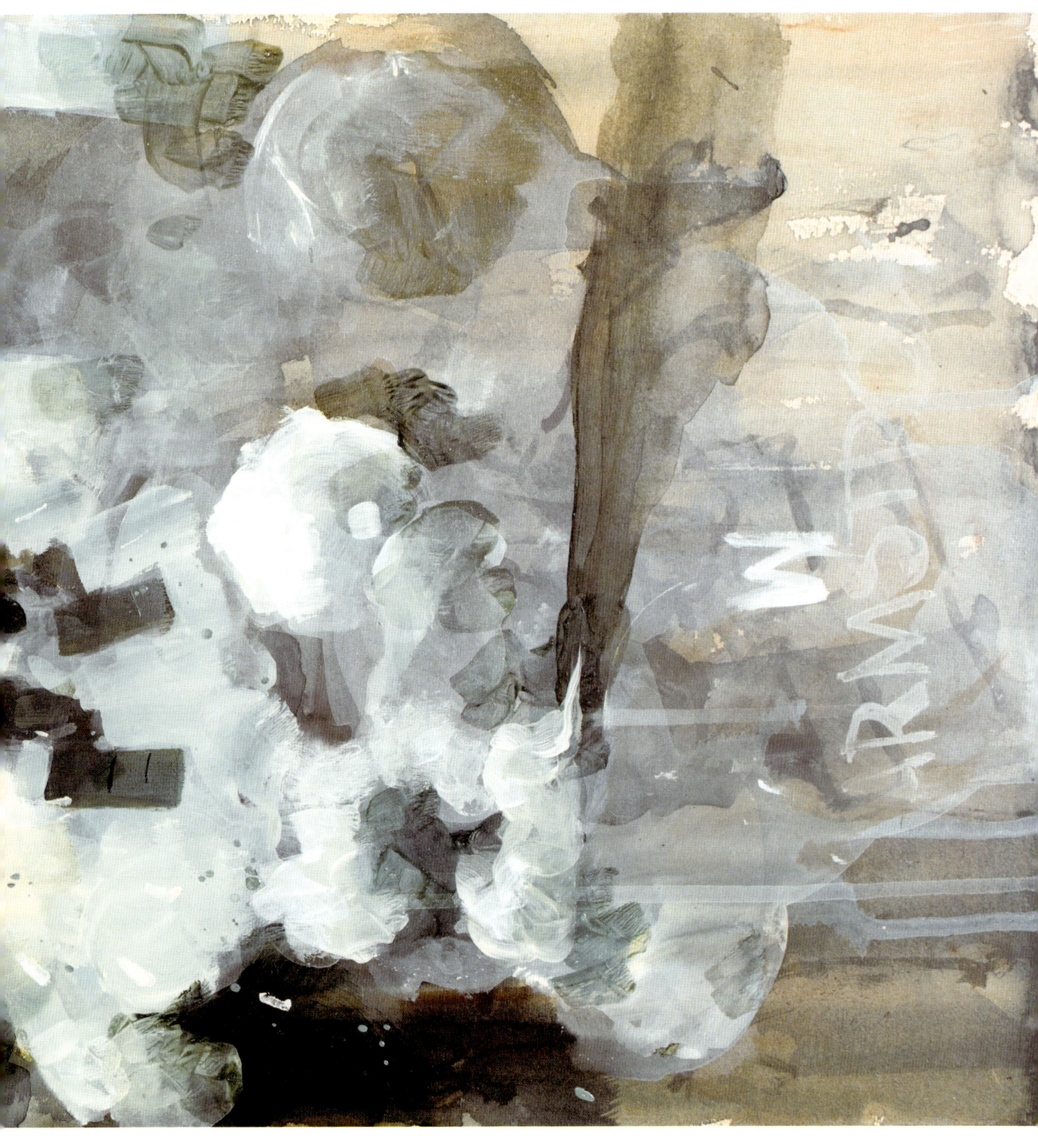

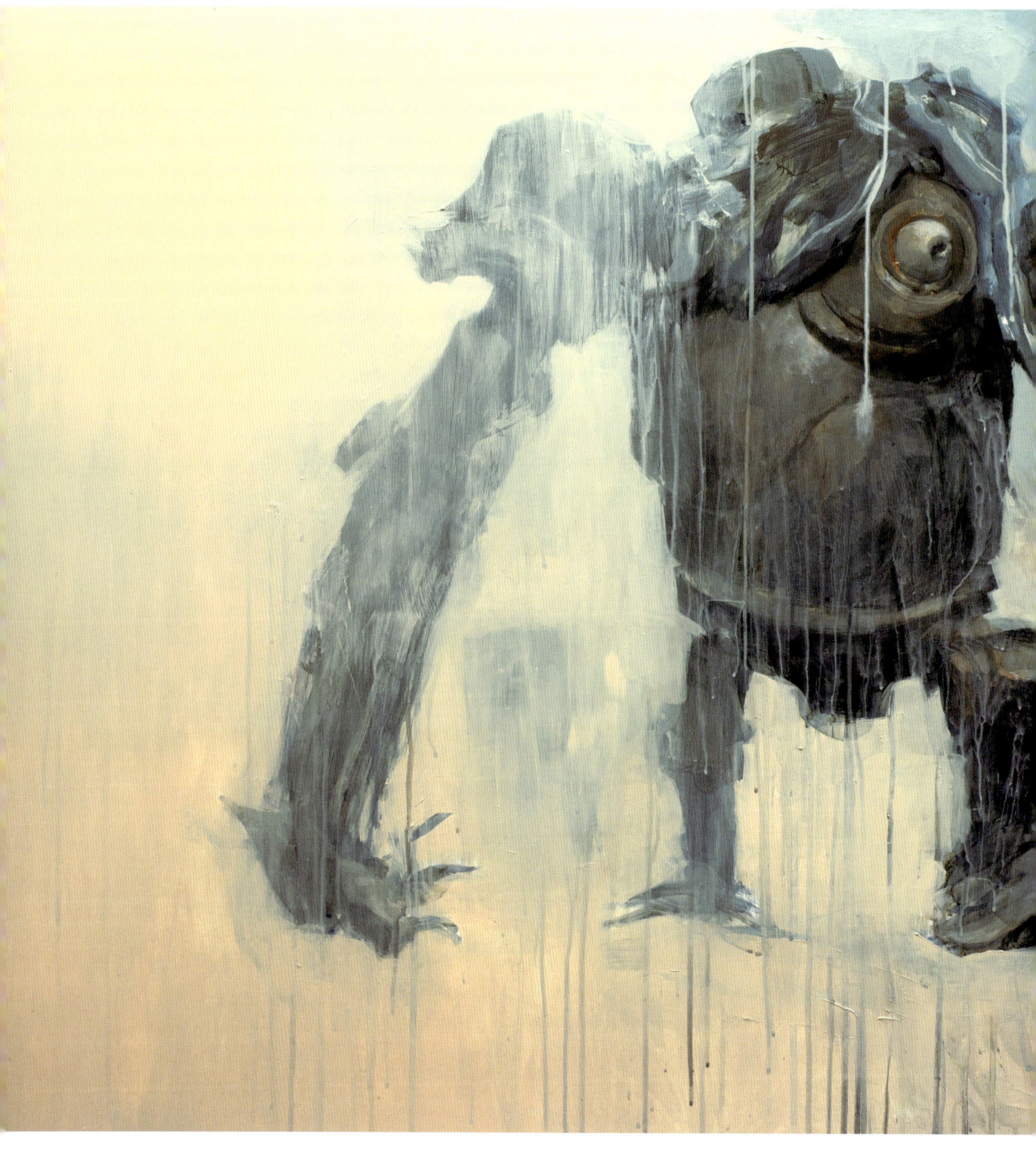

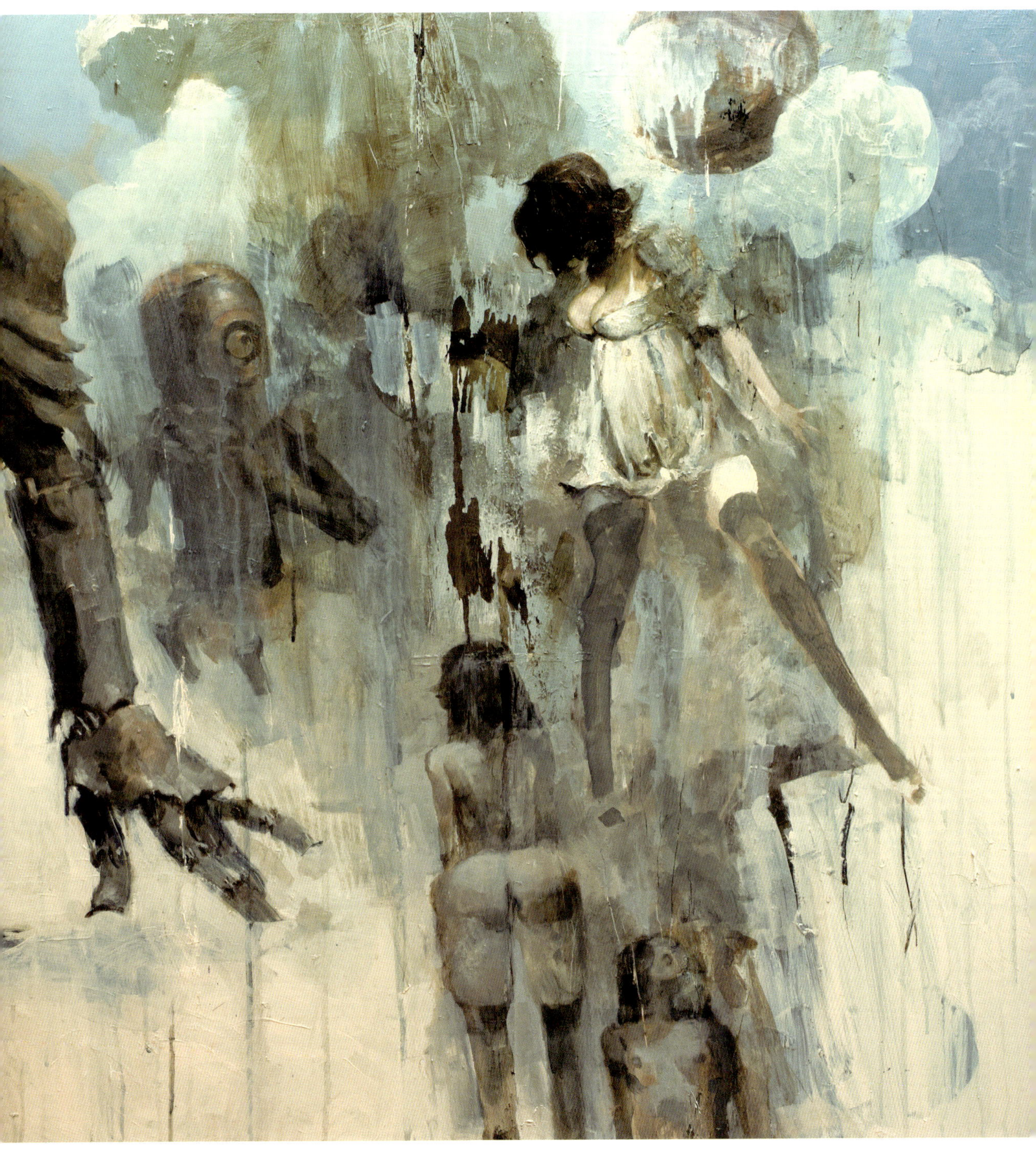

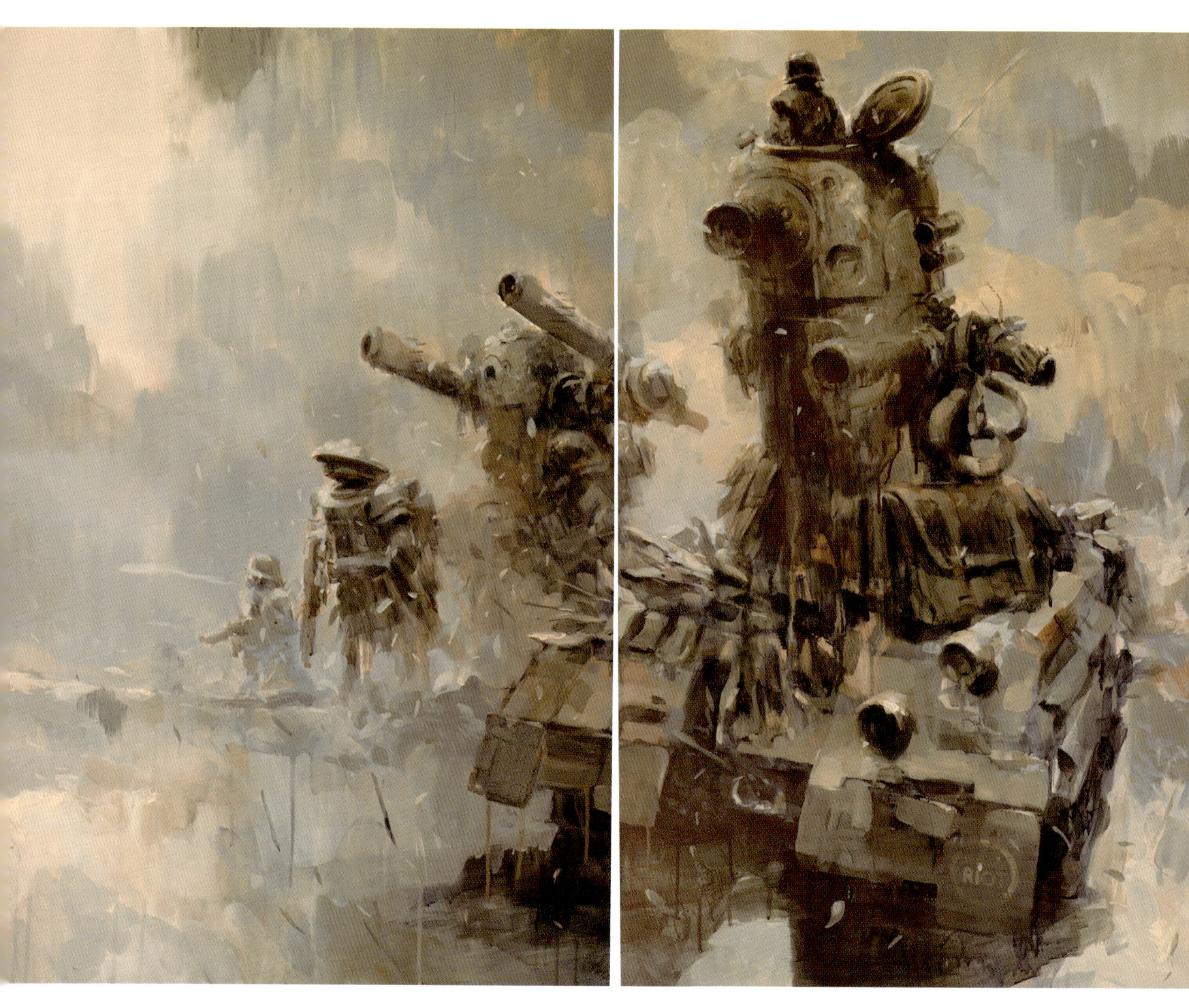

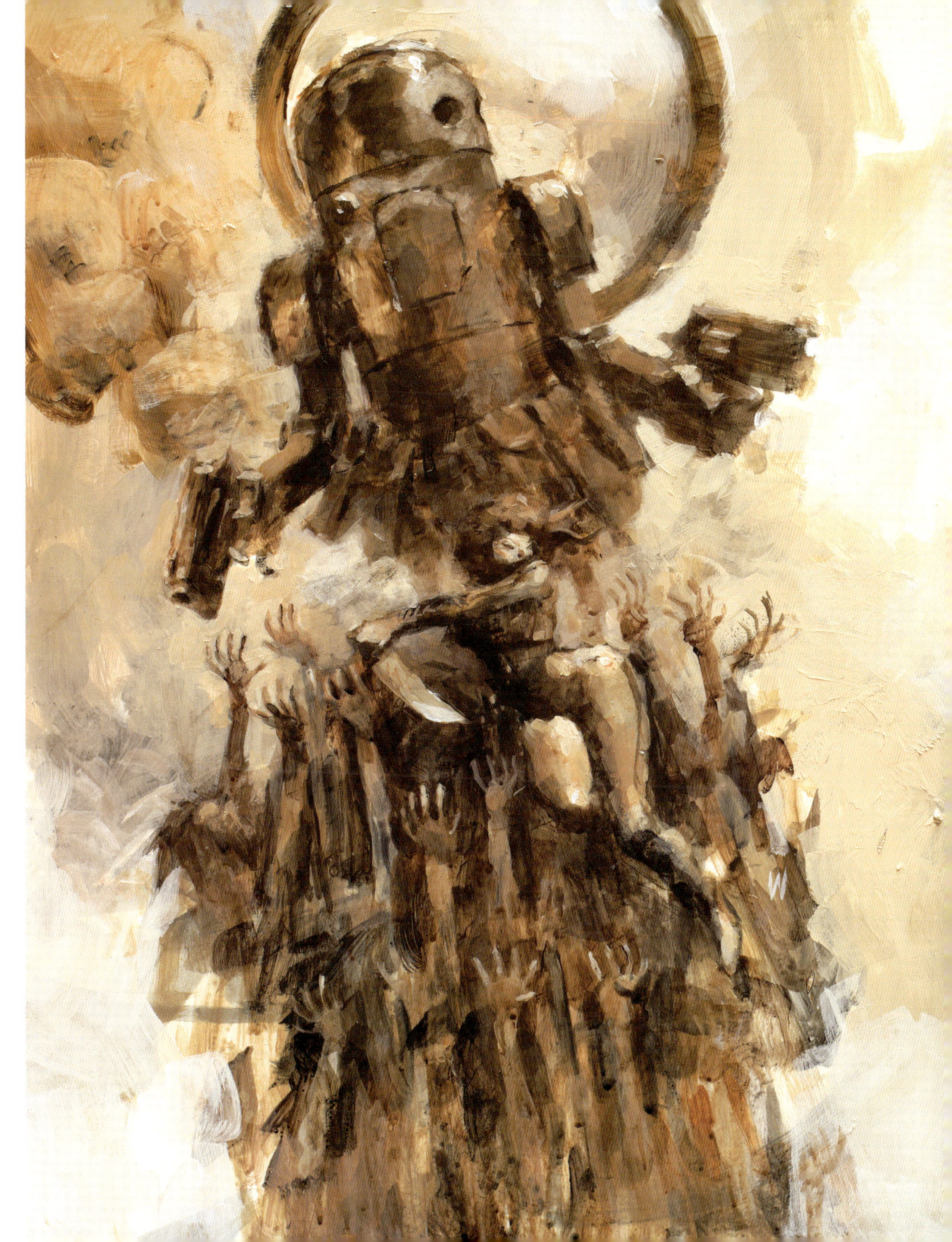

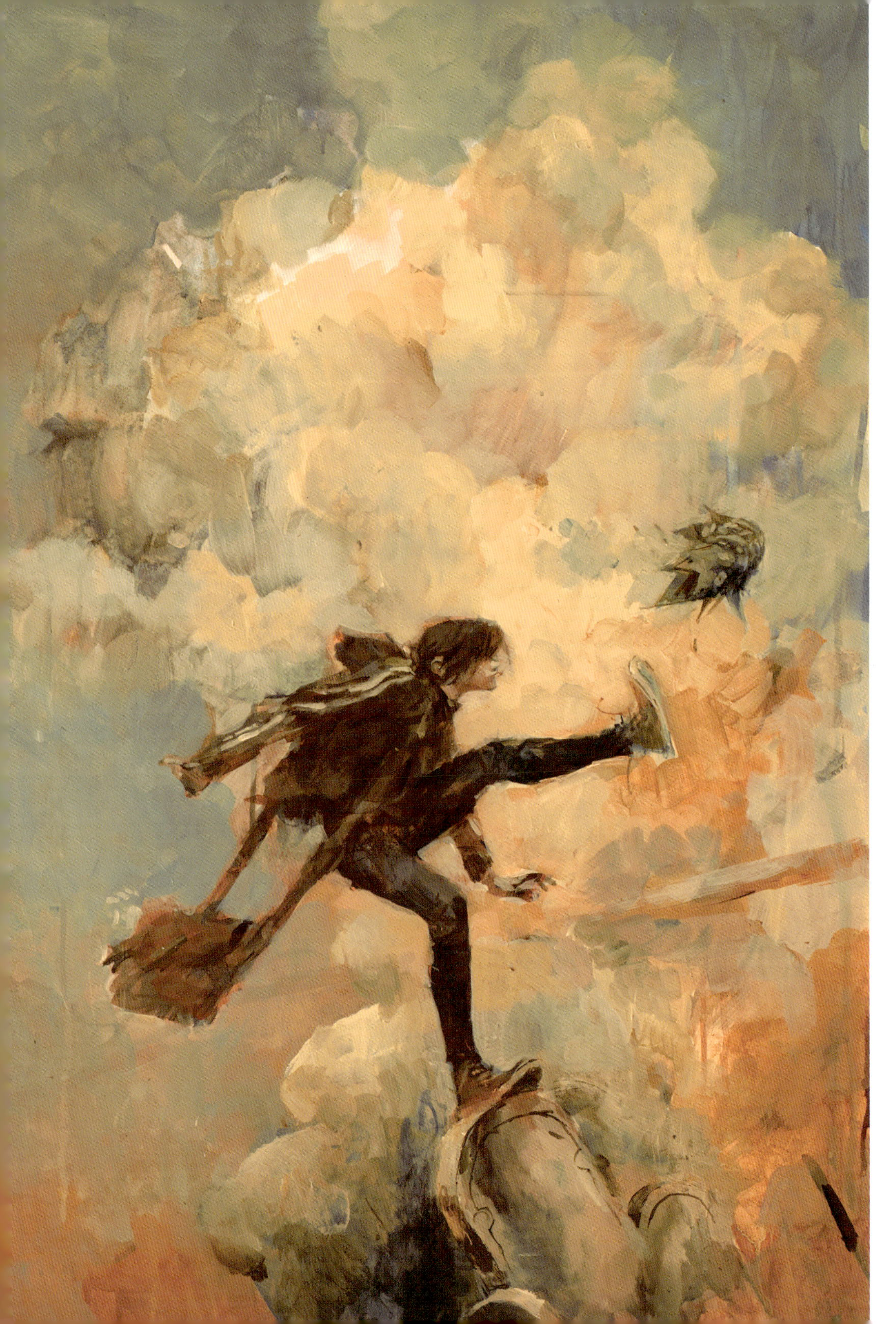

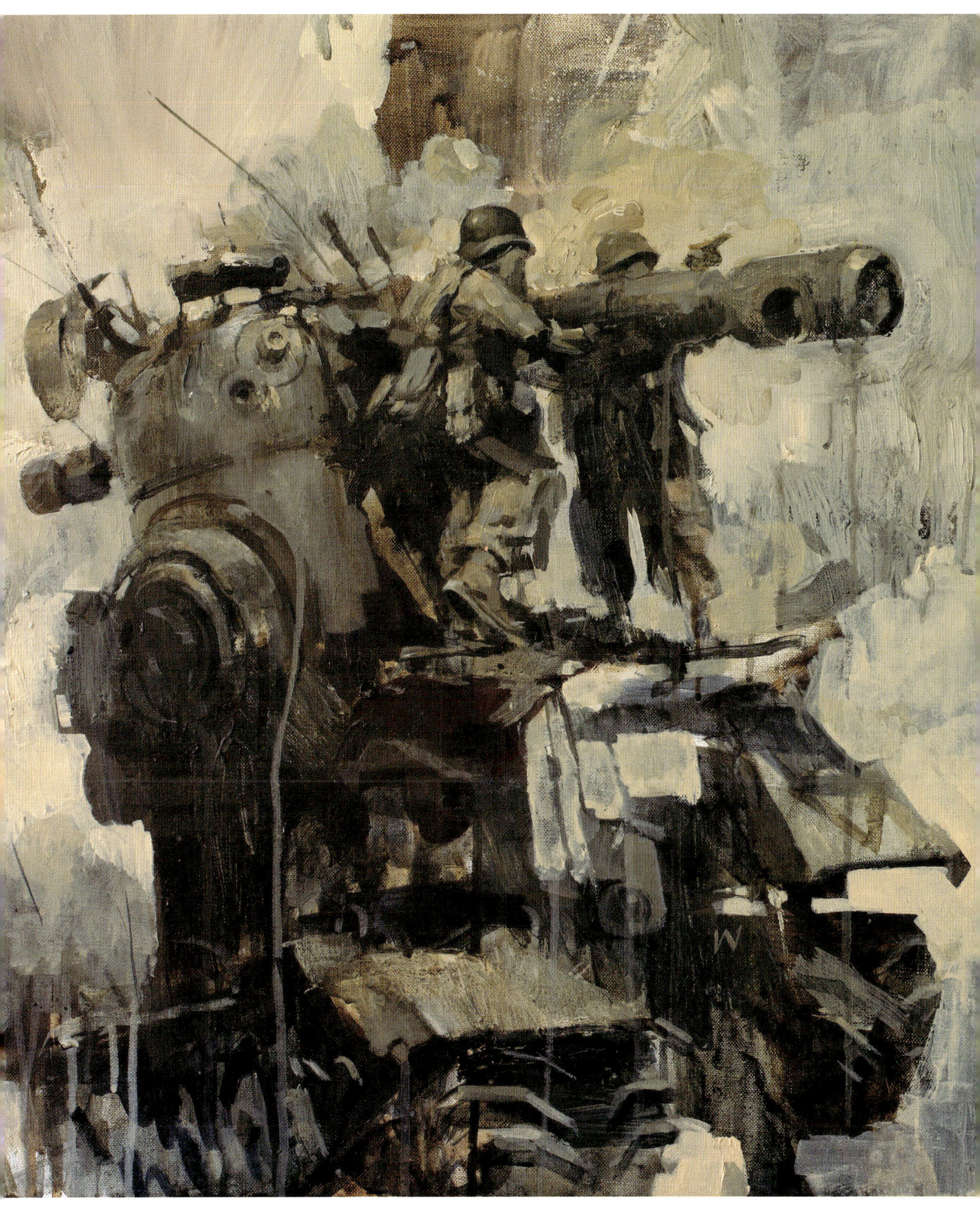

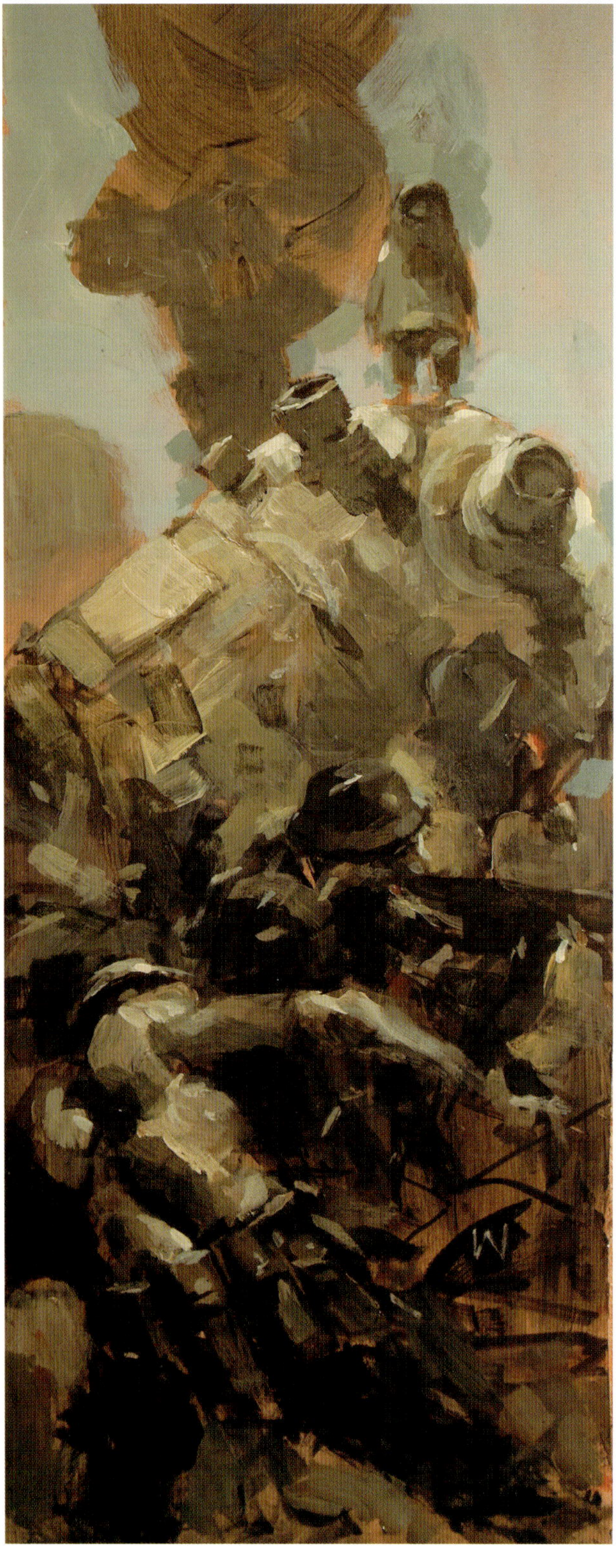

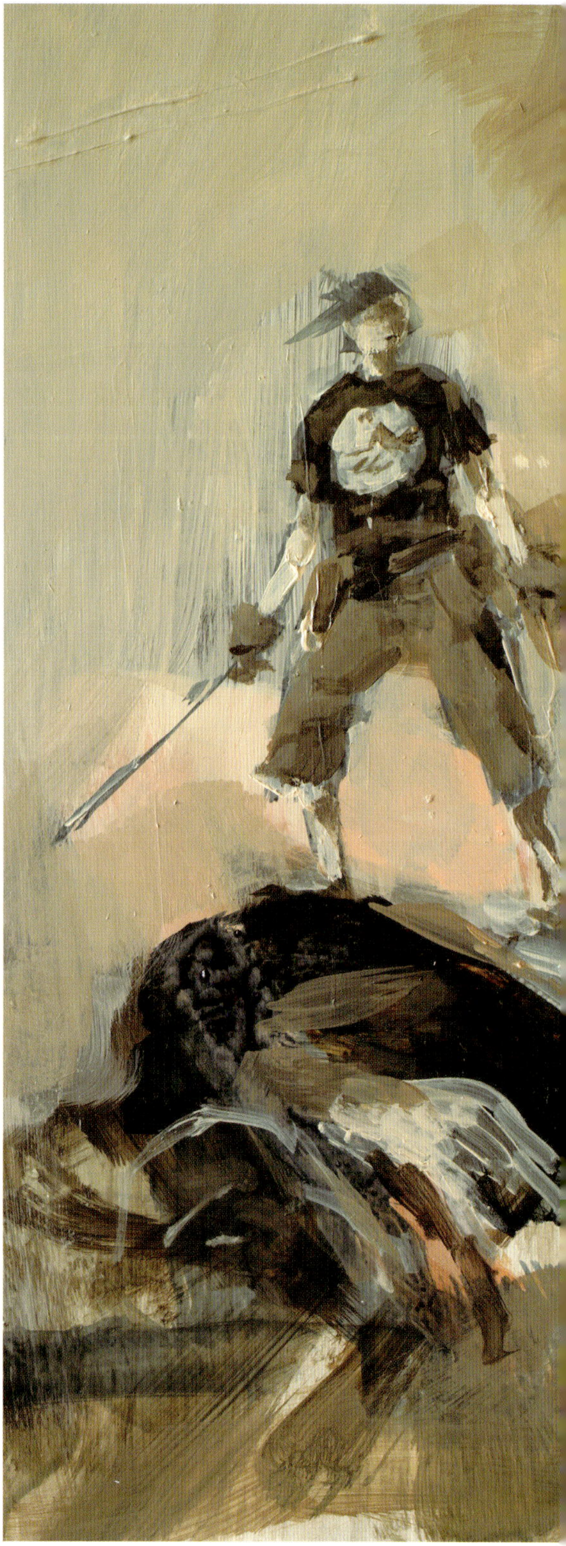

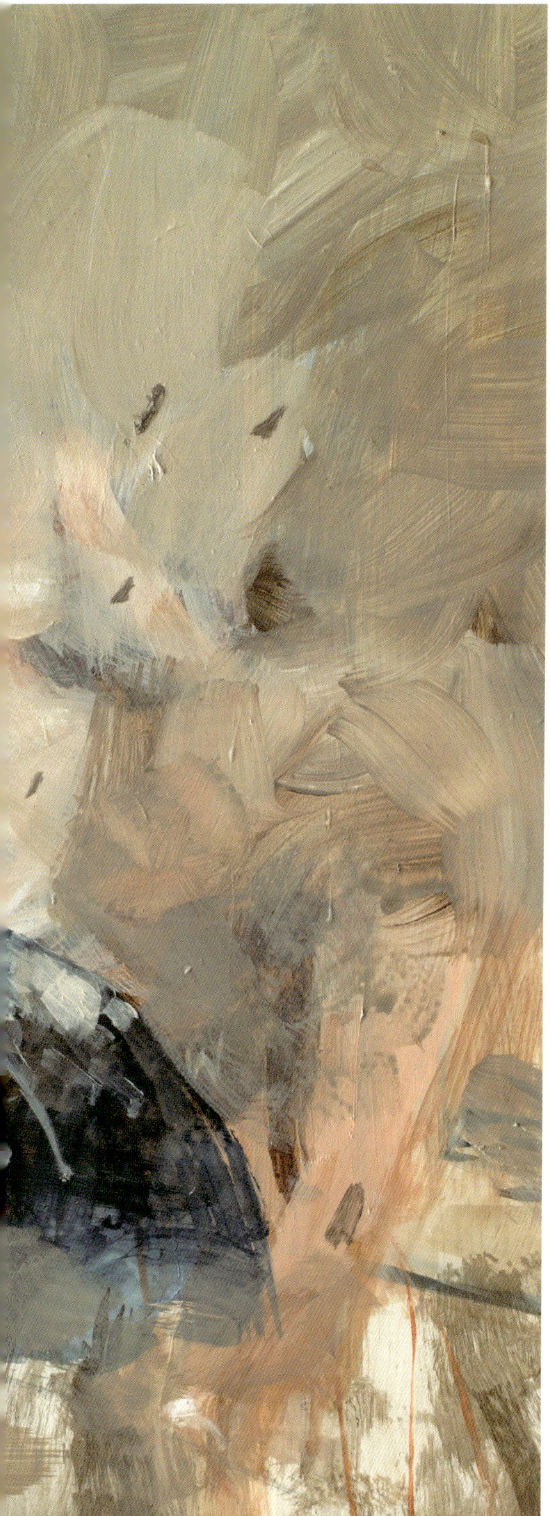

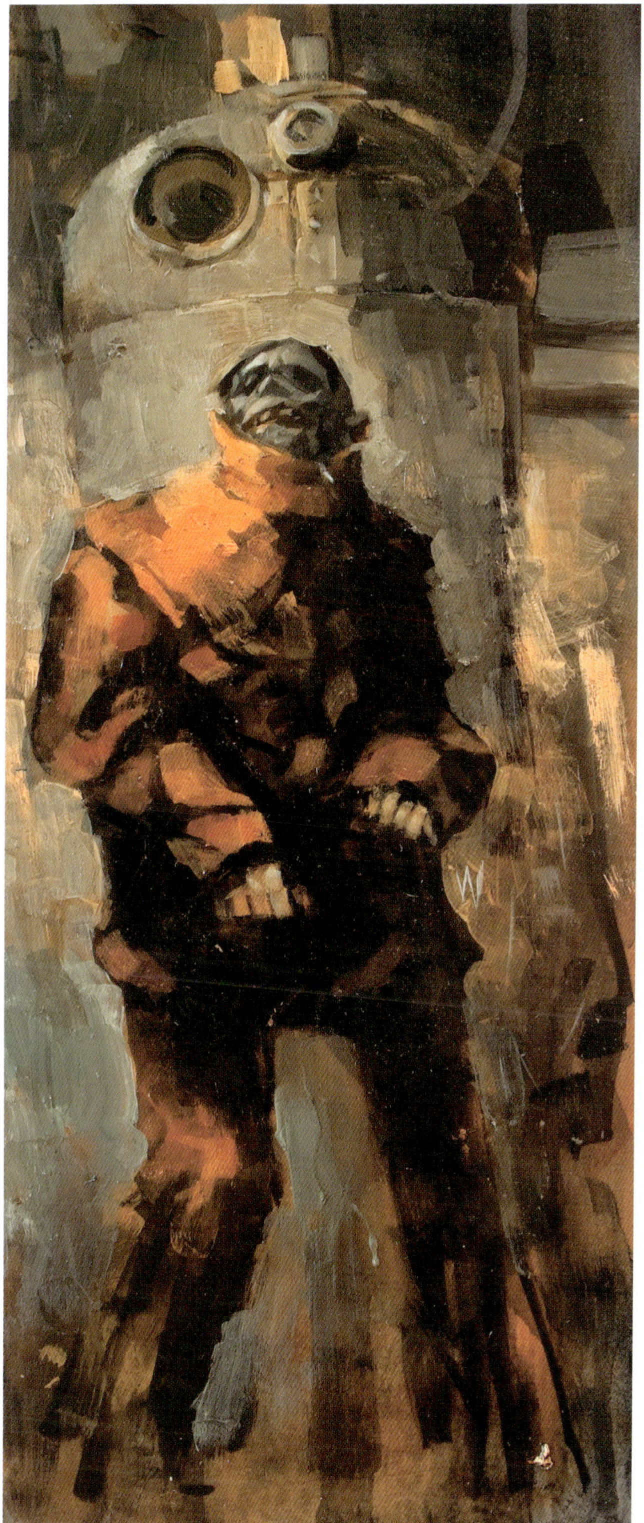

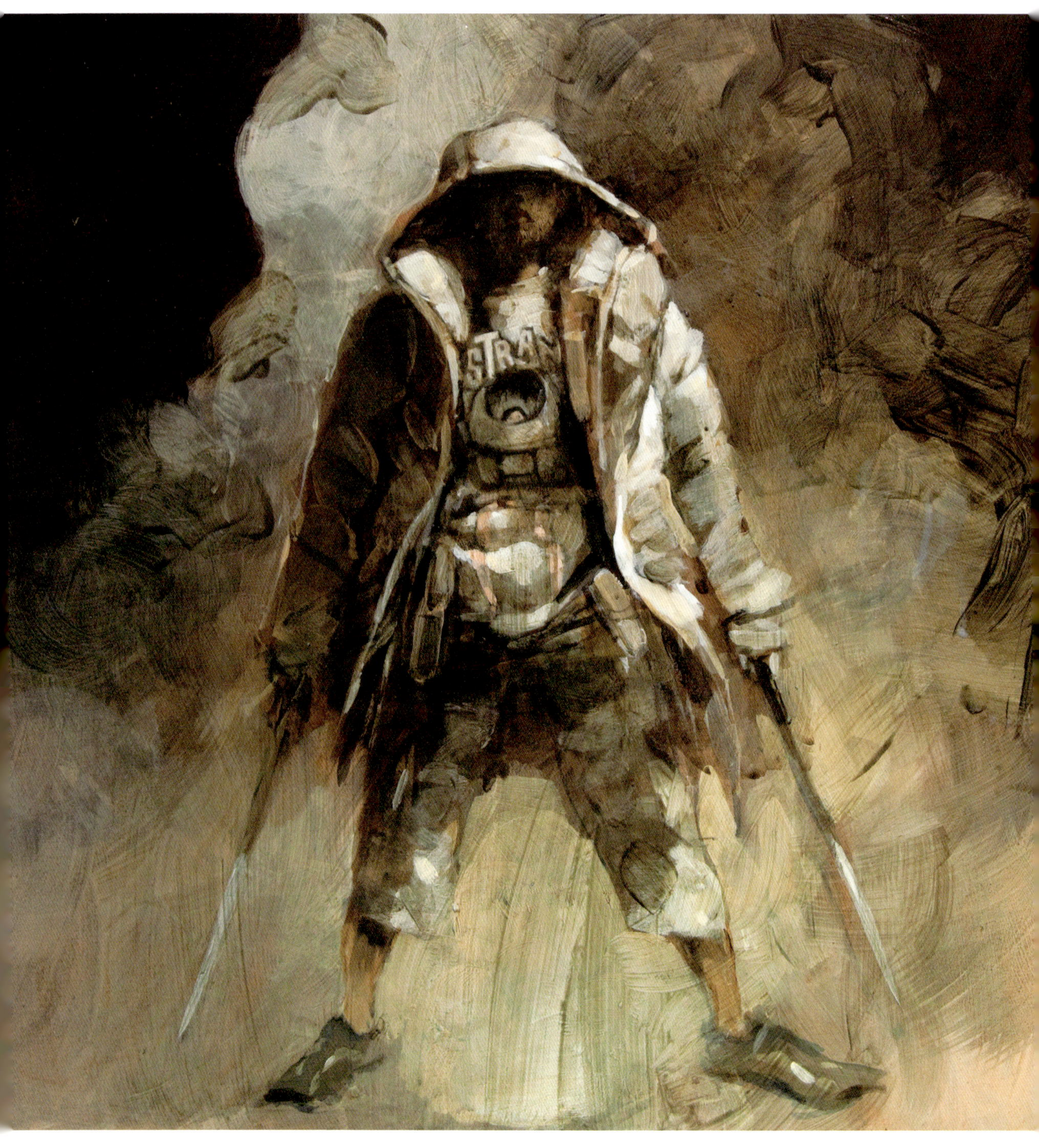

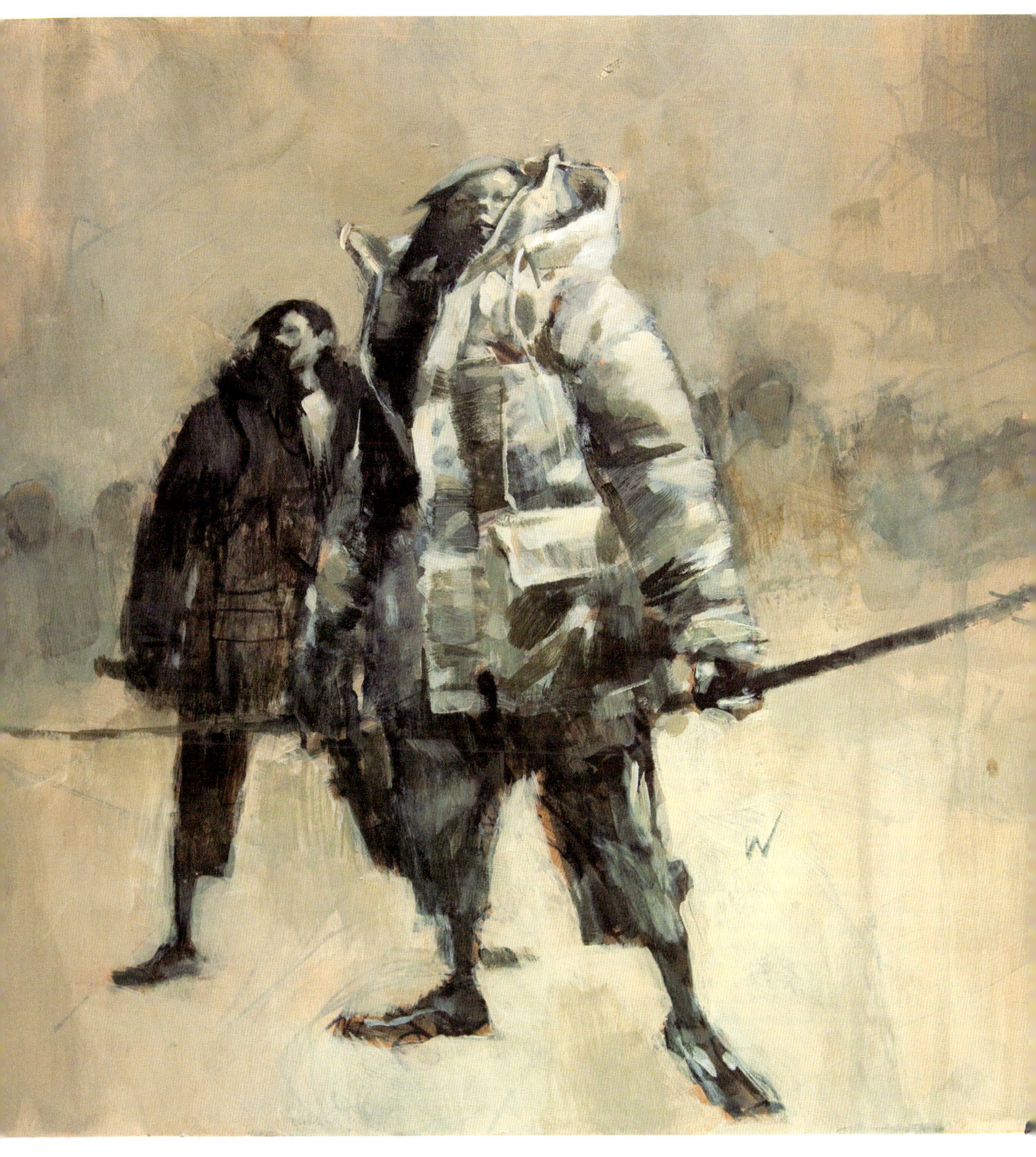

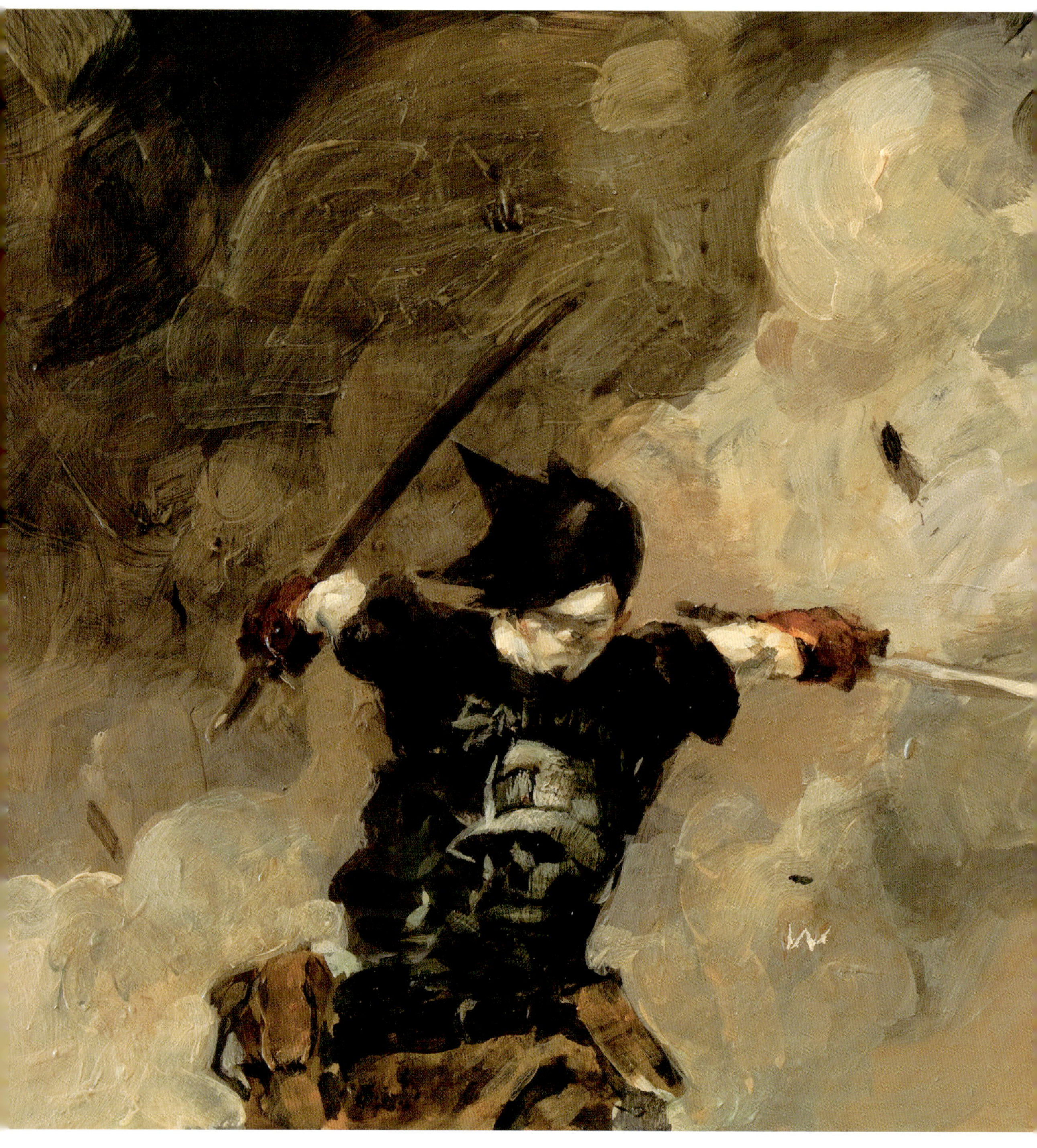

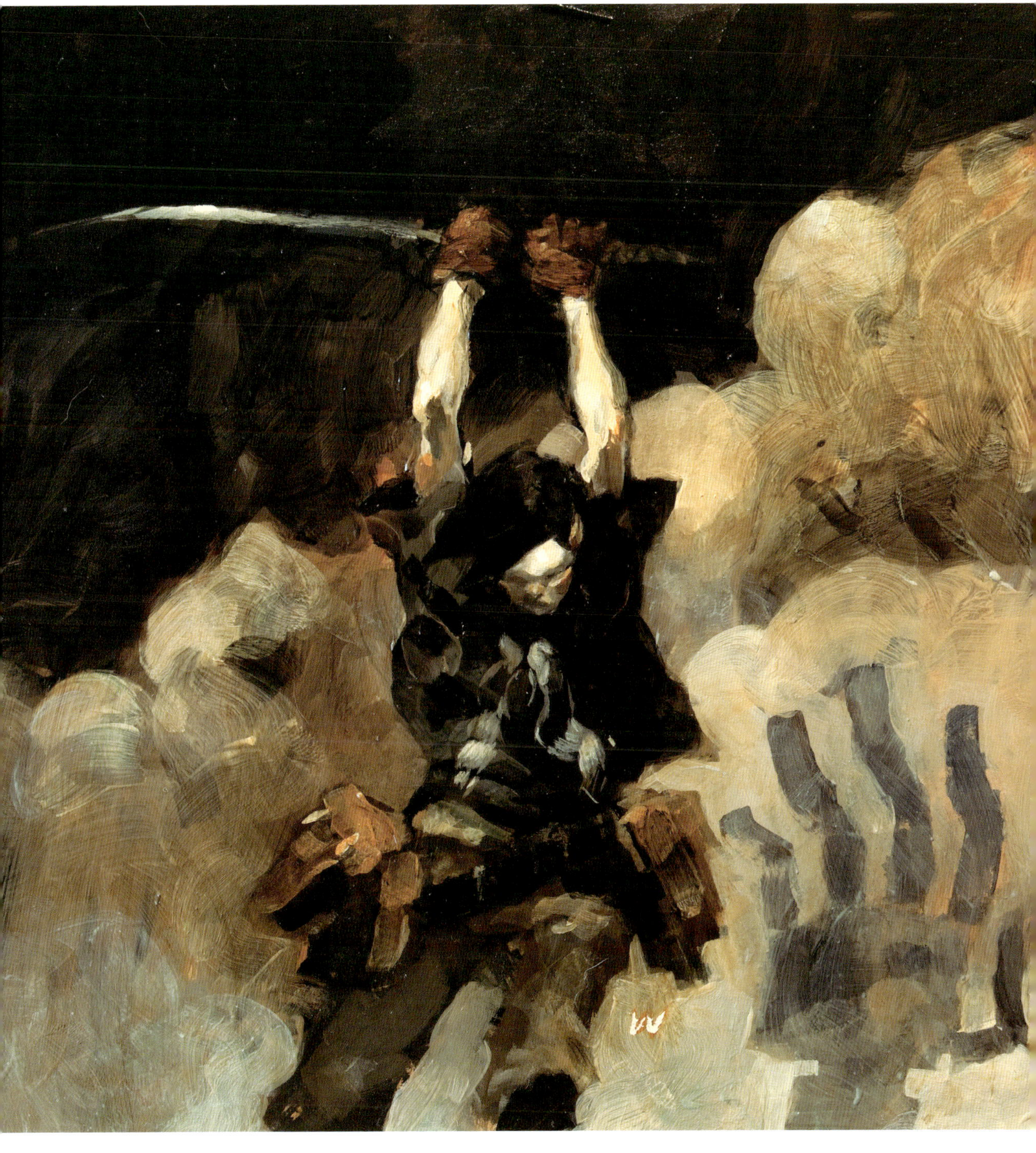

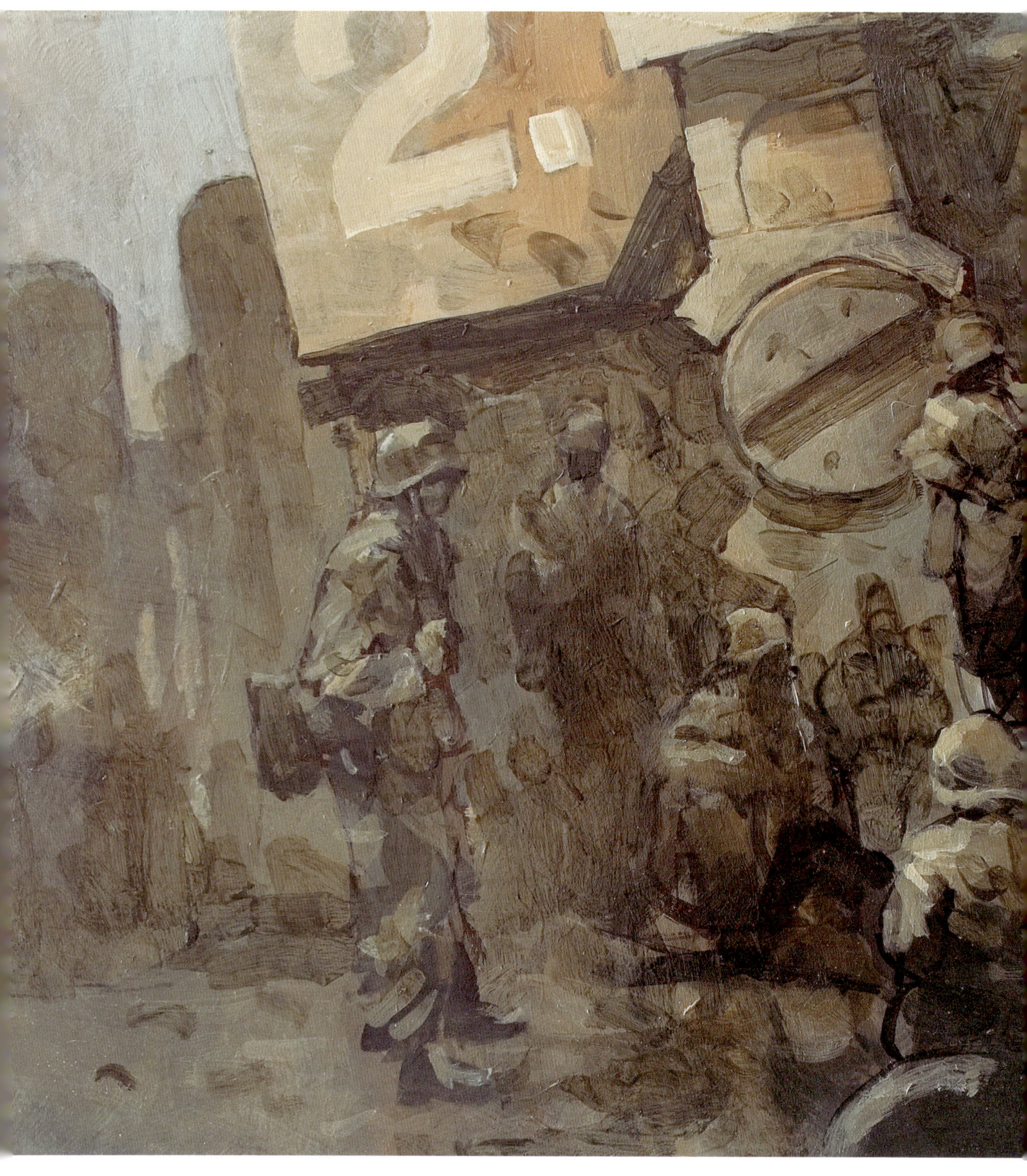

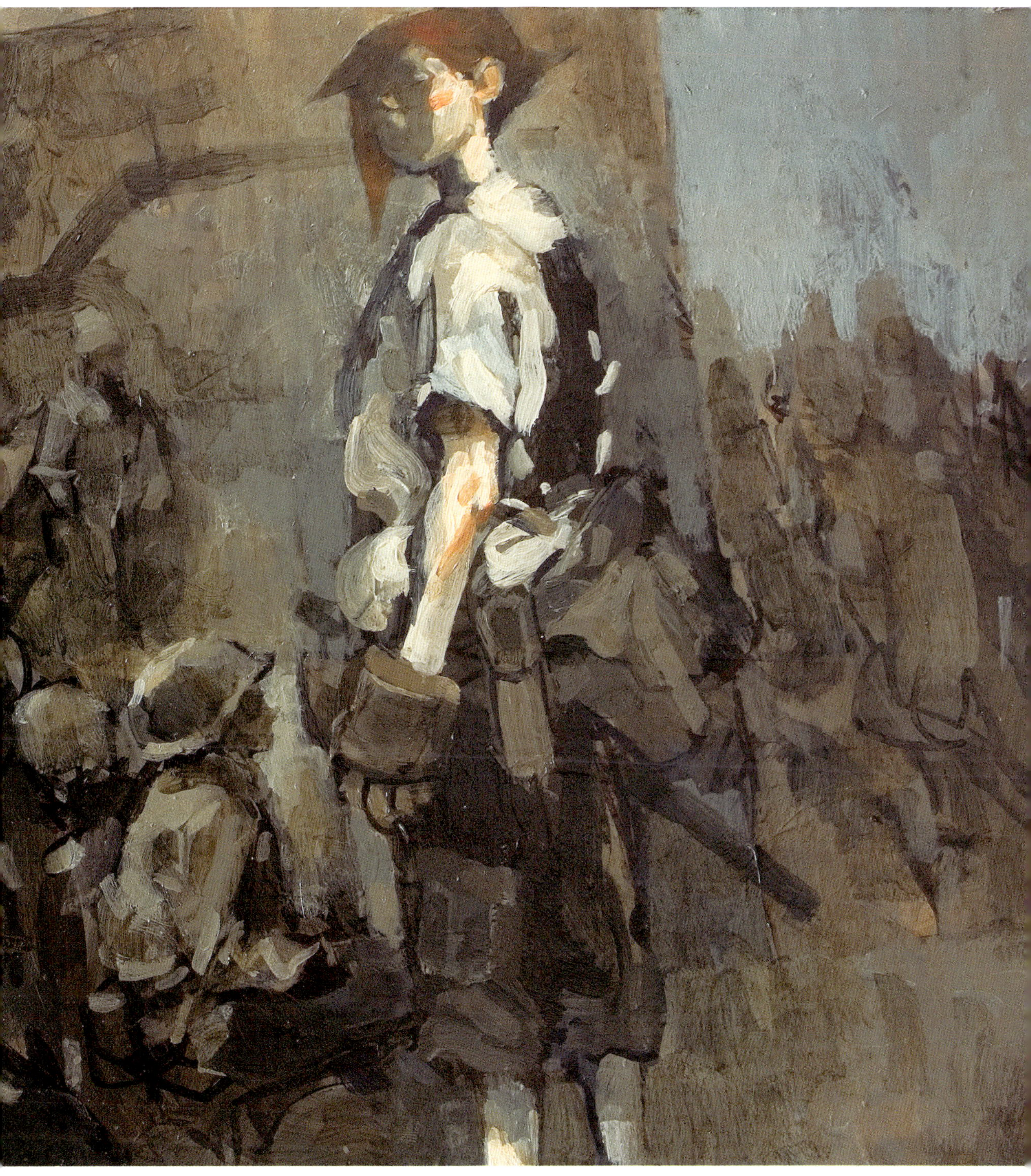

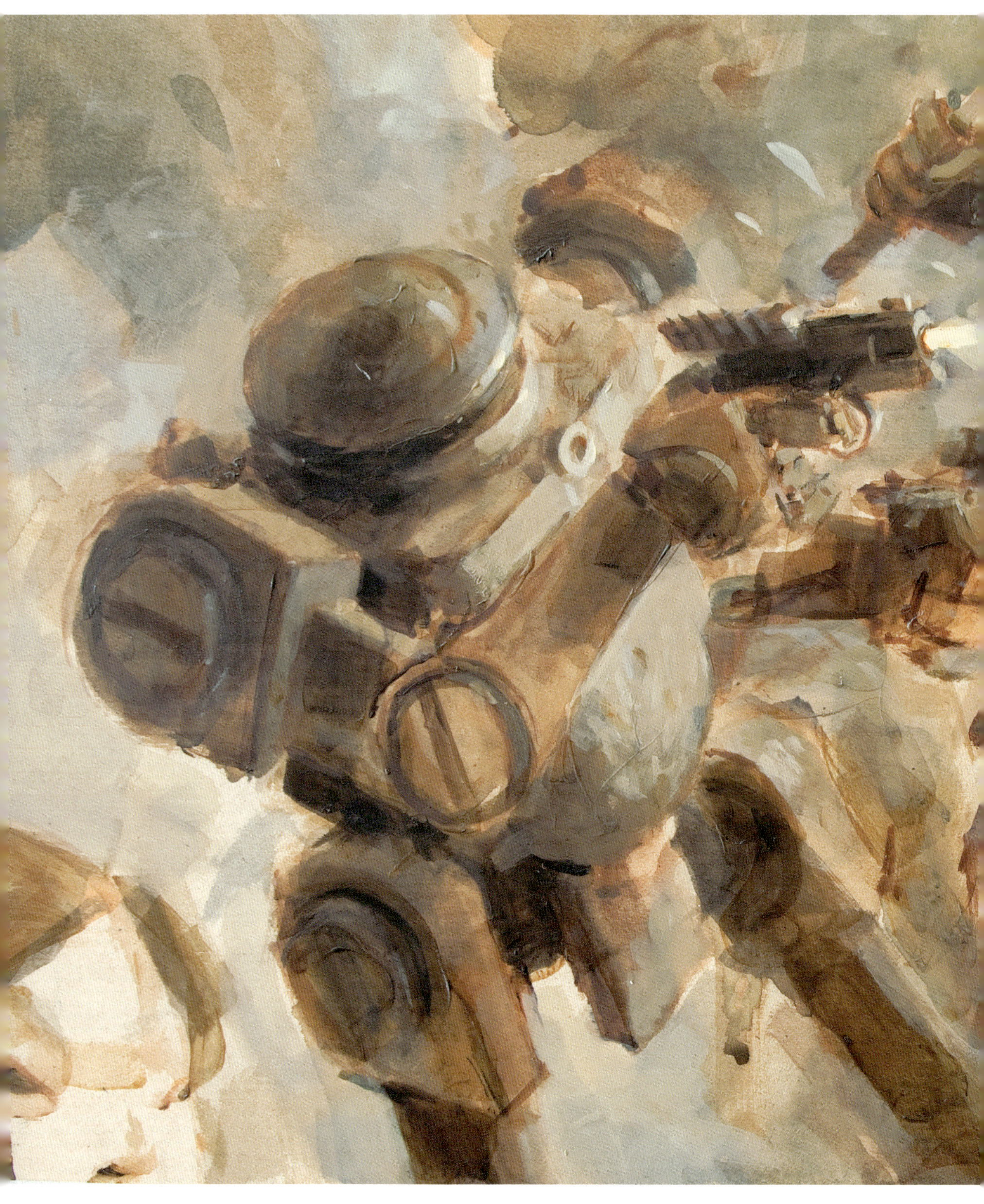

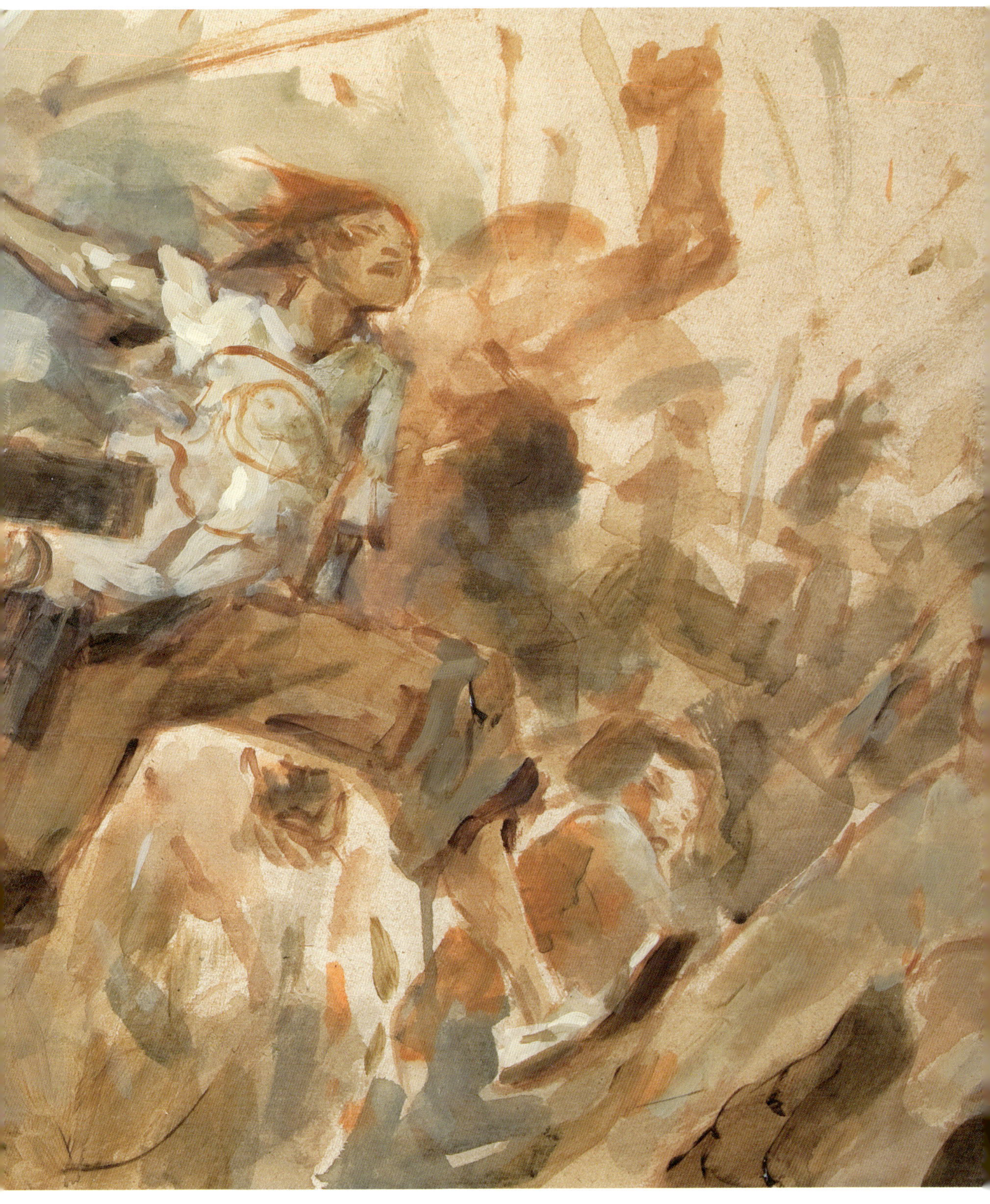

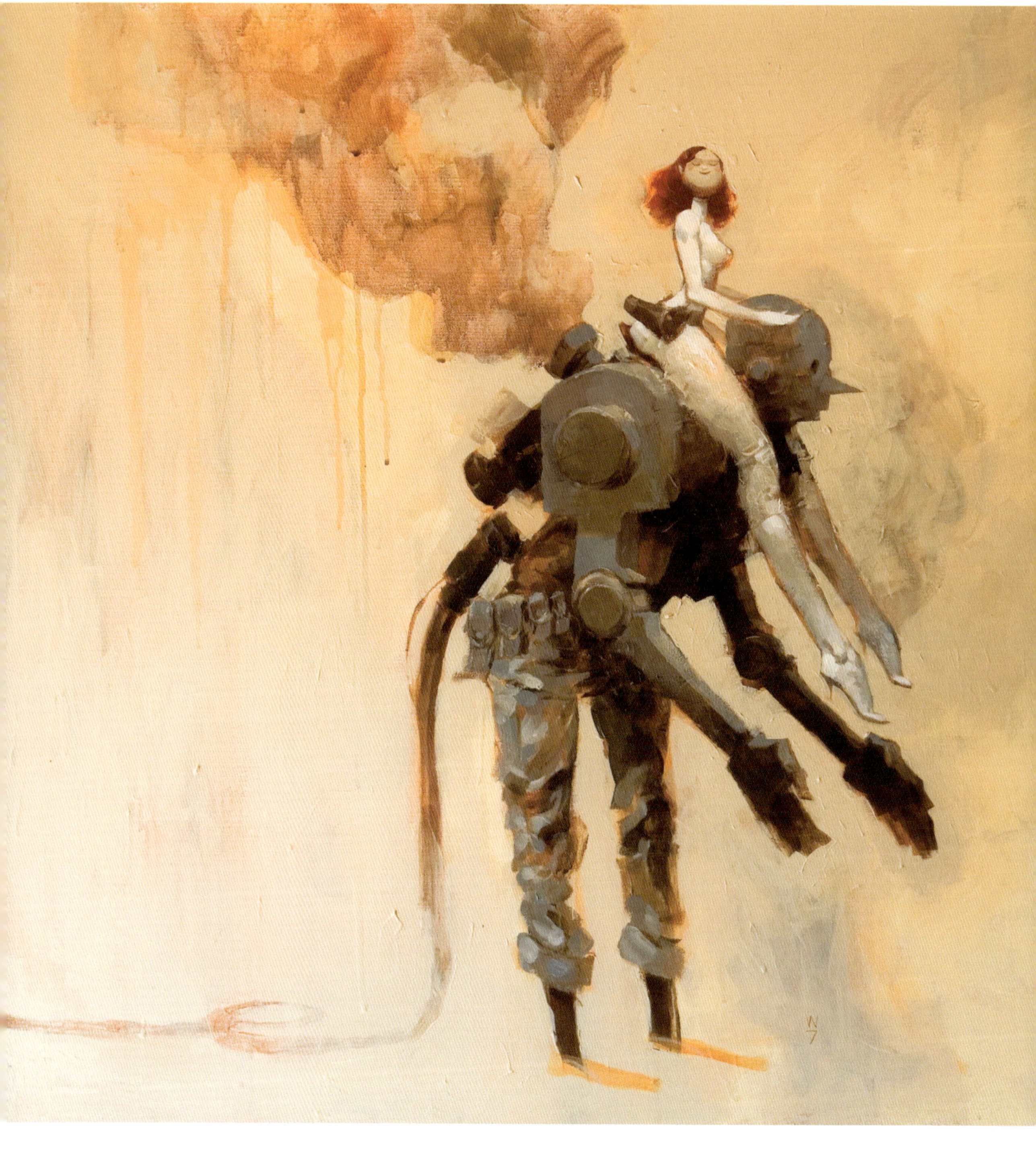

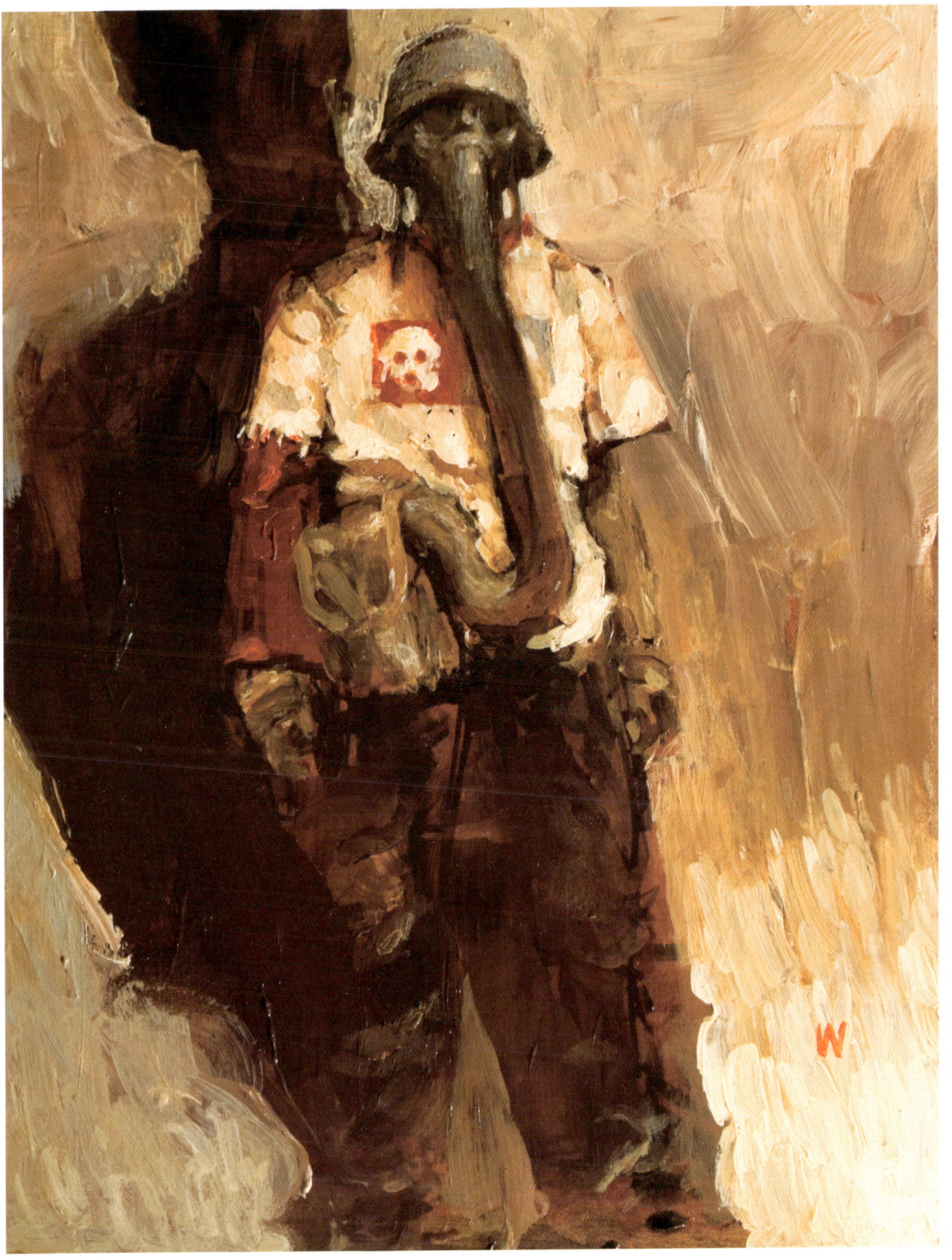

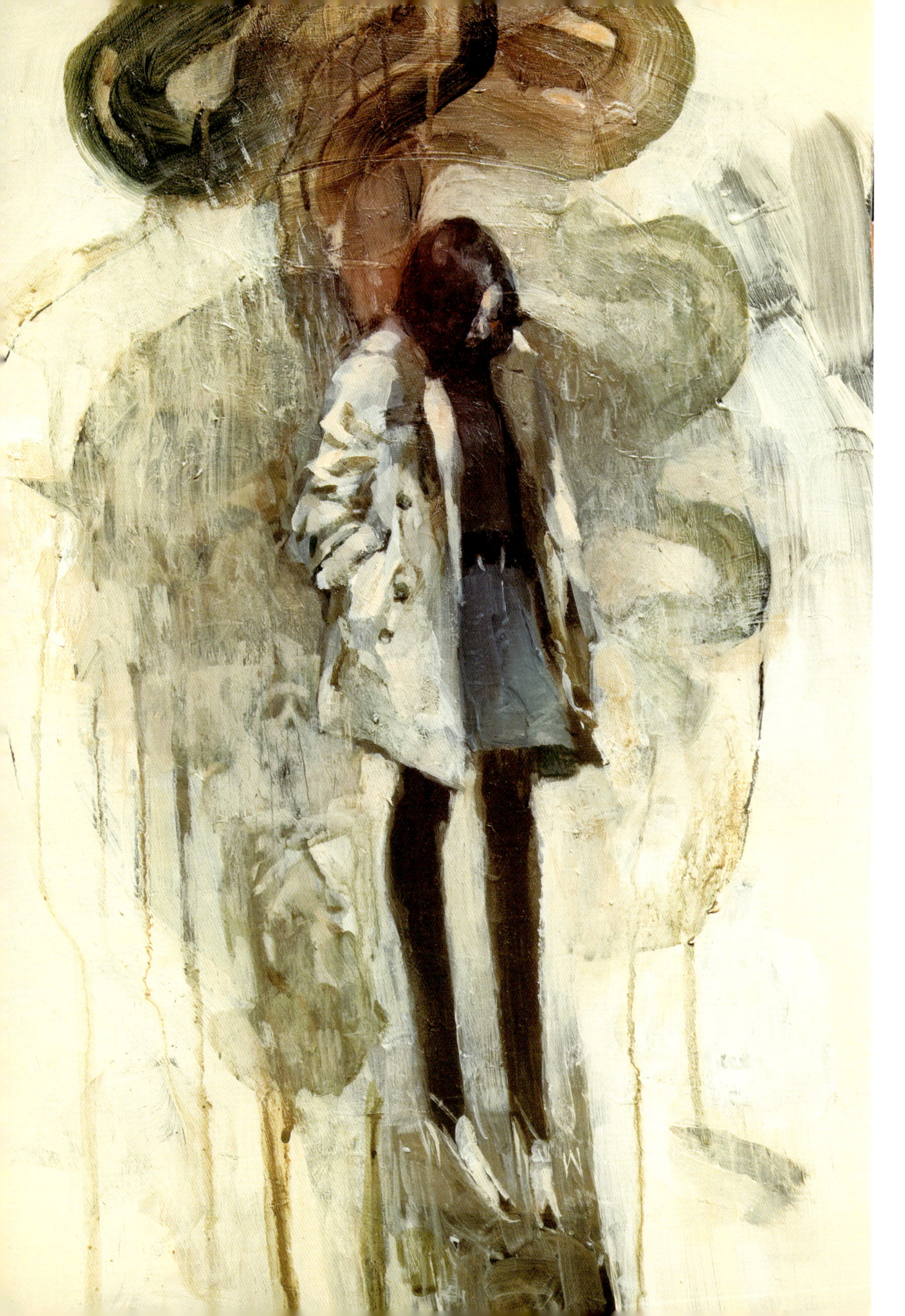

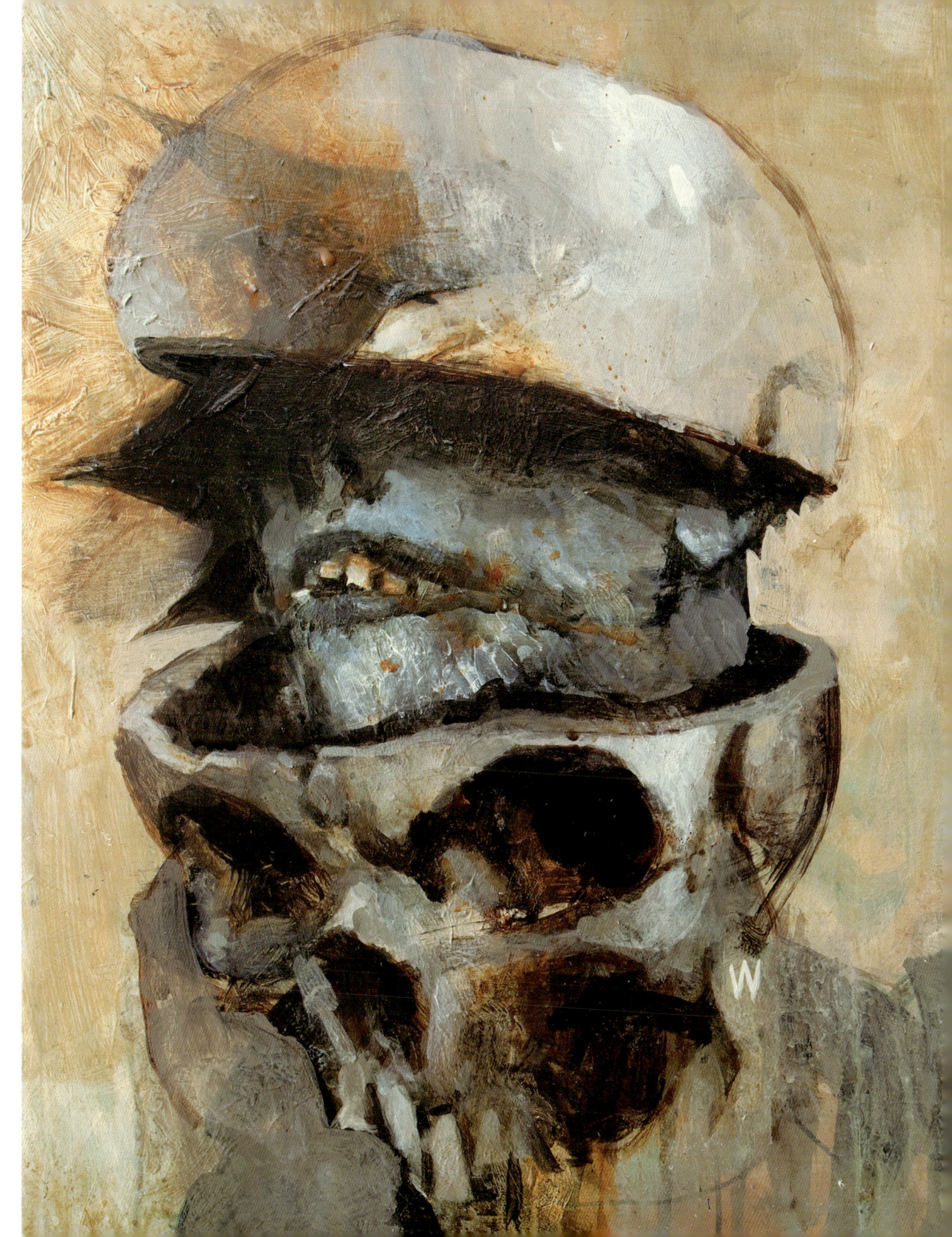

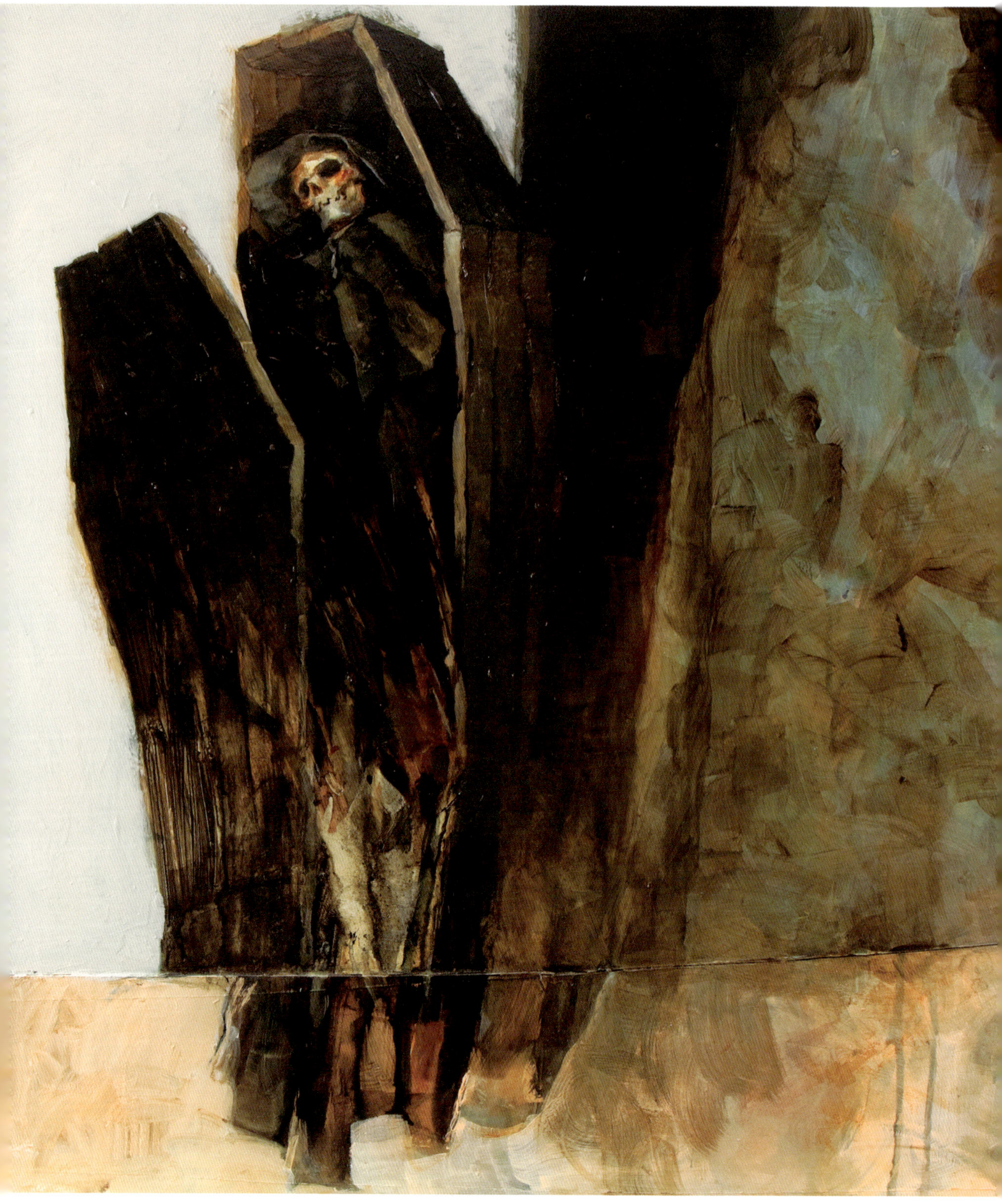

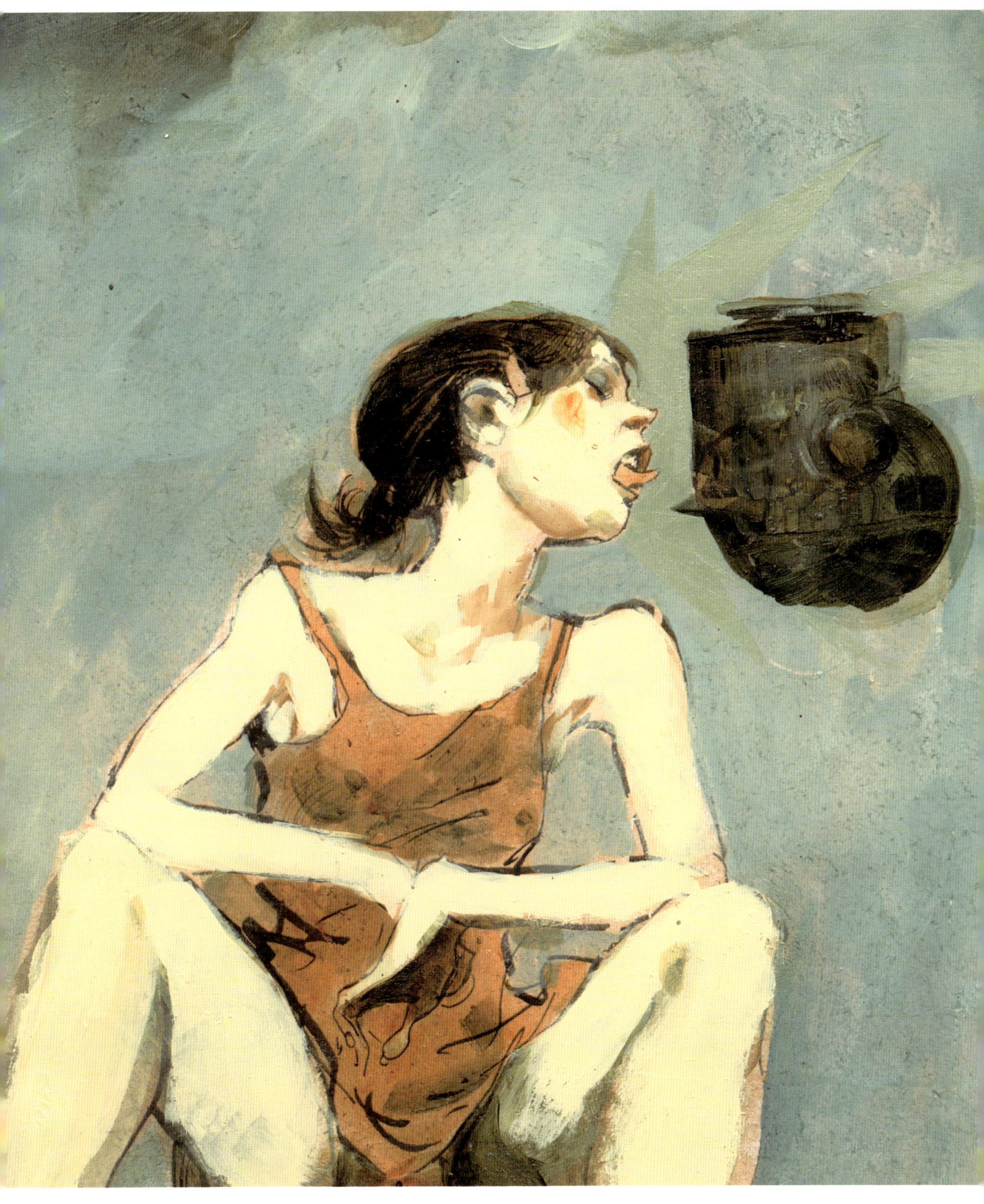

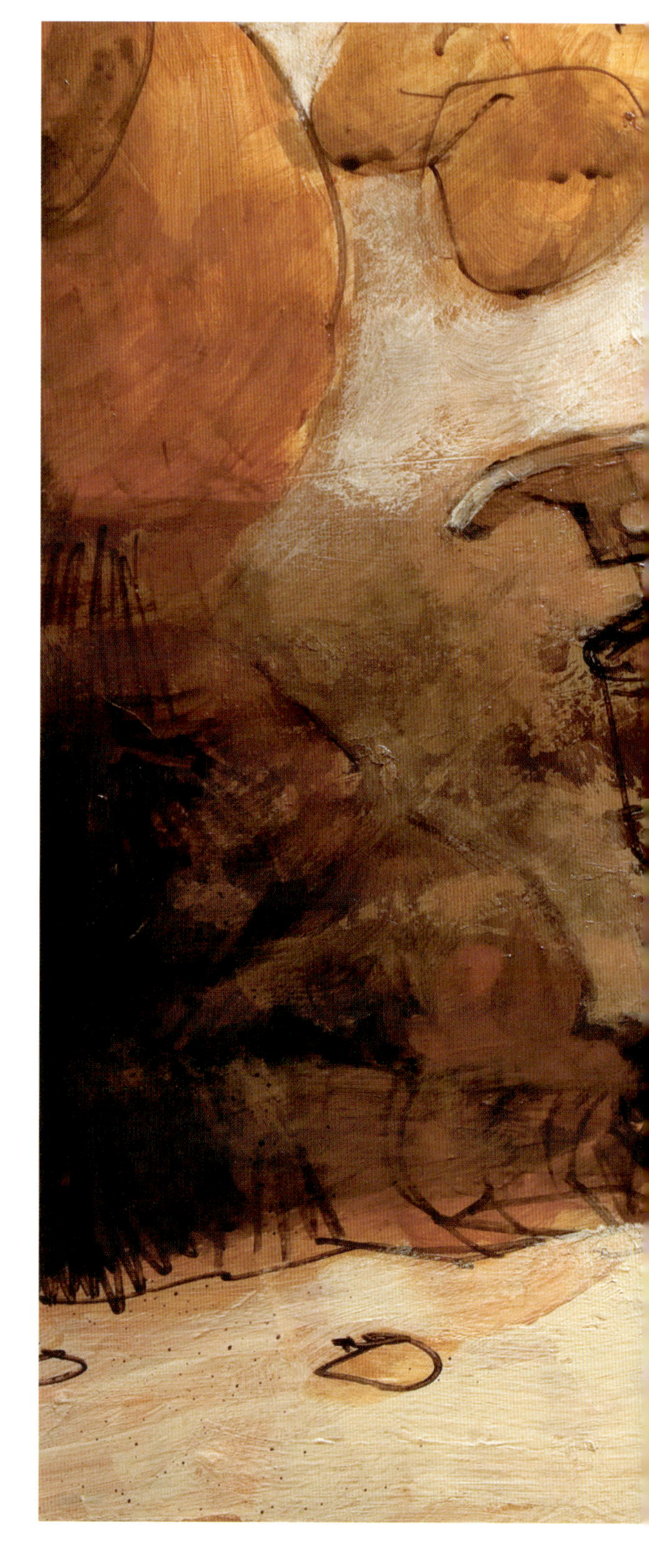

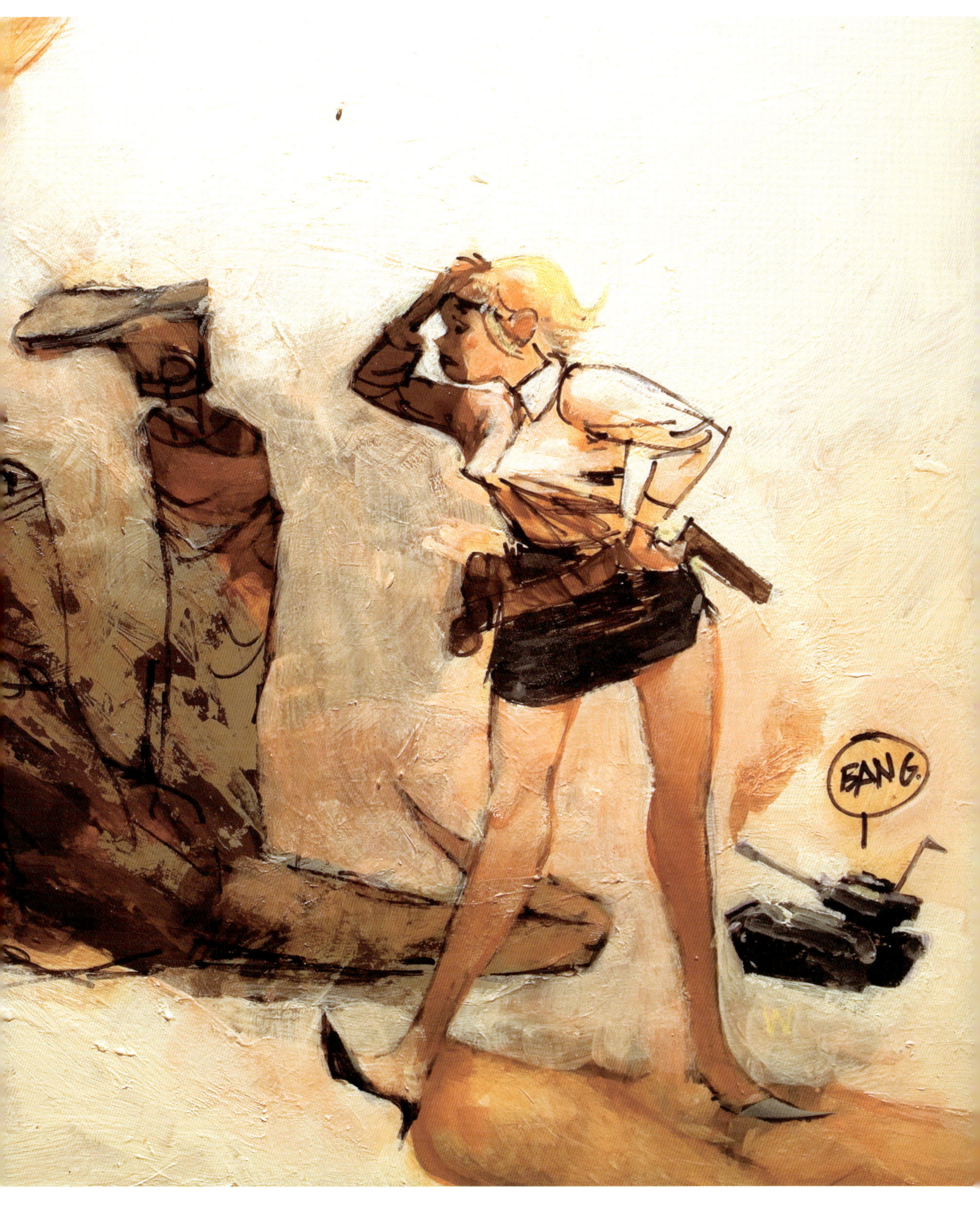
BAN G.

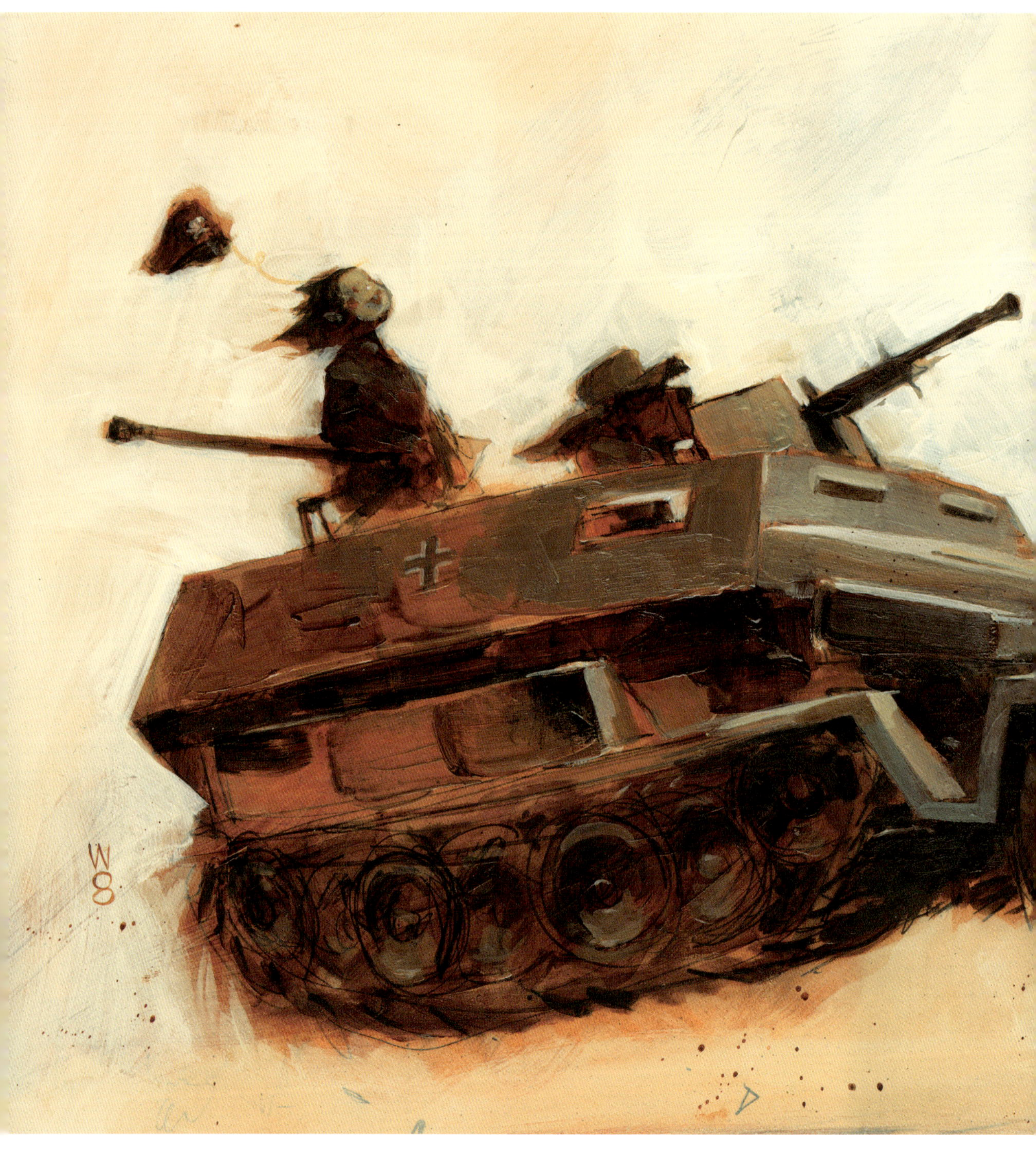

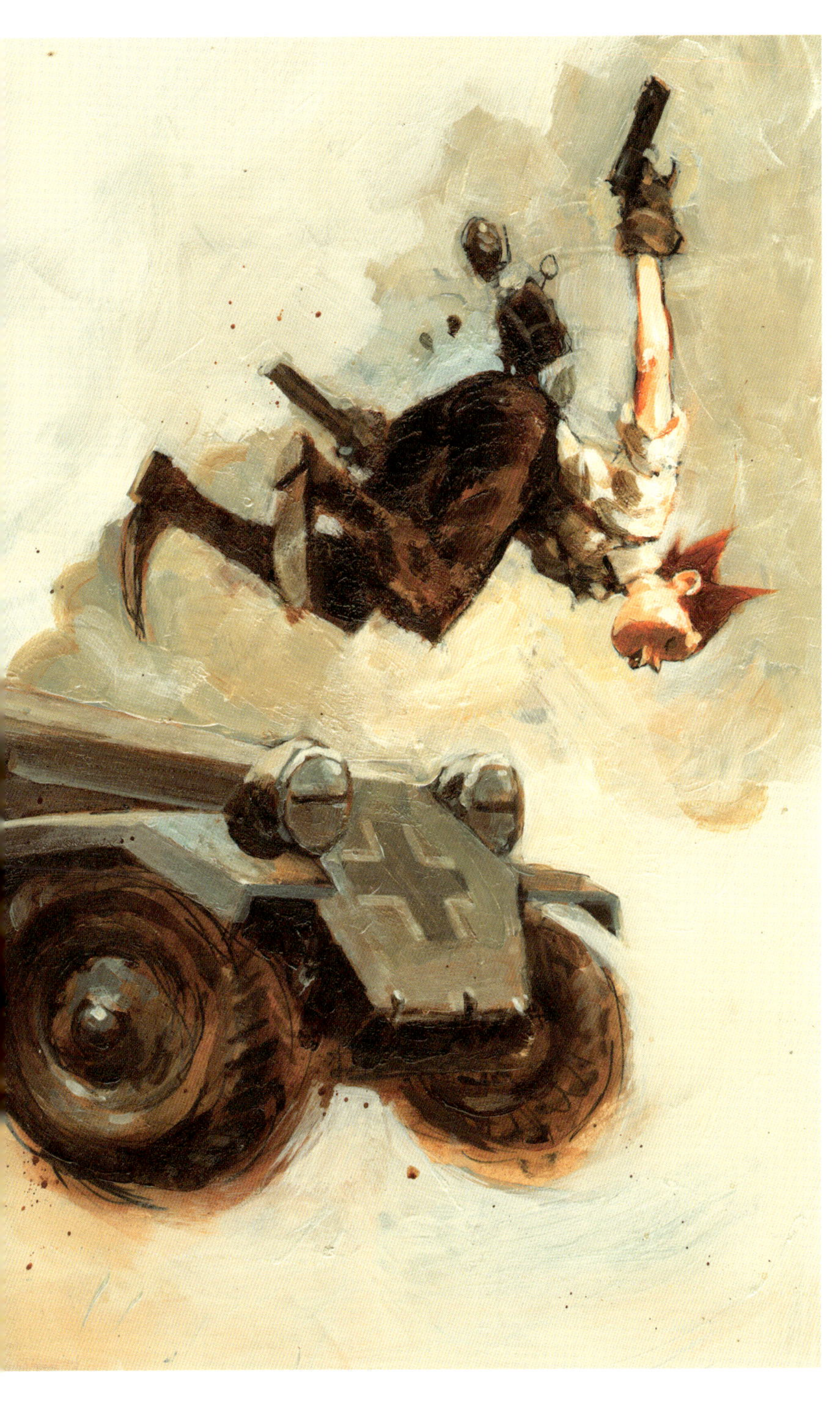

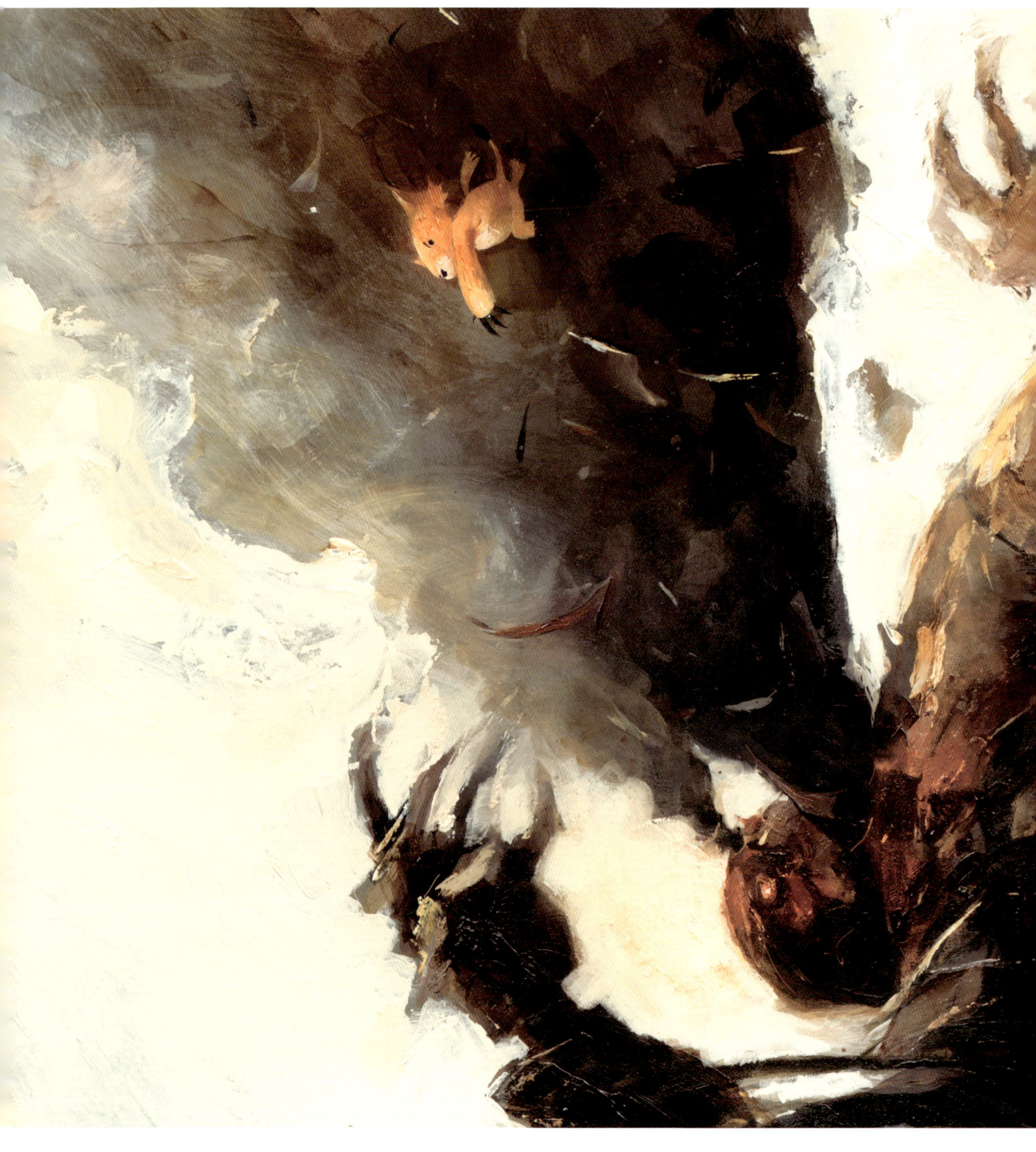

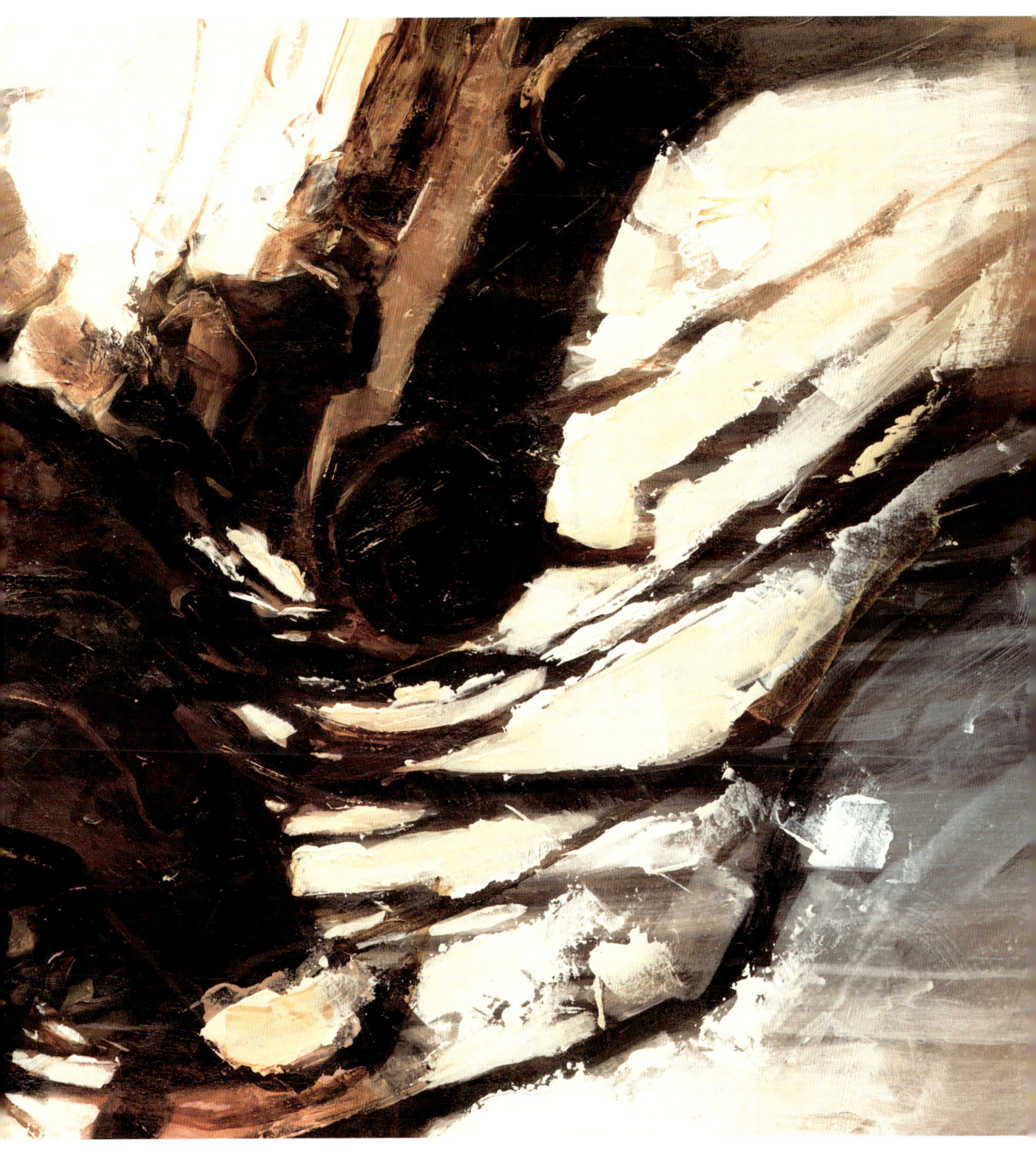

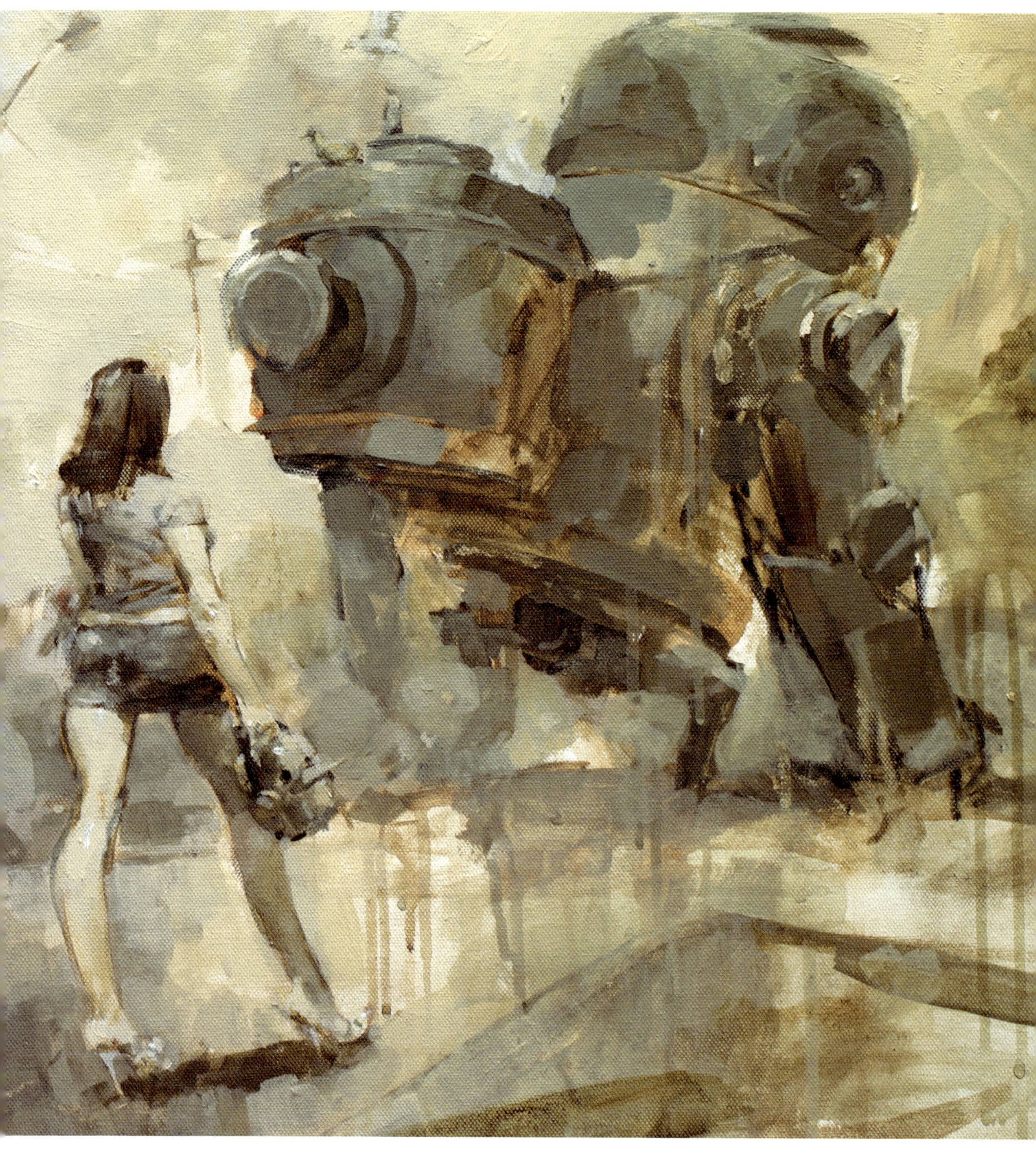

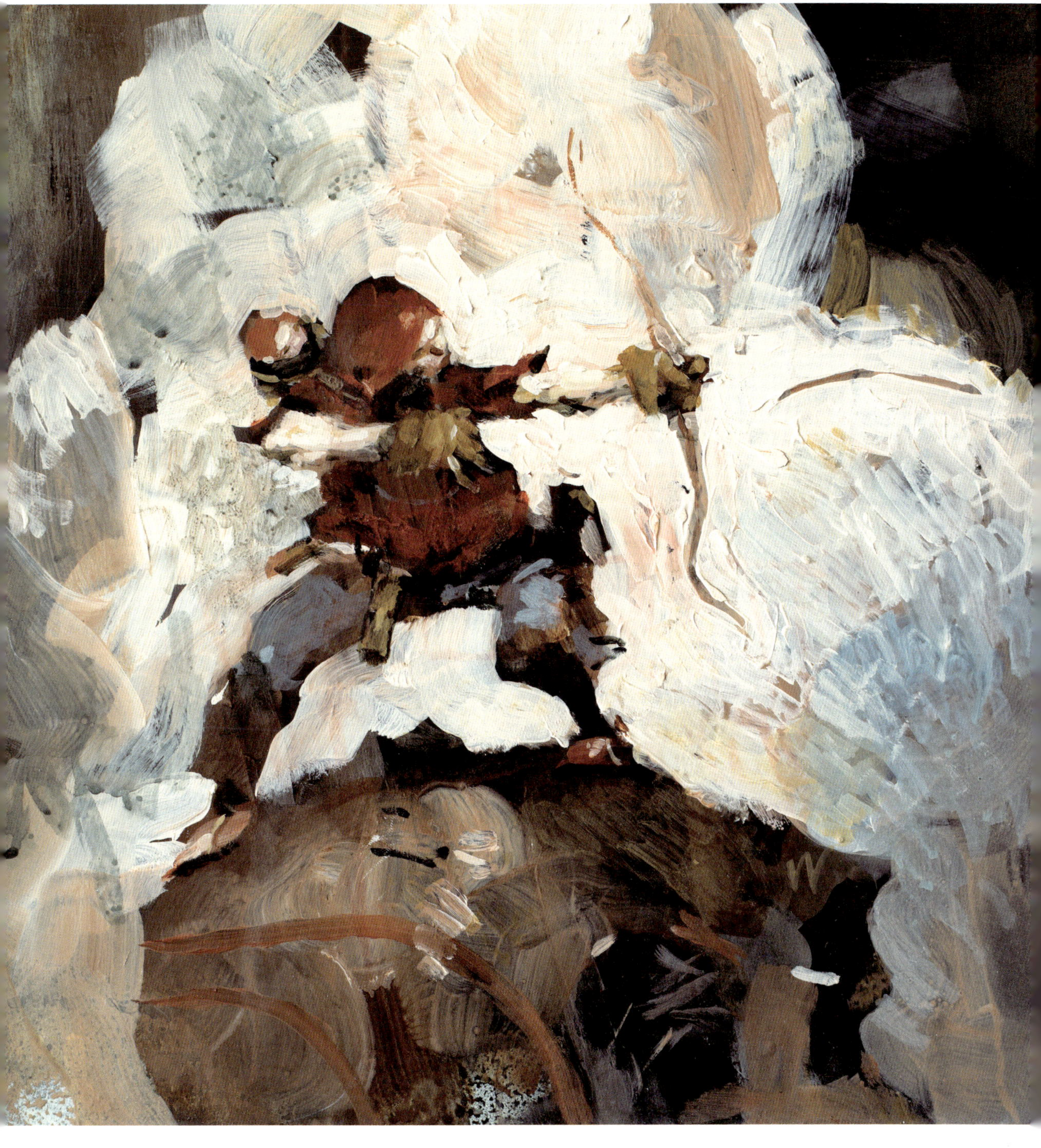

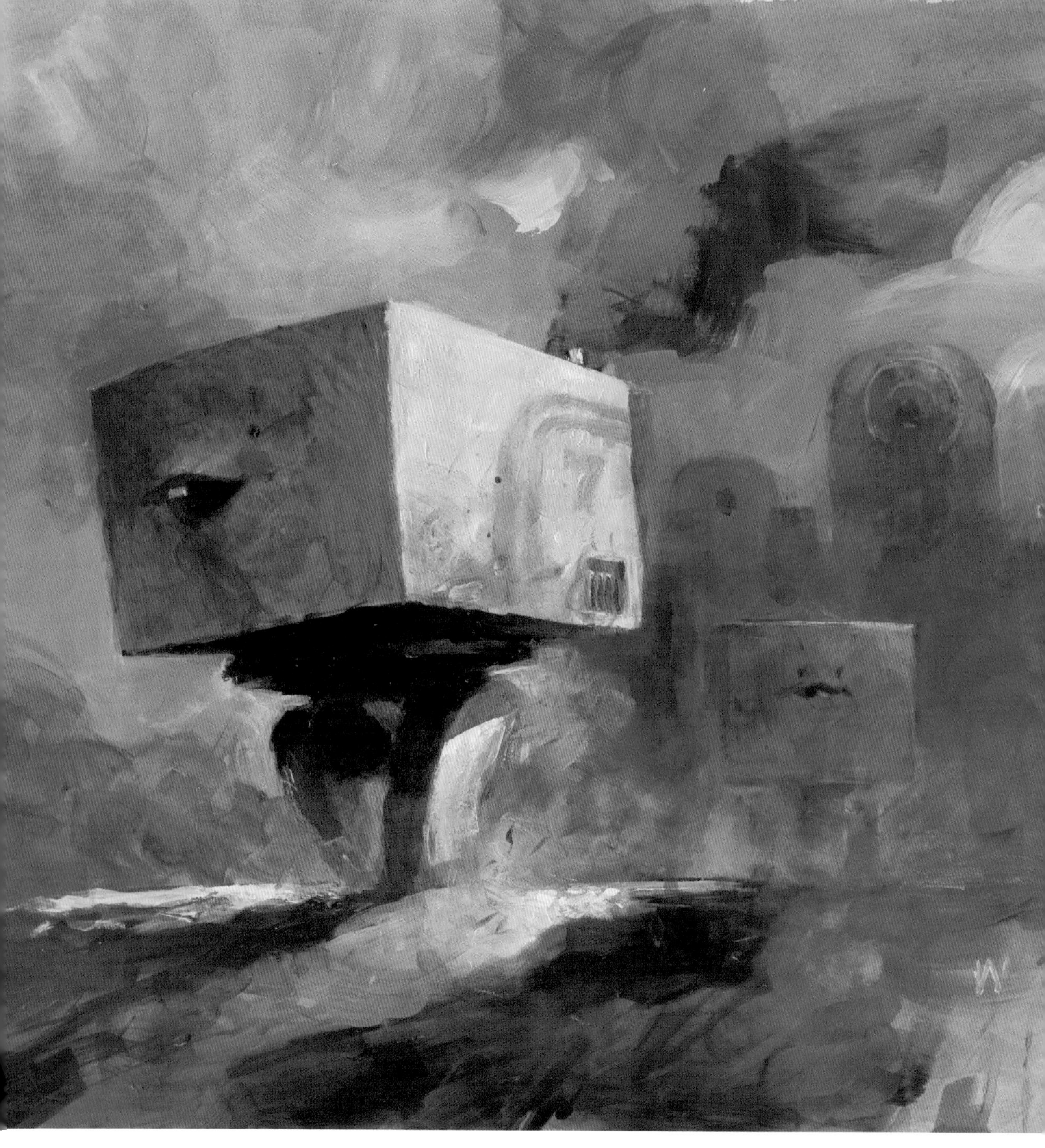

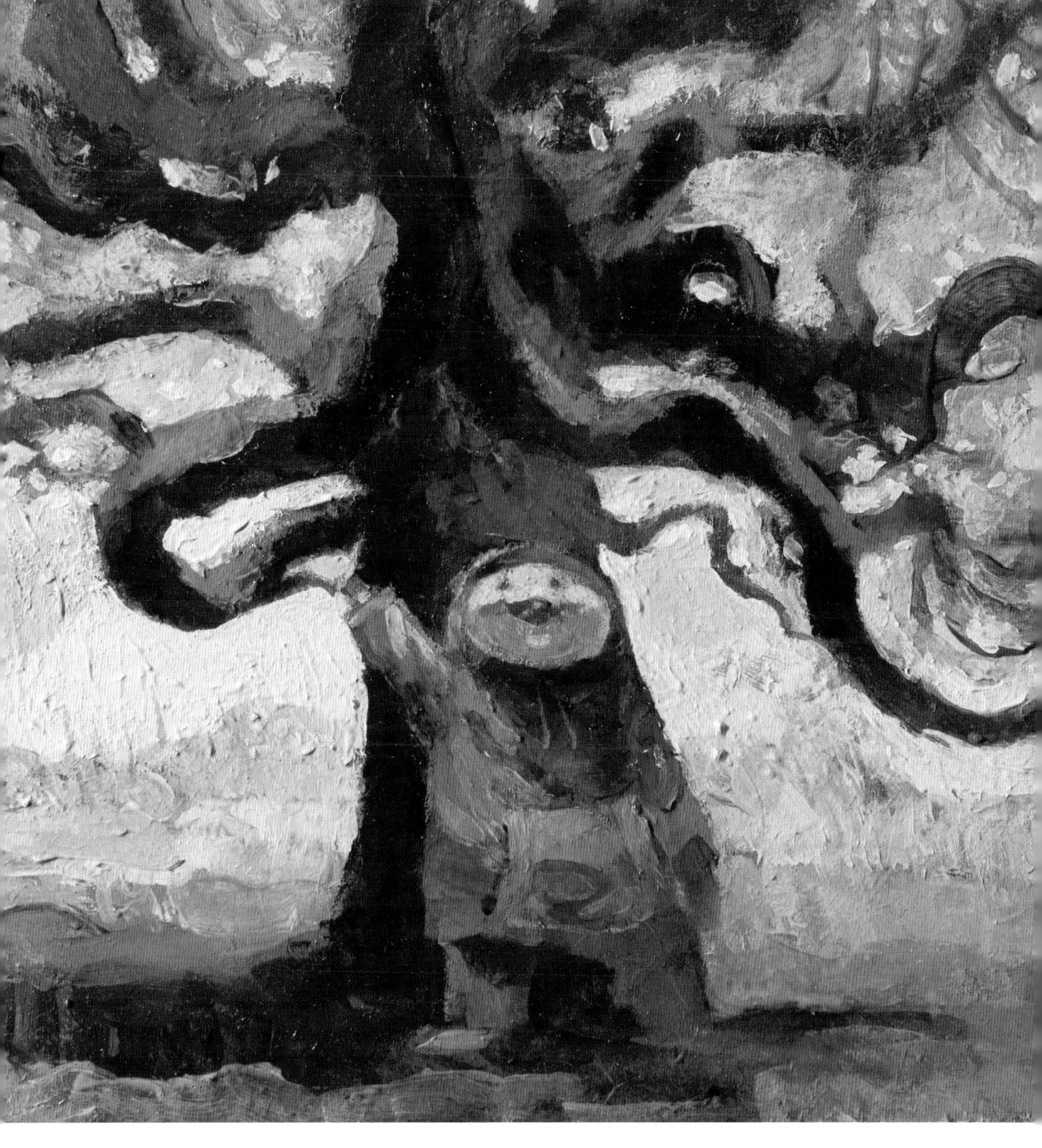

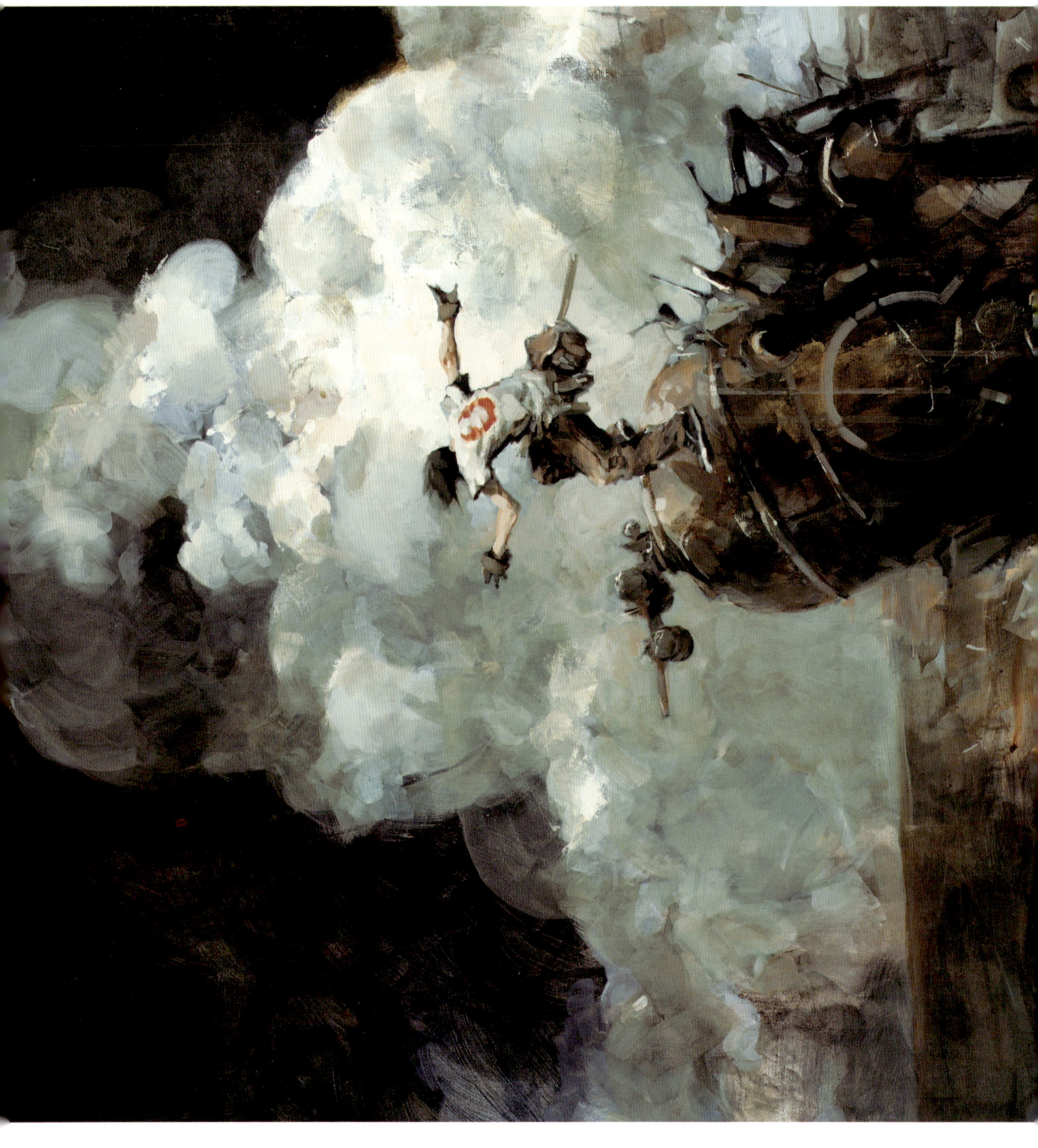

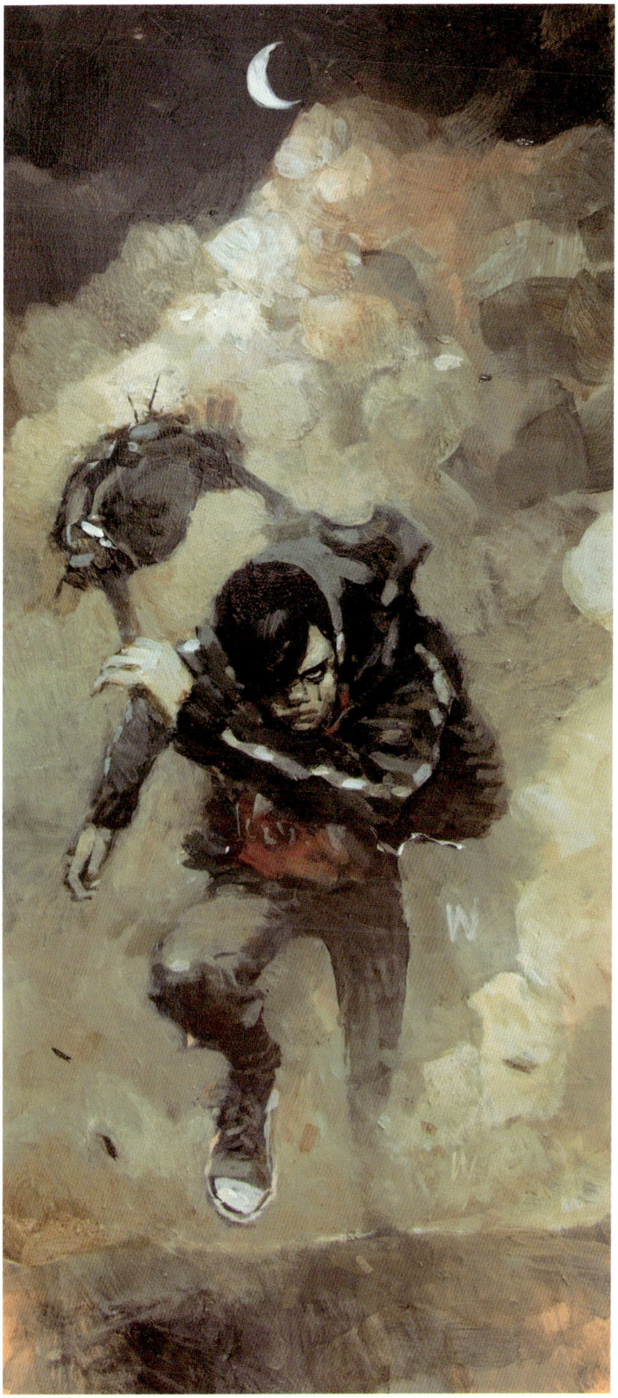

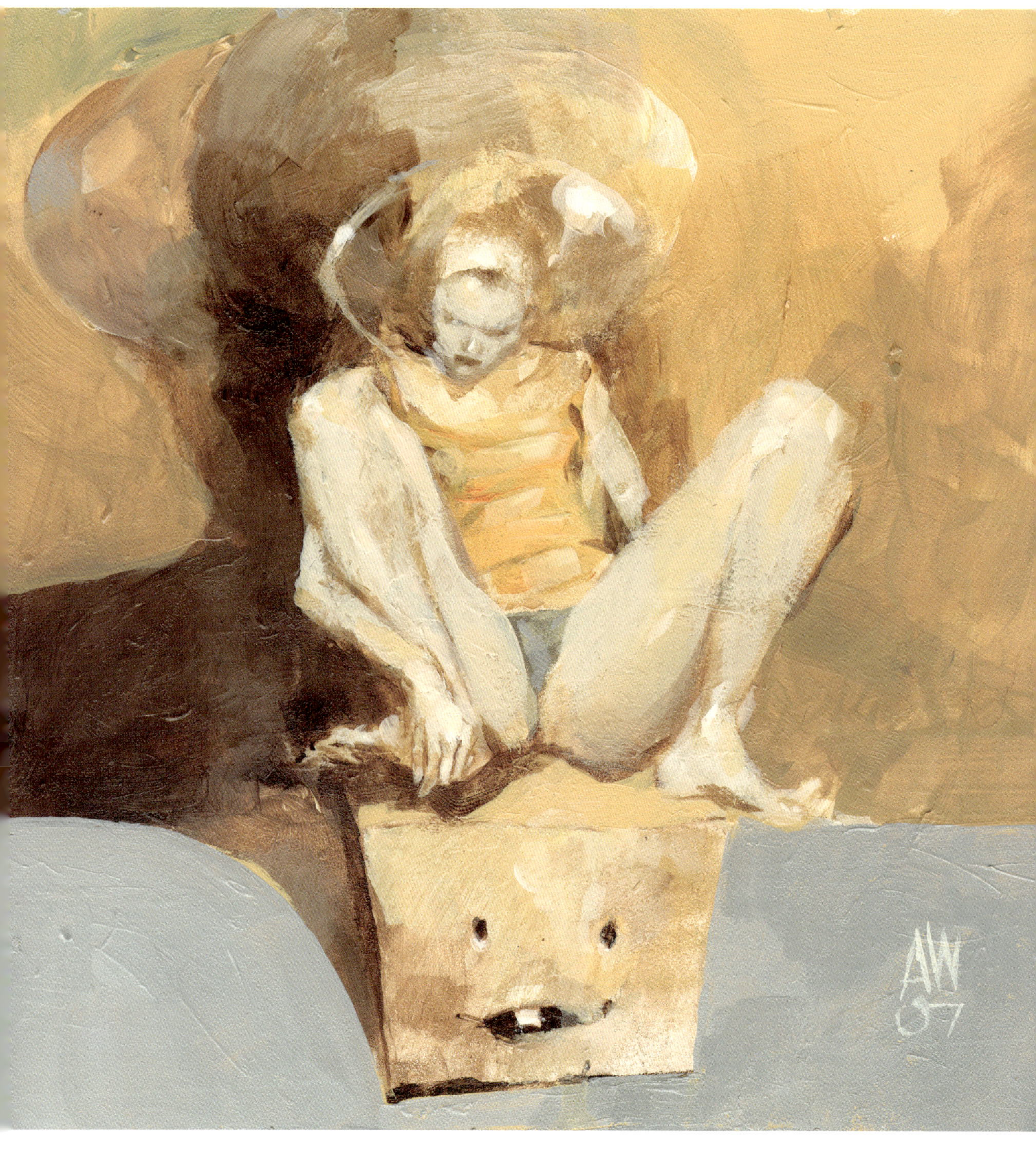

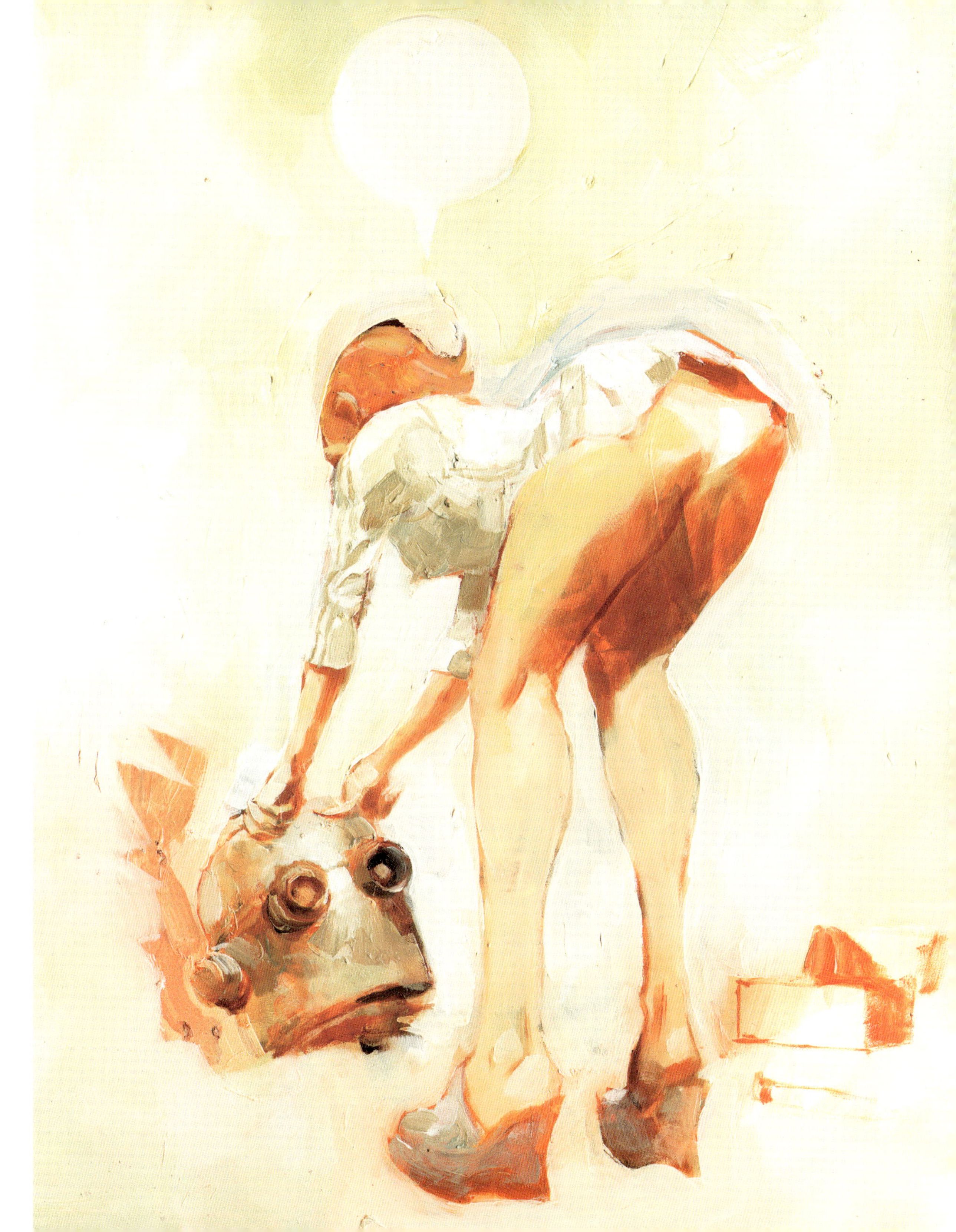

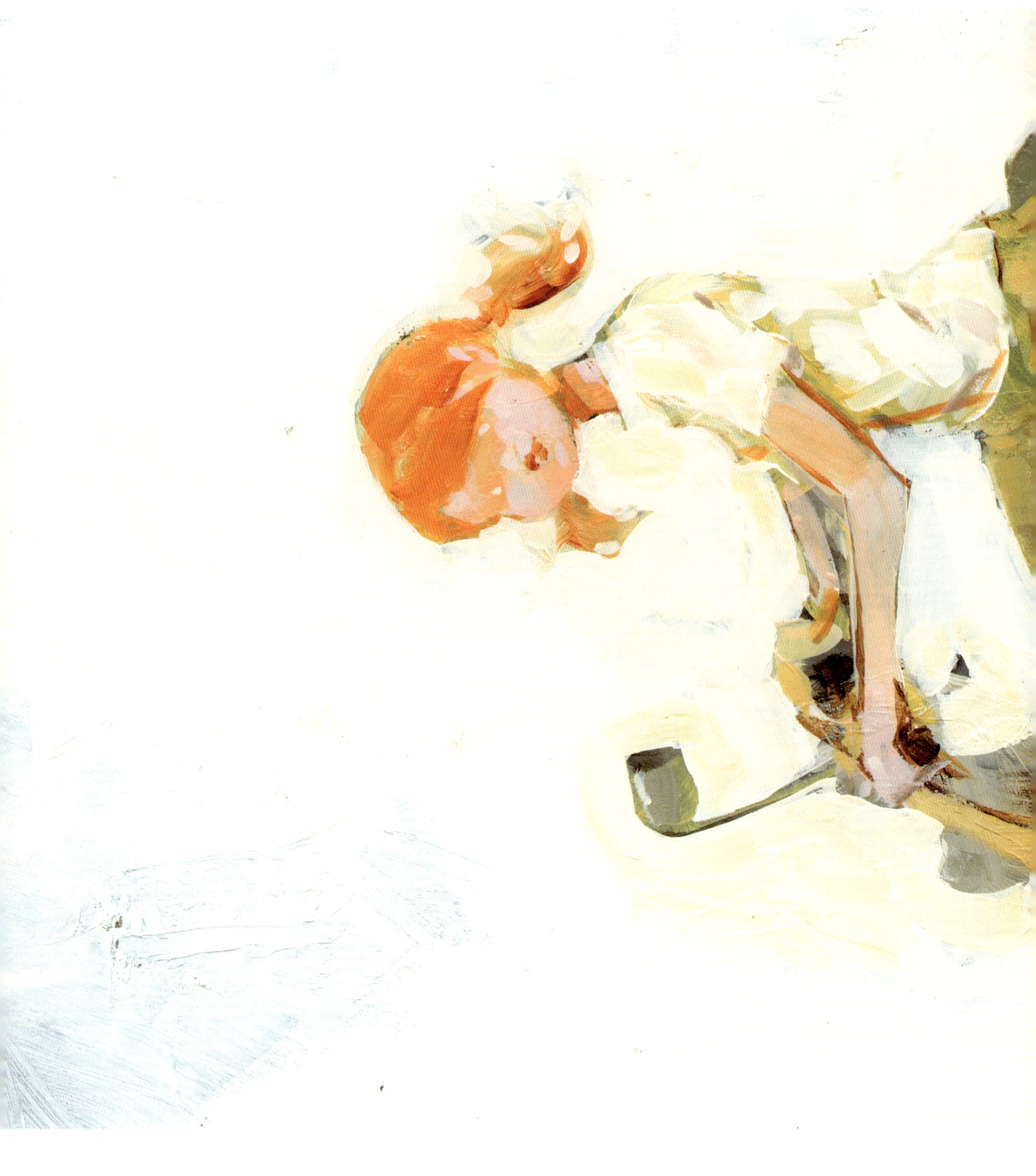

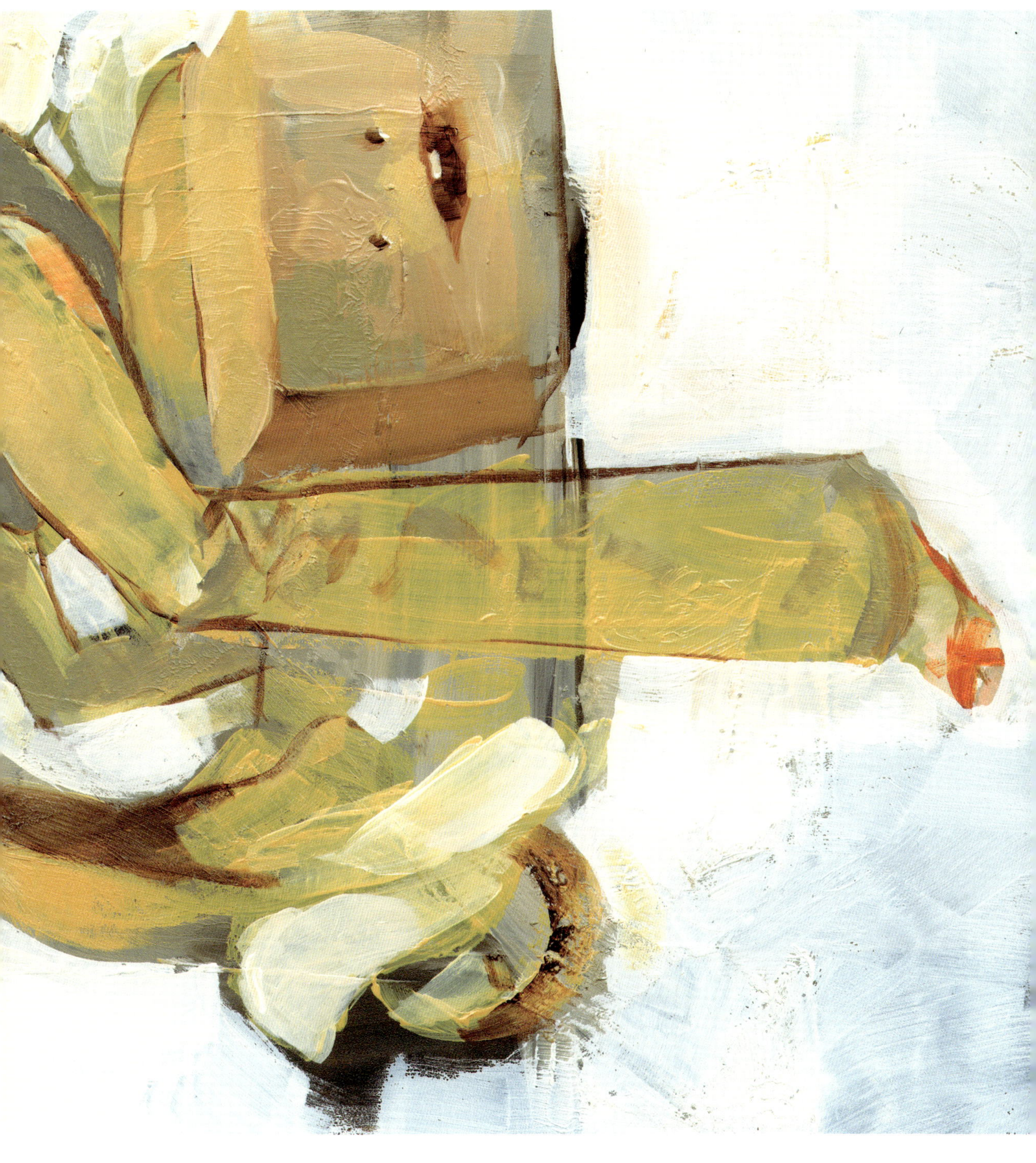

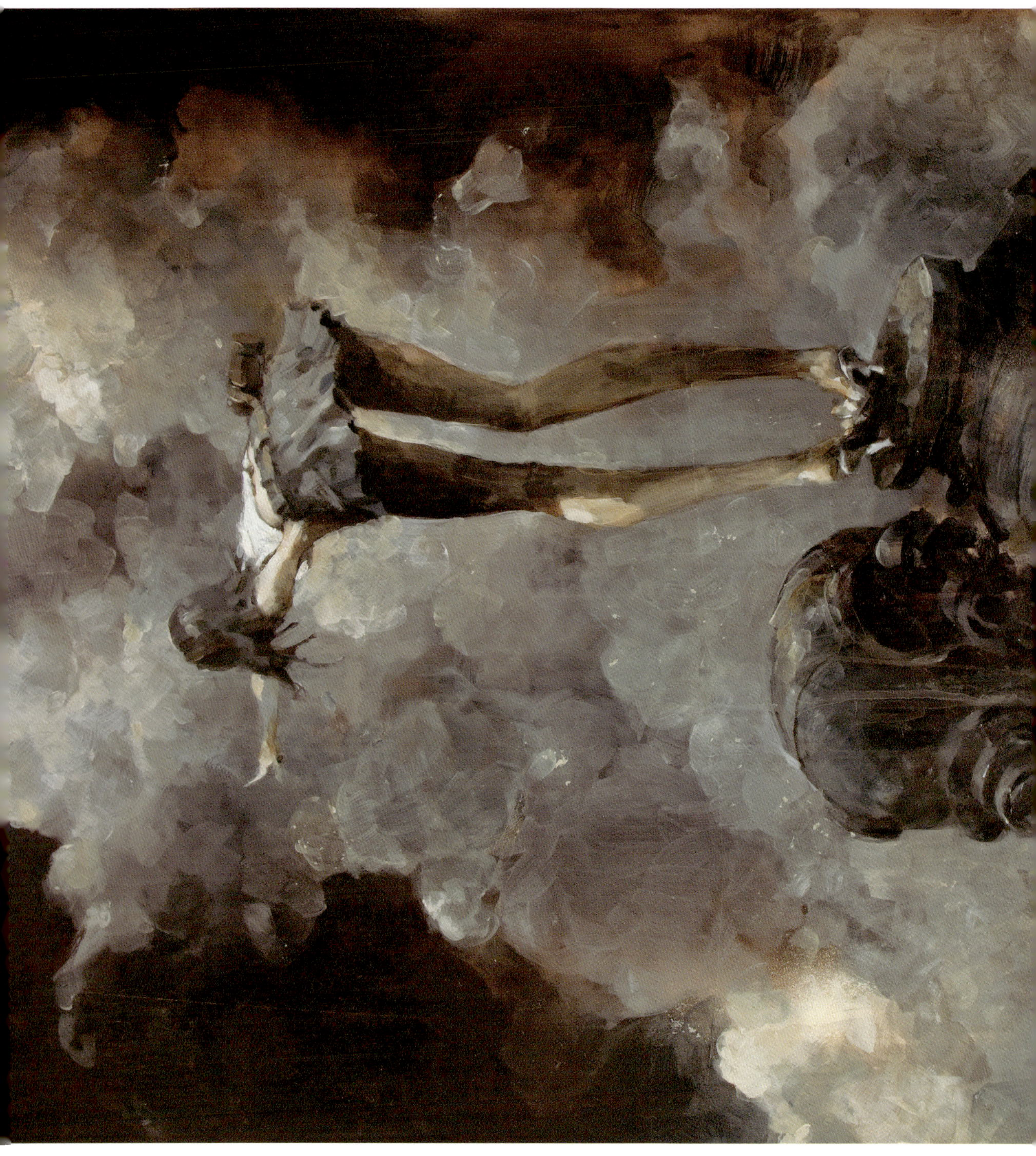

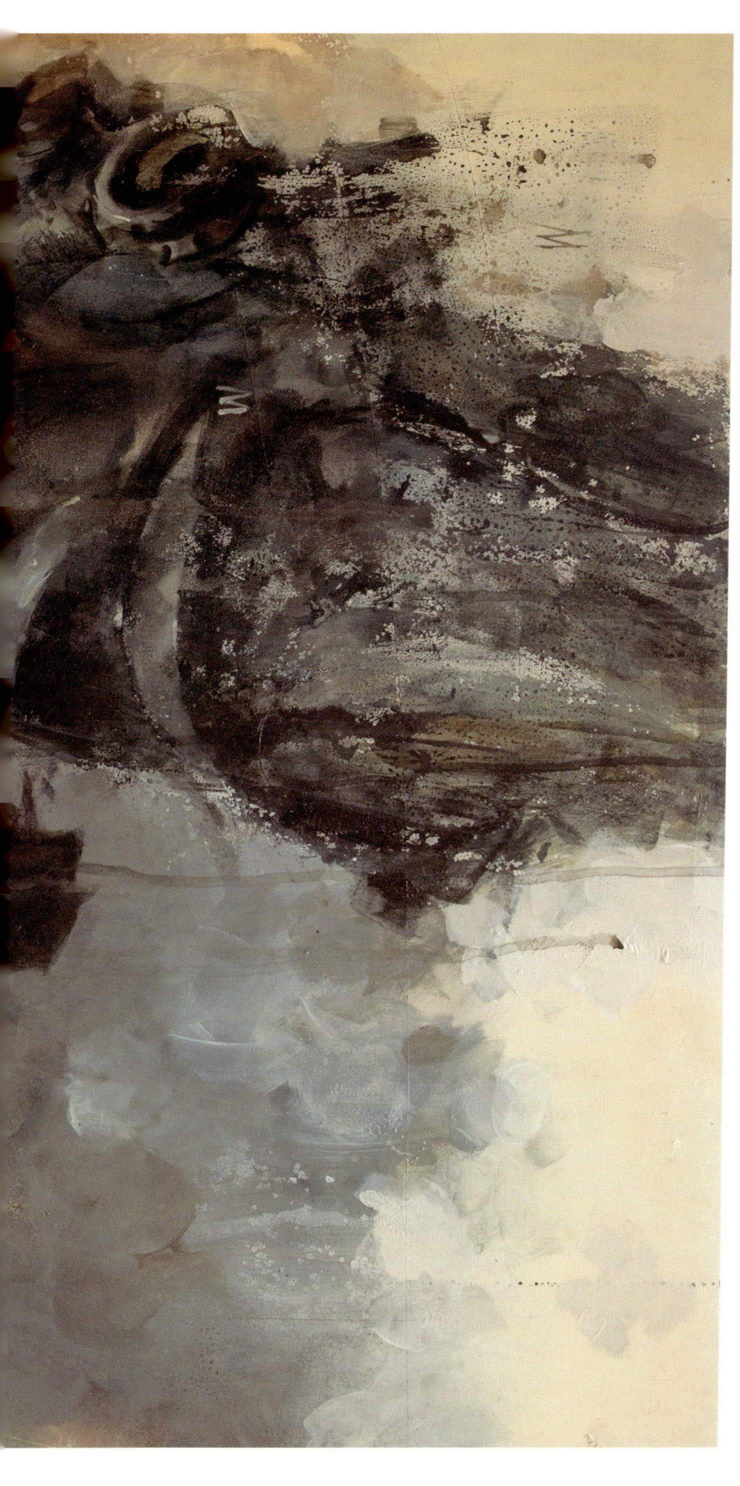

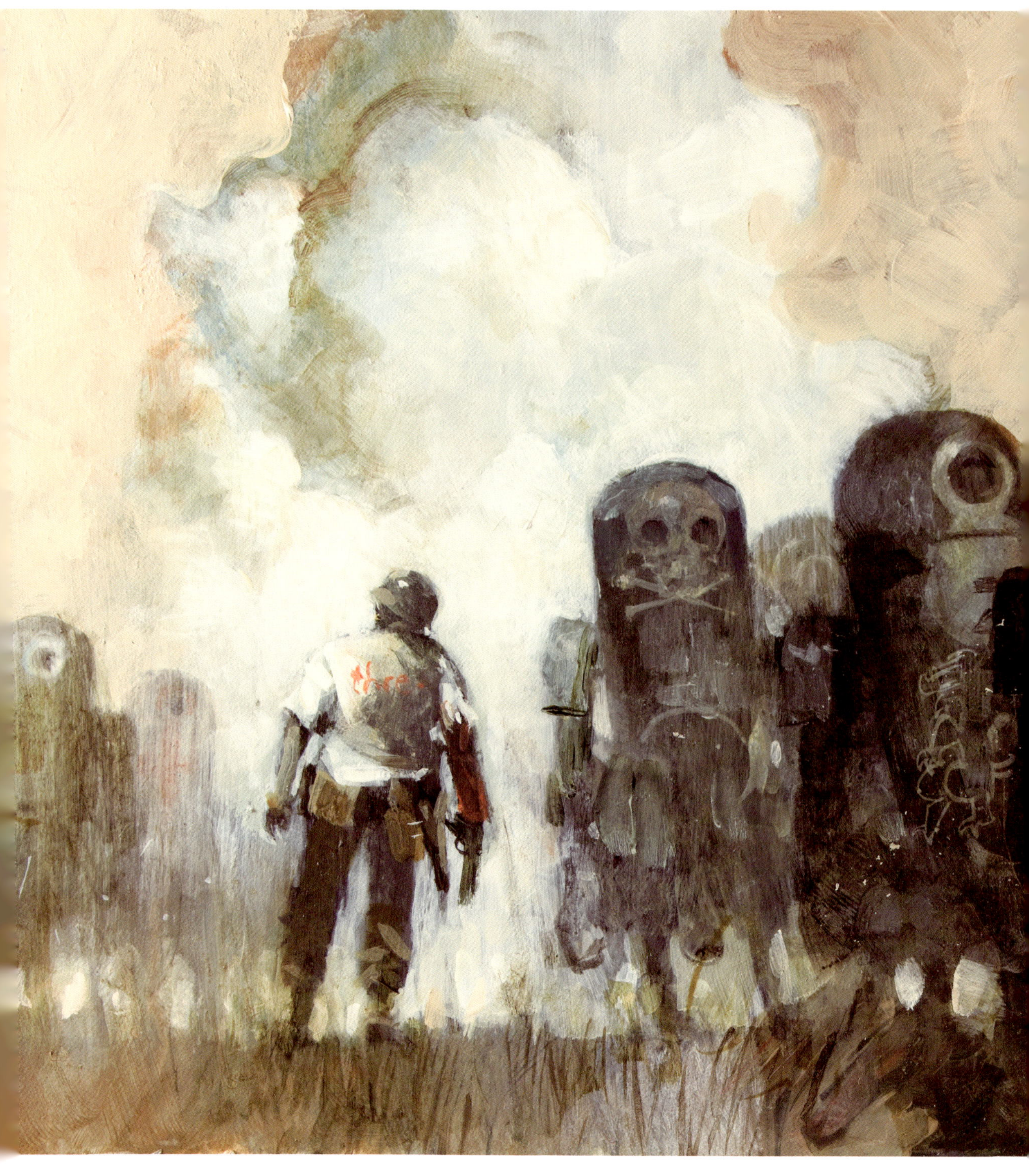

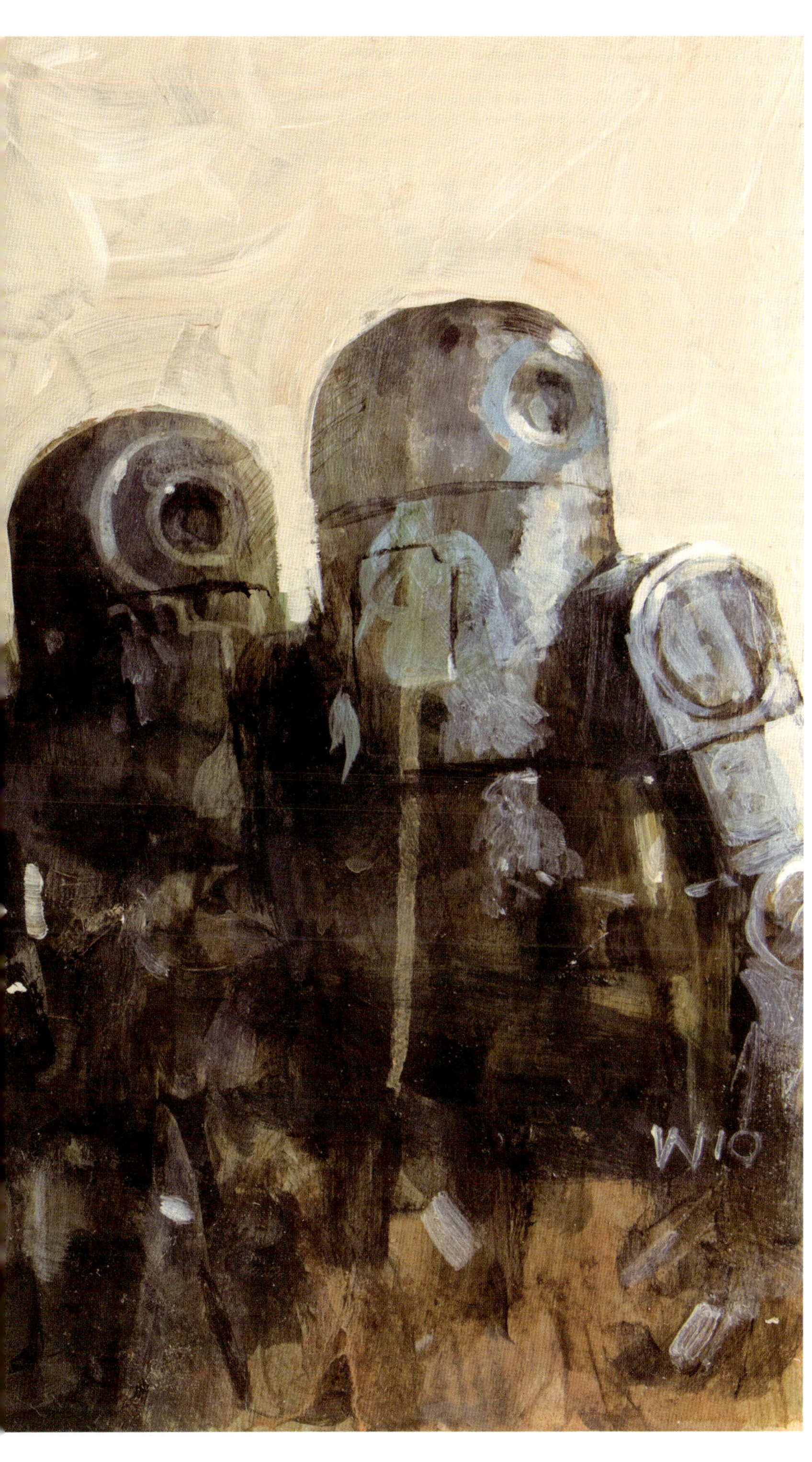

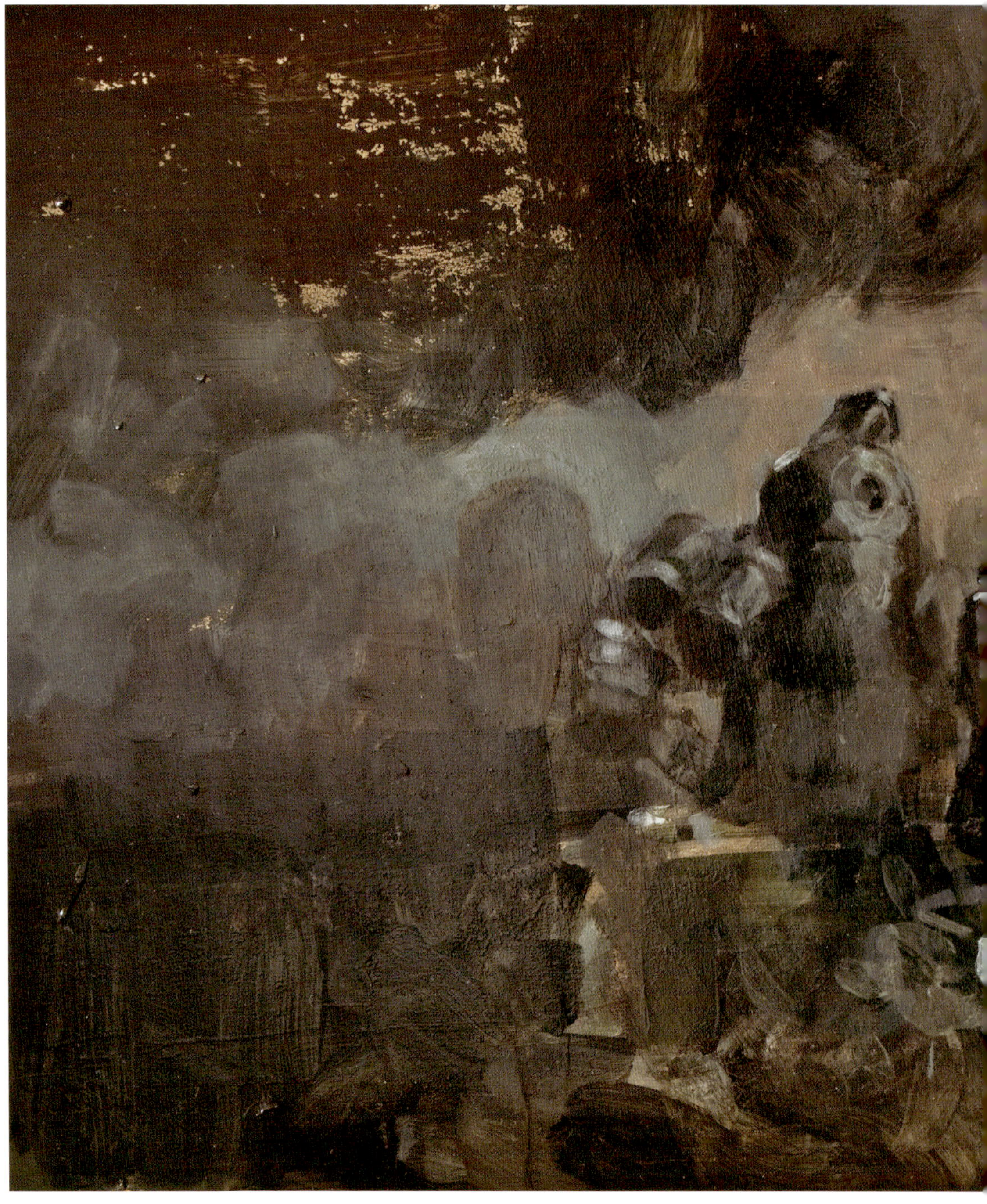

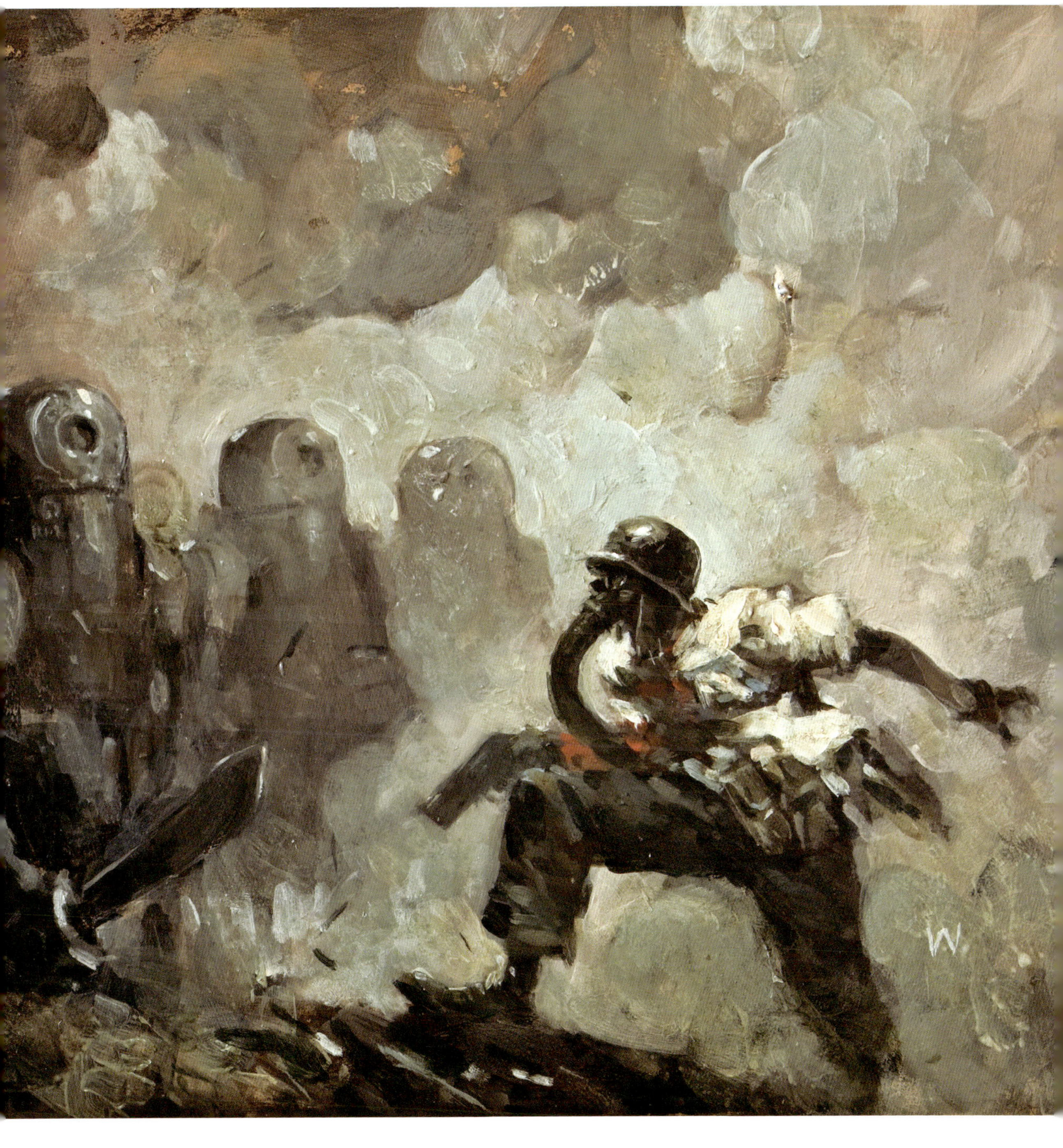

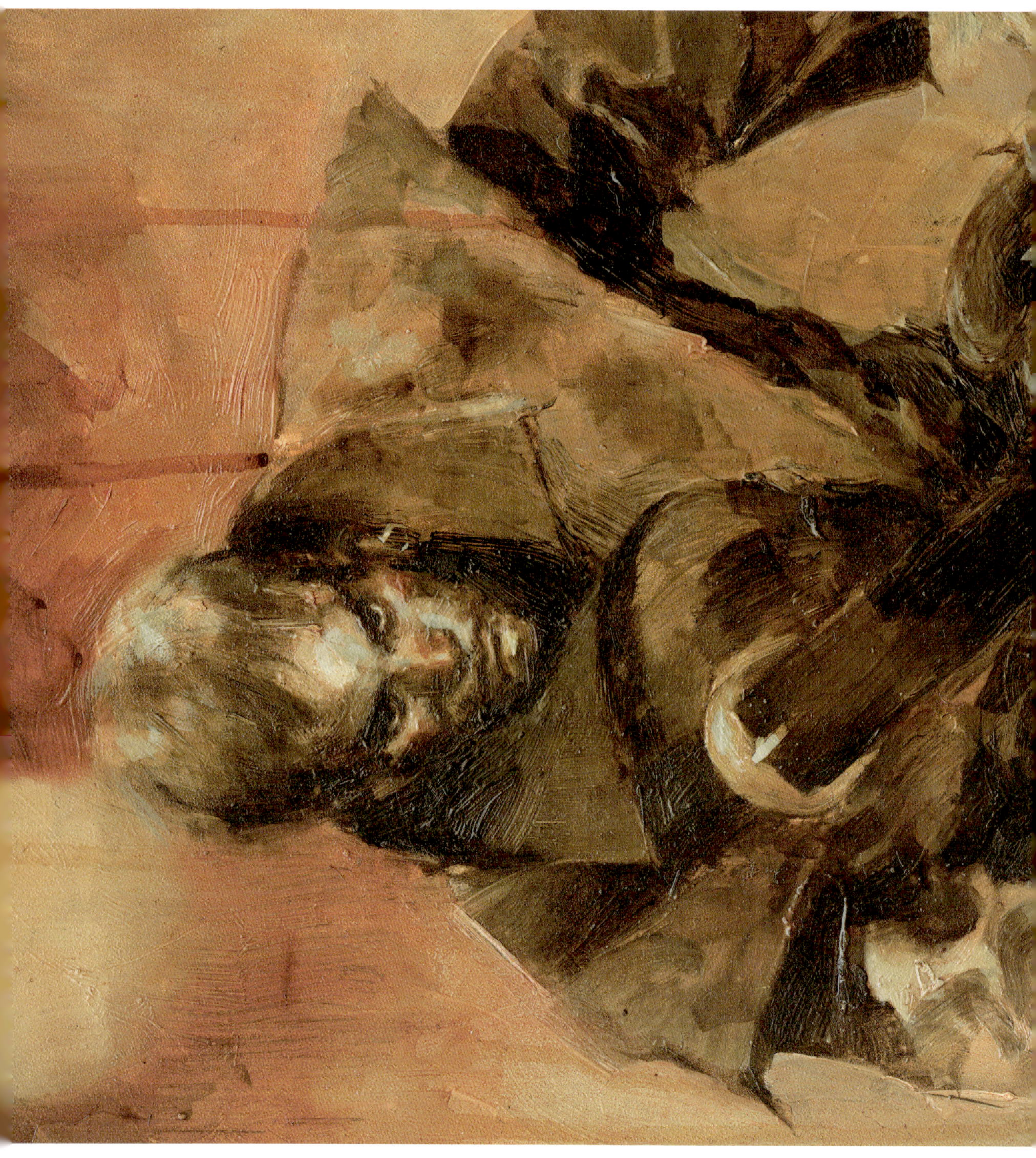

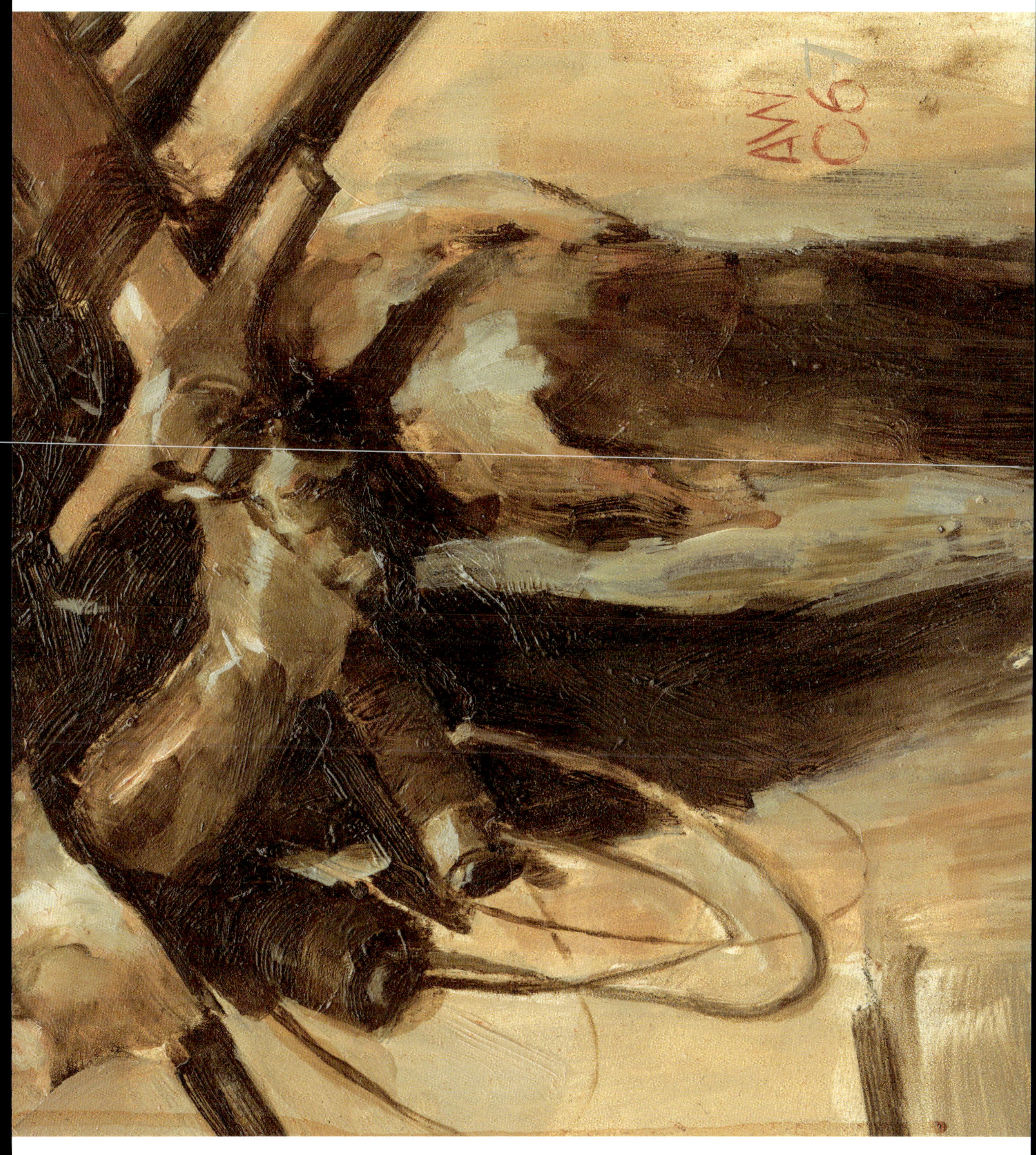

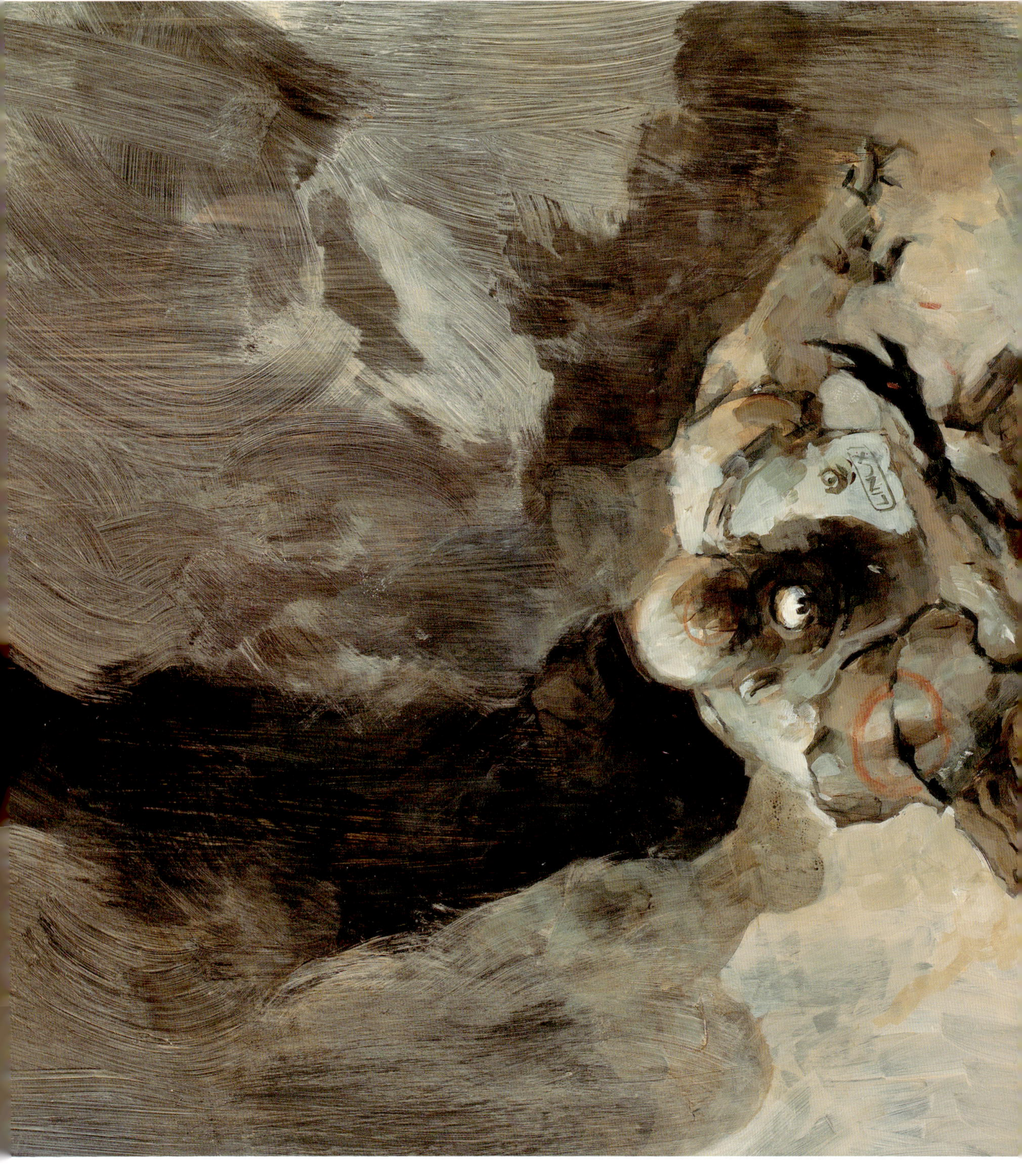

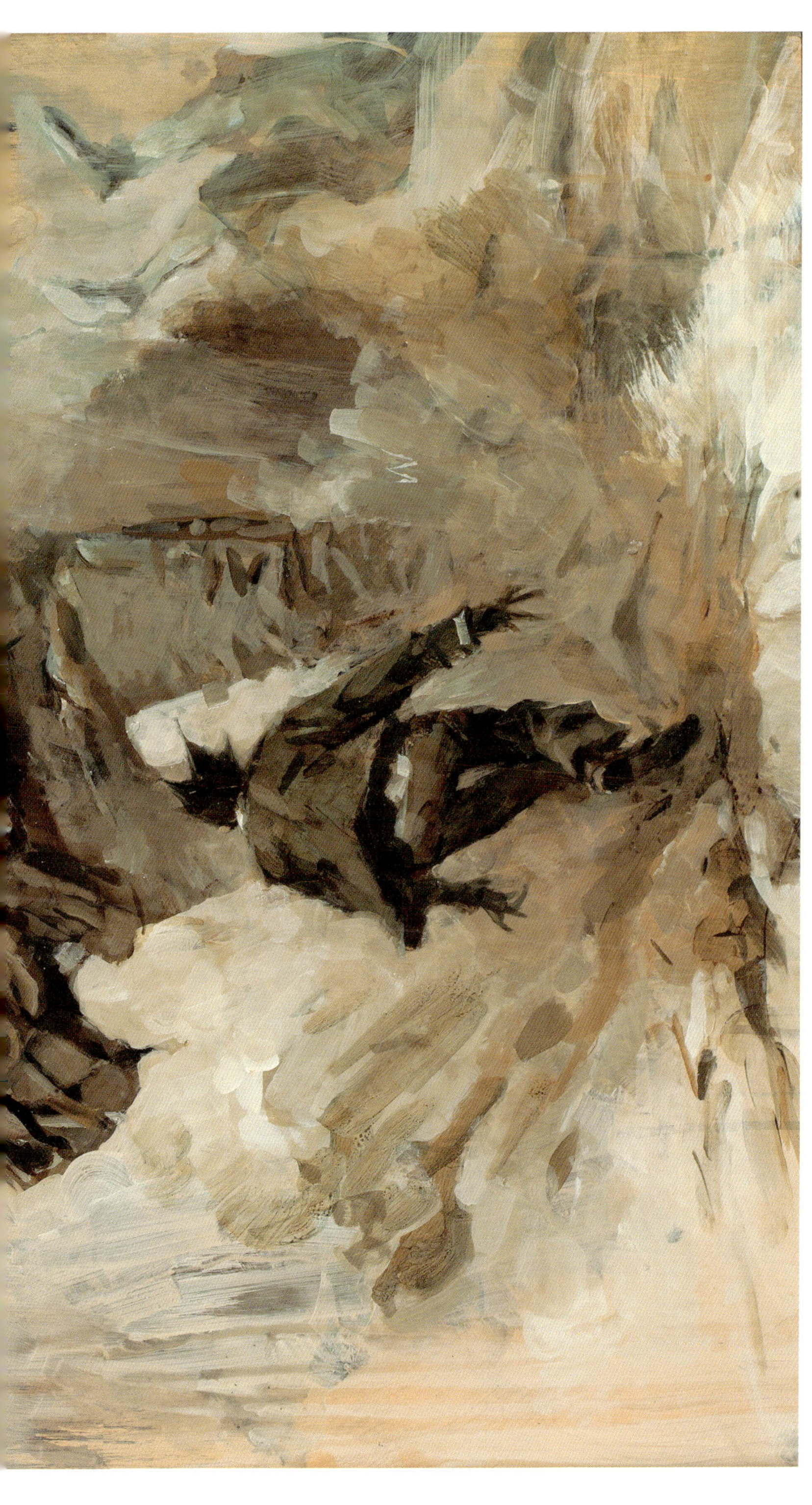

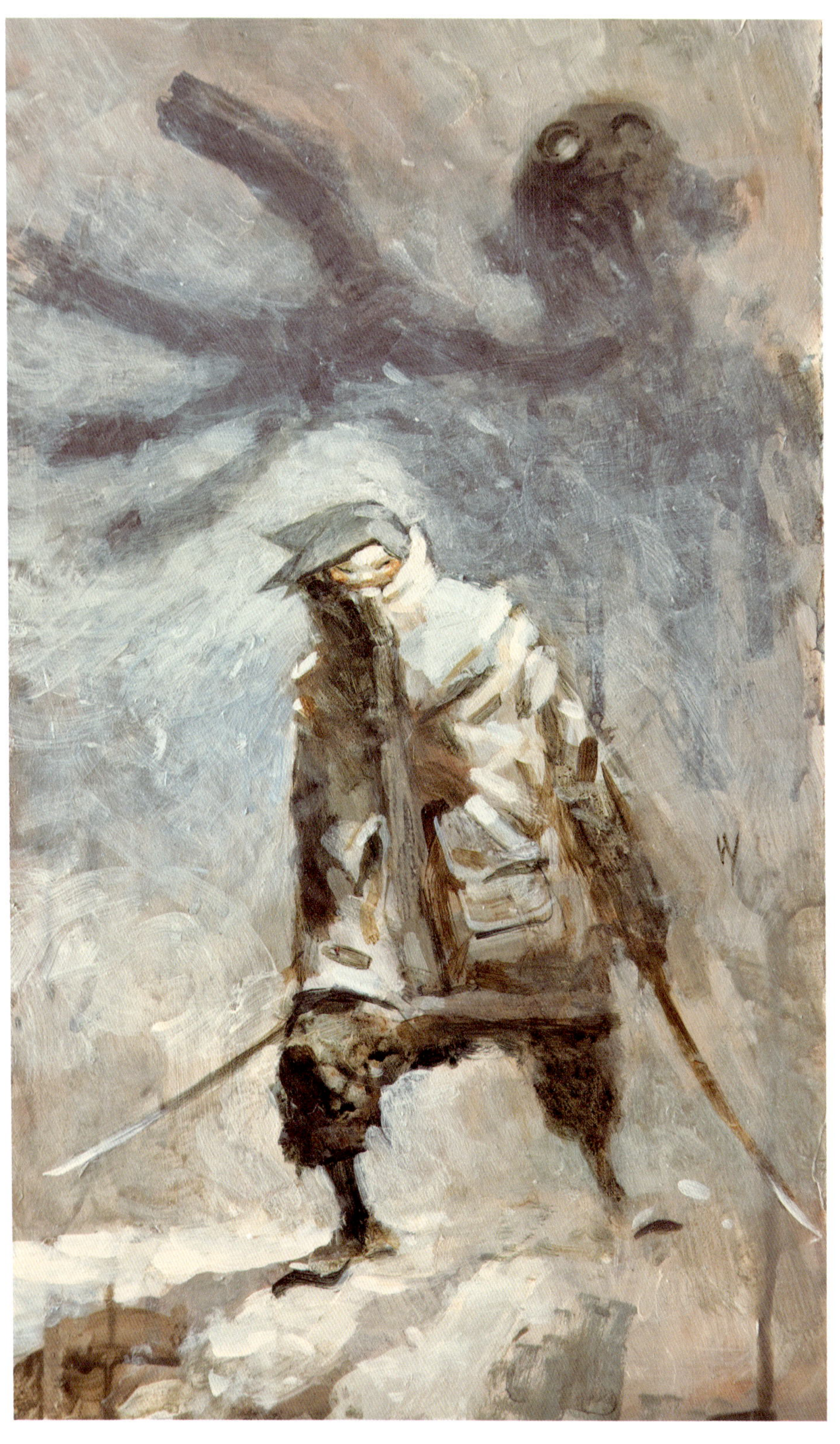

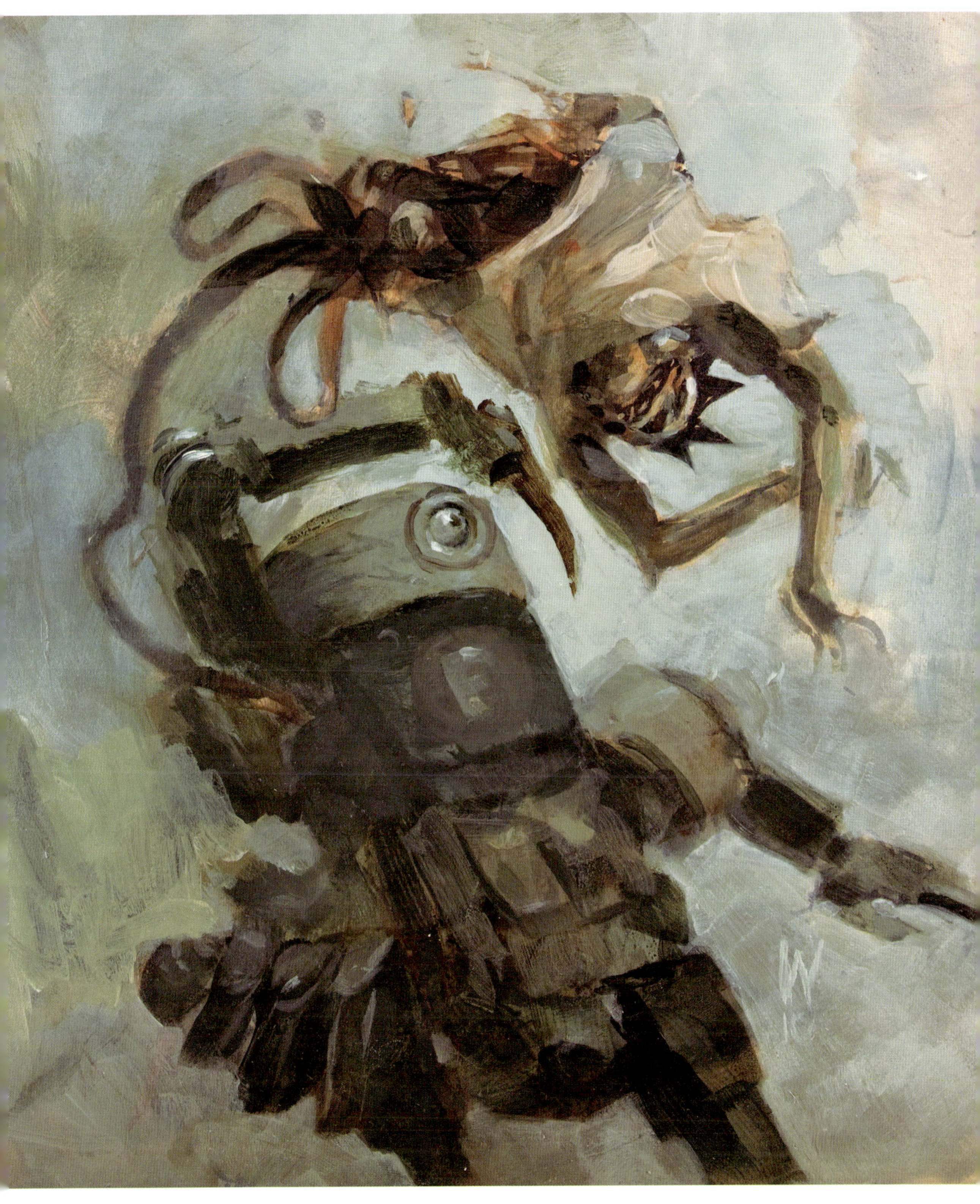

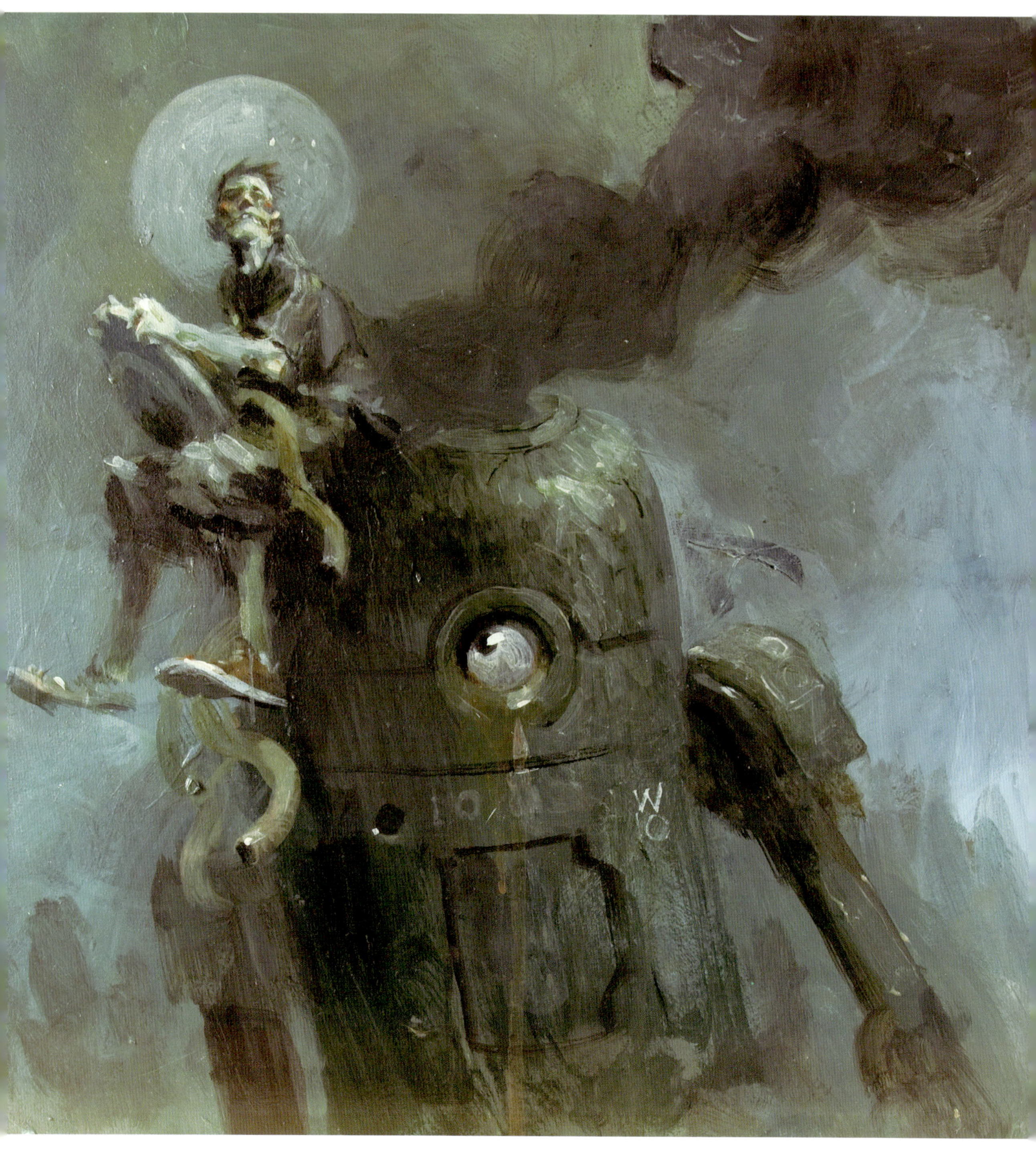

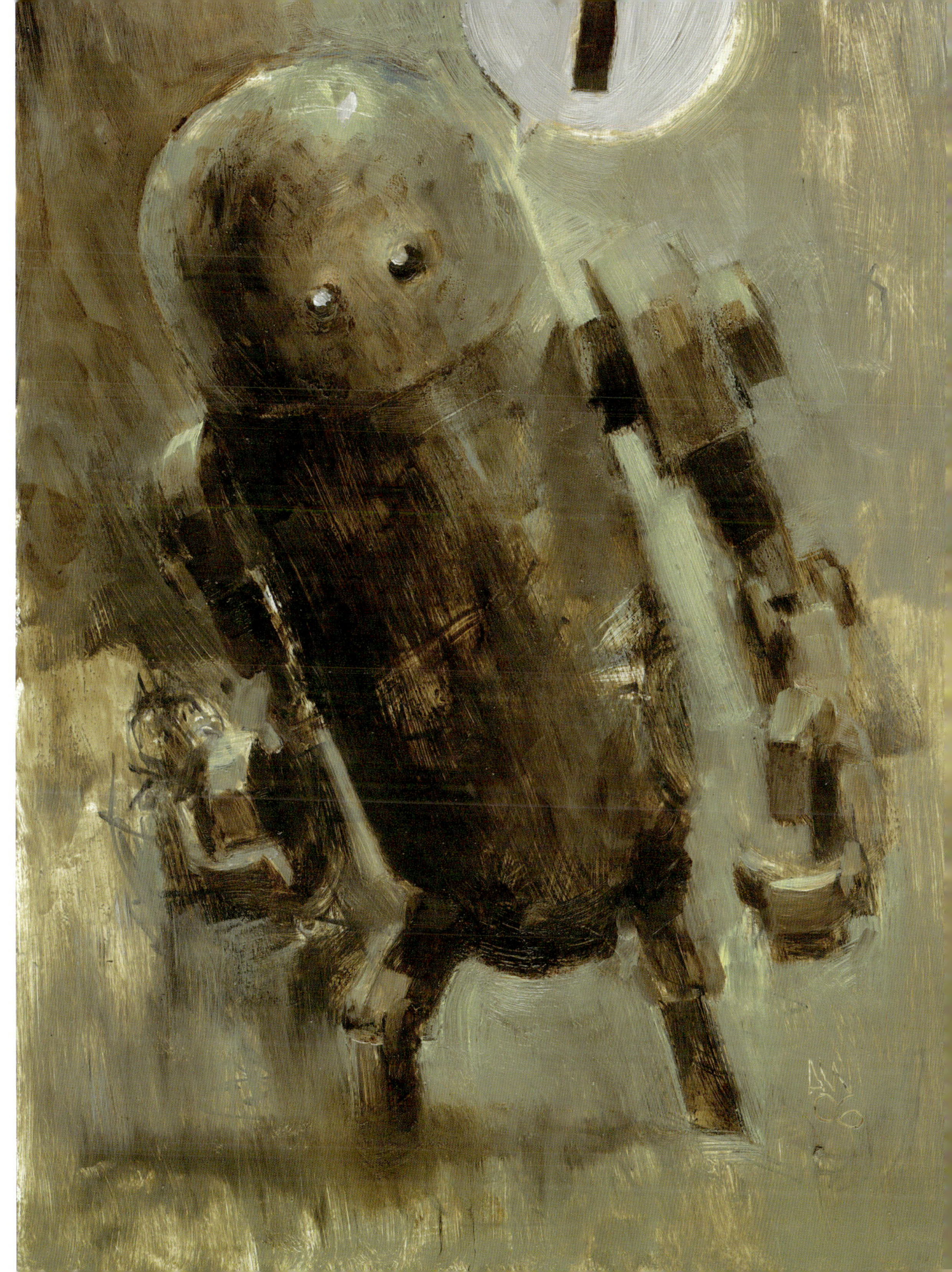

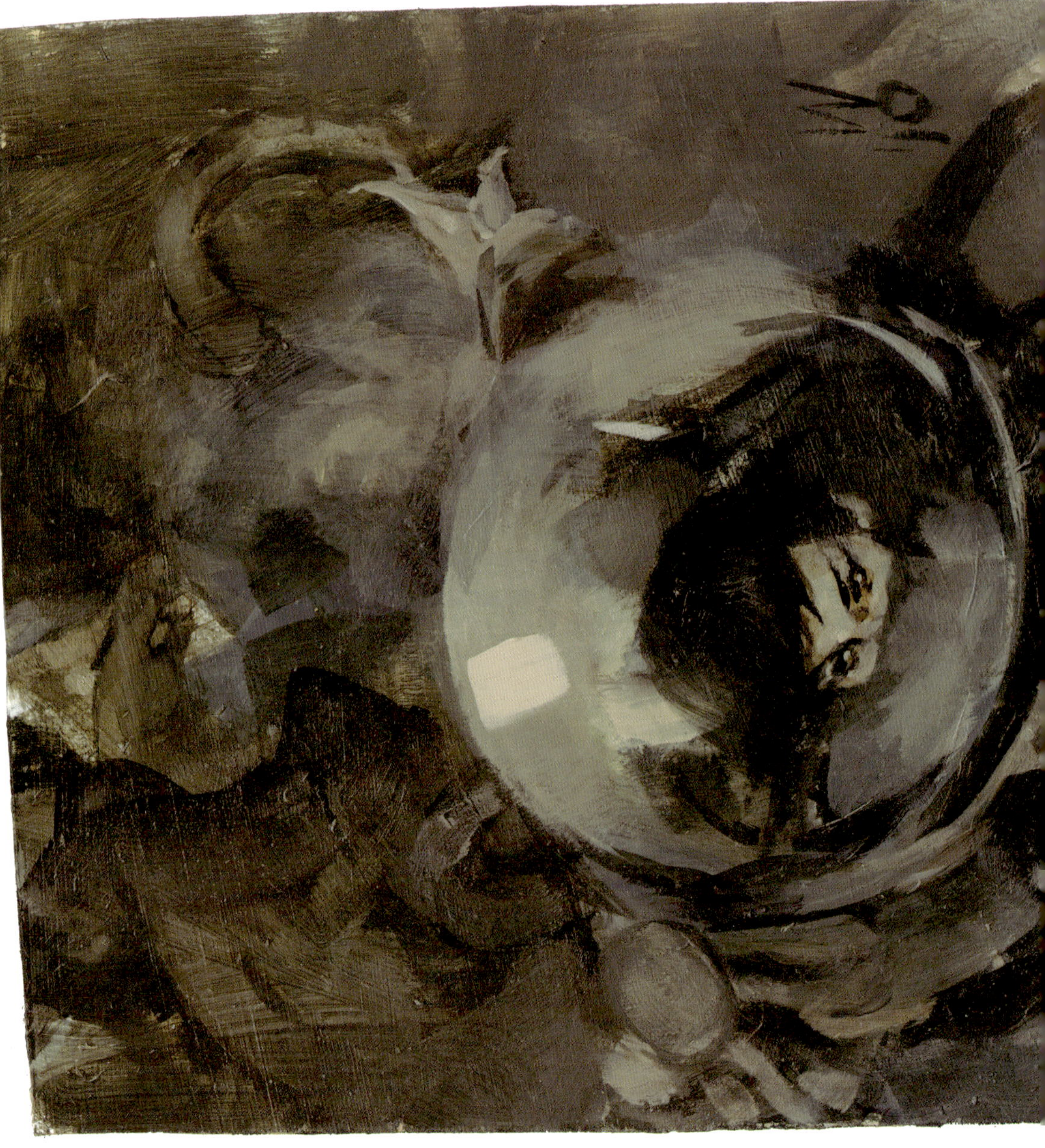

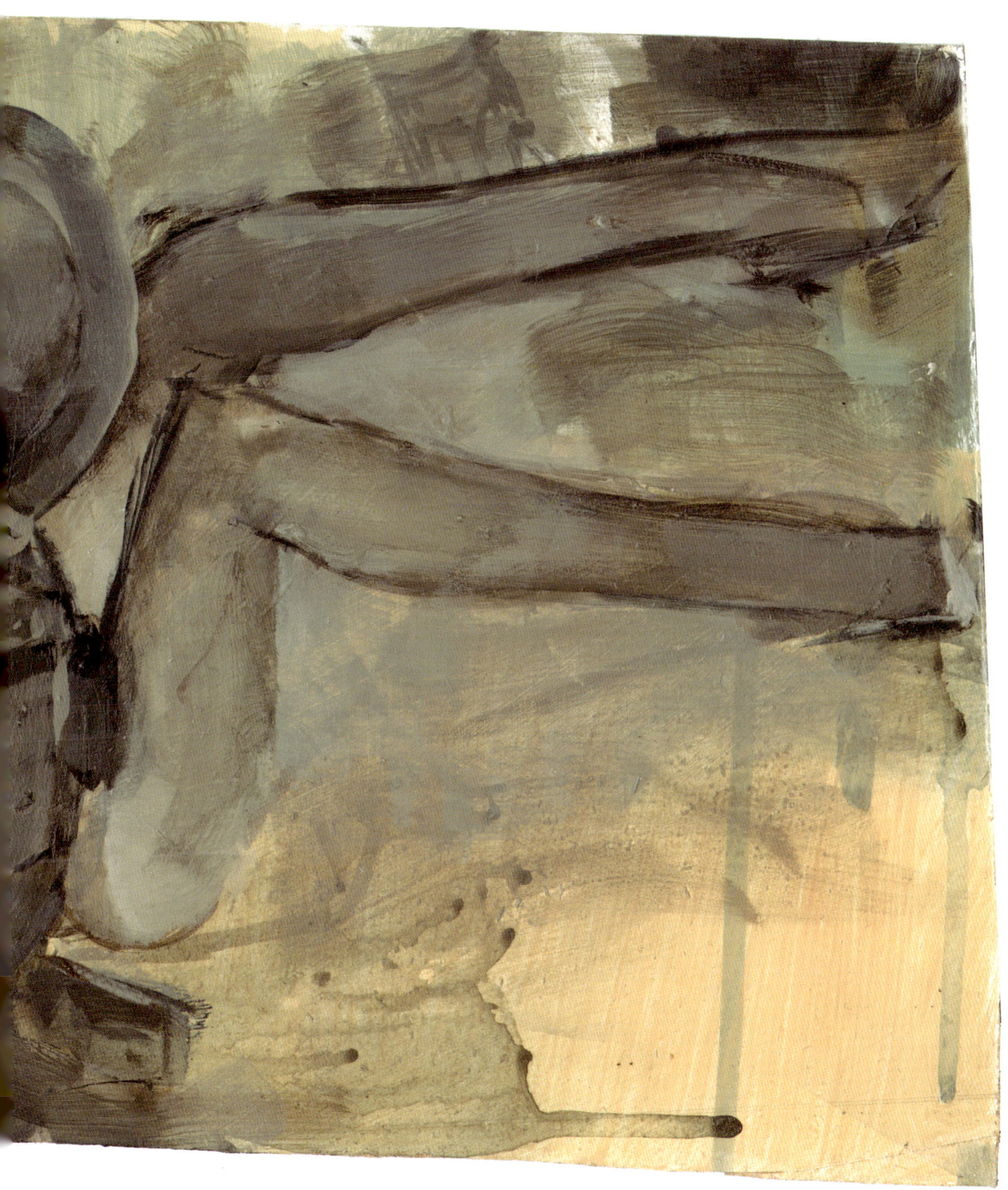

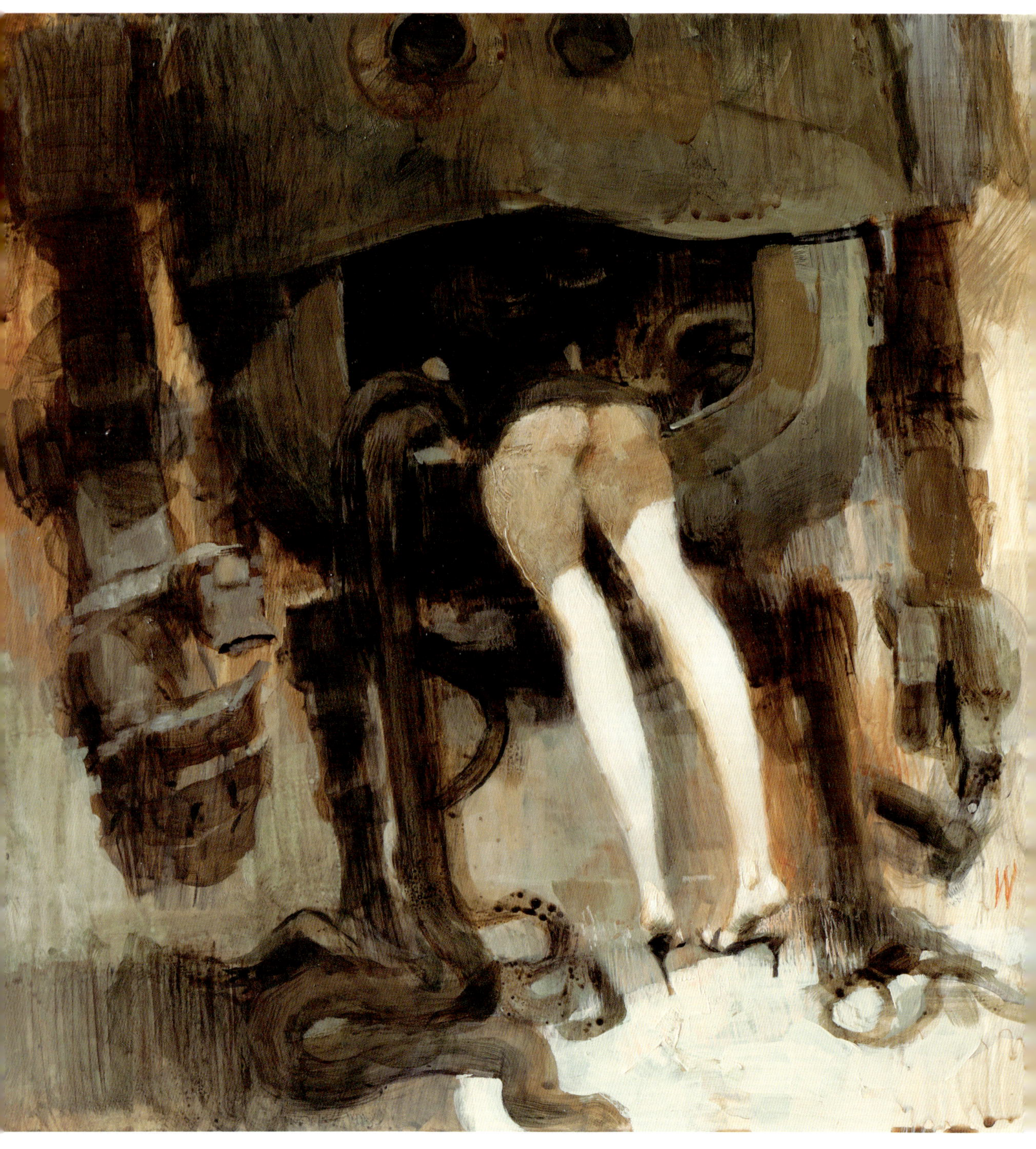

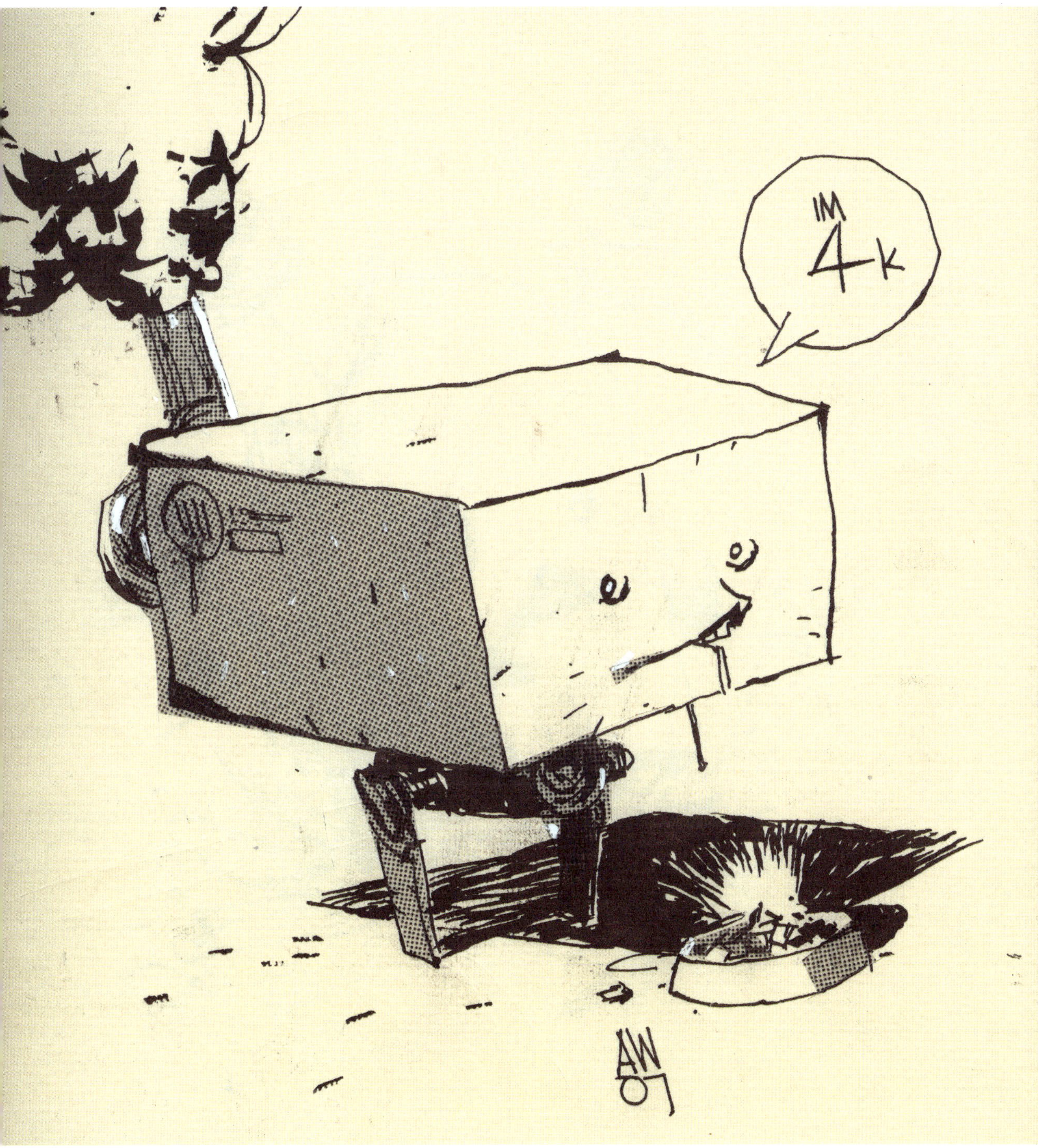

IM
4 k

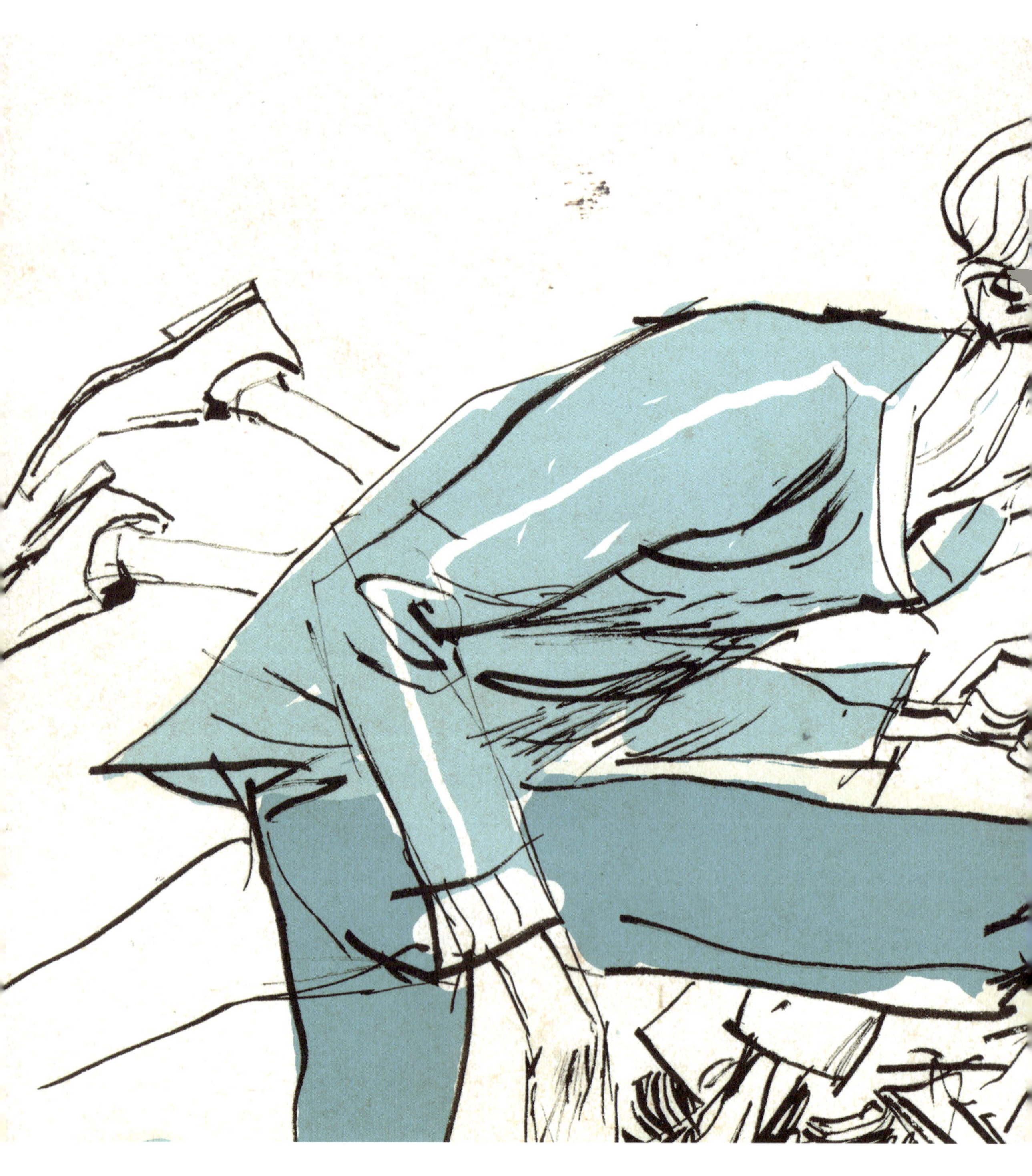

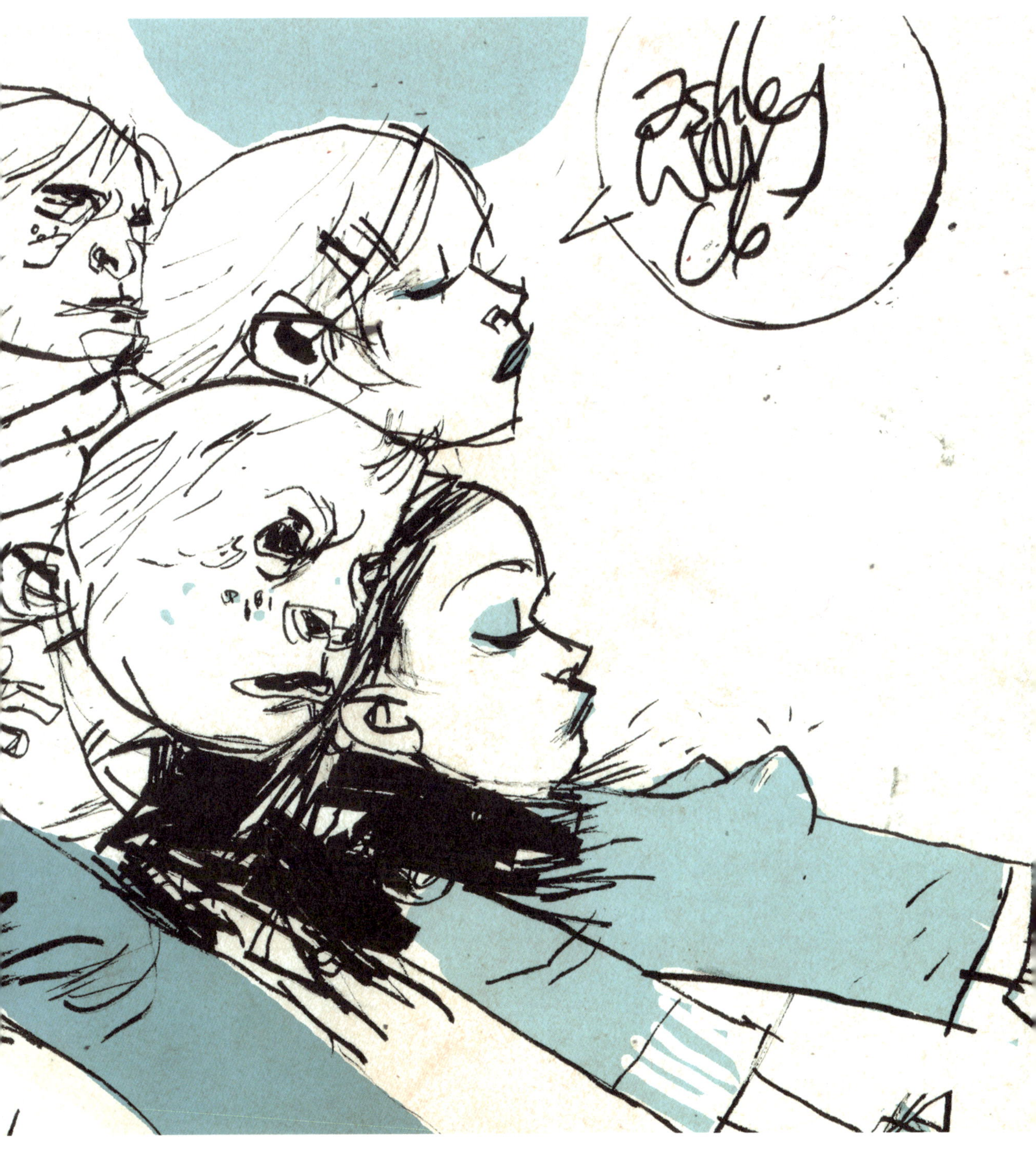

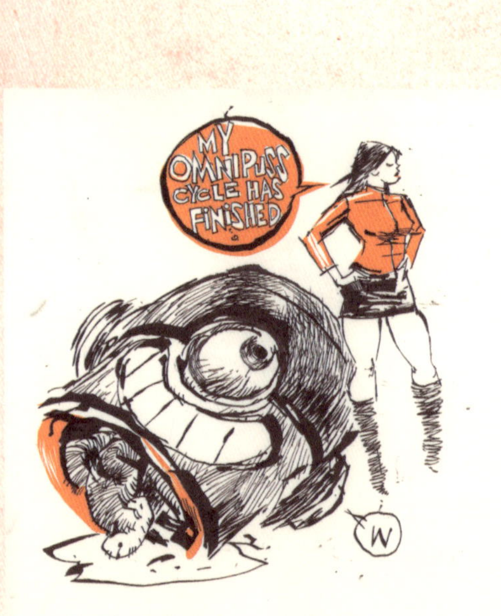

MY OMNIPUSS CYCLE HAS FINISHED

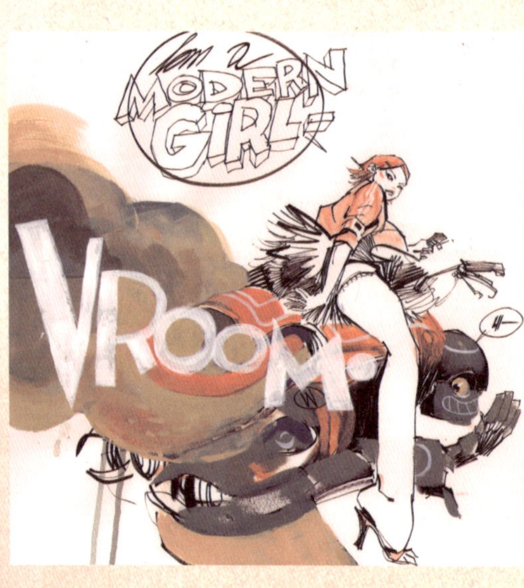

MODERN GIRL
VROOM

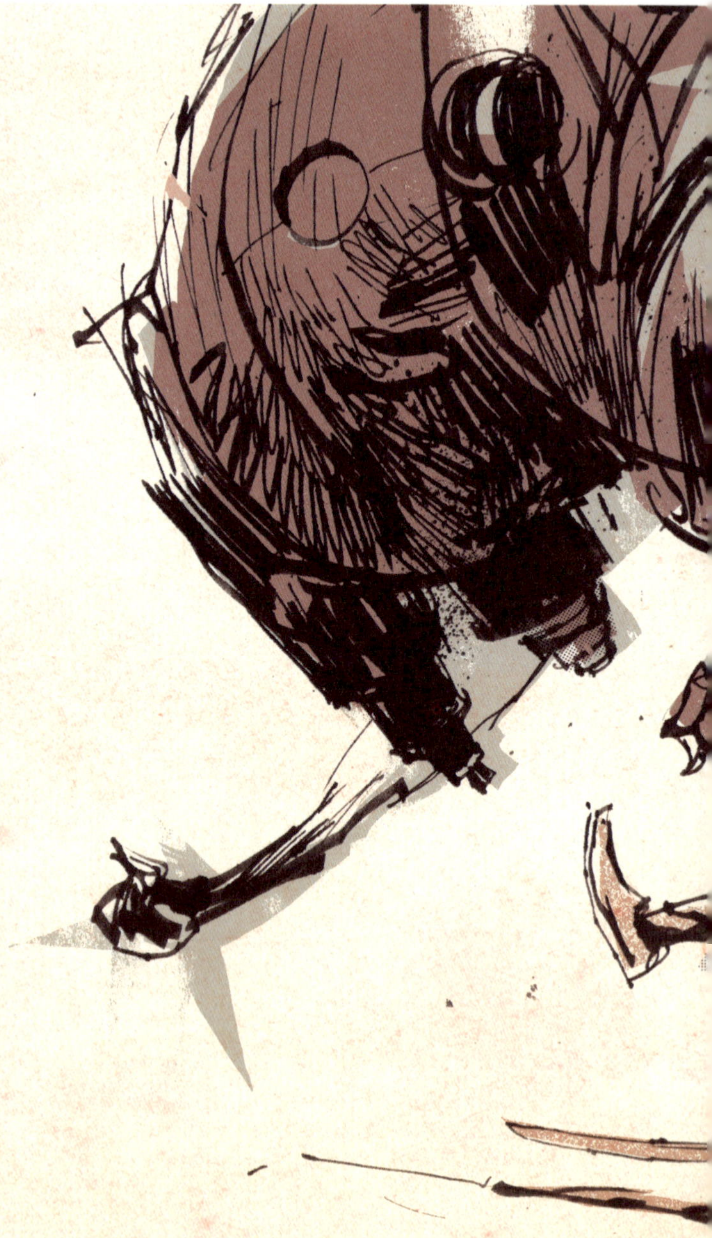

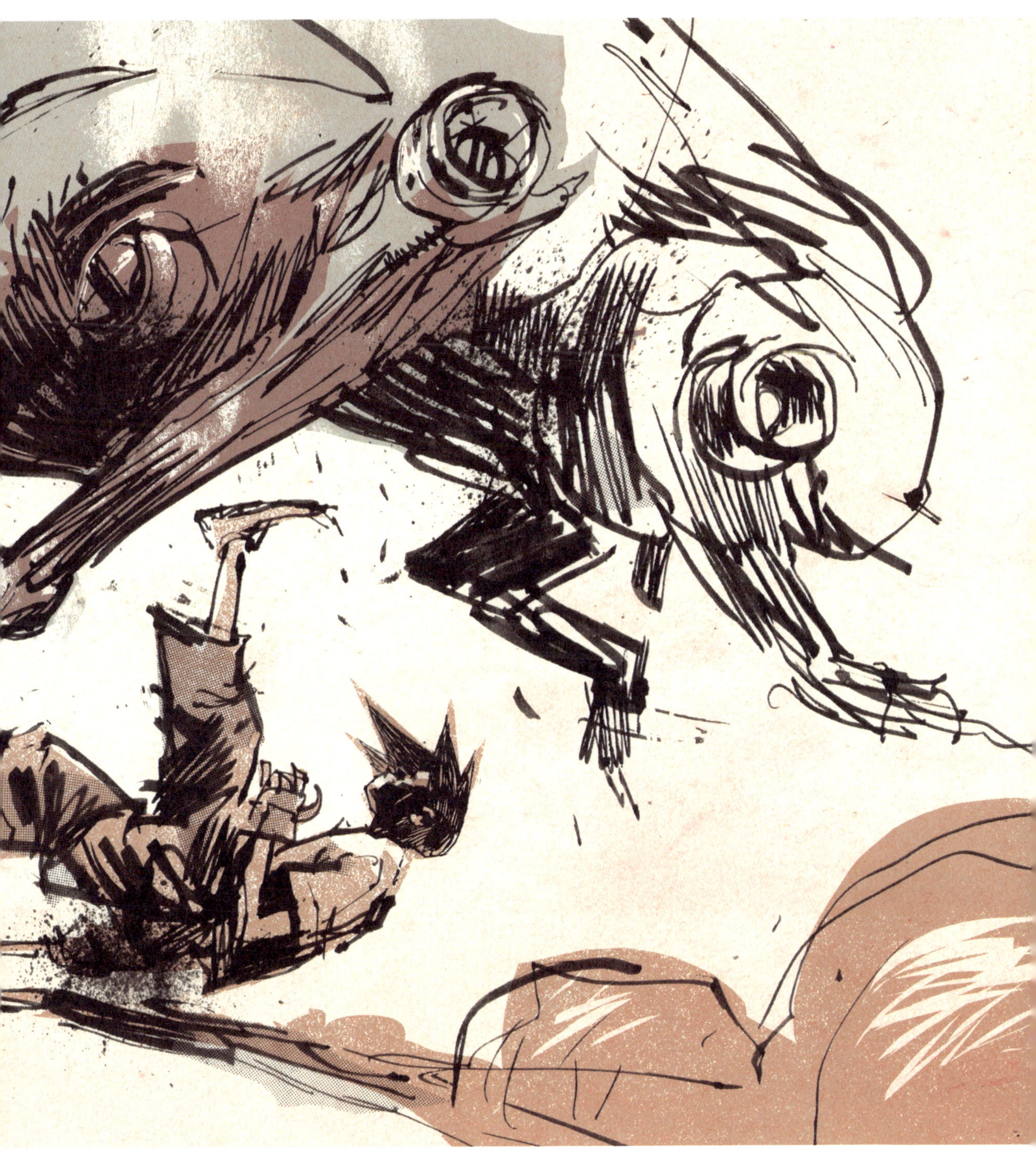

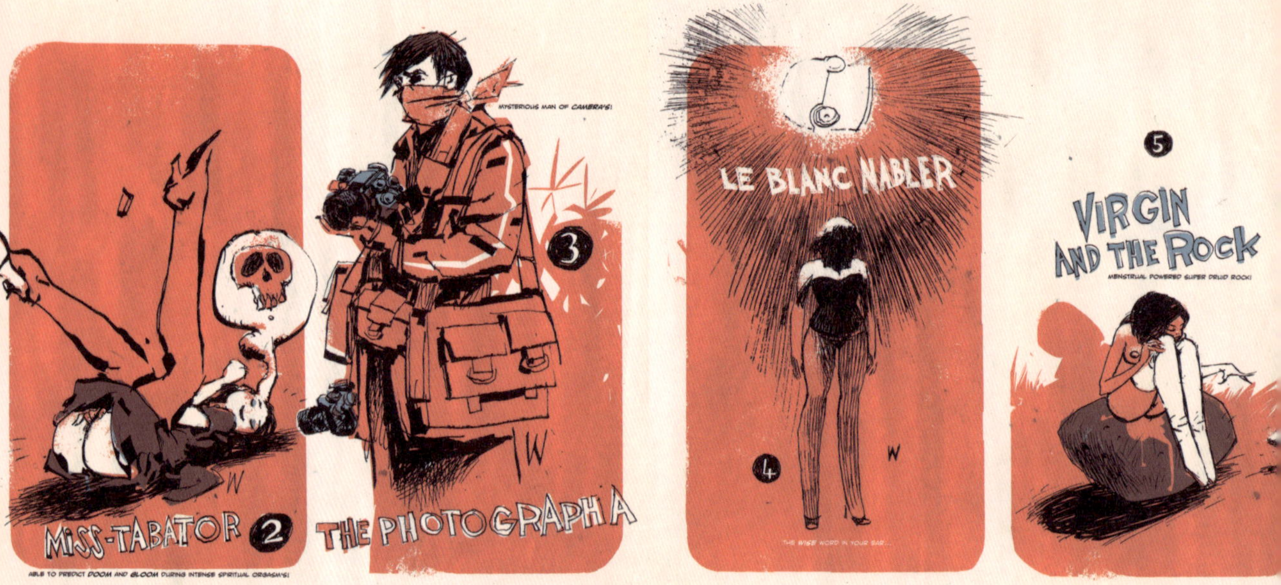

MISS-TABATOR 2
ABLE TO PREDICT DOOM AND BLOOM DURING INTENSE SPIRITUAL ORGASM'S!
MYSTERIOUS MAN OF CAMERA'S!
THE PHOTOGRAPH A 3
LE BLANC NABLER 4
THE BASE WORD IN YOUR BAG....
5
VIRGIN AND THE ROCK
MENSTRUAL POWERED SUPER DRUG ROCK!
BIZARRE BIRTH DEFECT LEAD'S TO CRAZY SENSITIVE LEGS THAT CAN HEAR, TASTE AND KICK BALL'S! 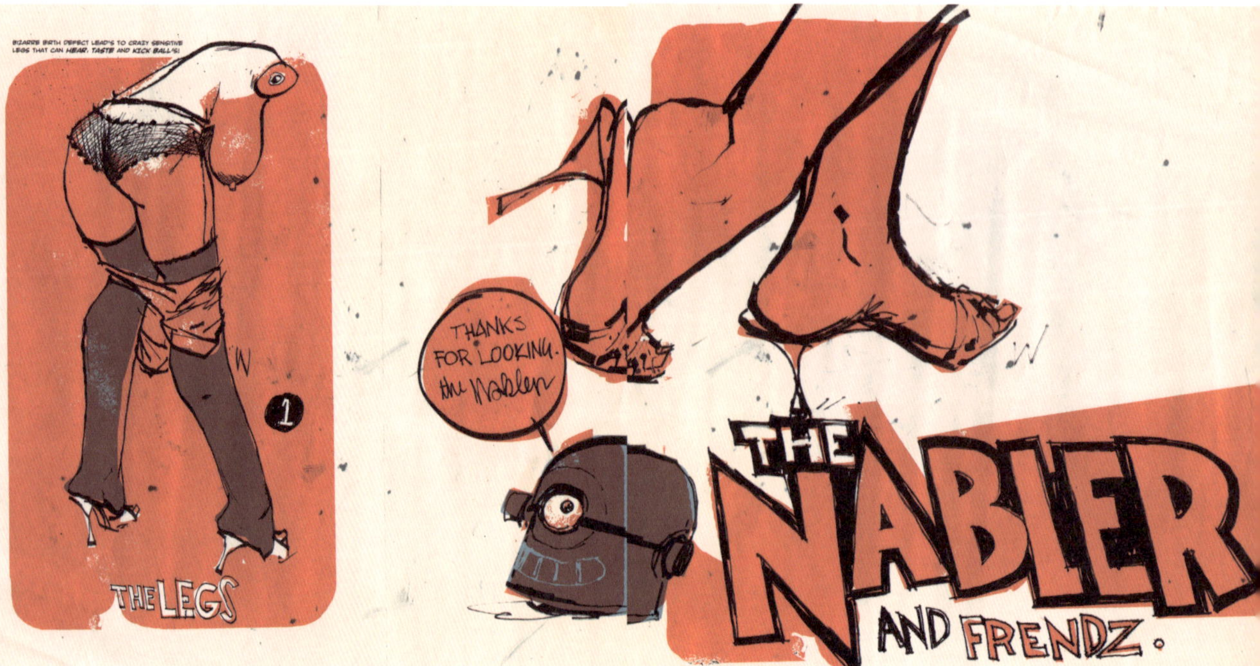
THE LEGS 1
THANKS FOR LOOKING. the Nabler
THE NABLER AND FRENDZ.

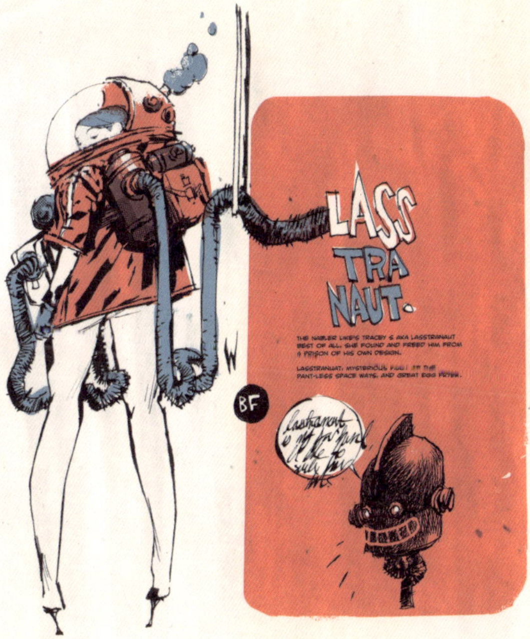

LASS TRA NAUT.
THE NABLER LIKES TRACEY'S AKA LASSTRANAUT BEST OF ALL. SHE FOUND AND FREED HIM FROM A PRISON OF HIS OWN DESIGN.
LASSTRANAUT: MYSTERIOUS FUEL AT THE PANT-LESS SPACE WAYS. AND GREAT EGG FRYER.
BF 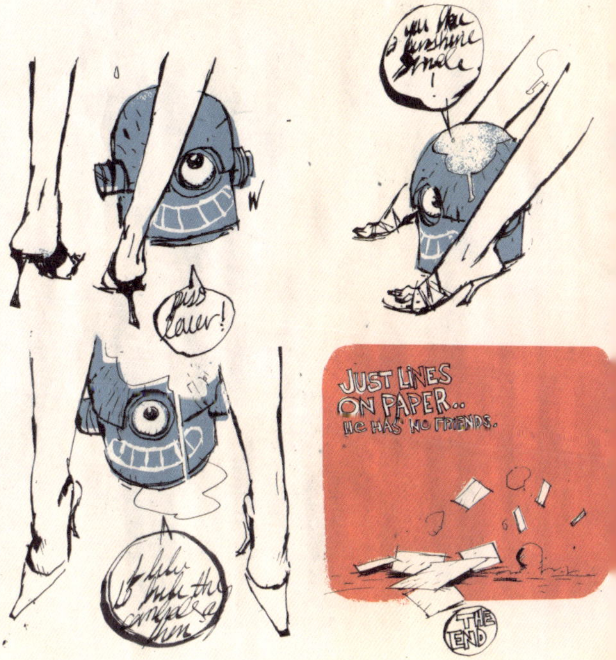
a Sunshine Smile
piss leaver!
JUST LINES ON PAPER.. HE HAS NO FRIENDS.
THE END

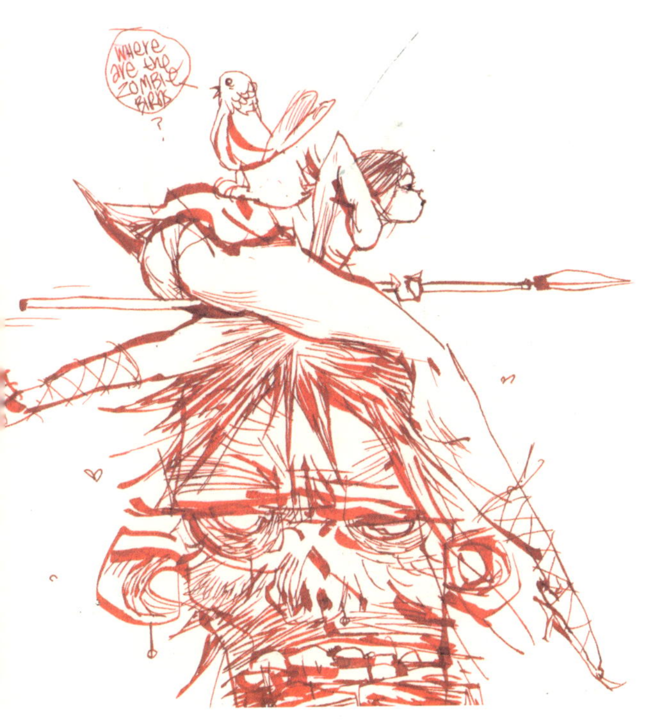

where are the zombie birds?

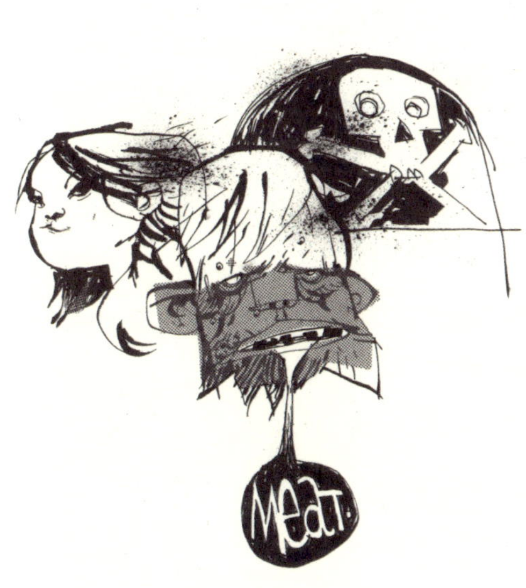

MEaT

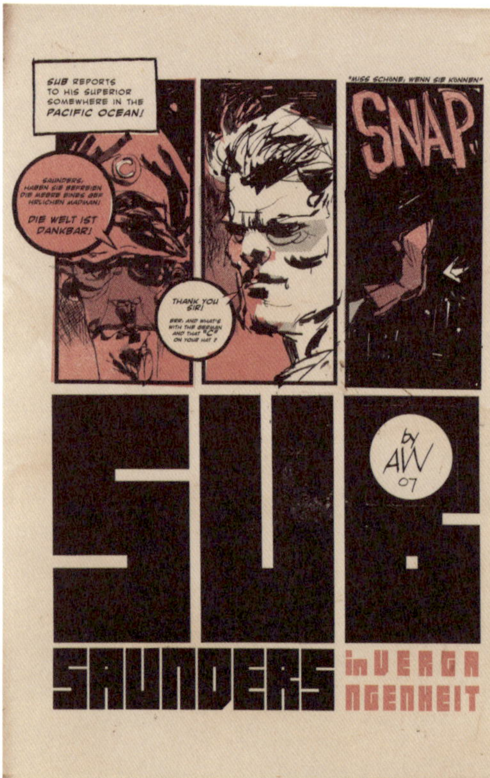

SUB REPORTS TO HIS SUPERIOR SOMEWHERE IN THE PACIFIC OCEAN!

MISS SCHÖNE, WENN SIE KÖNNEN

SAUNDERS, HABEN SIE BEFREIEN DIE MEERE EINES DER HRLICHEN MADMAN! DIE WELT IST DANKBAR!

THANK YOU SIR! BRR. AND WHAT'S WITH THE ... ON YOUR HAT?

SNAP

SUB. SAUNDERS in VERGANGENHEIT

by AW 07

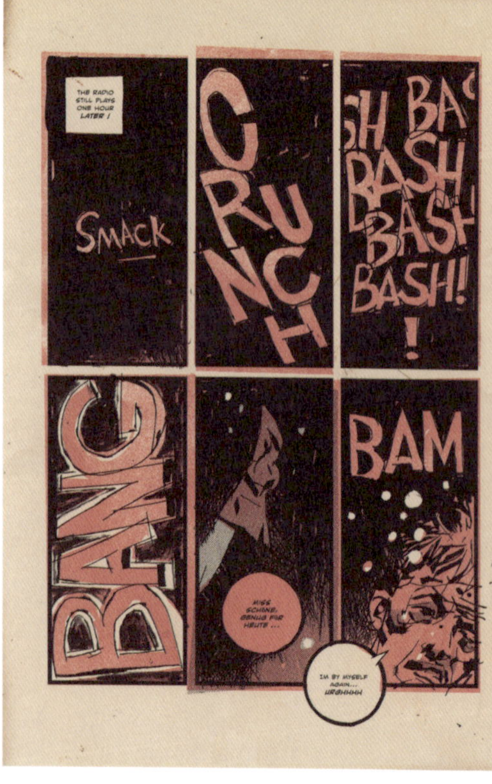

THE RADIO STILL PLAYS ONE HOUR LATER!

SMACK

CRUNCH

SH BA... BASH BASH BASH!

BANG

BAM

MISS SCHÖNE, GENUG FÜR HEUTE ...

IM BY MYSELF AGAIN... URGHHHH

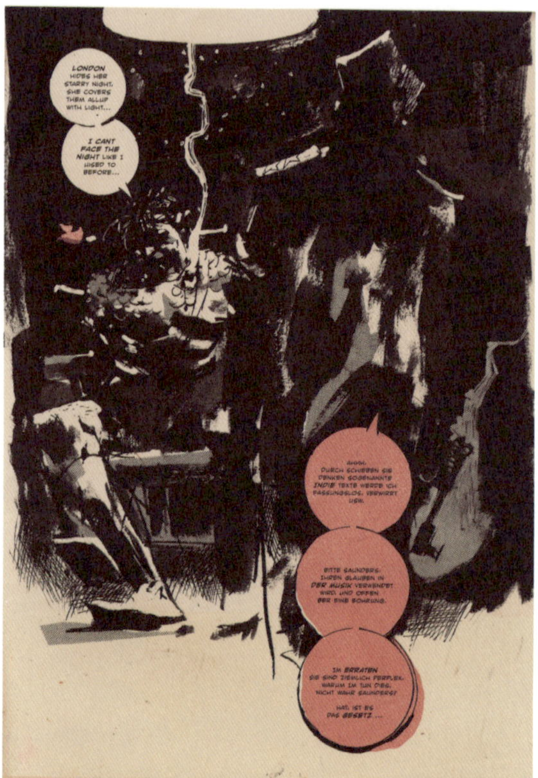

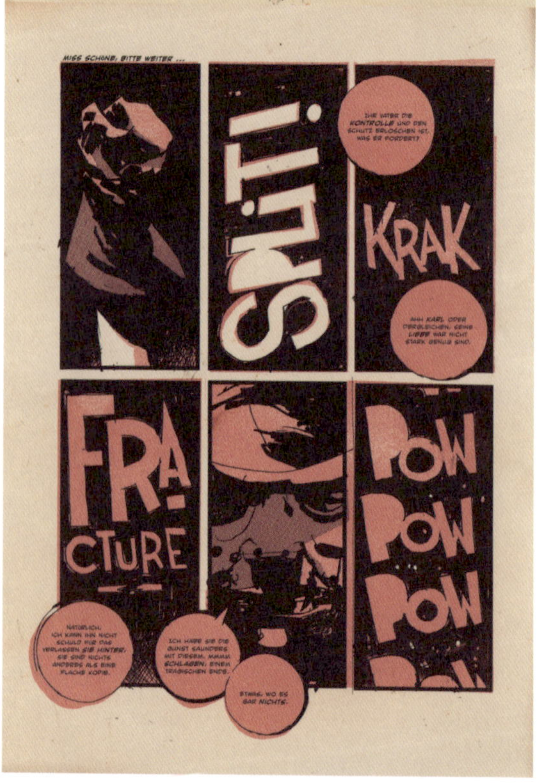

LONDON HIDES HER STARRY NIGHT, SHE COVERS THEM ALL UP WITH LIGHT...

I CANT FACE THE NIGHT LIKE I USED TO BEFORE...

WOHL... DURCH SCHREIEN SIE DENKEN SOGENANNTE INDIE TEXTE WERDE ICH FASSUNGSLOS, IRRWIRRT VOR...

BITTE SAUNDERS, IHREN GLAUBEN IN DER MUSIK VERWENDET WIRD. UND OFFEN FÜR EINE BOHRUNG.

ICH BERATEN SIE SIND ZIEMLICH PERPLEX, WARUM DA SUK DIES NICHT MEHR SAUNDERS? HA!, IST ES DAS GESETZ ...

MISS SCHÖNE, BITTE WEITER ...

IHR WISST DIE KONTROLLE UND DEN SCHUTZ ERLOSCHEN IST, WAS ER FORDERT?

AHH KARL ODER DERGLEICHEN, SEINE LIEBE WAR NICHT STARK GENUG SIND.

SPLIT!

KRAK

FRA-CTURE

POW POW POW

NATÜRLICH. ICH KANN IHN NICHT SCHULD FÜR DAS VERLASSEN SIE HINTER, SIE SIND NICHTS ANDERES ALS EINE FLACHE KOPIE.

ICH HABE SIE DIE GUNST SAUNDERS MIT DIESEM, MMMM, SCHLAGEN, EINEM TRAGISCHEN ENDE.

ETWAS, WO ES GAR NICHTS.

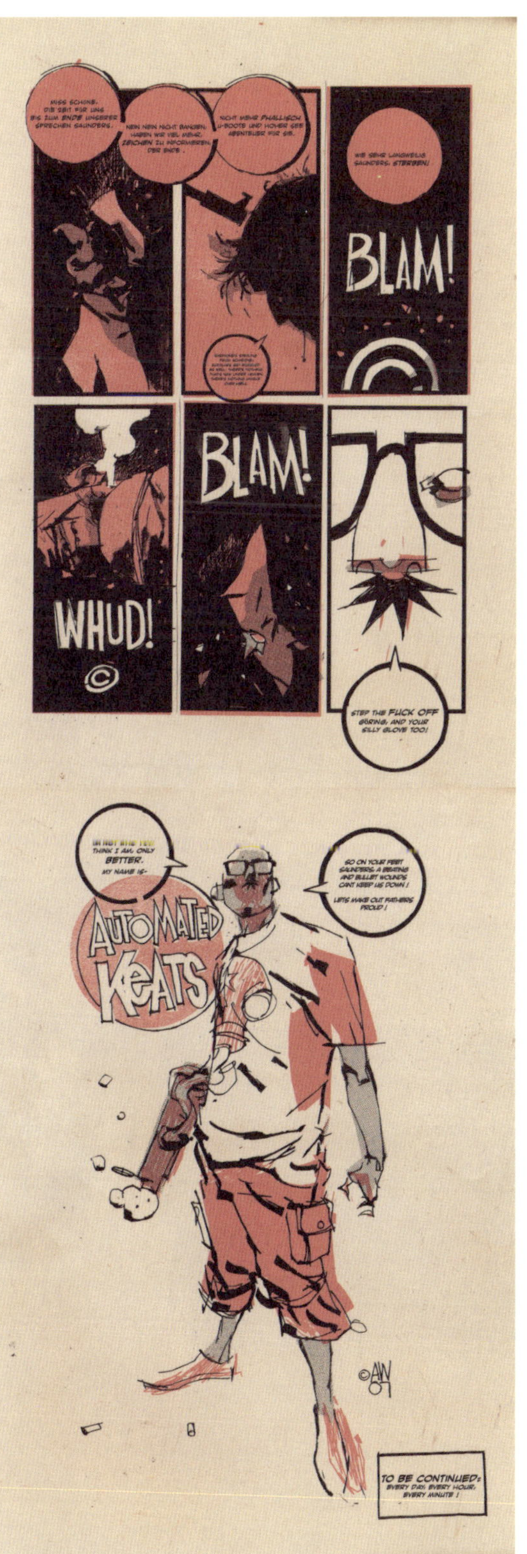

MISS SCHÖNE, DIE ZEIT FÜR UNS BIS ZUM ENDE UNSERER SPRECHEN SAUNDERS.
NEIN NEIN NICHT BANGEN, HABEN WIR VIEL MEHR, ZEICHEN ZU INFORMIEREN, DER ENDE.
NICHT MEHR PHALLISCH U-BOOTS UND HOHER SEE ABENTEUER FÜR SIE.
WIE SEHR LANGWEILIG SAUNDERS, STERBEN!
BLAM!
BLAM!
WHUD!
STEP THE FUCK OFF ØBRING, AND YOUR SILLY GLOVE TOO!
I'M NOT WHO YOU THINK I AM, ONLY BETTER. MY NAME IS—
AUTOMATED KEATS
GO ON YOUR FEET SAUNDERS, A BEATING AND BULLET WOUNDS CAN'T KEEP US DOWN!
LET'S MAKE OUT FATHERS PROUD!
TO BE CONTINUED: EVERY DAY, EVERY HOUR, EVERY MINUTE!

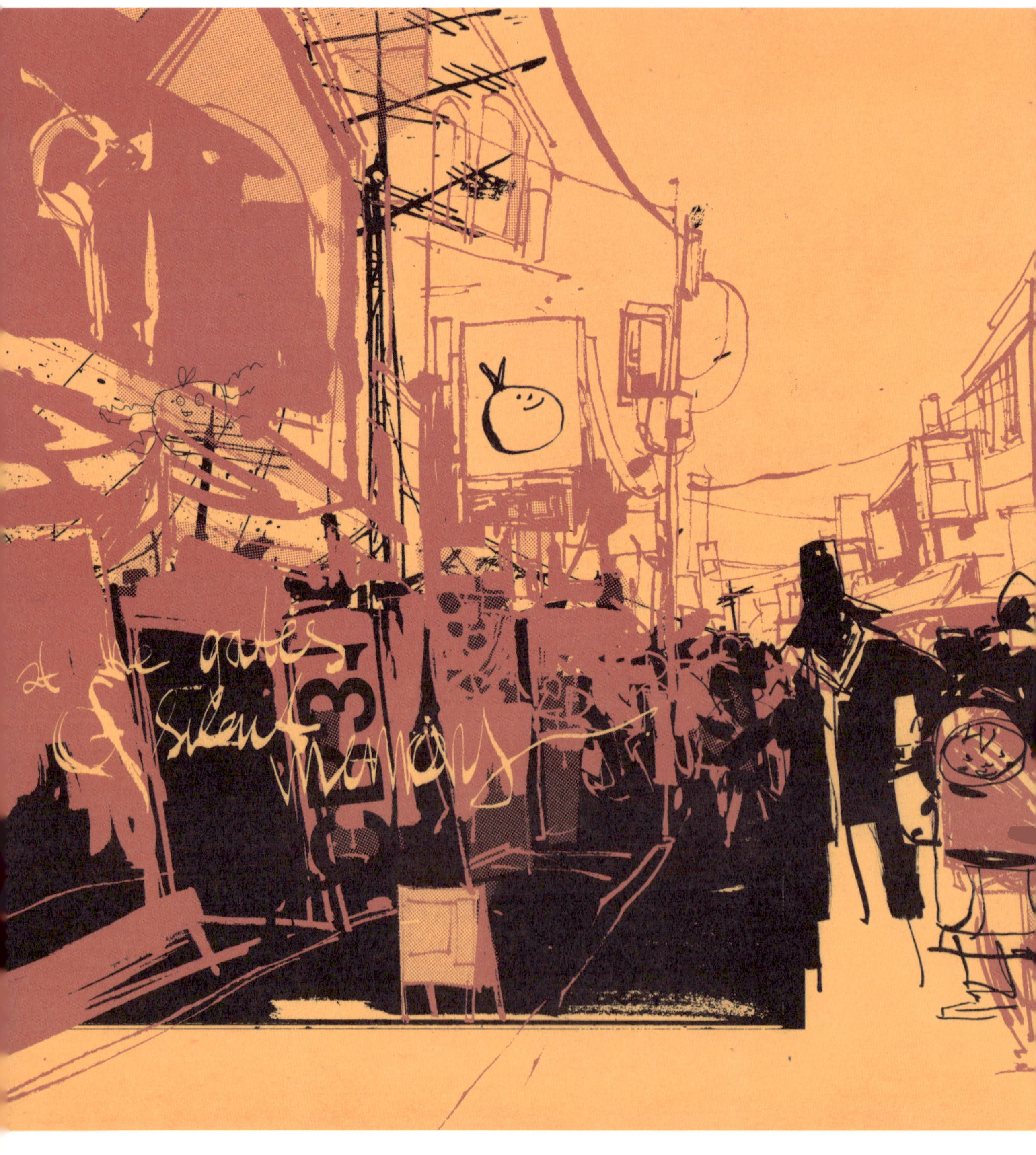
at the gates
silent
memory
3

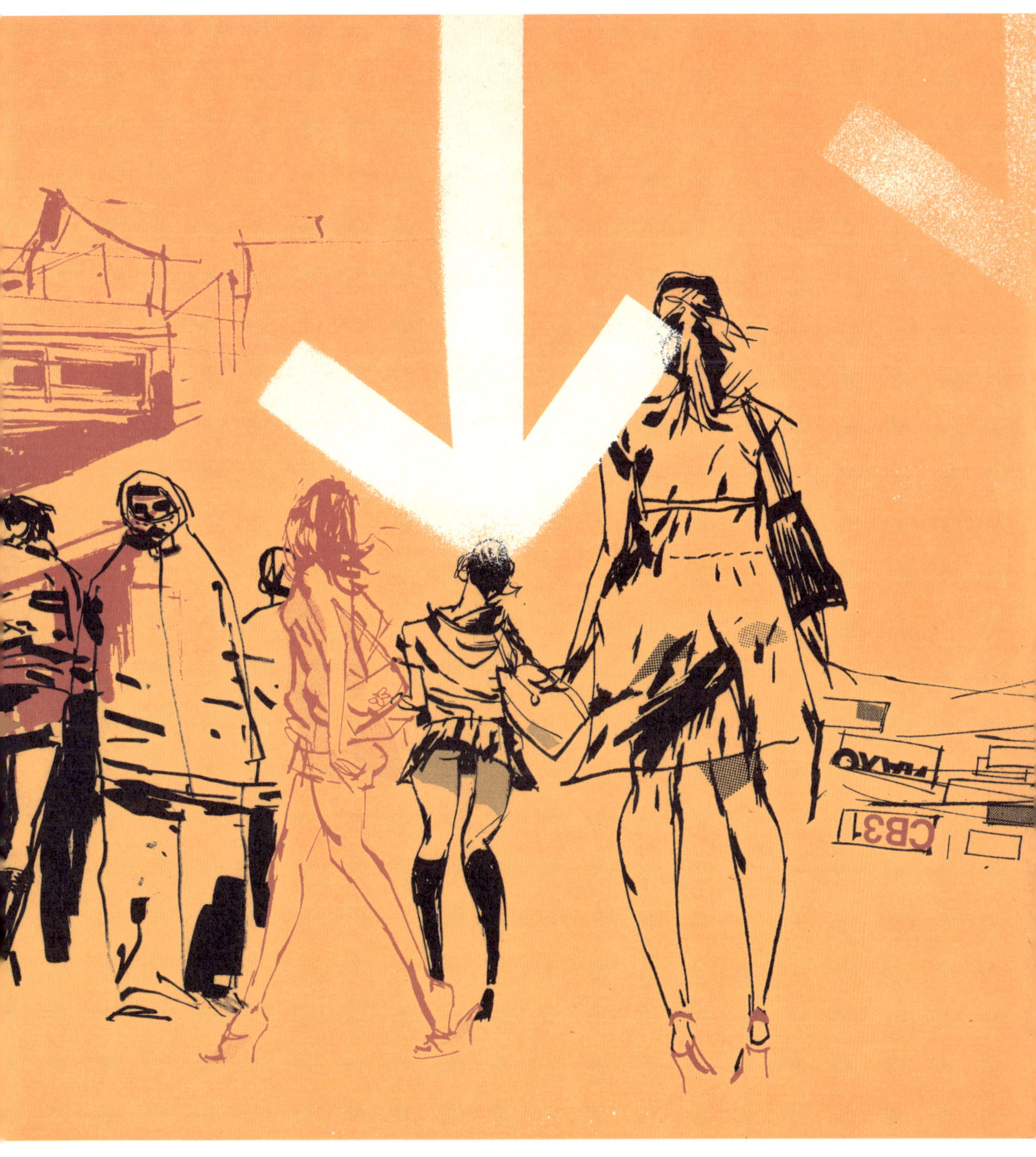

CB31

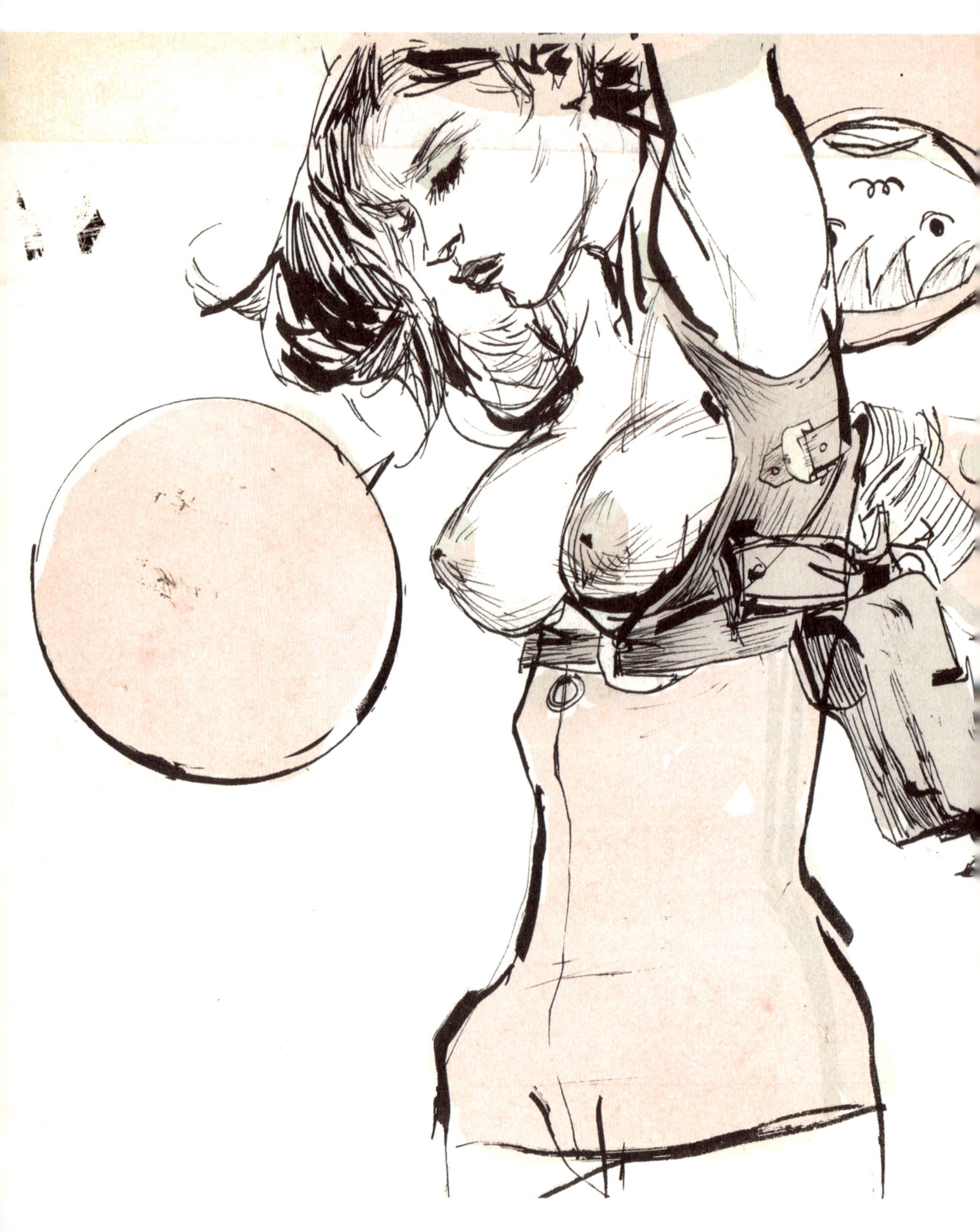

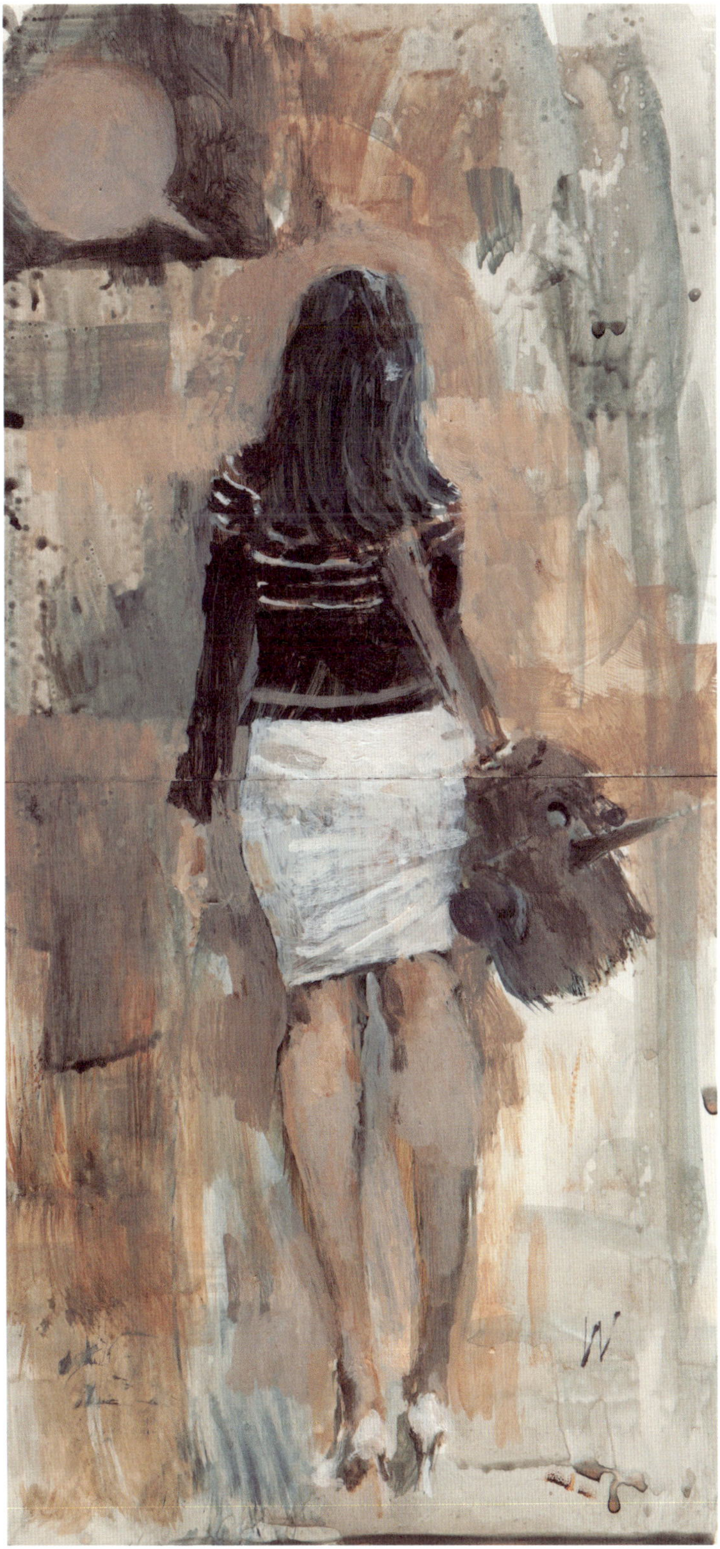

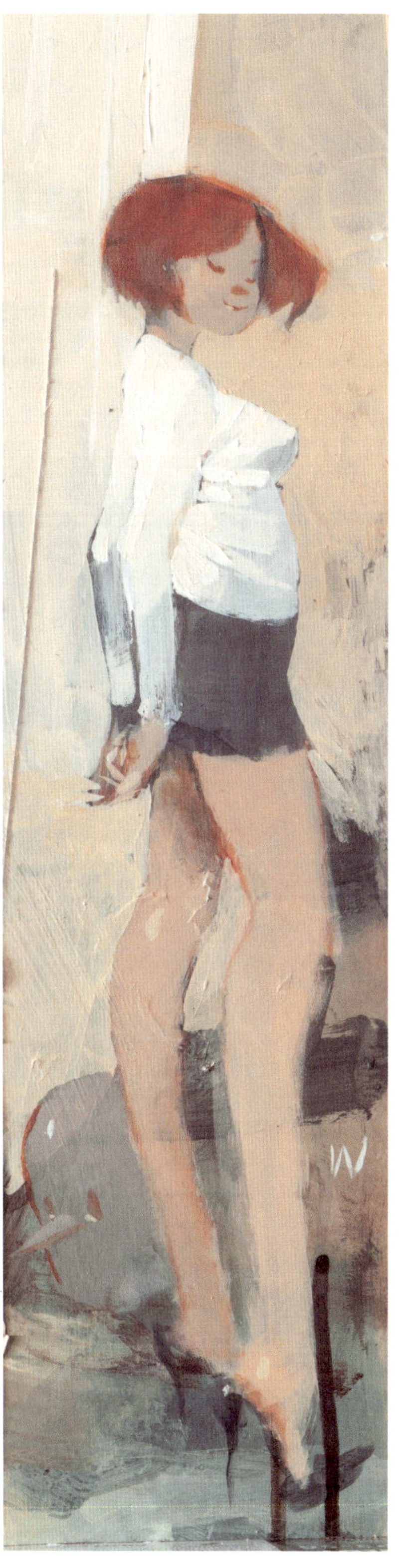

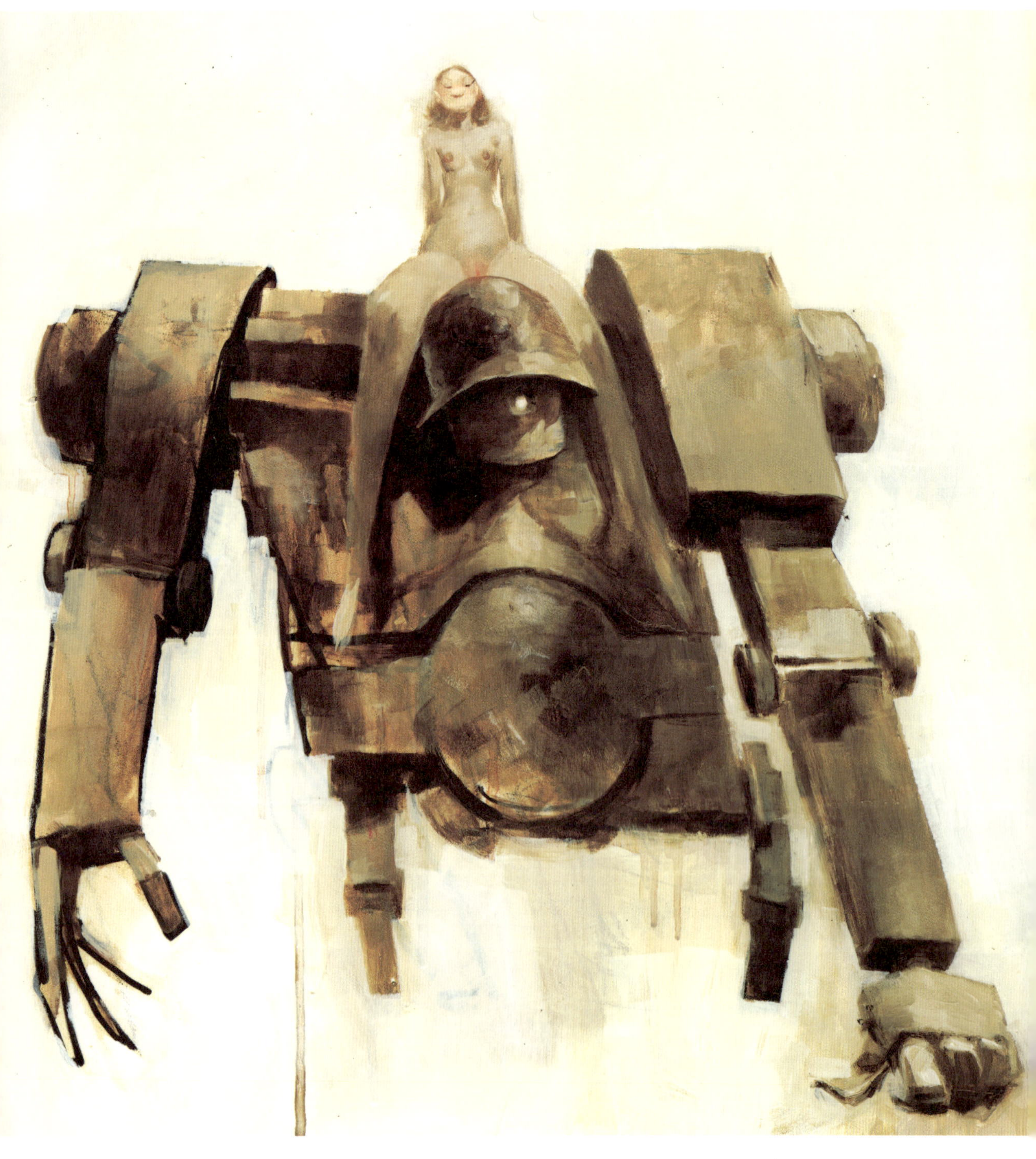

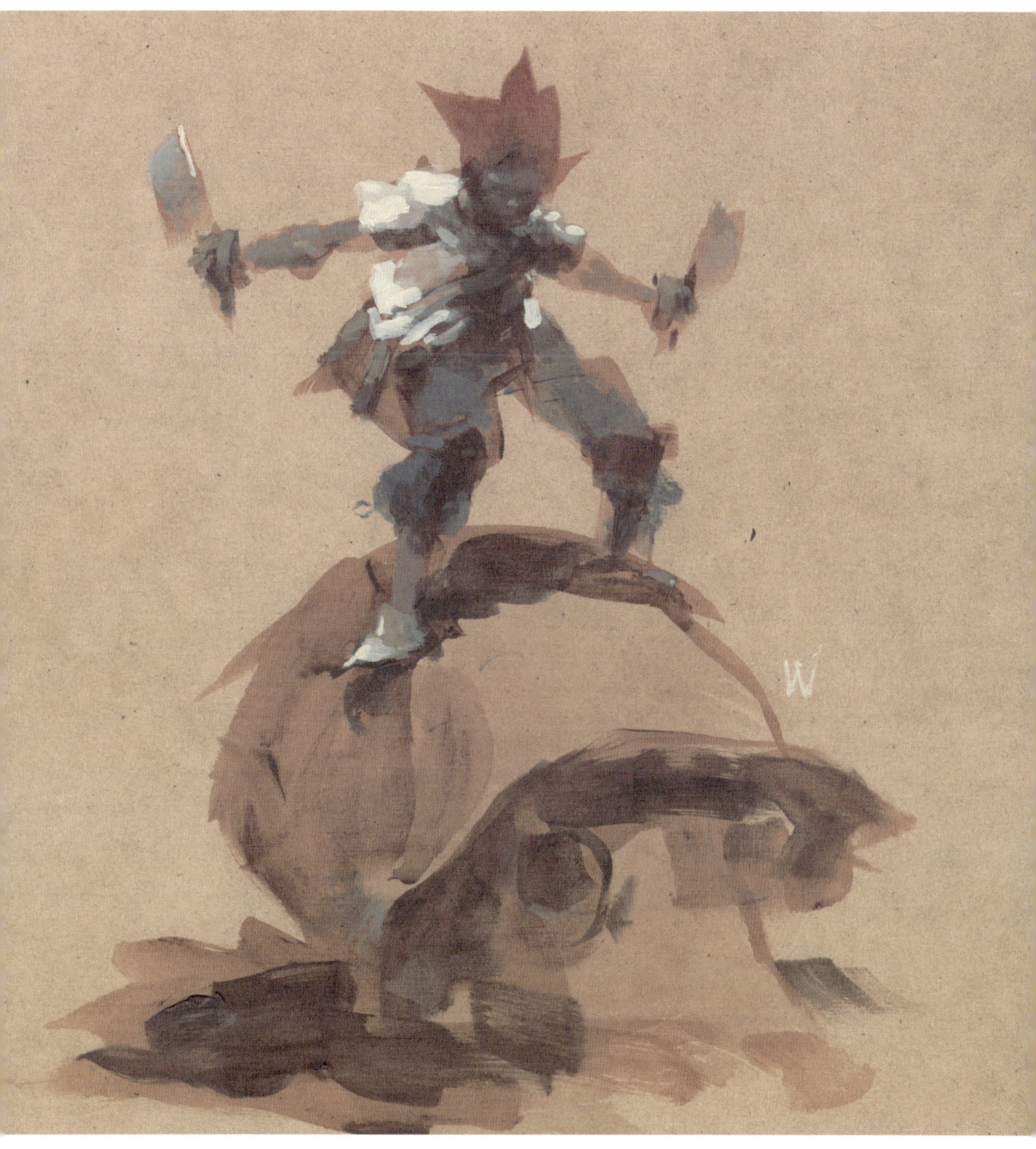

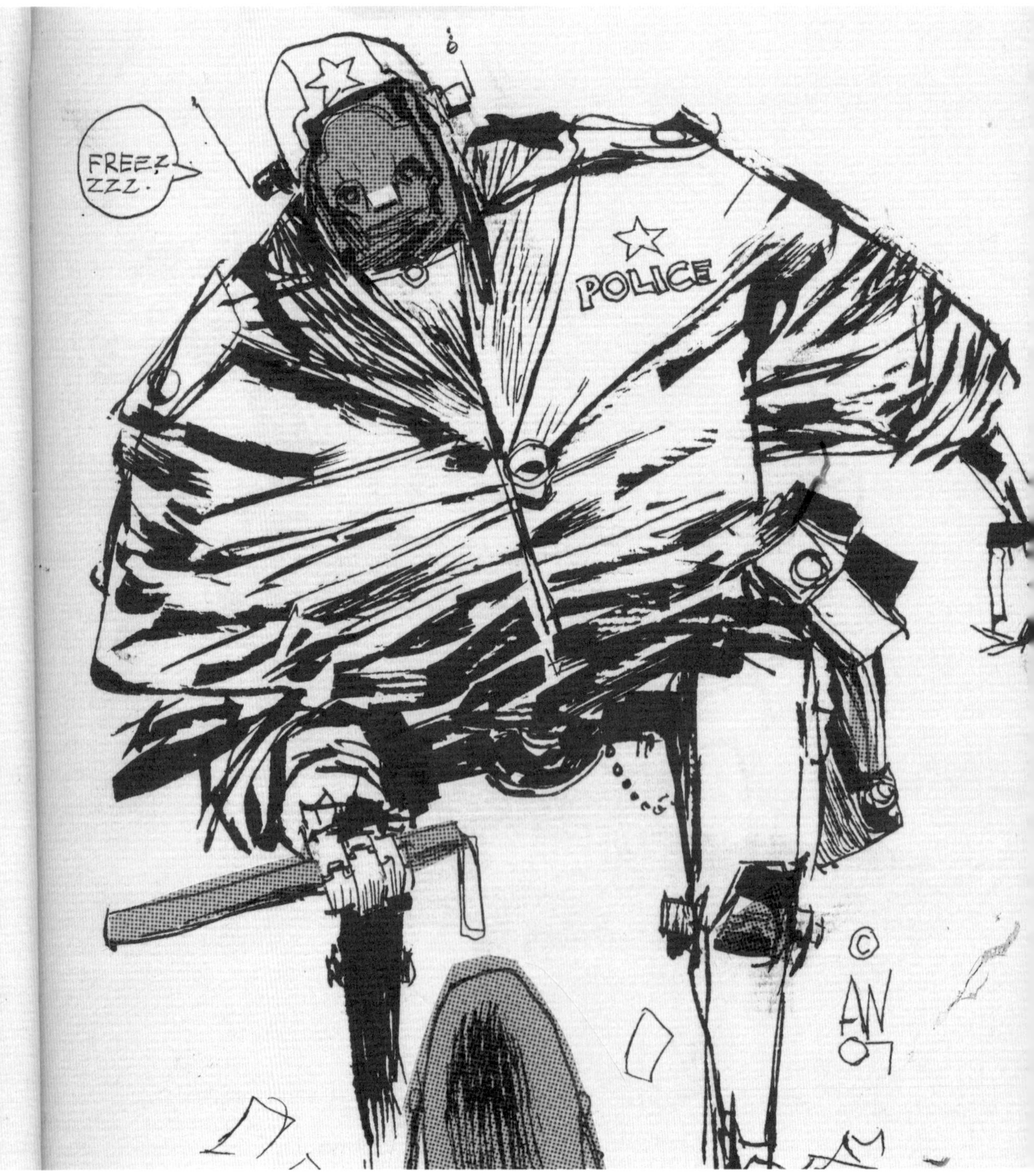

FREEZ
ZZZ.
POLICE

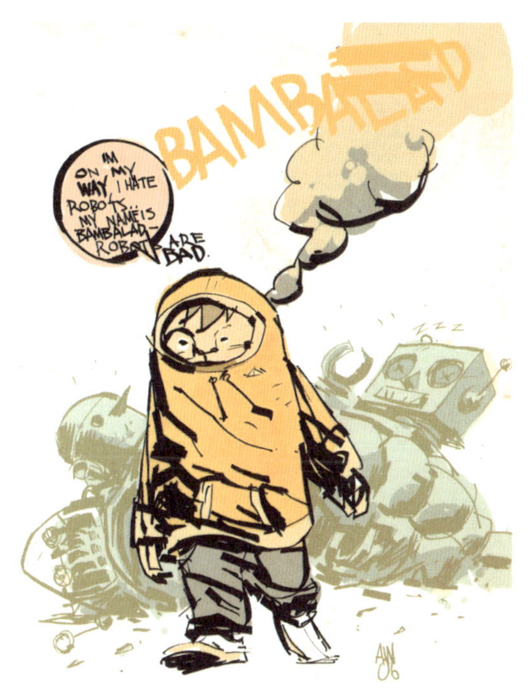
ON MY
WAY I HATE
ROBOTS
MY NAME IS
BAMBALAD -
ROBOTS ARE
BAD.
BAMBALAD
ZZZ

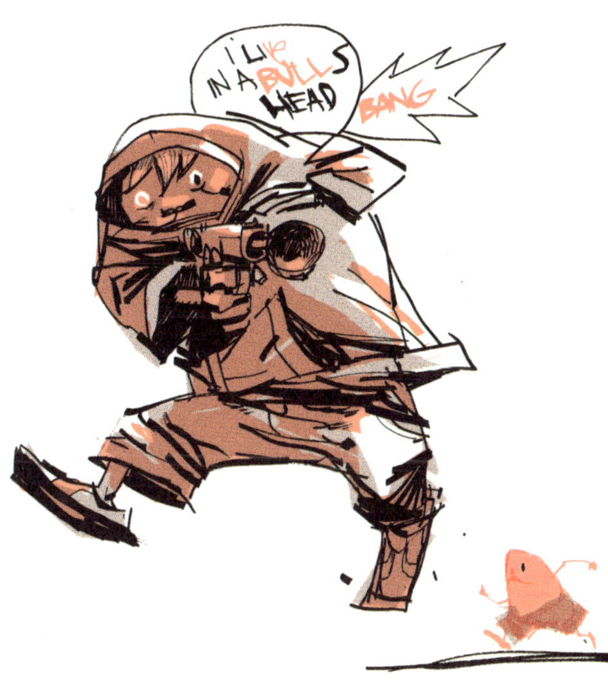
I LIVE
IN A BULLS
HEAD
BANG

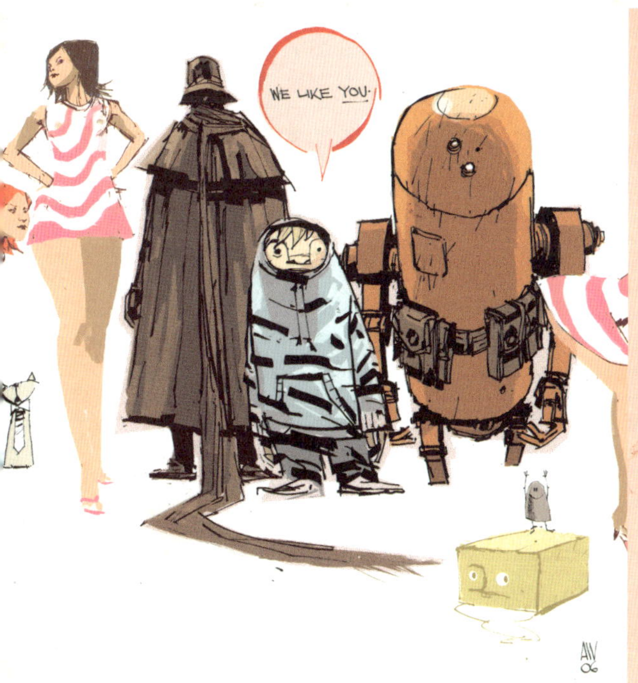
WE LIKE YOU.

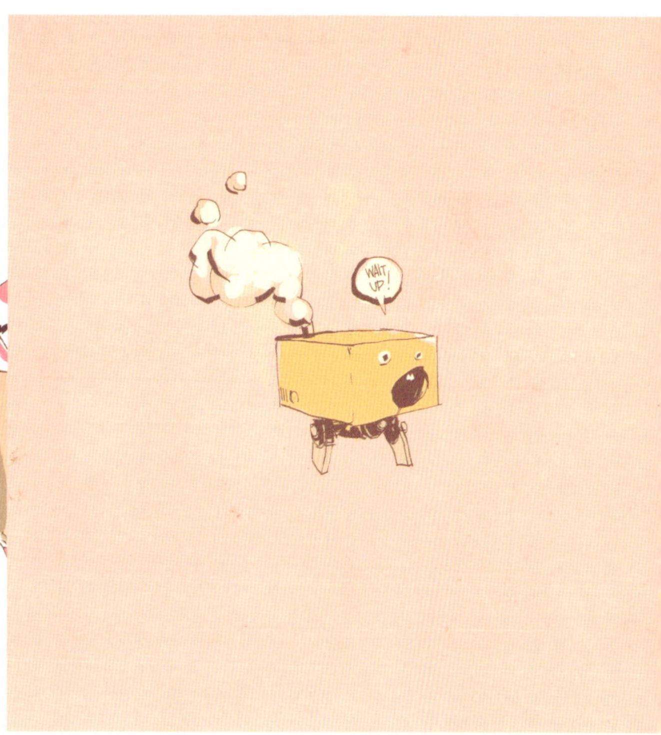
WAIT
UP!

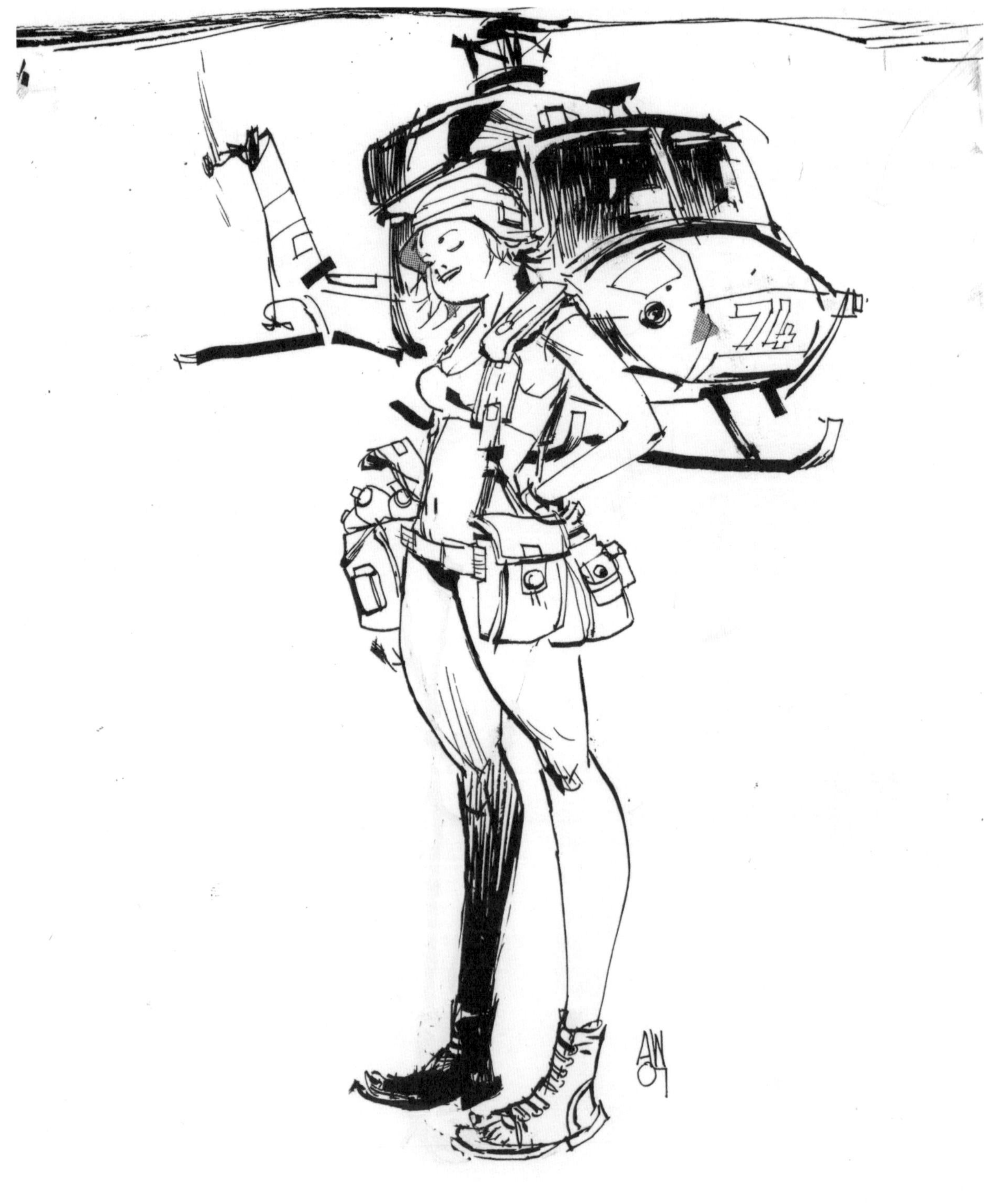

74

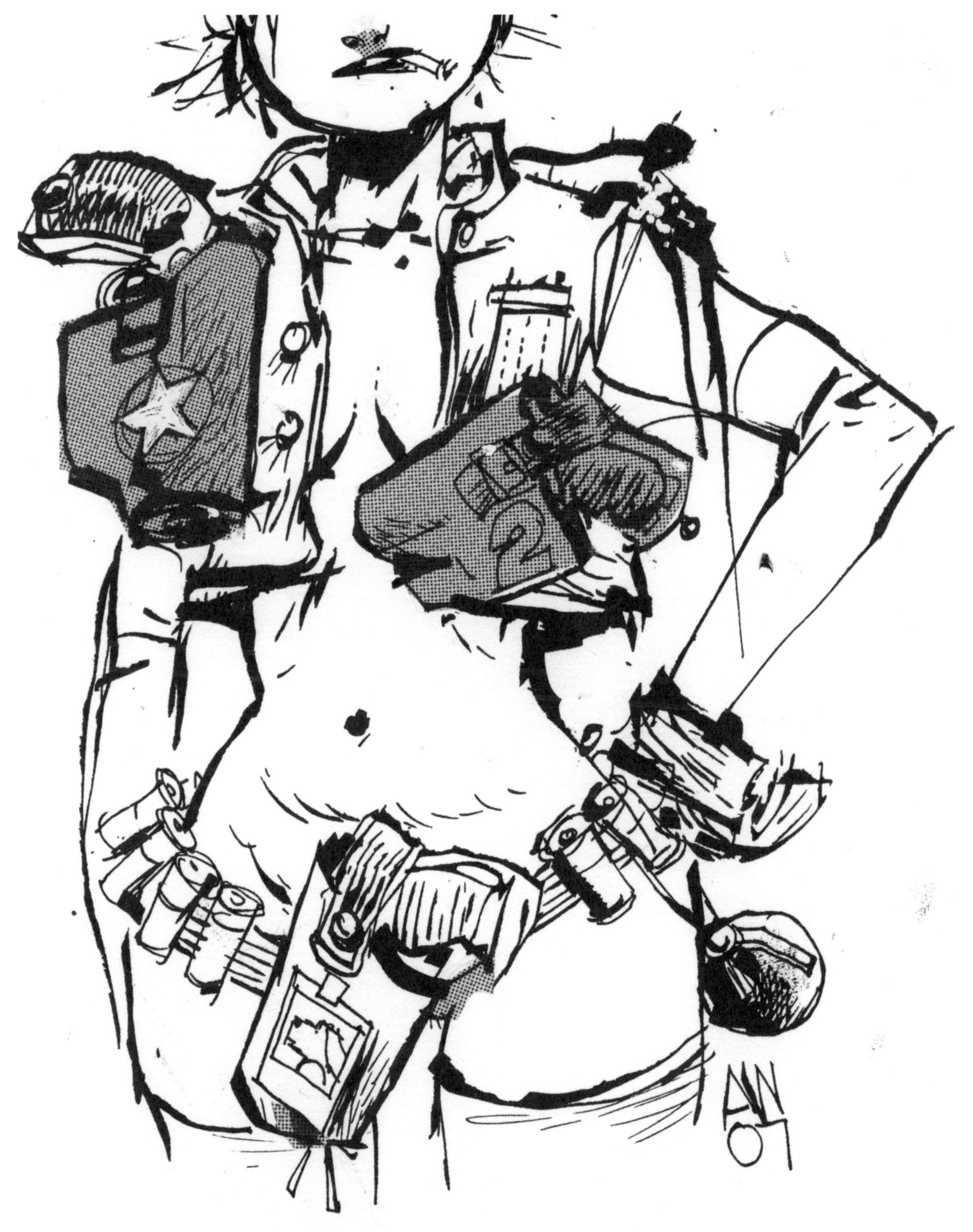

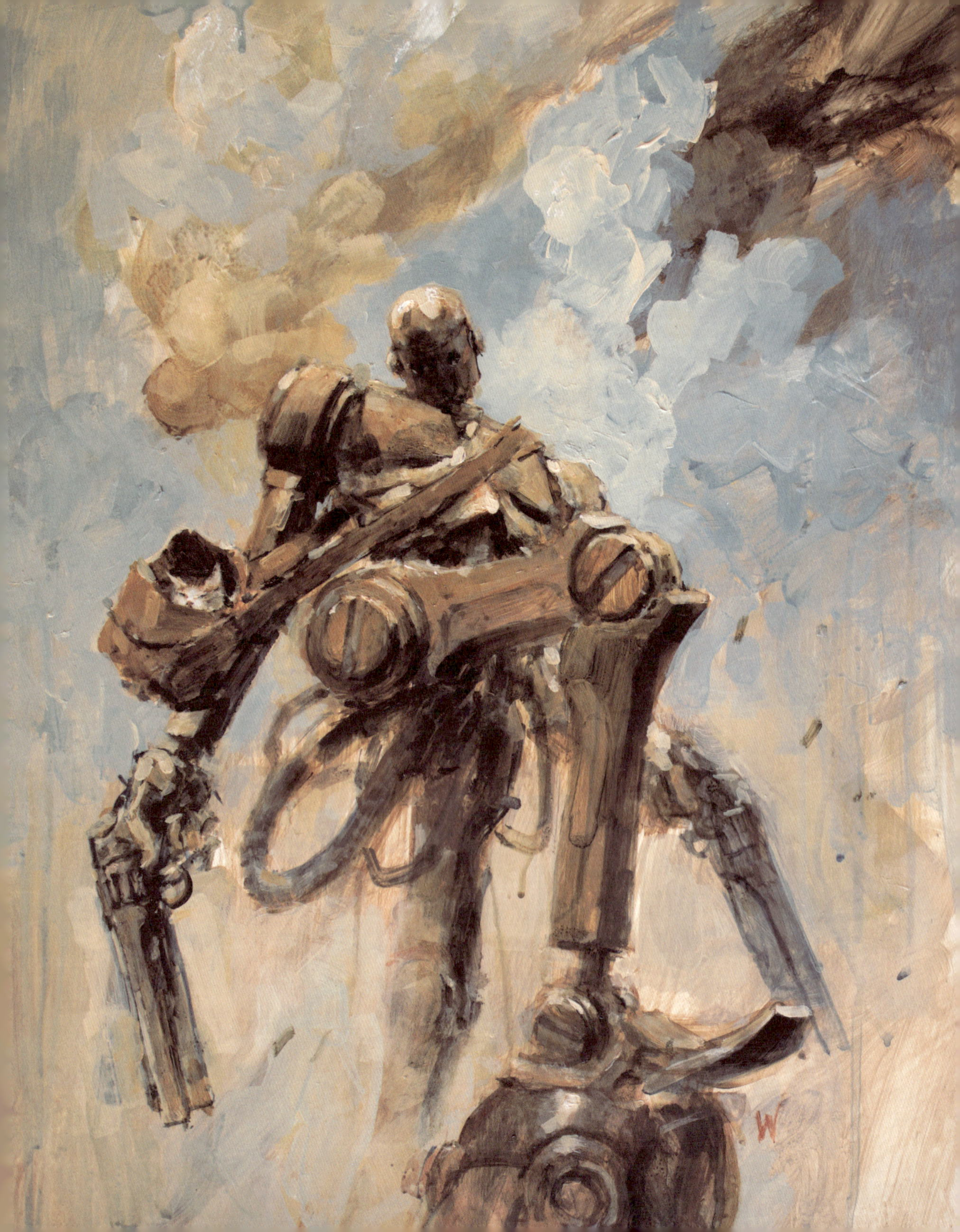

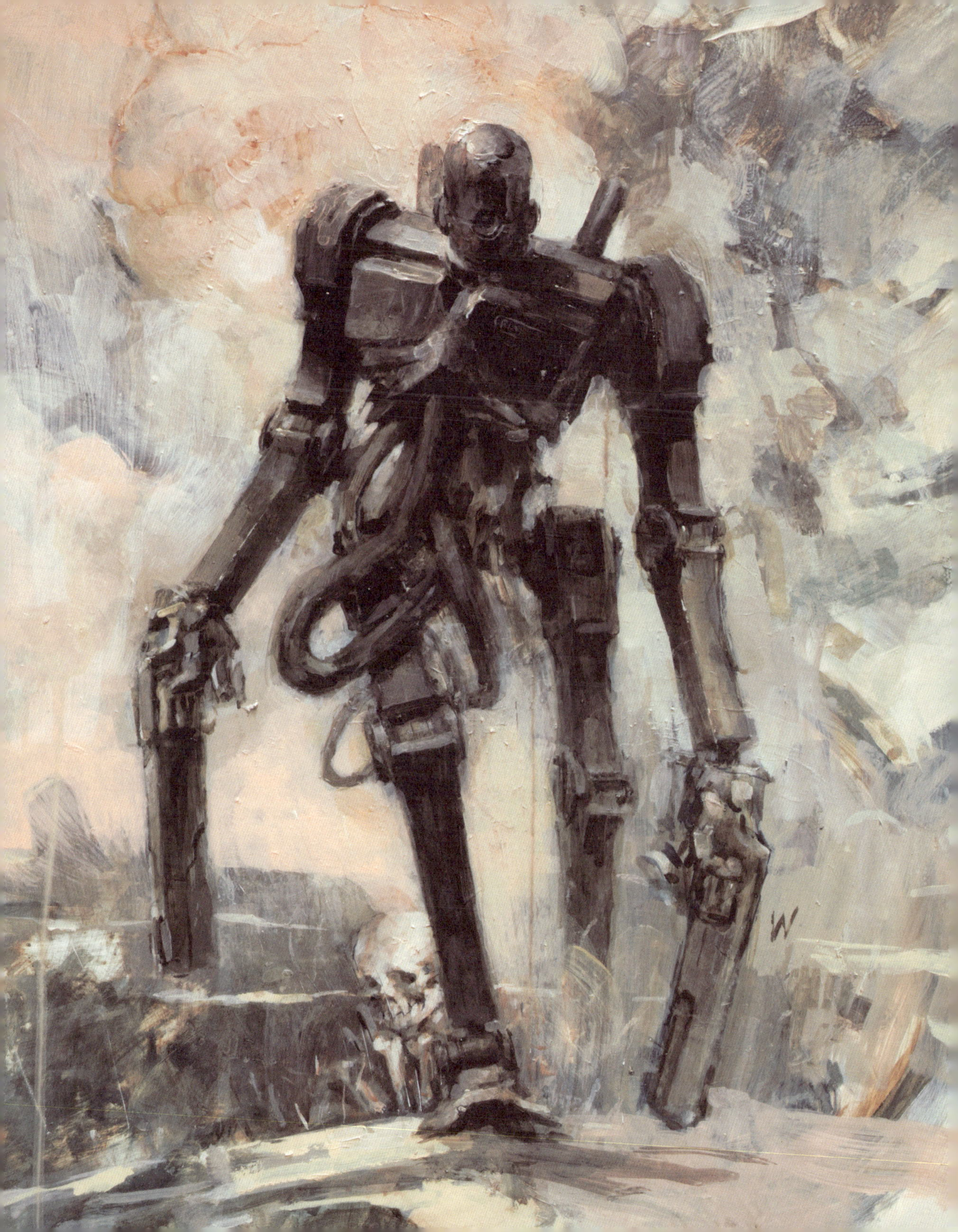

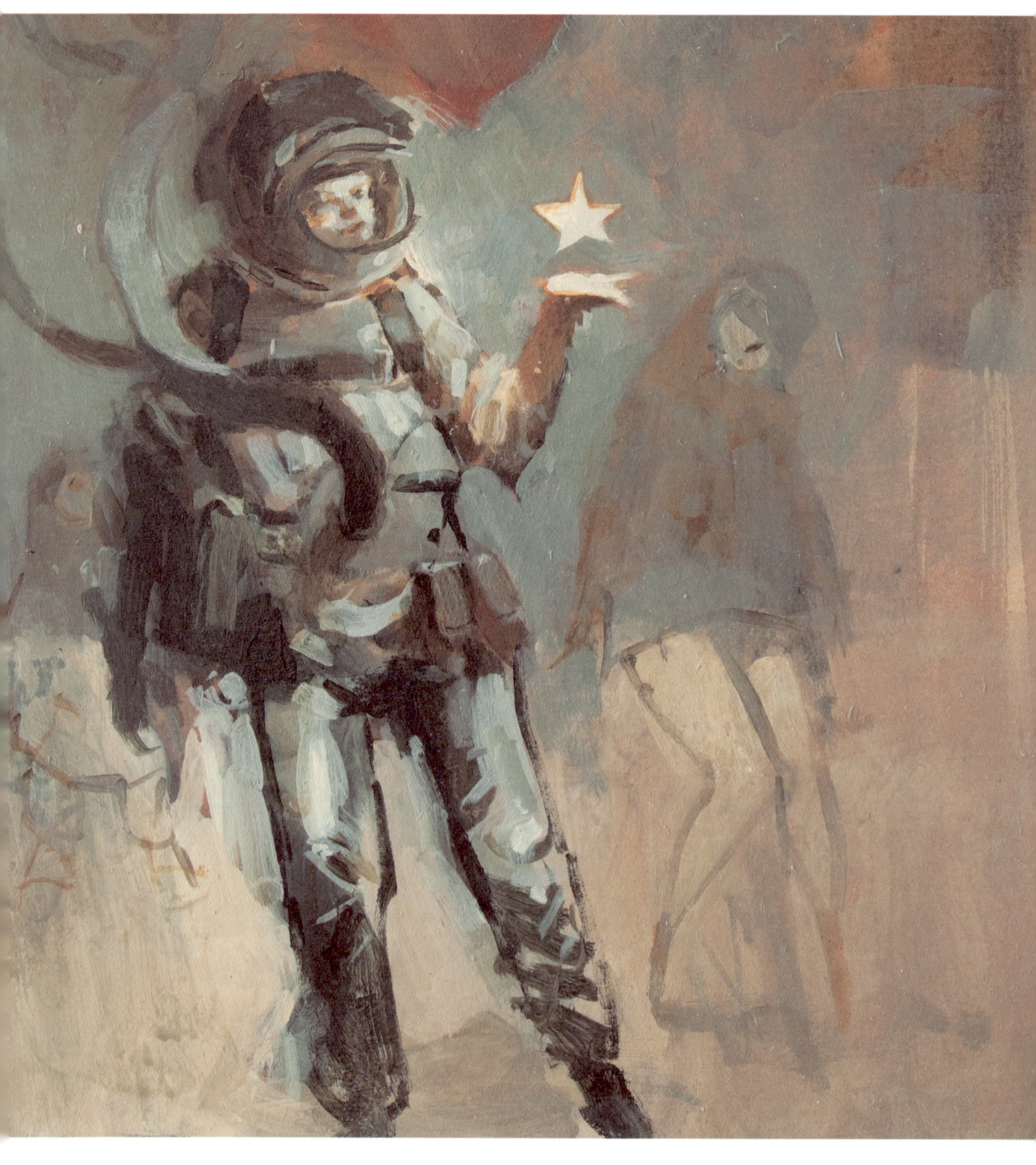

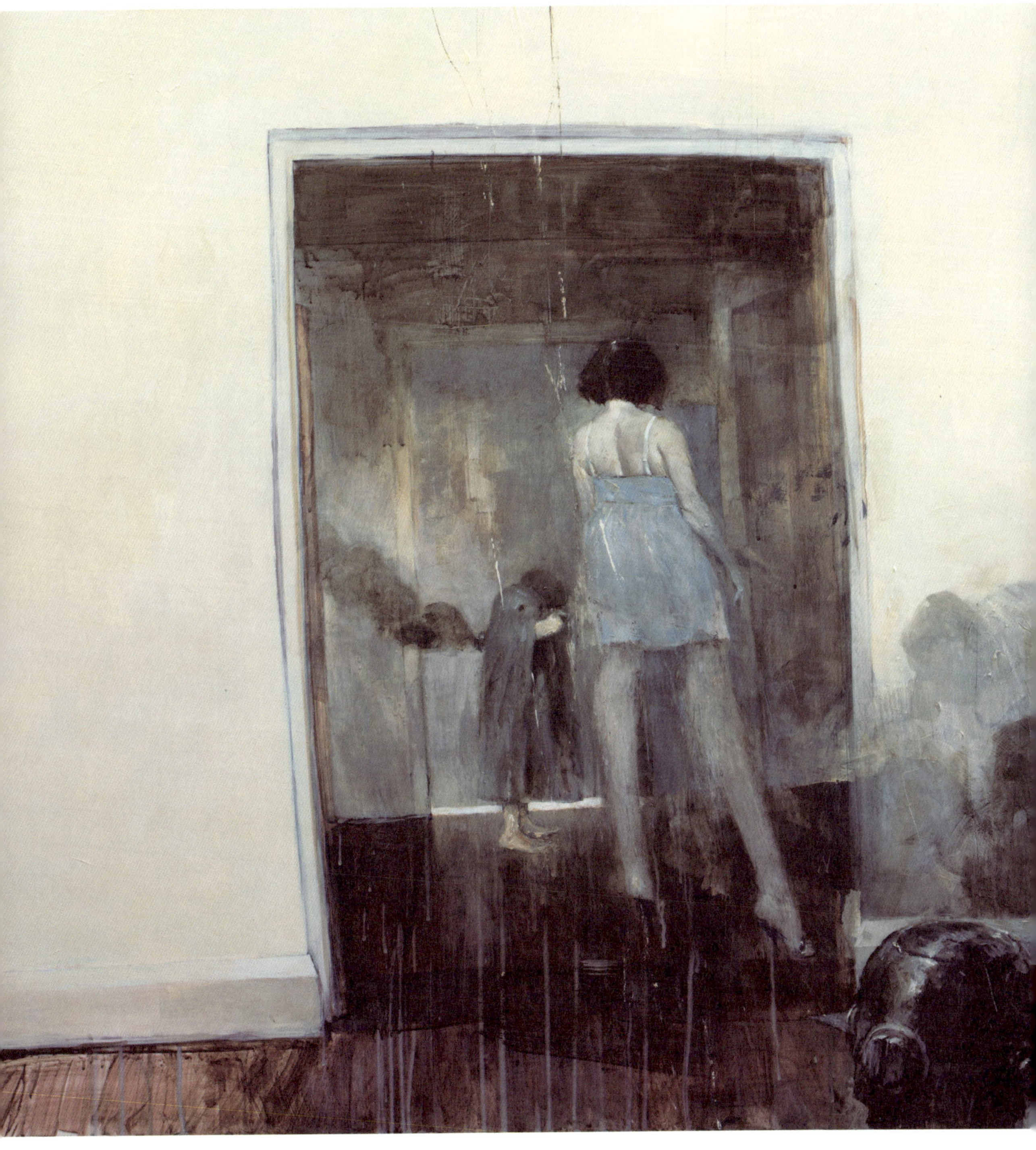

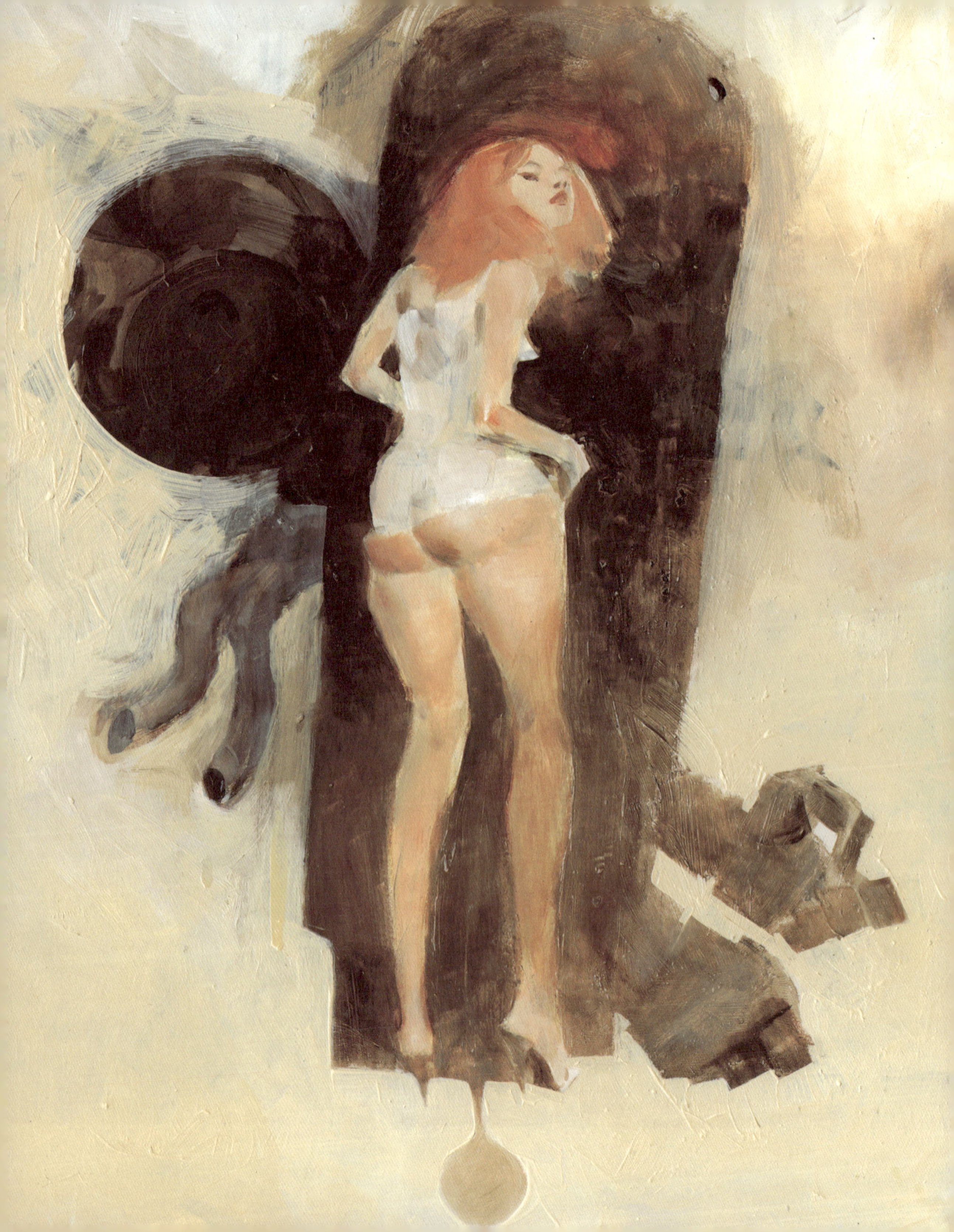

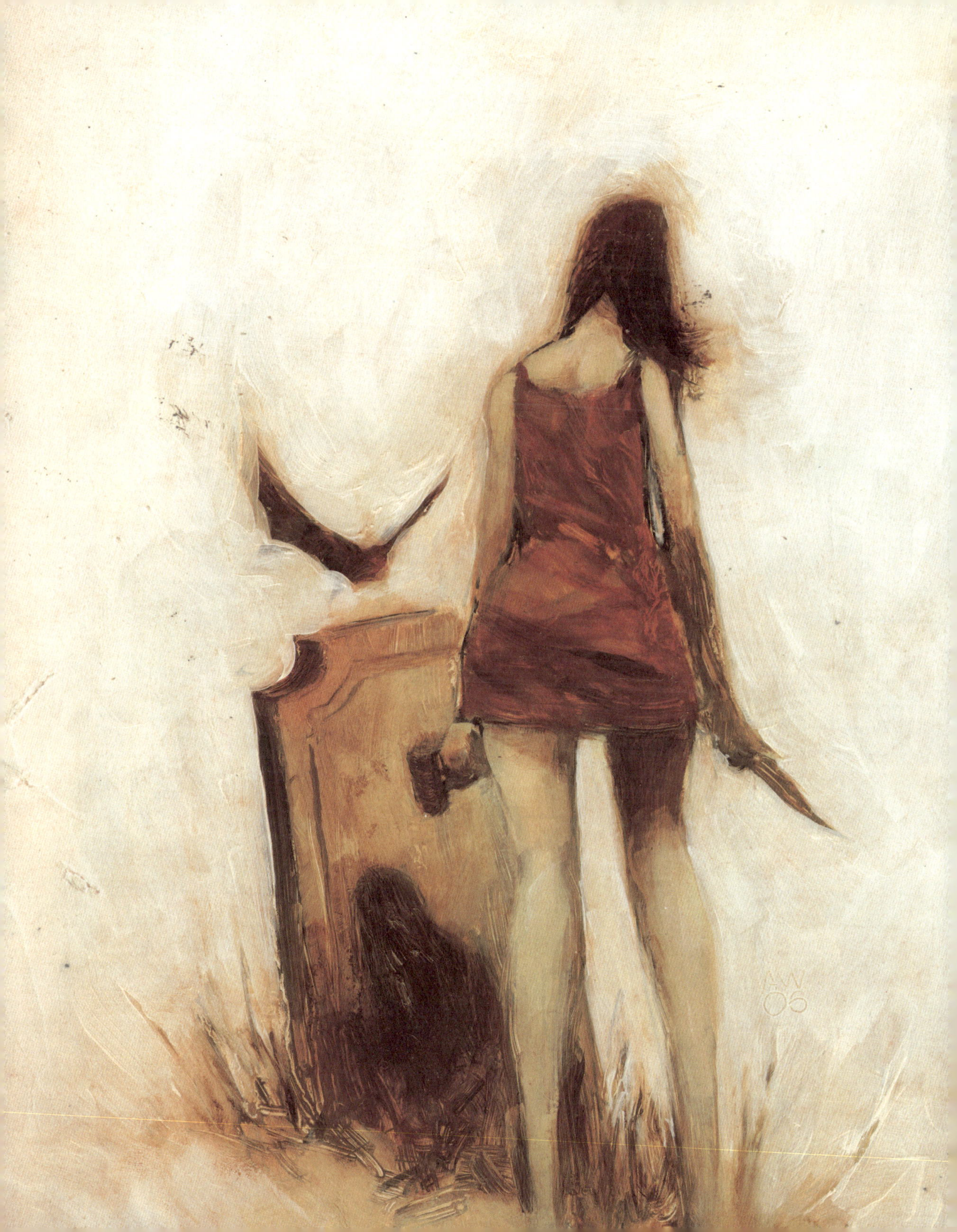

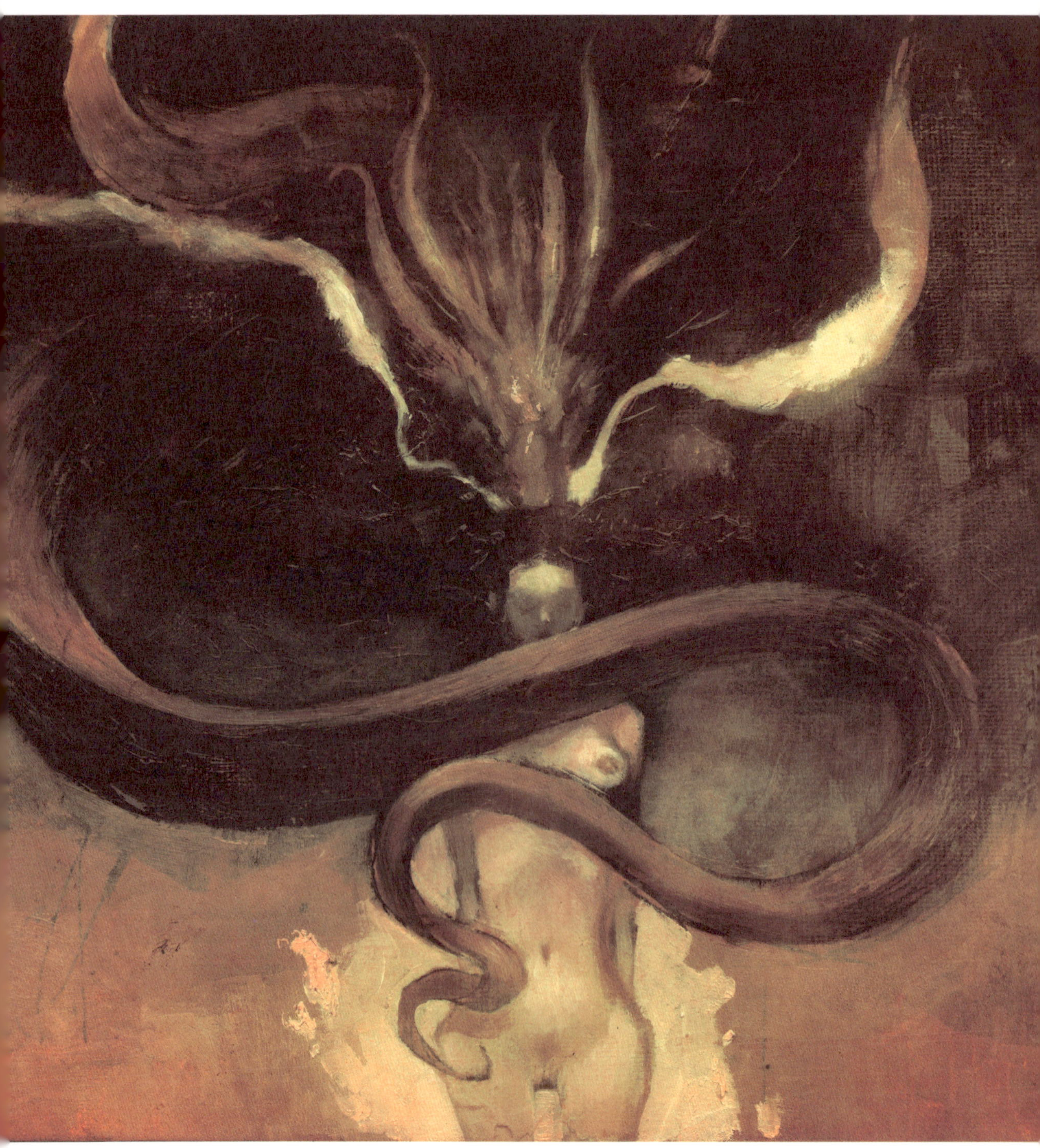

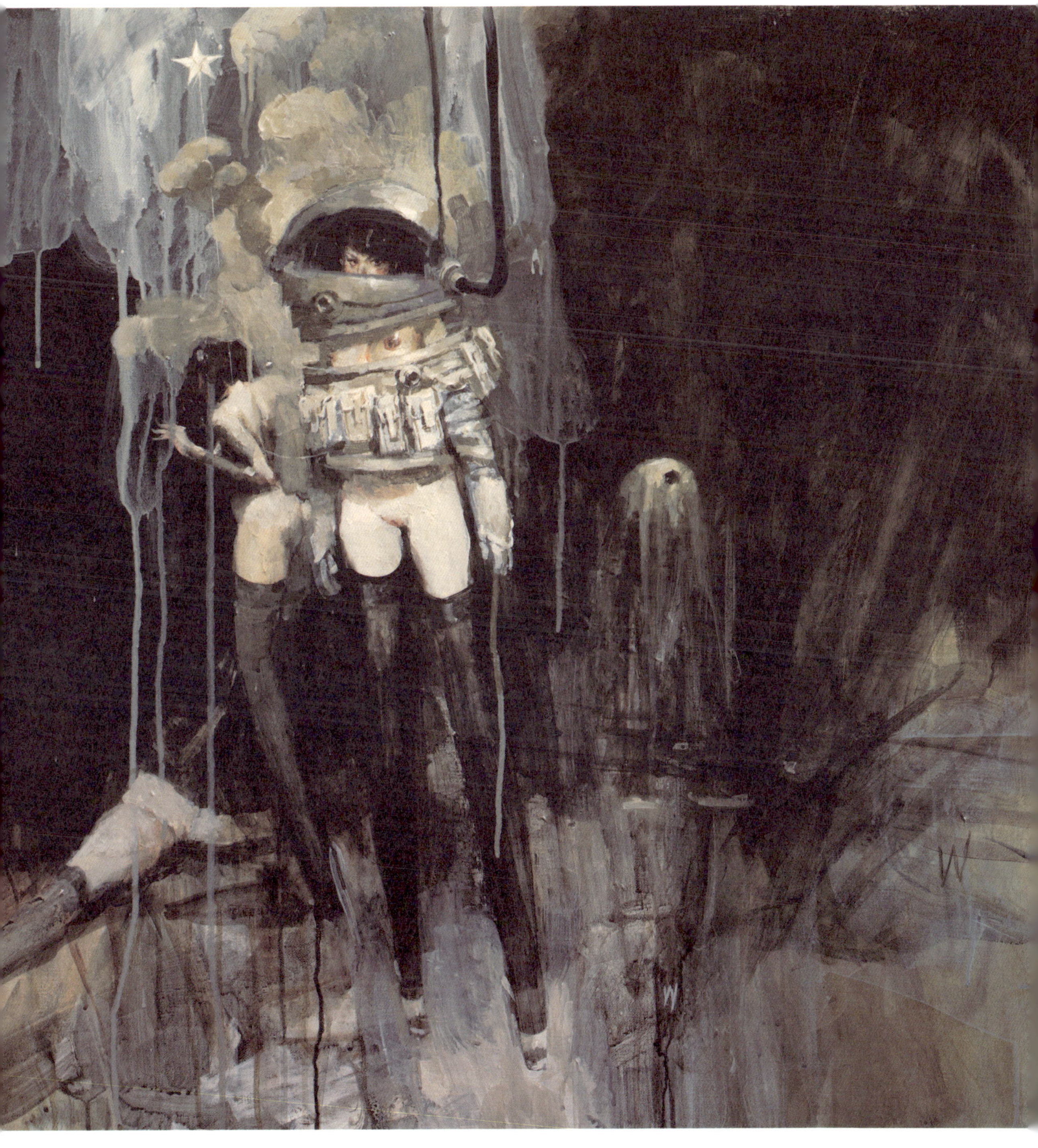

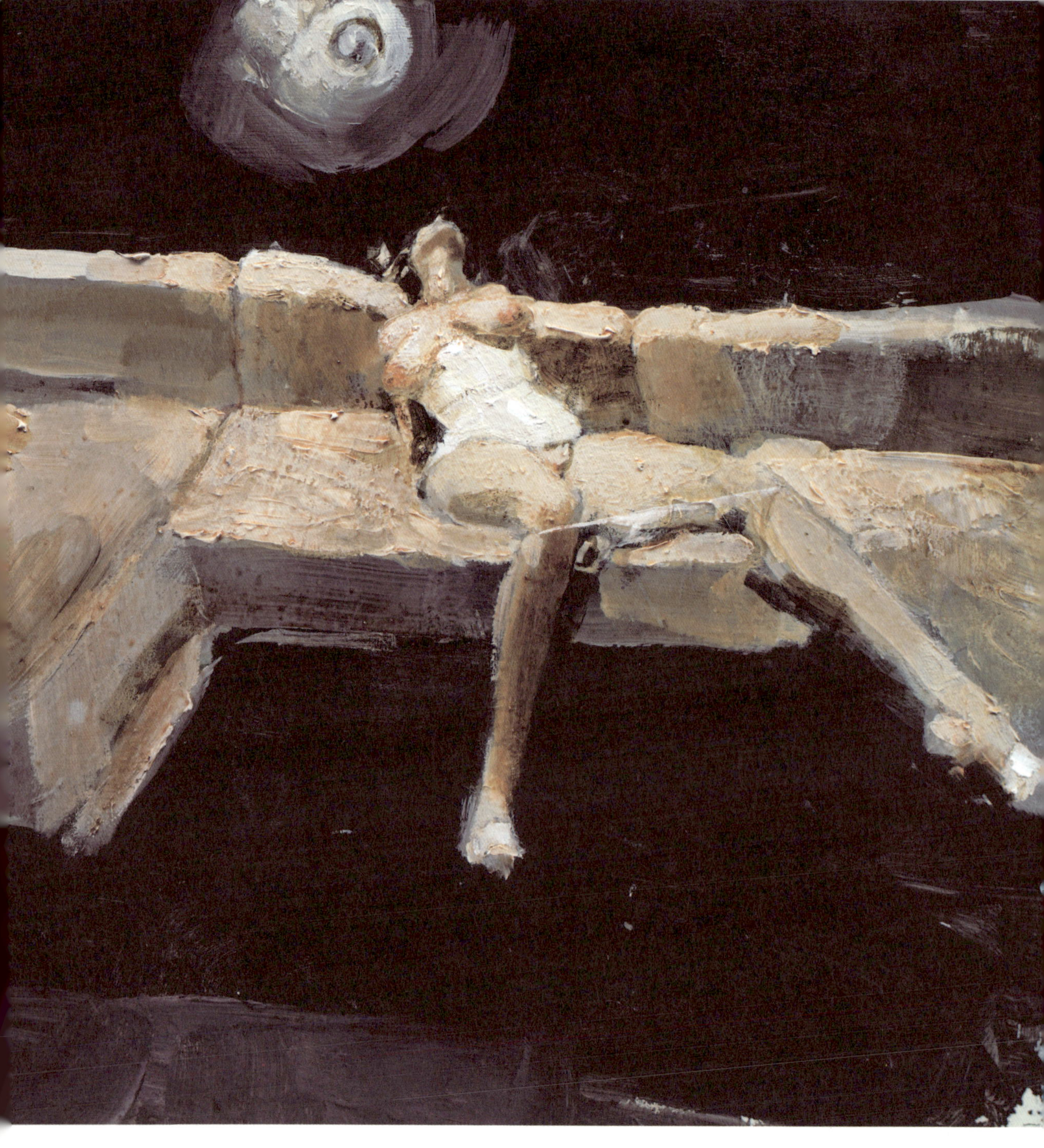

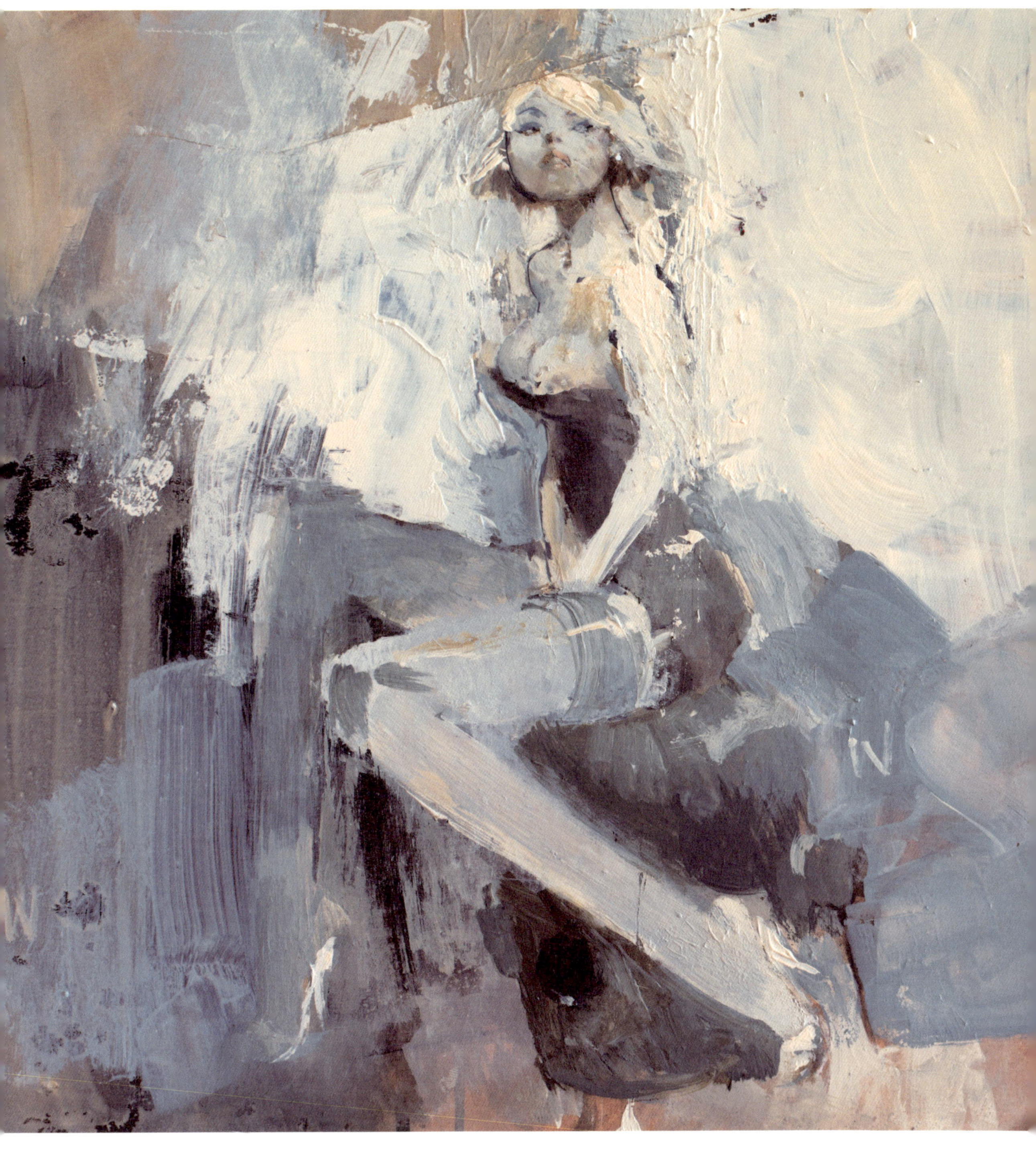

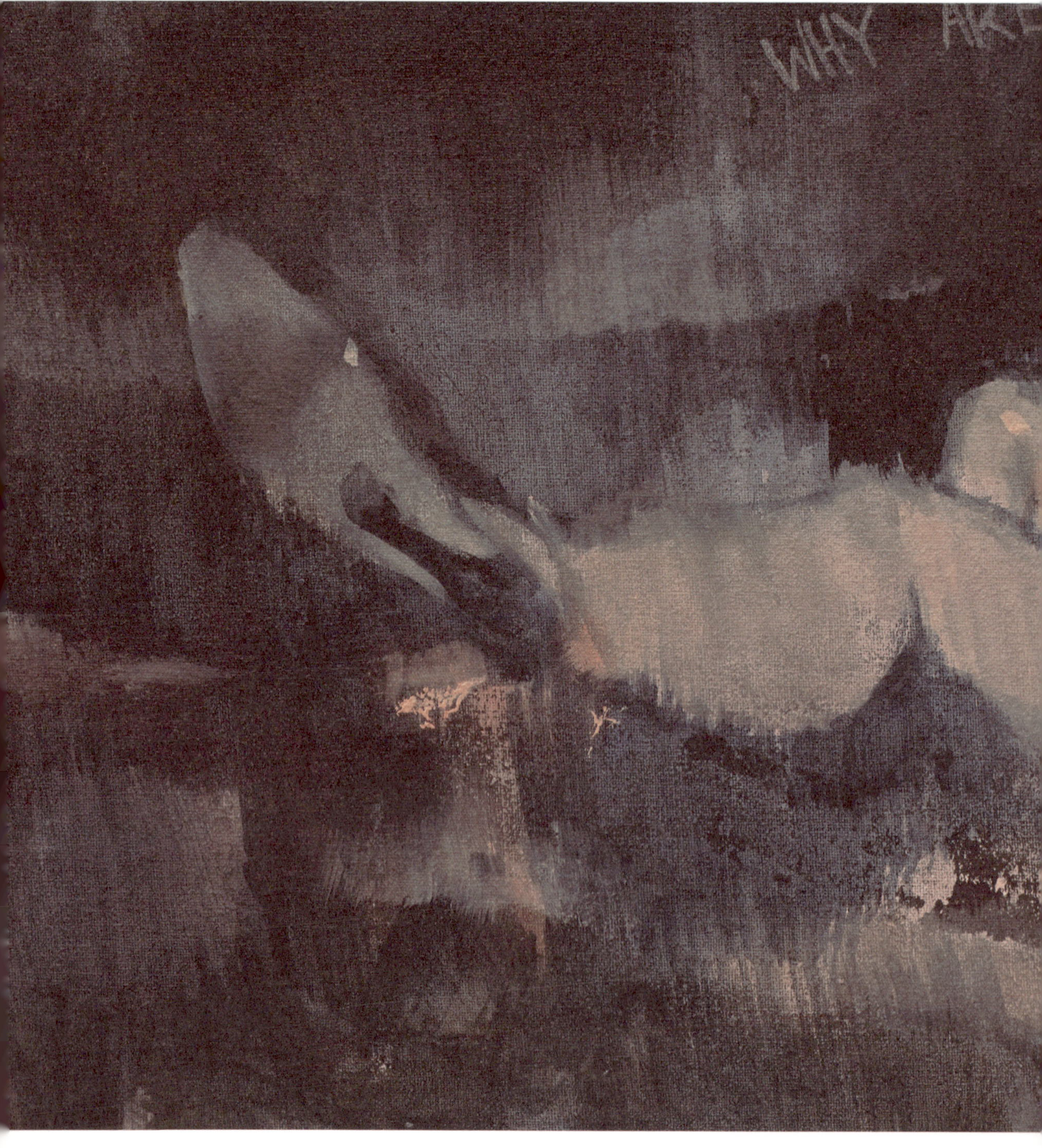
WHY ARE

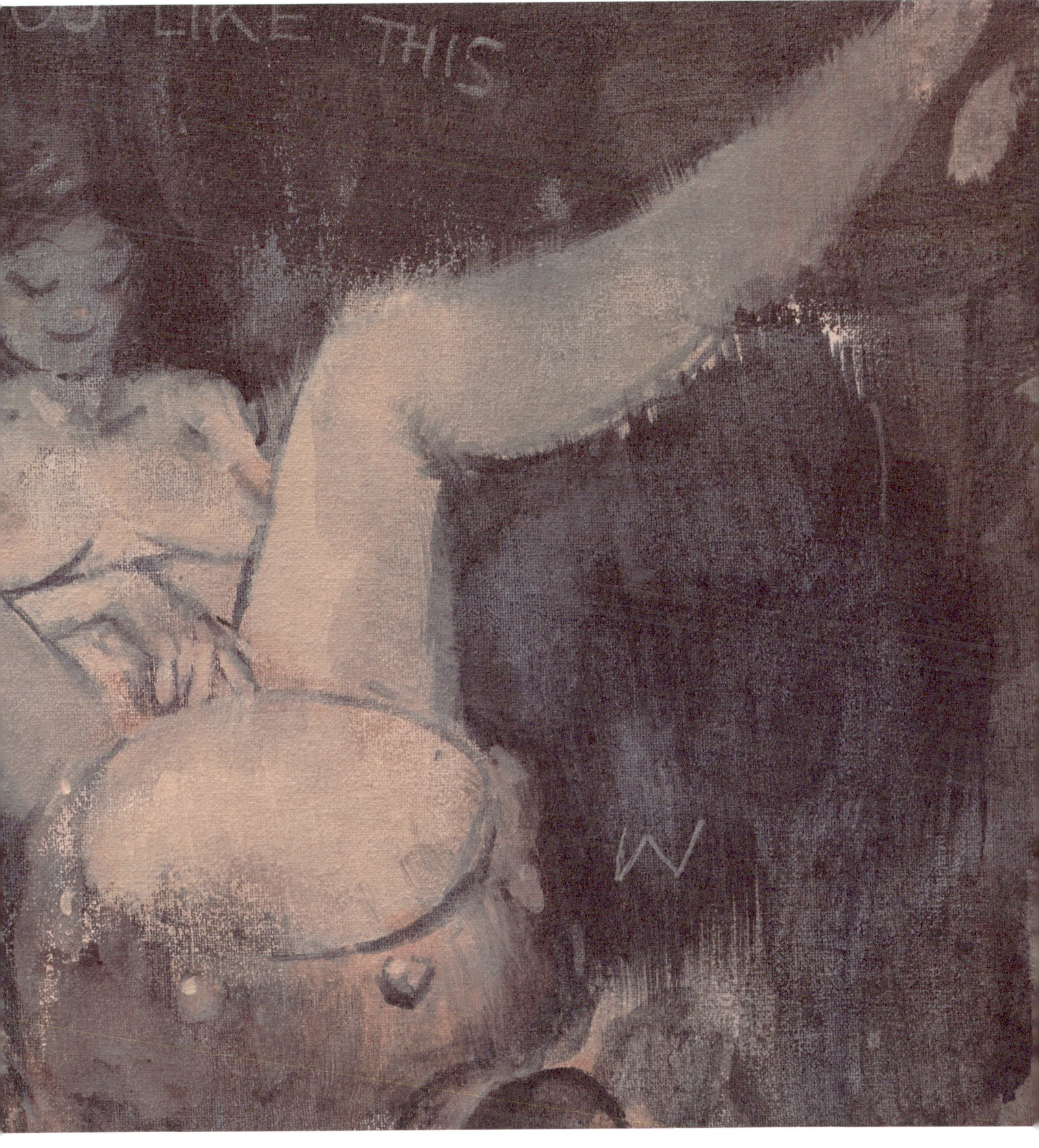
LIKE THIS

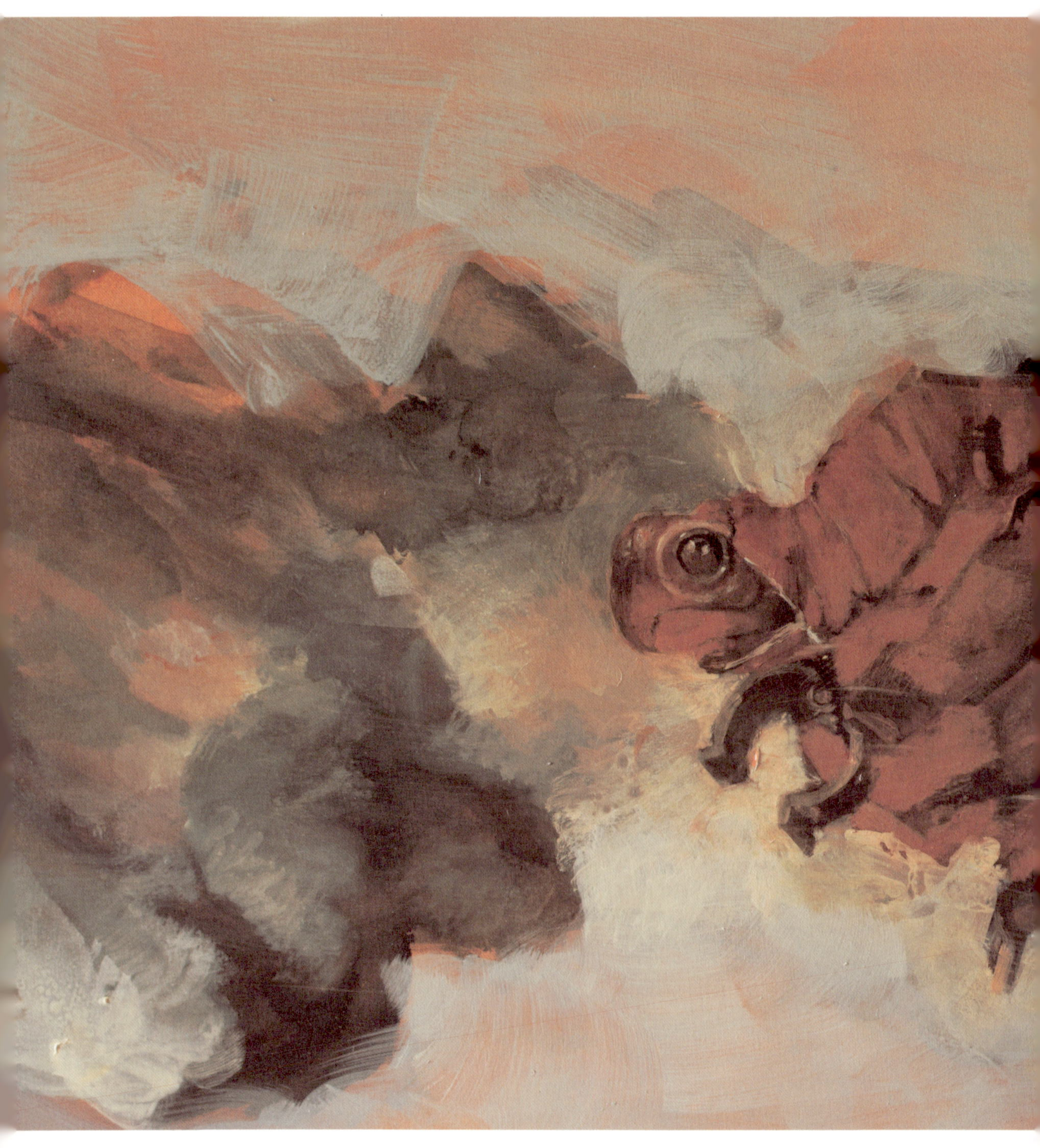

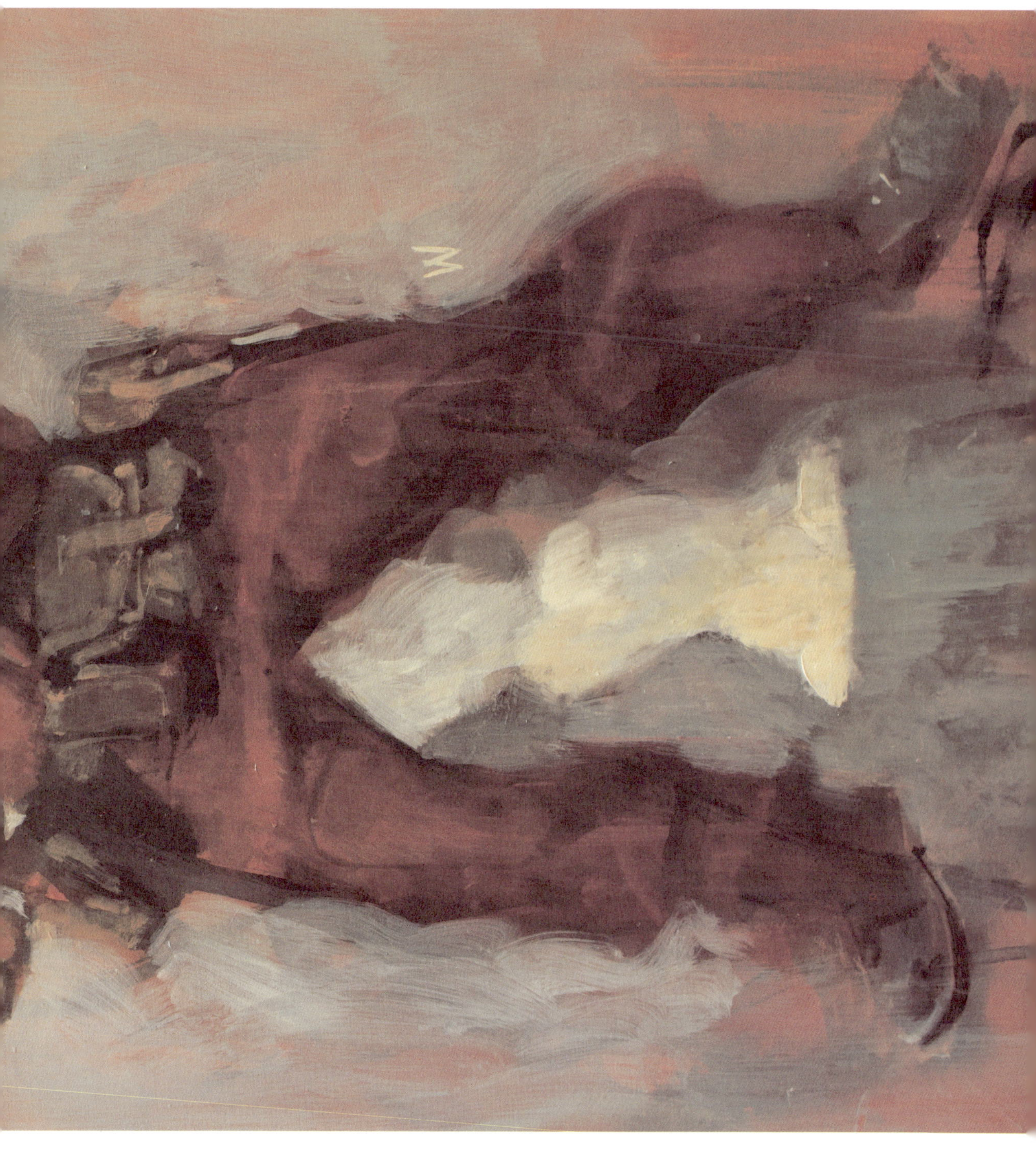

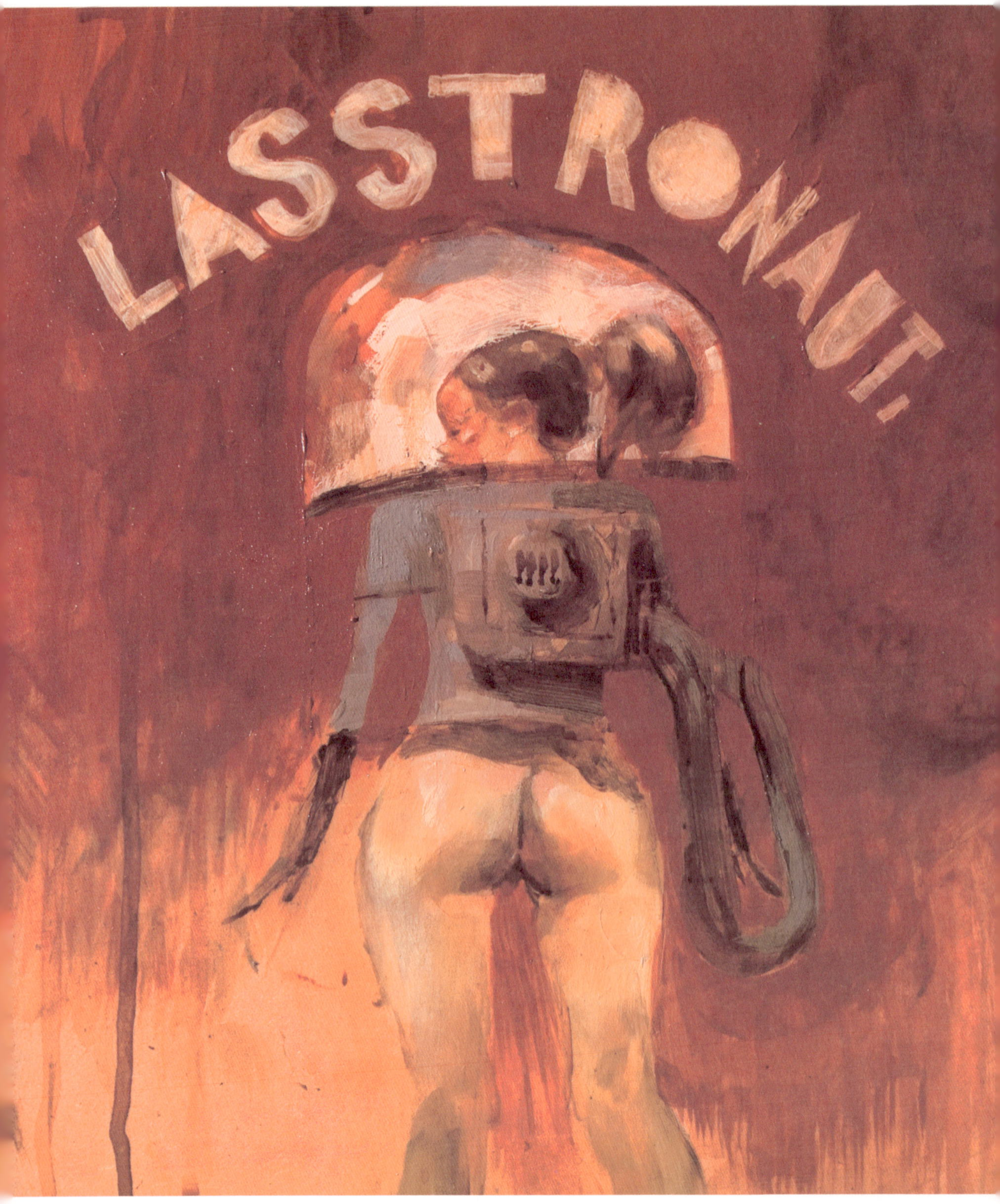

LASSTRONAUT.

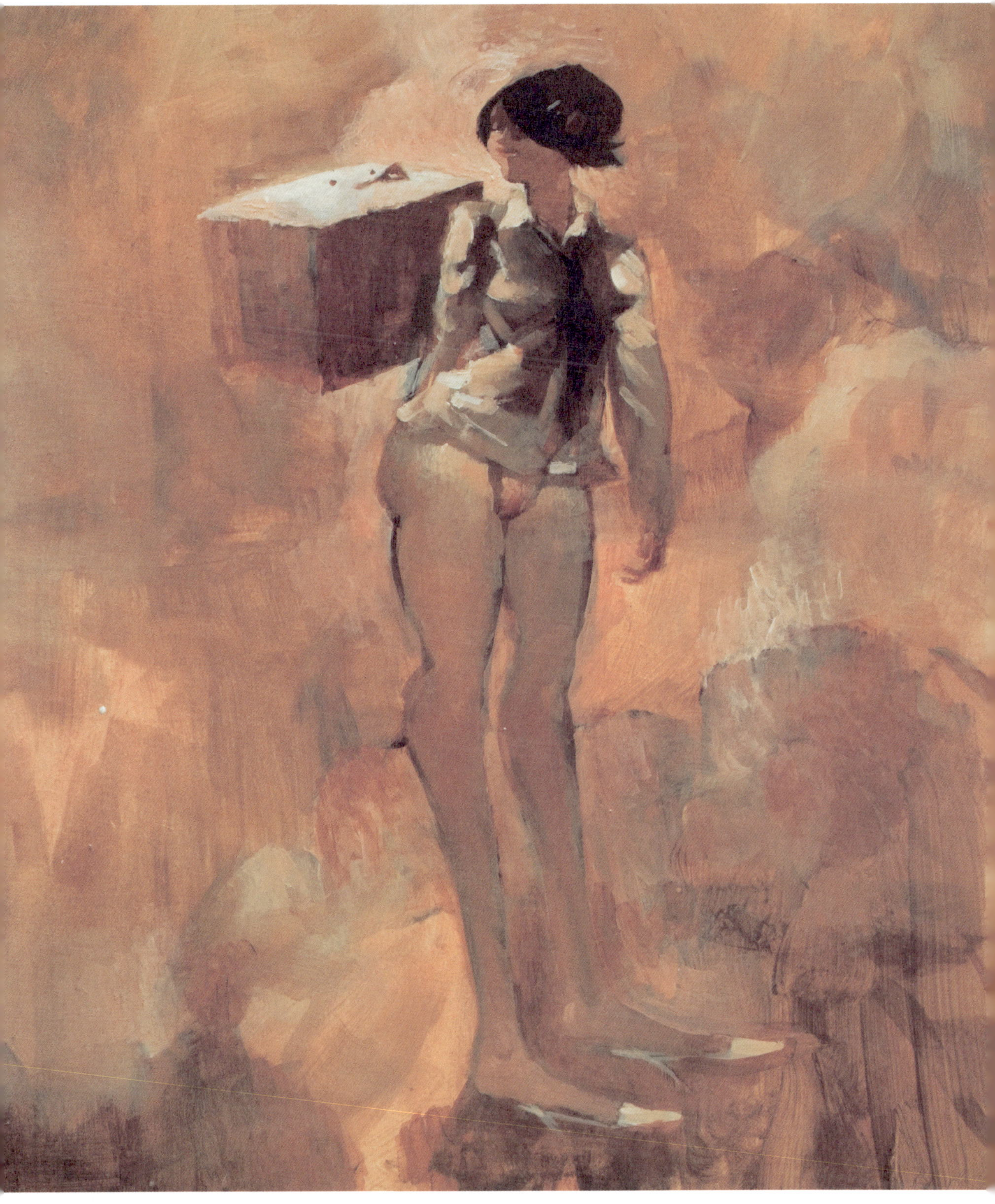

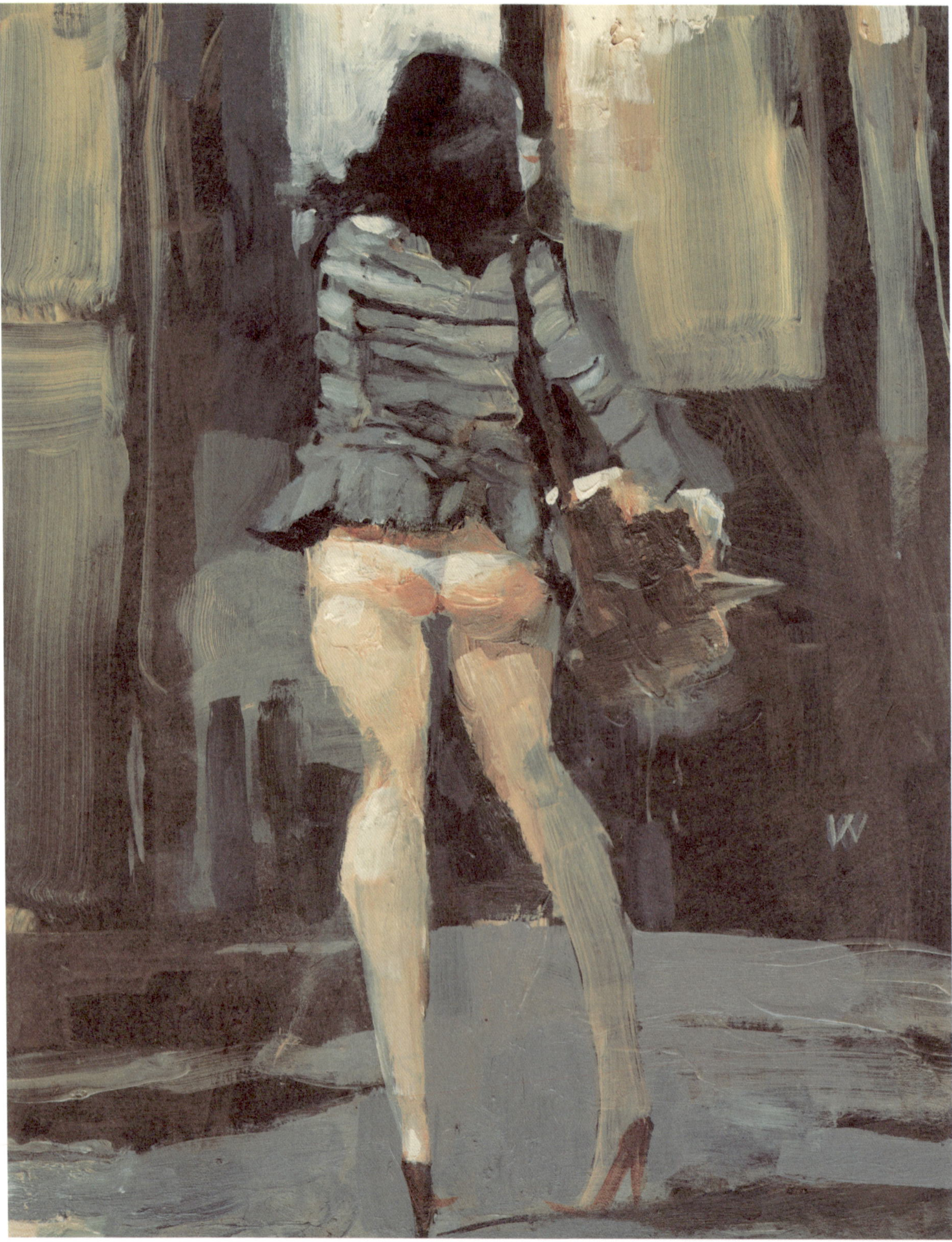

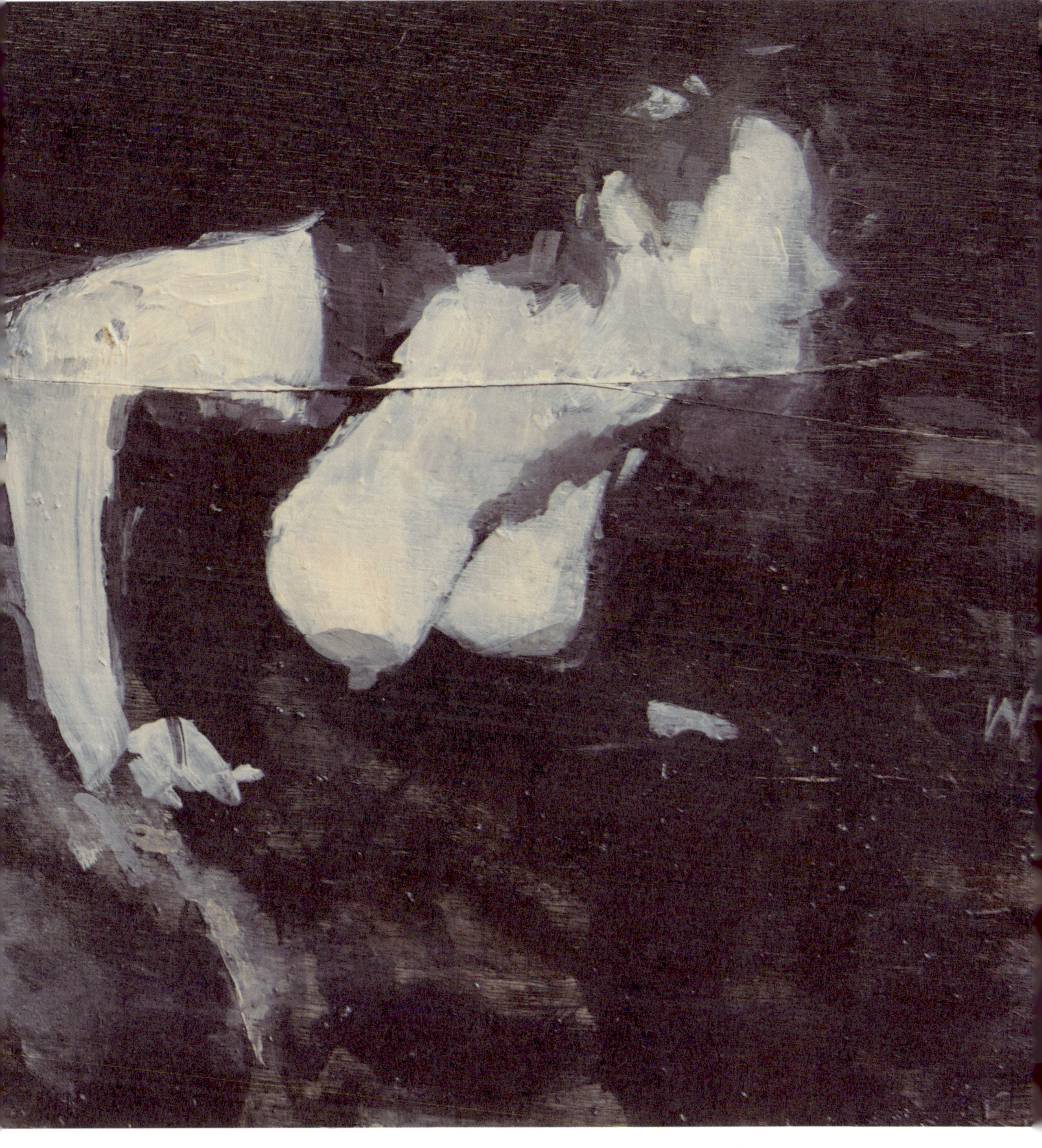

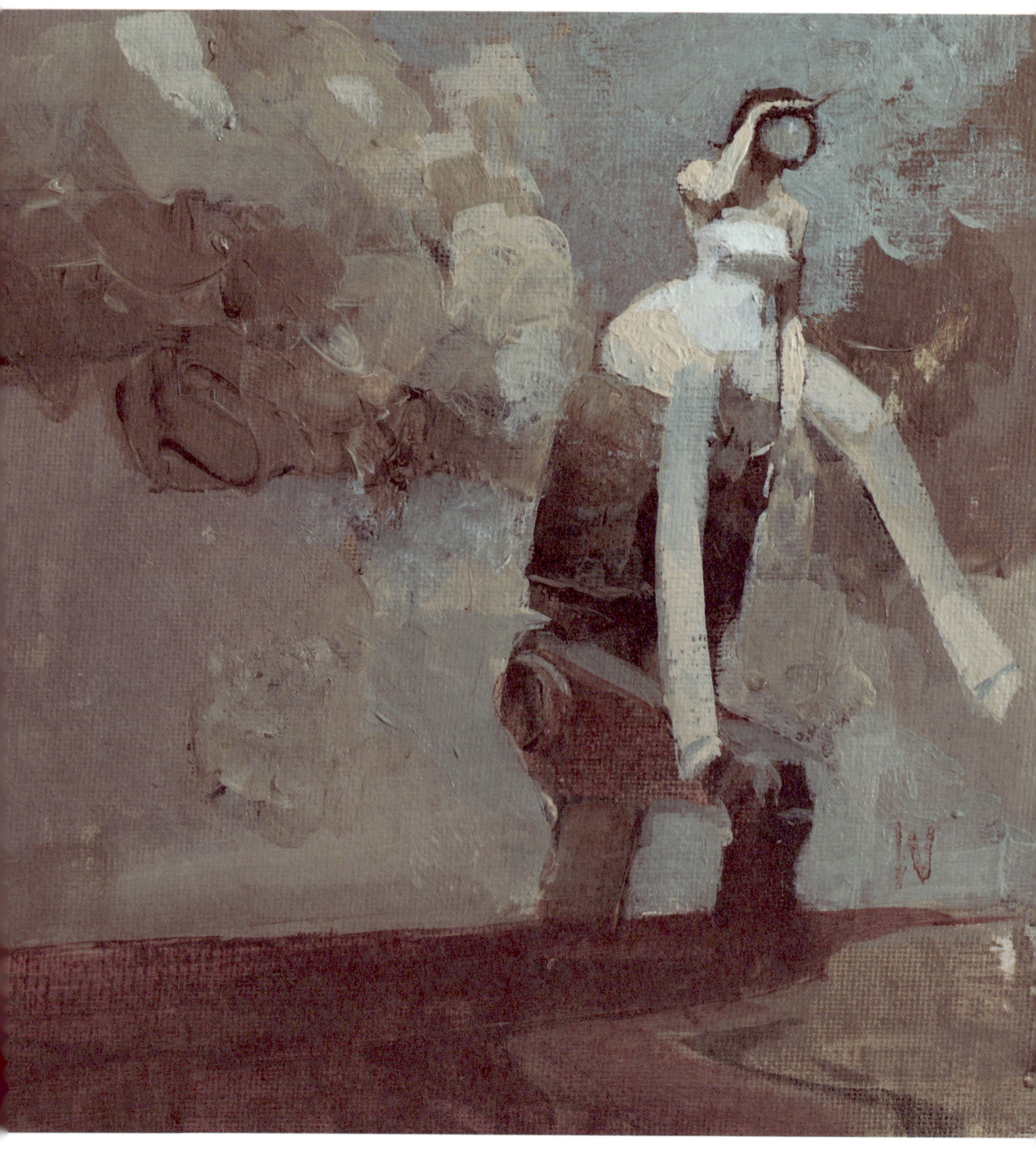

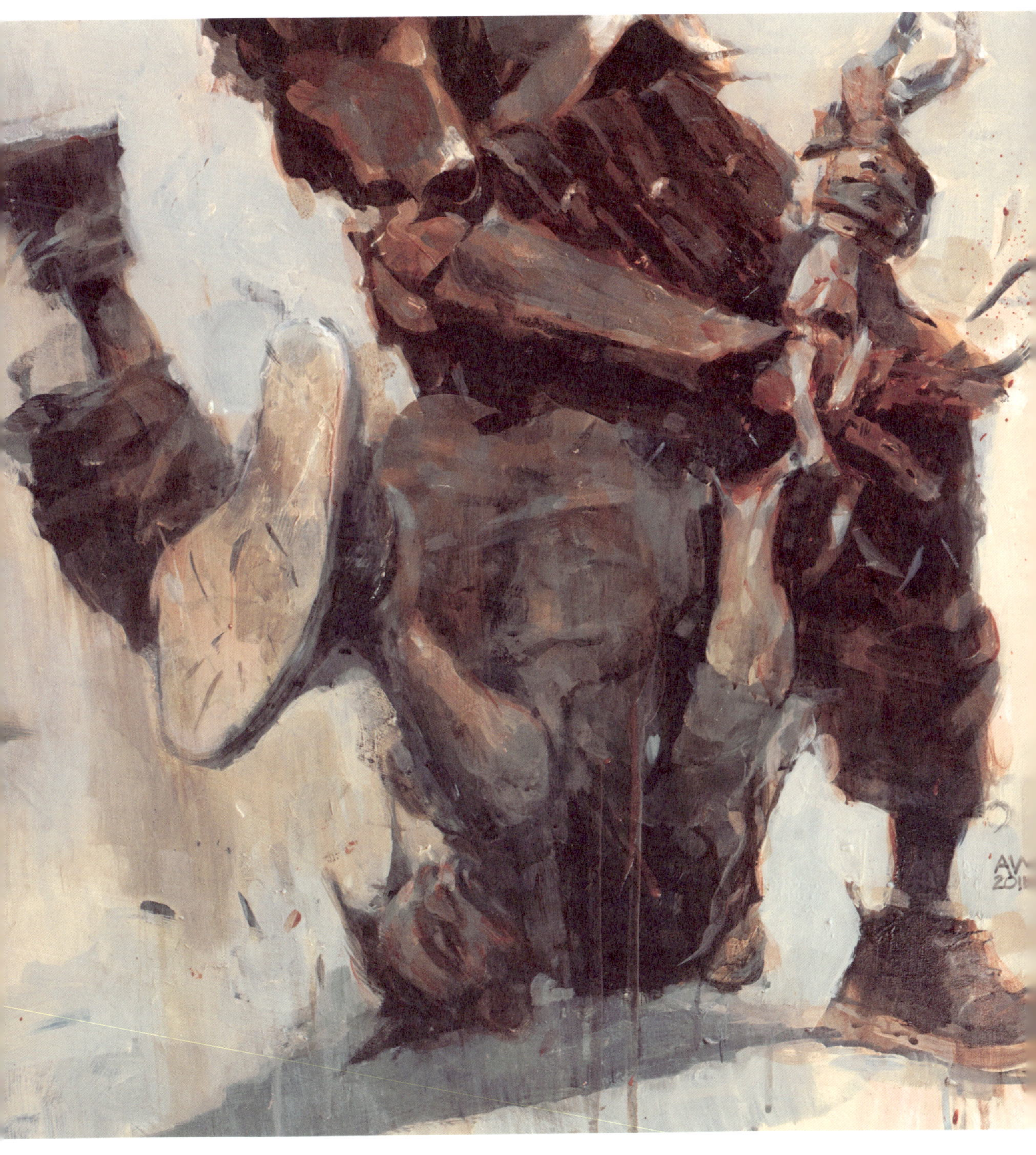

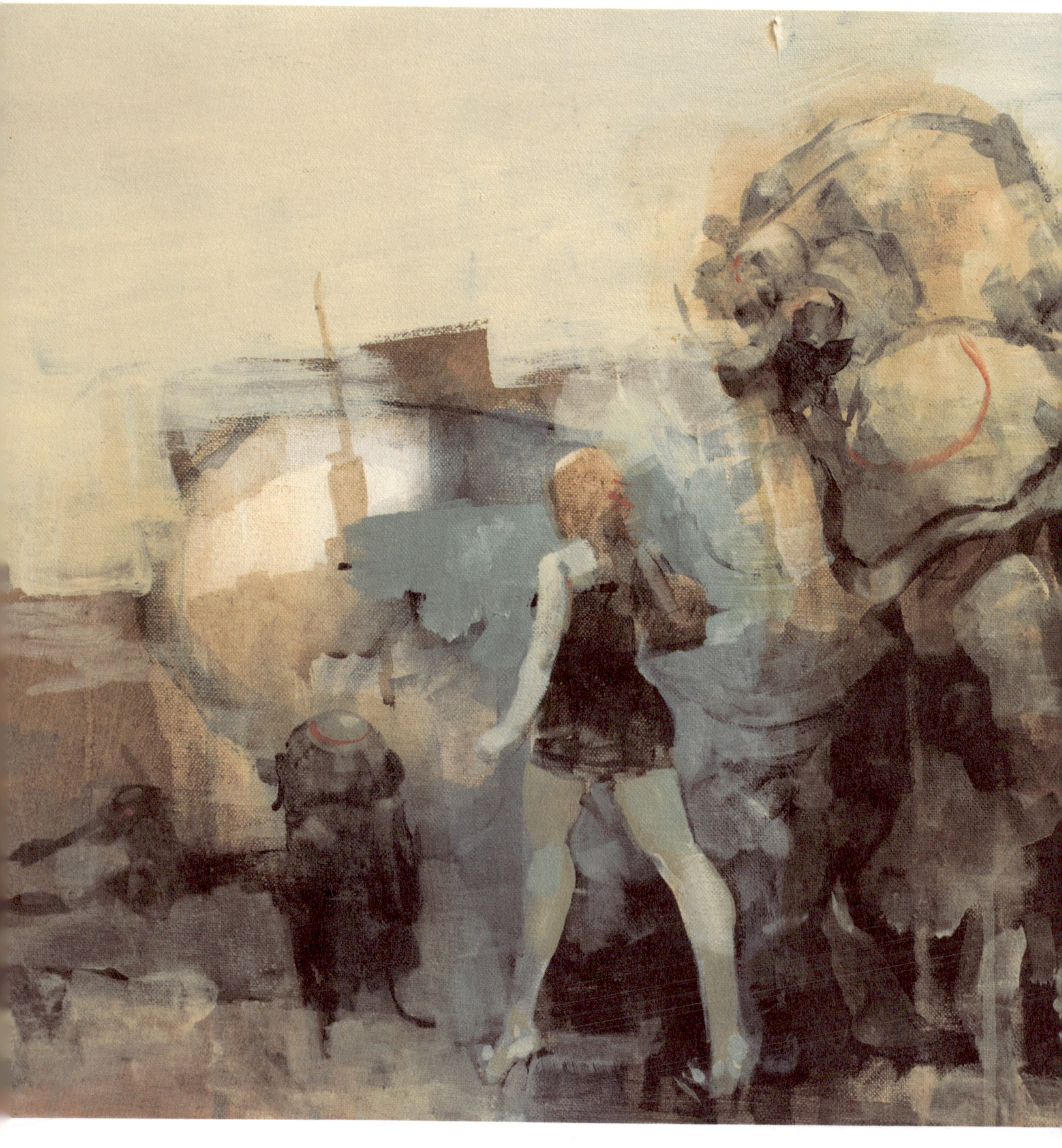

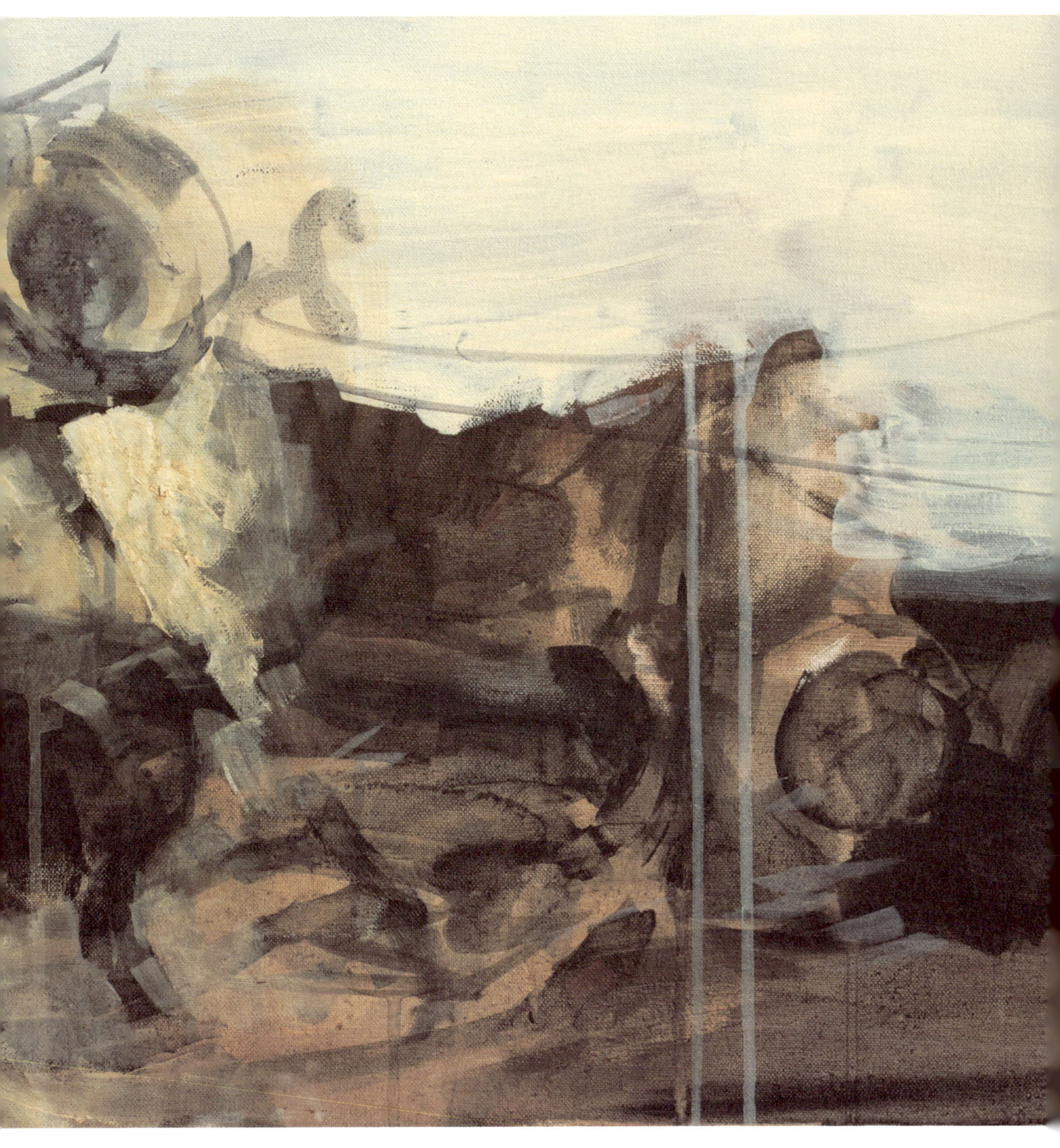

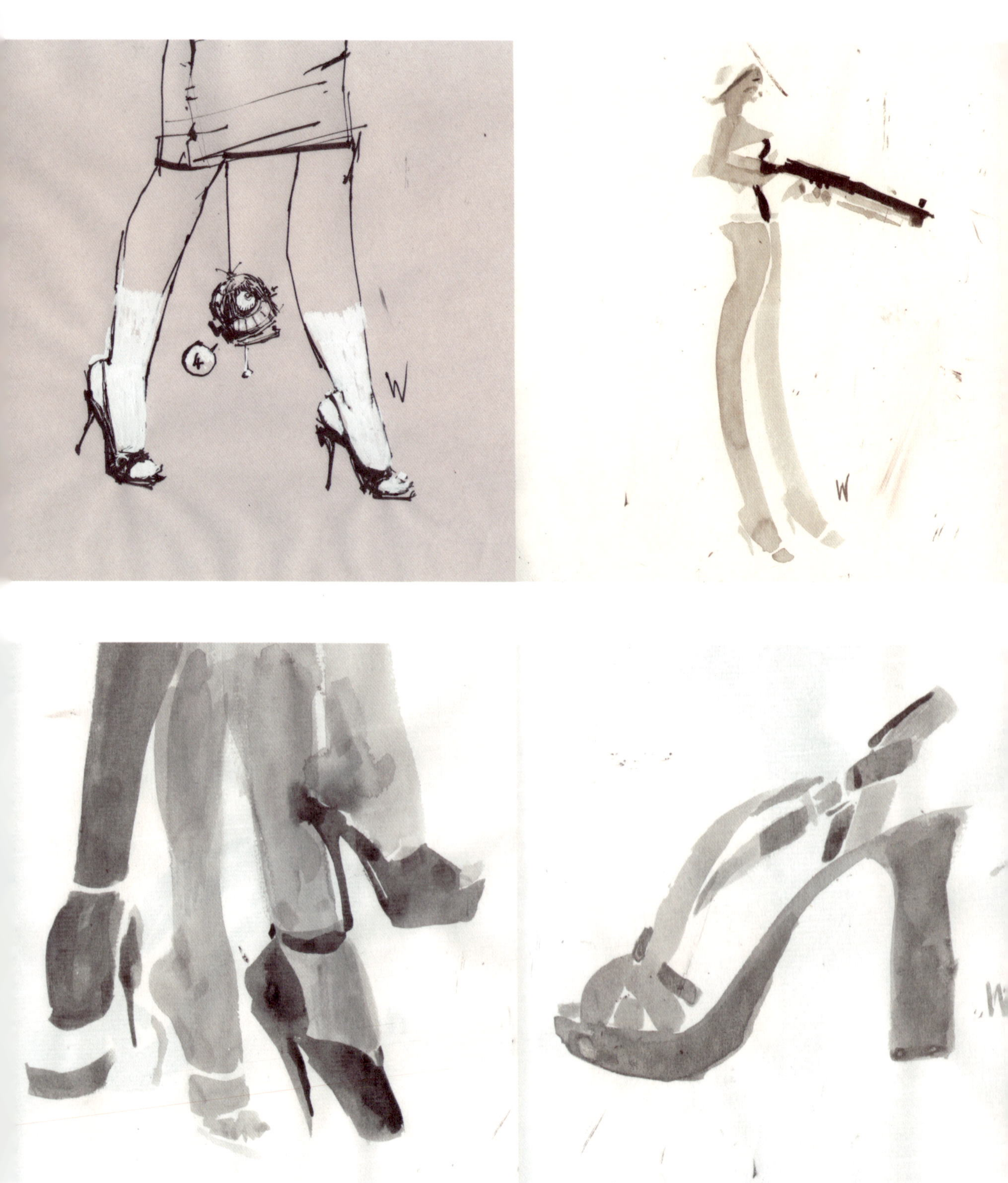

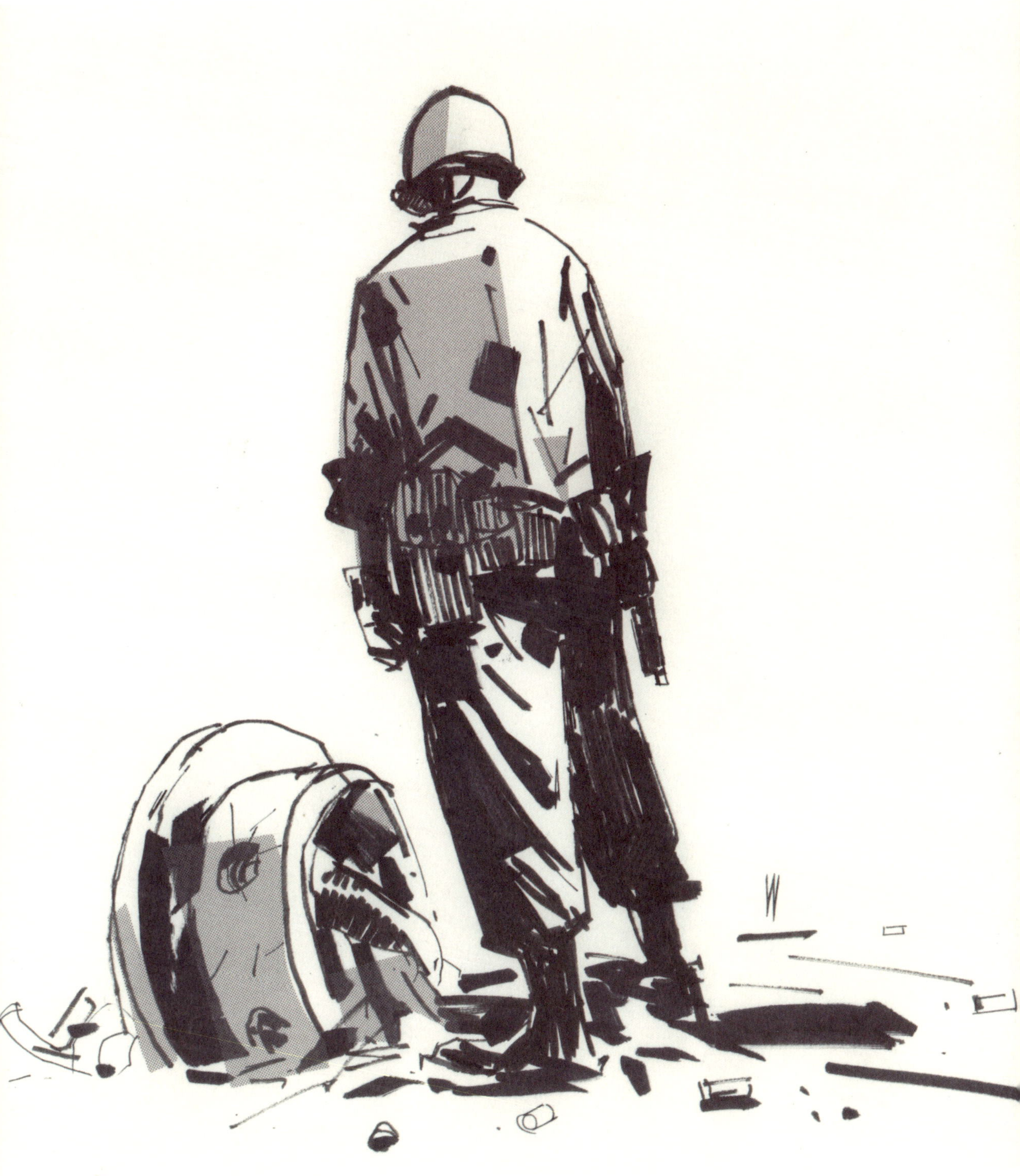

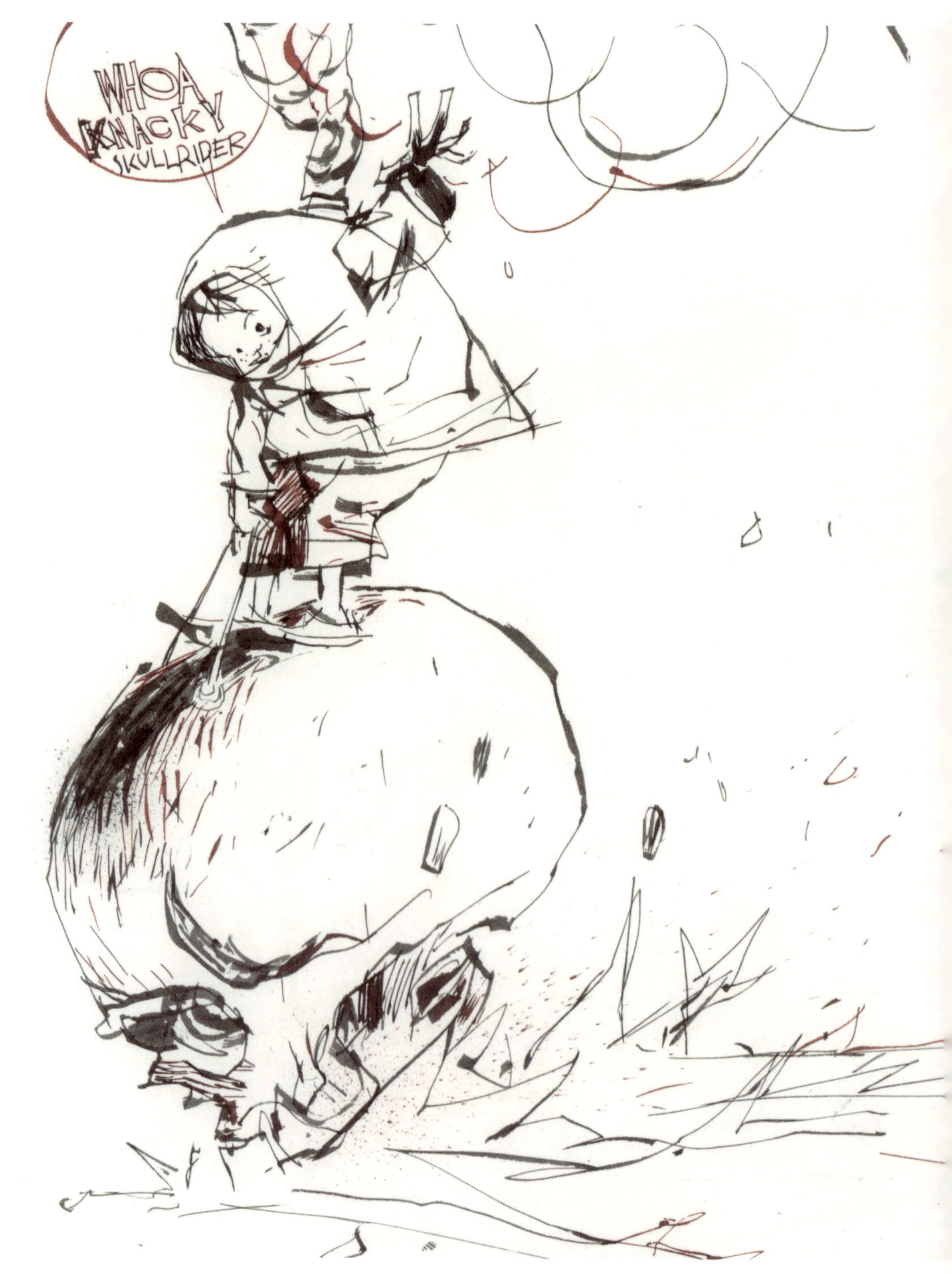

WHOA
KNACKY
SKULLRIDER

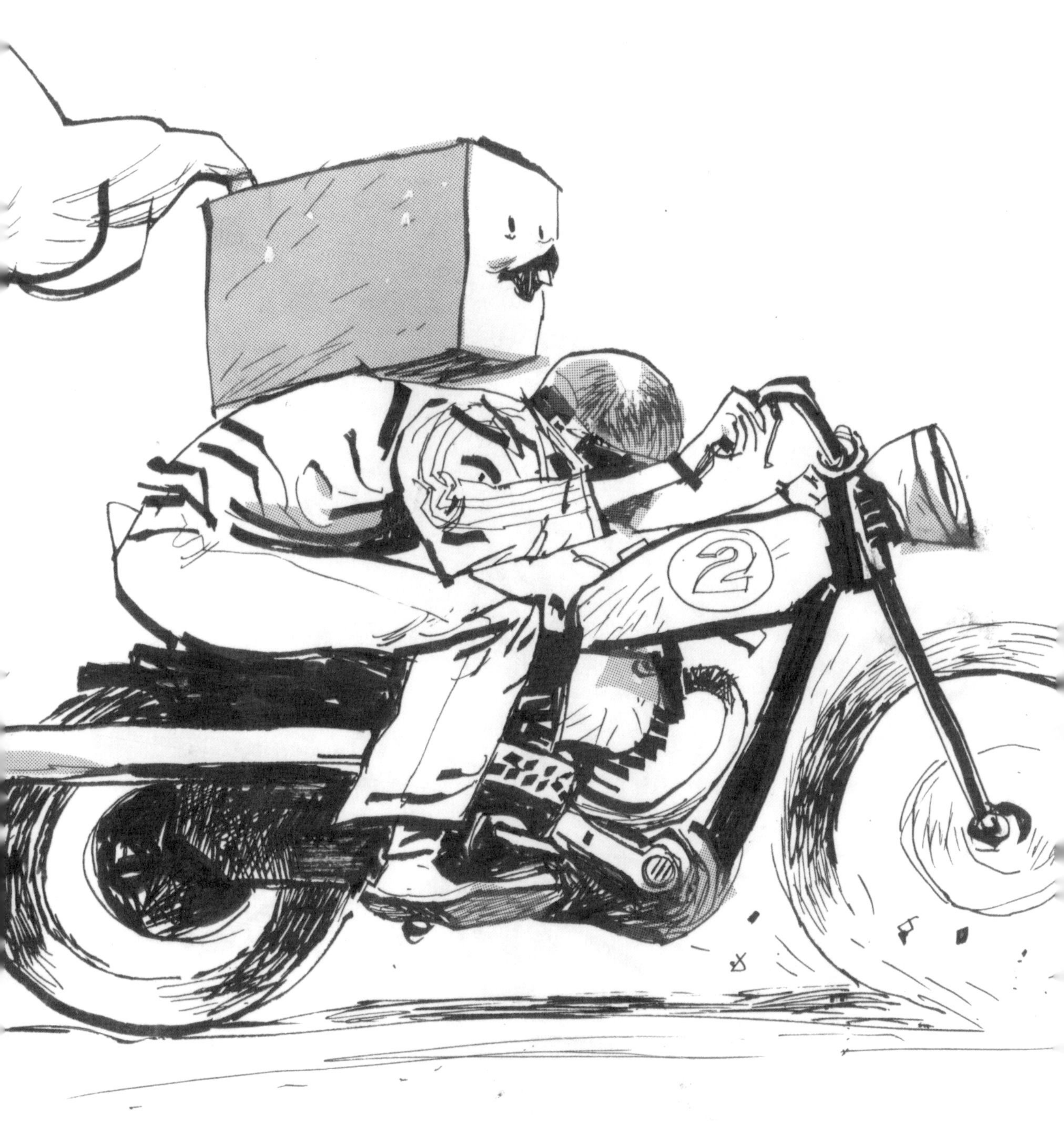

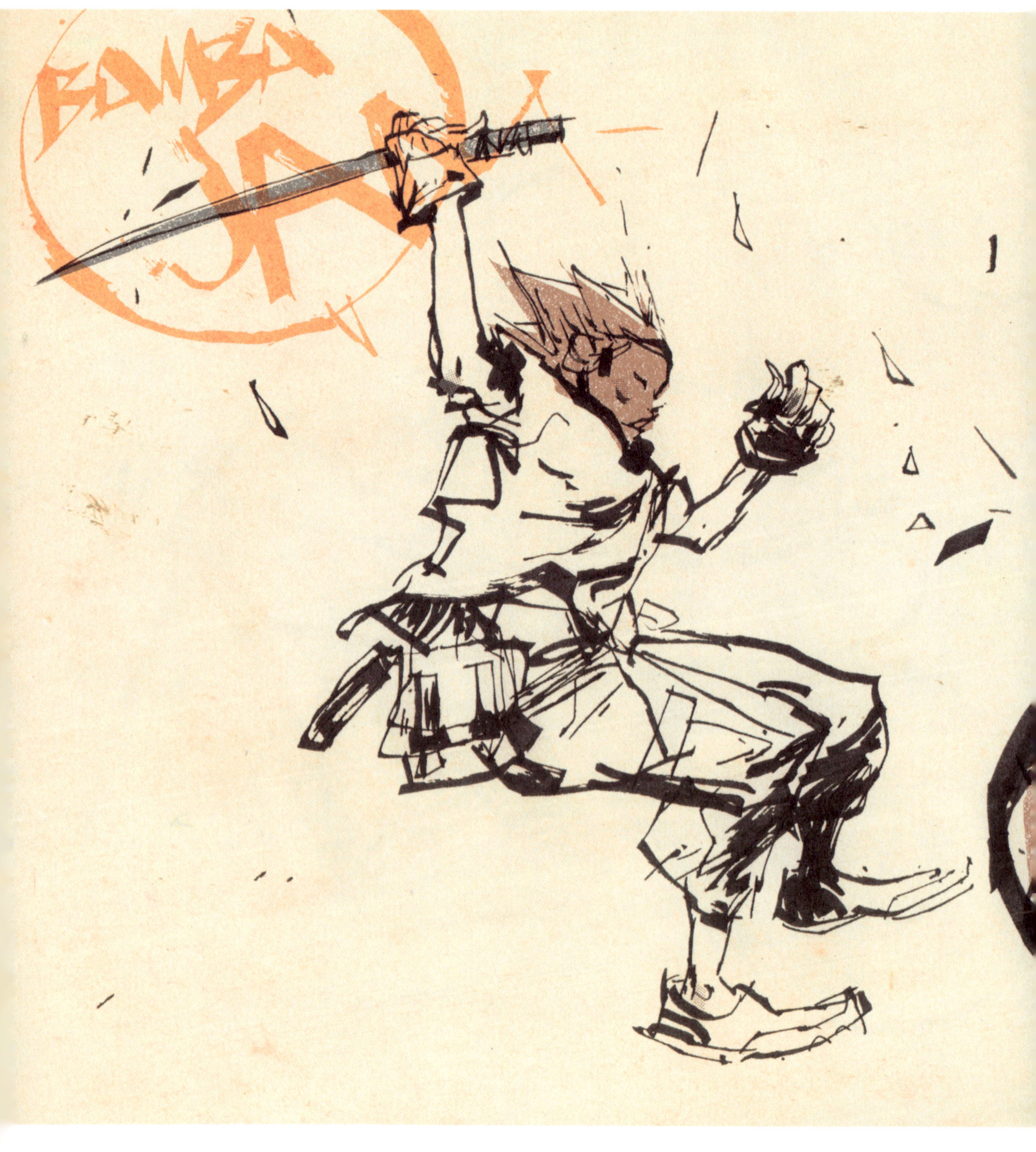
BOMBA
JACK

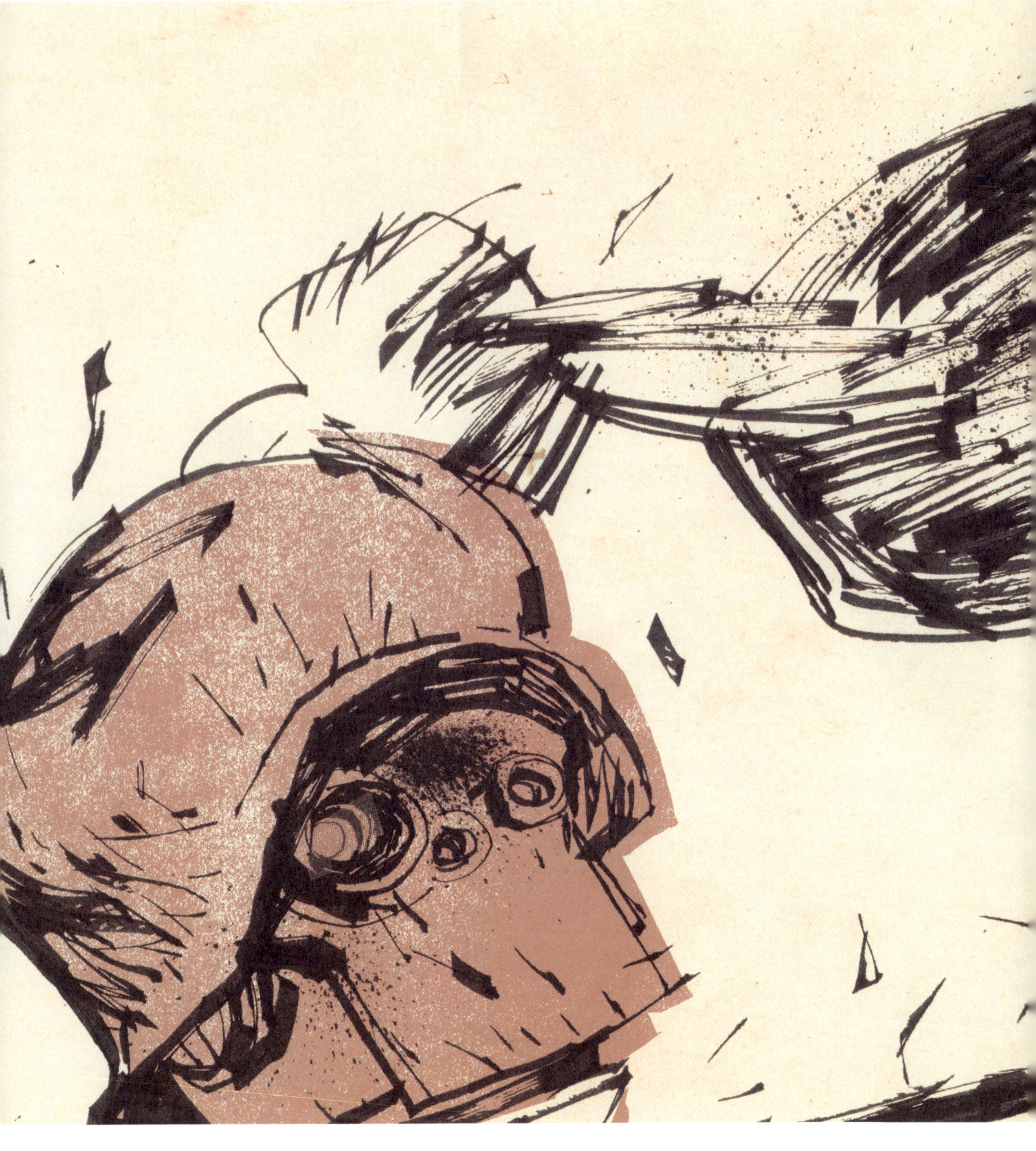

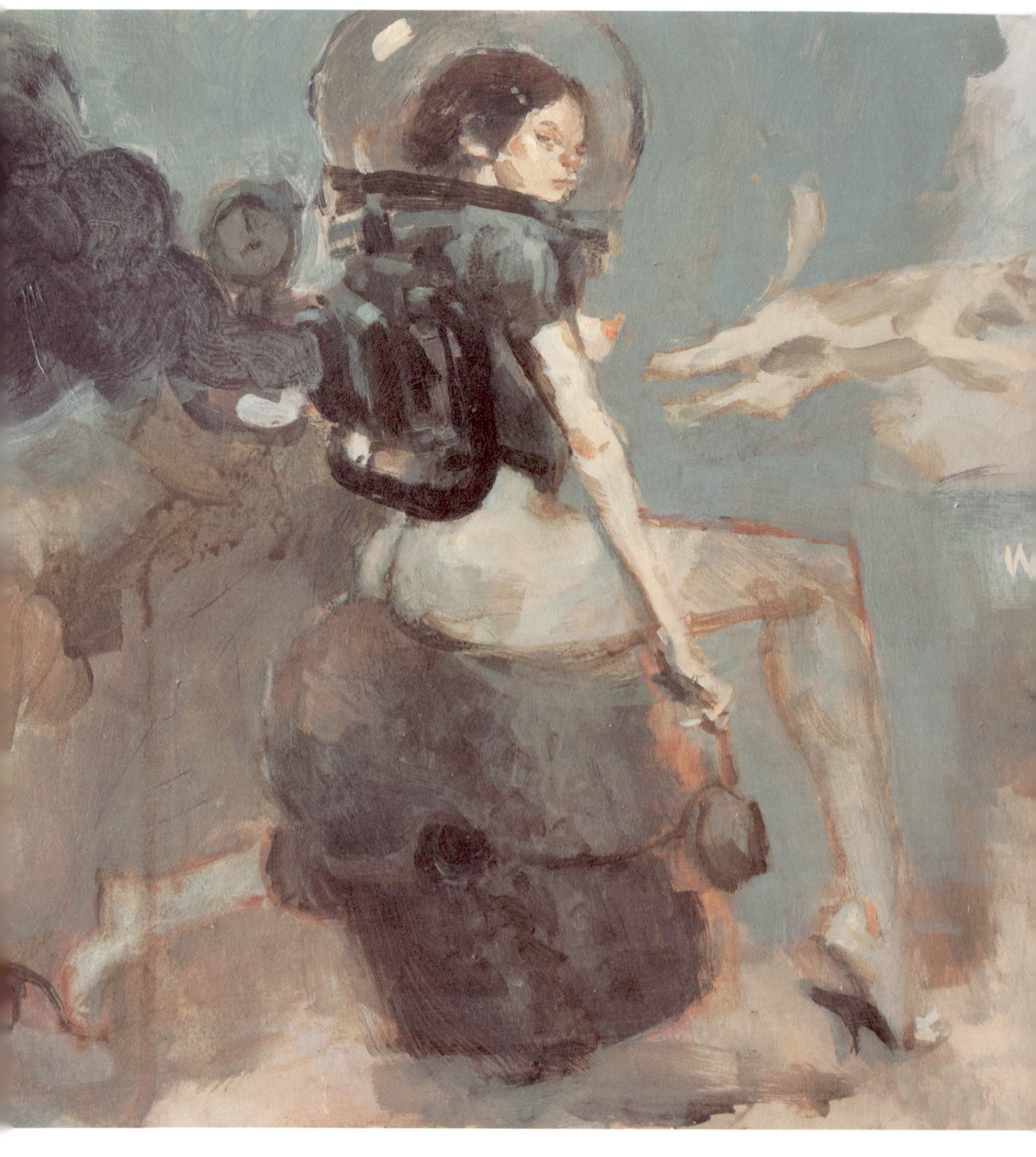

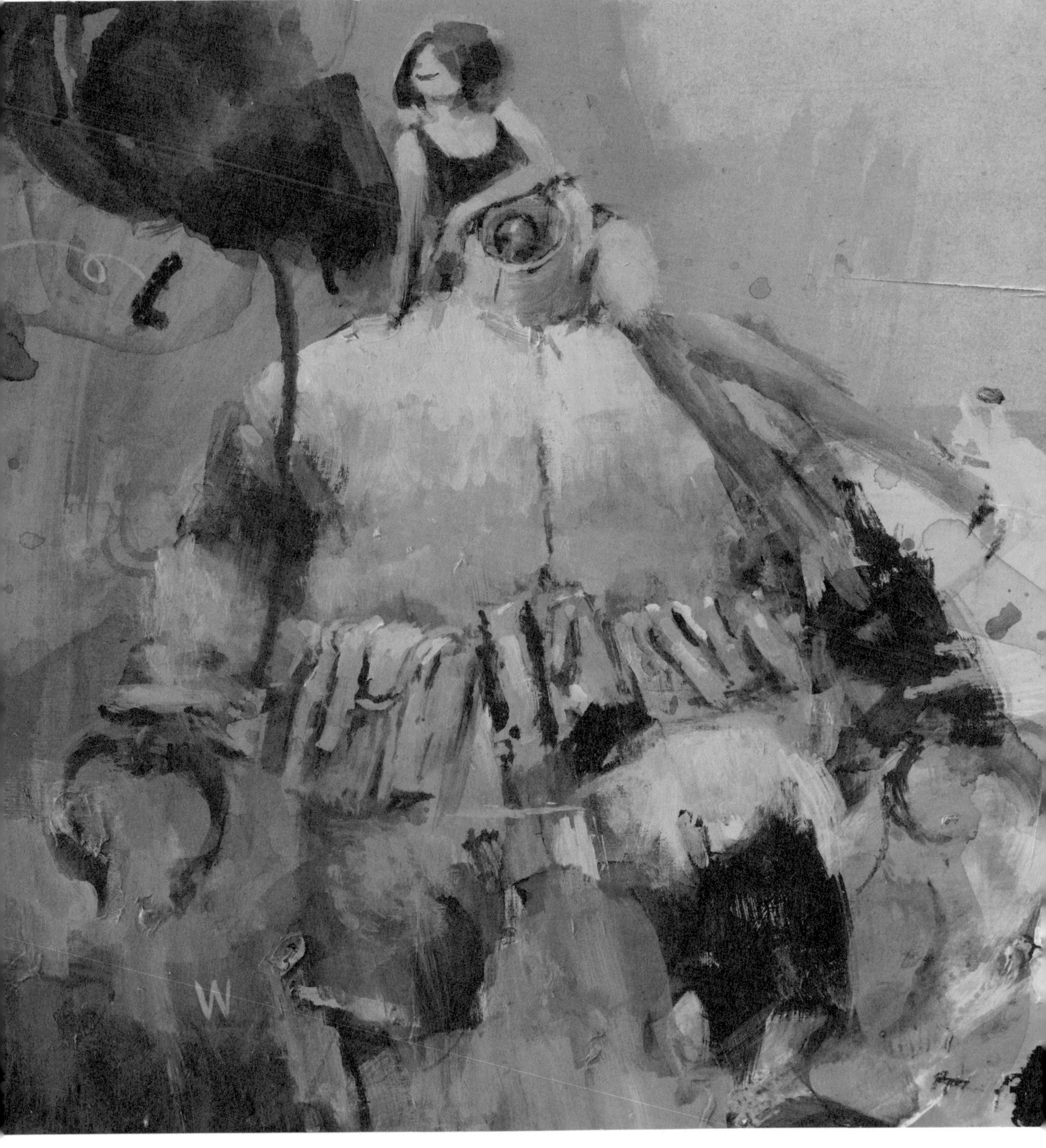

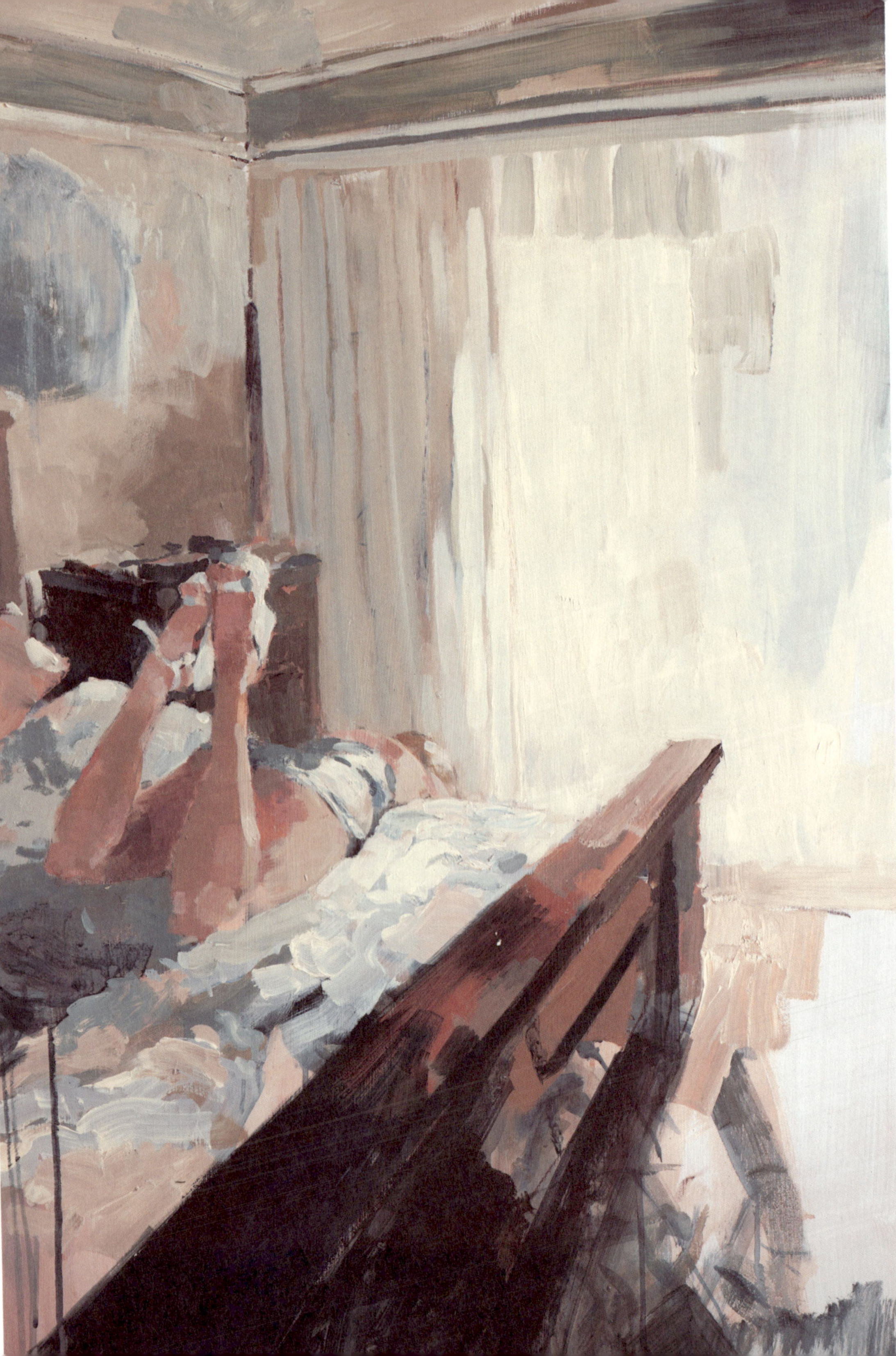

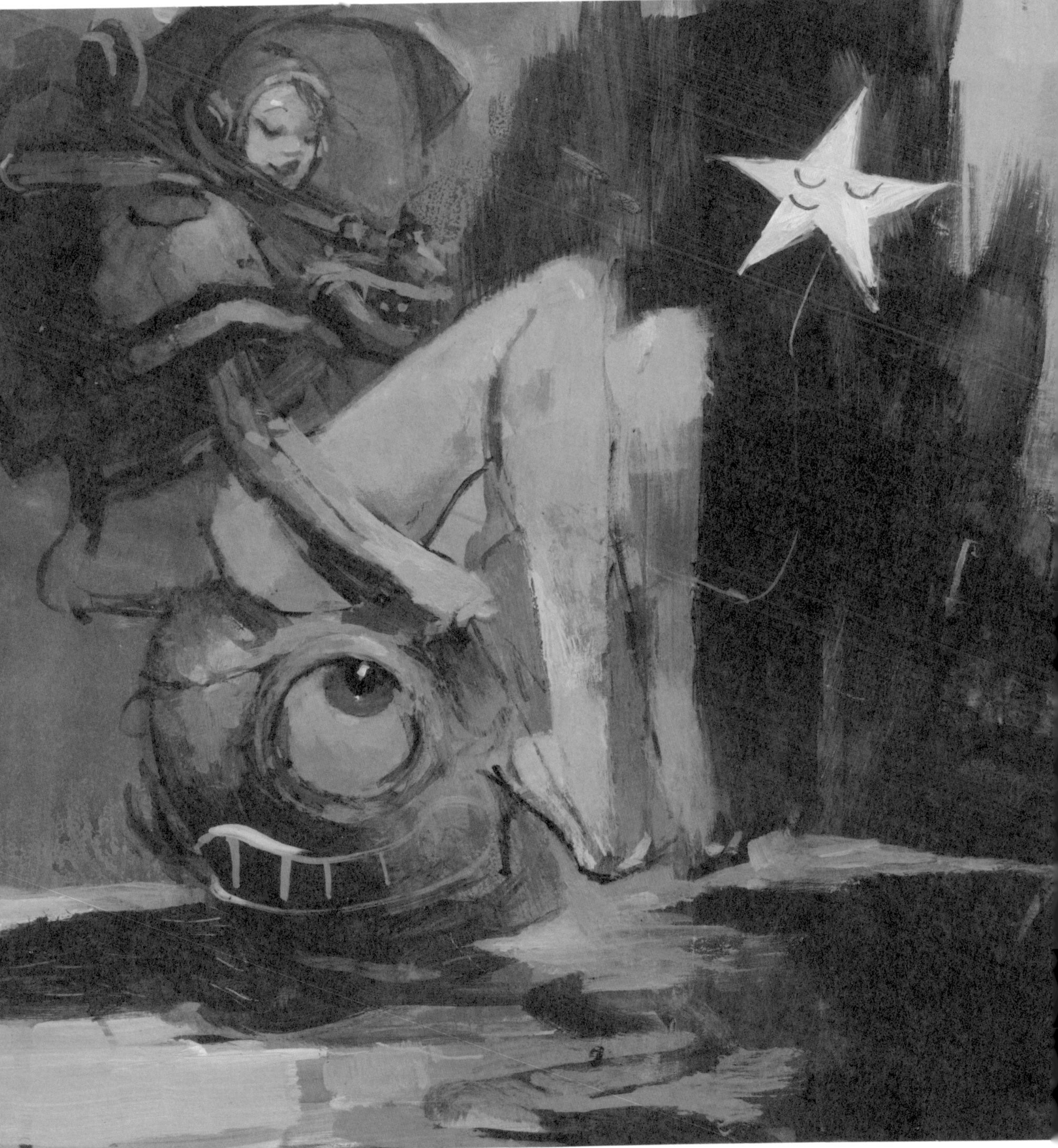

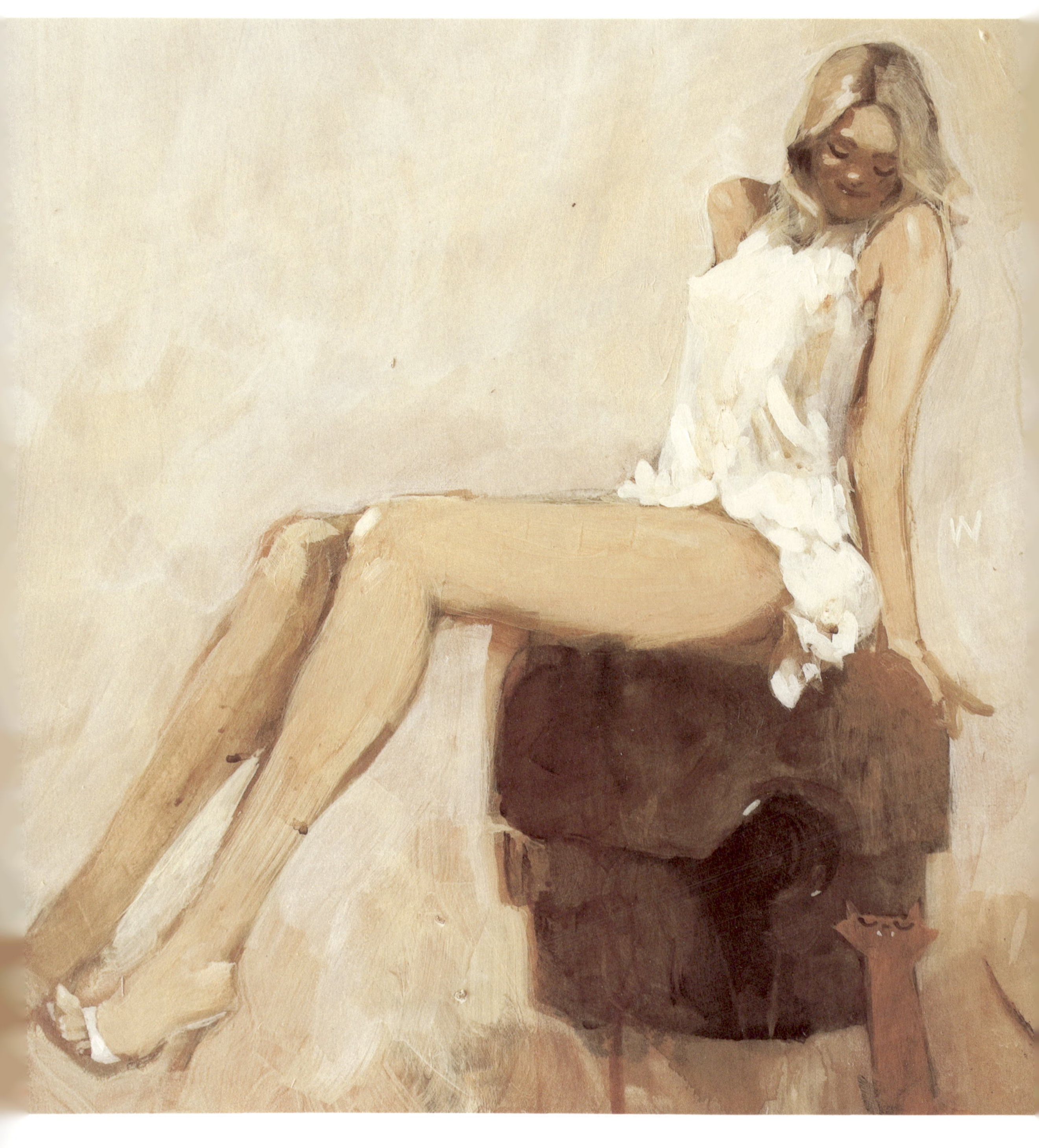

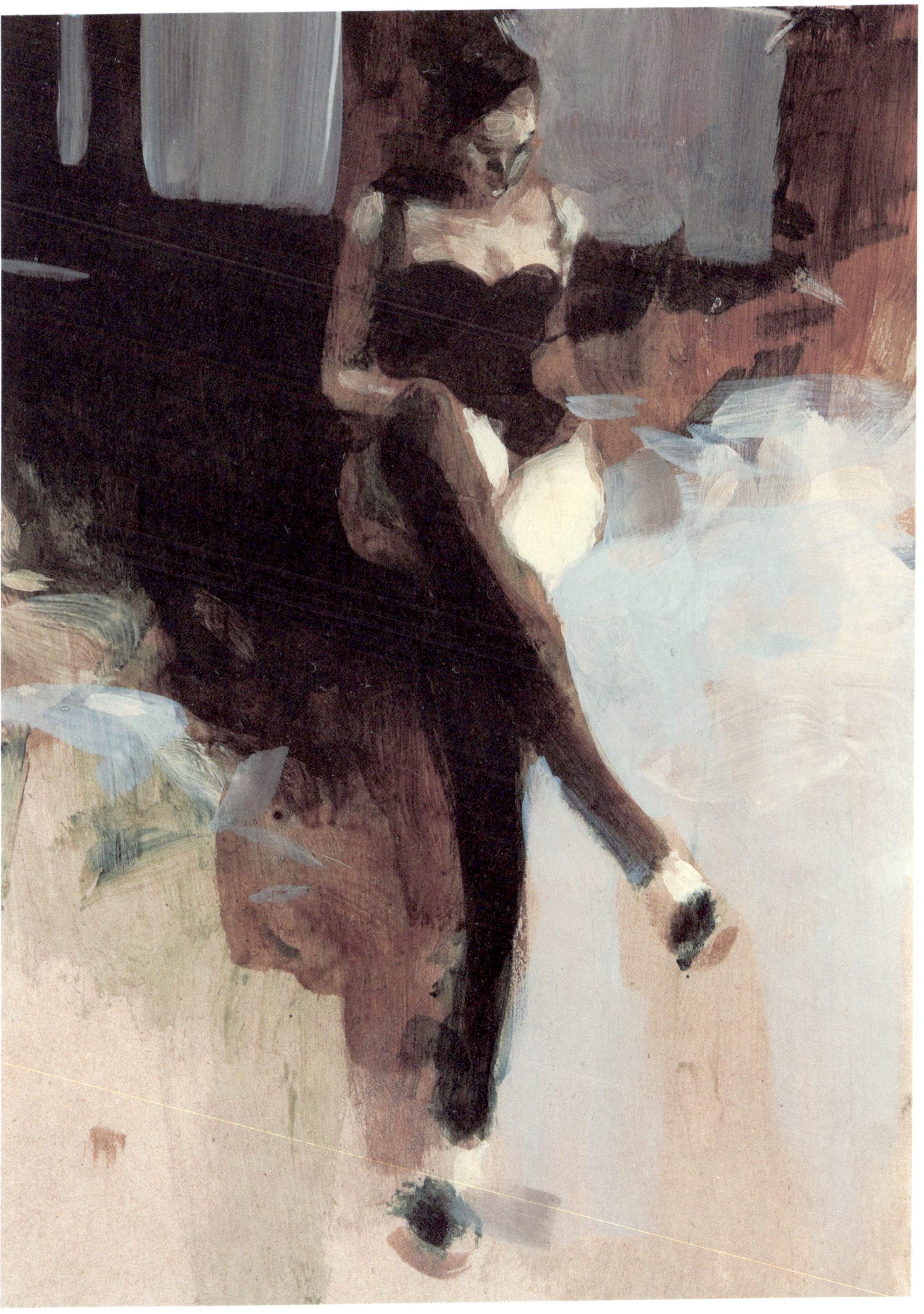

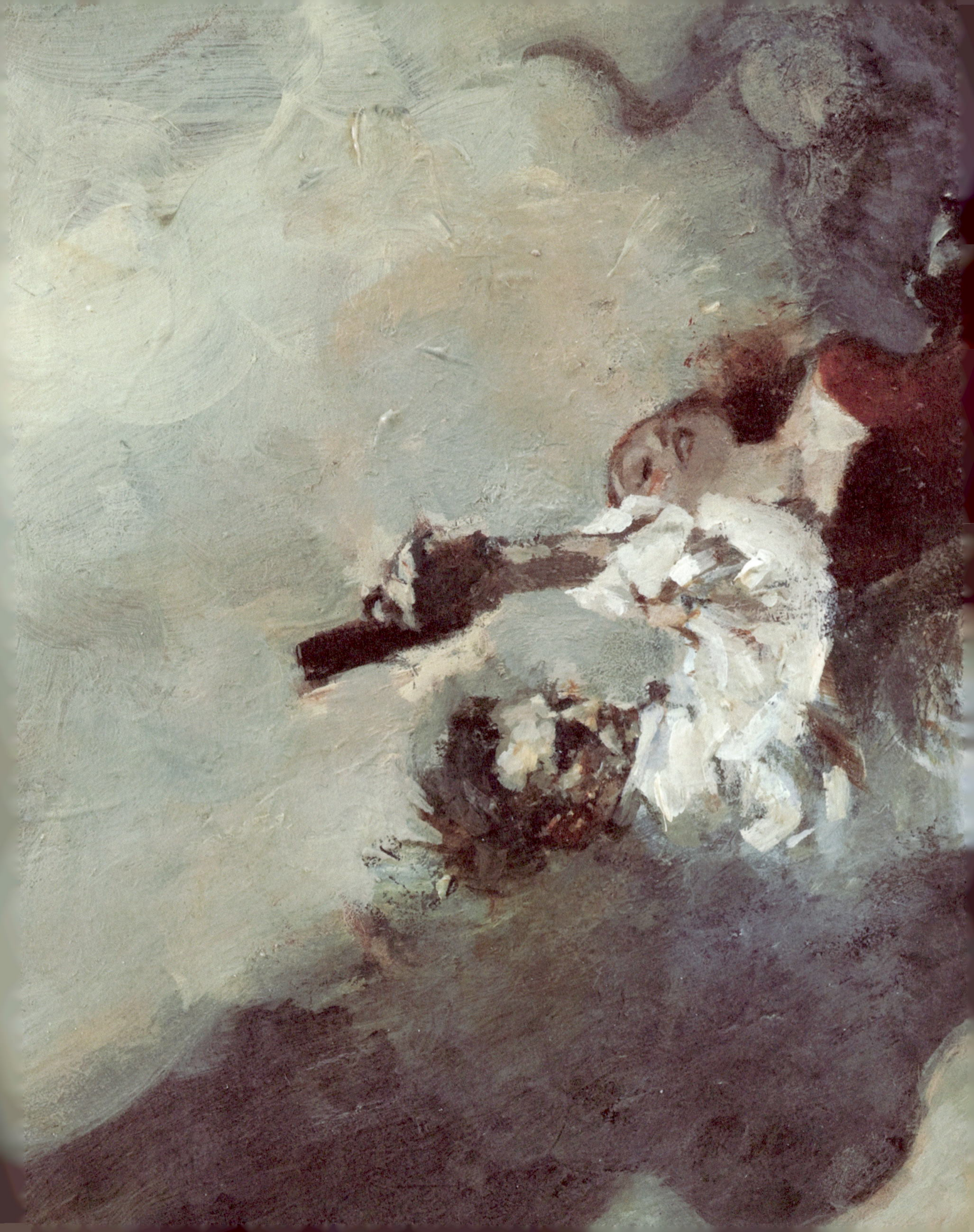

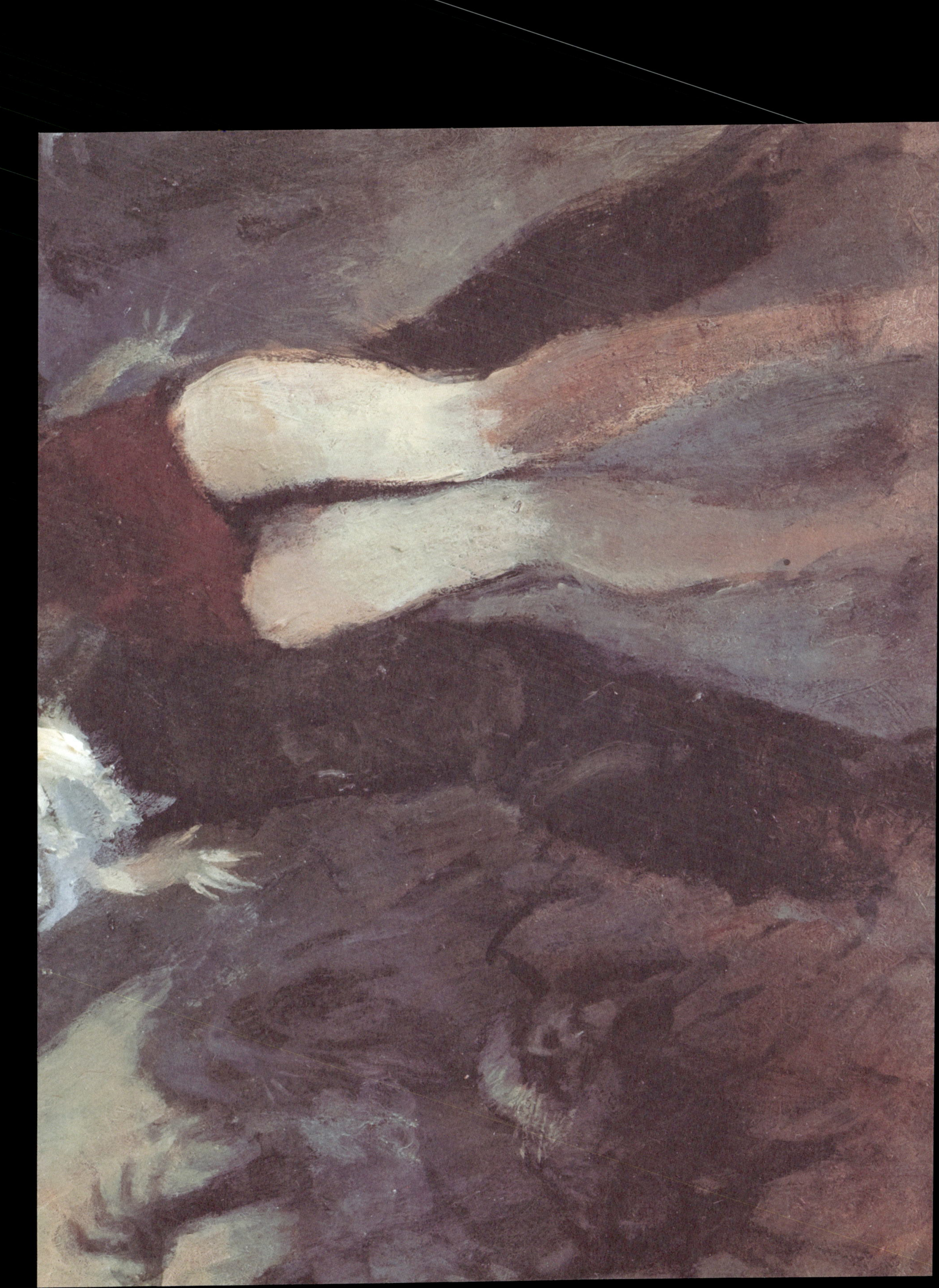

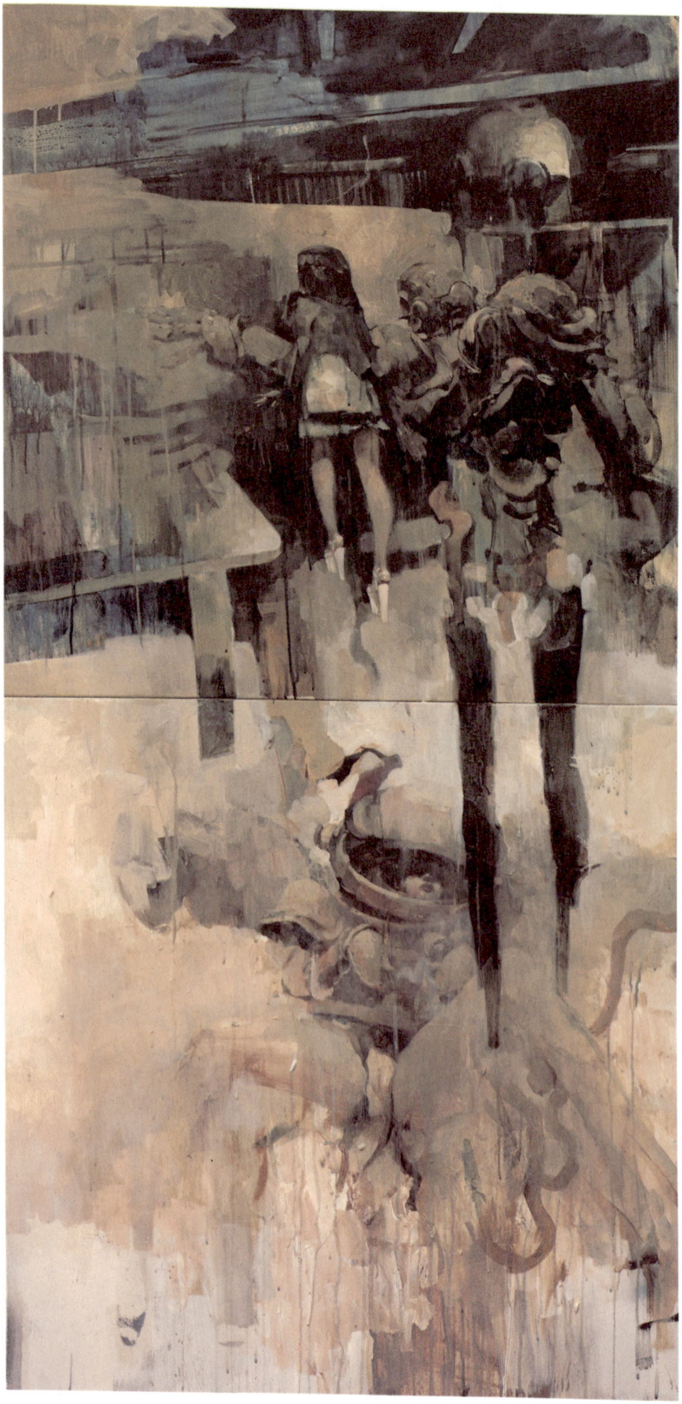

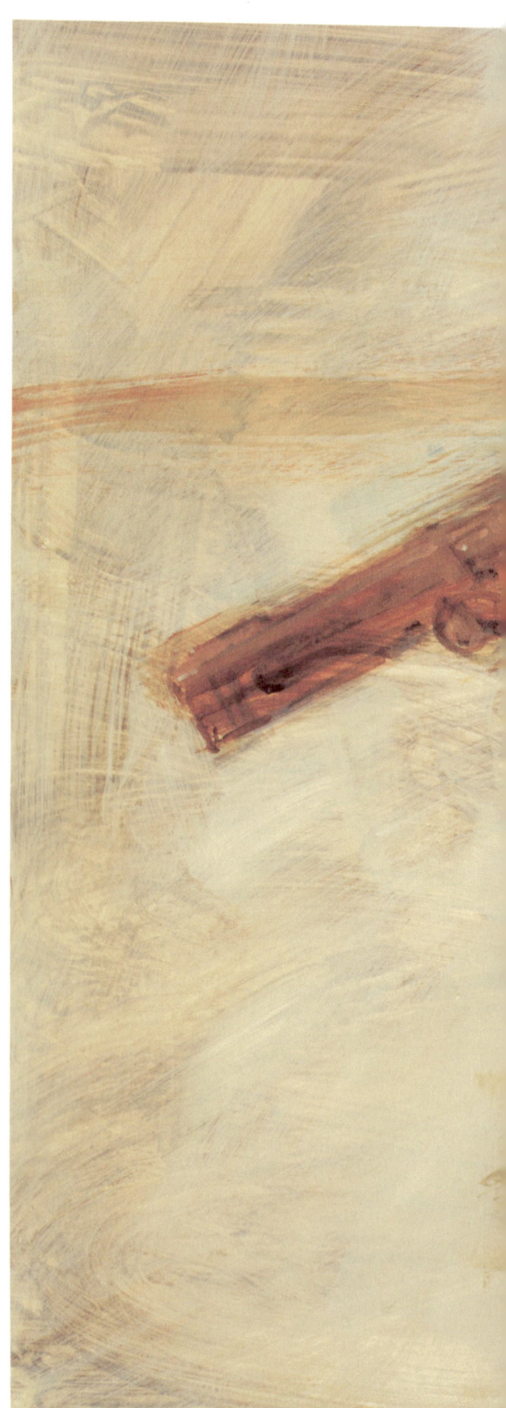

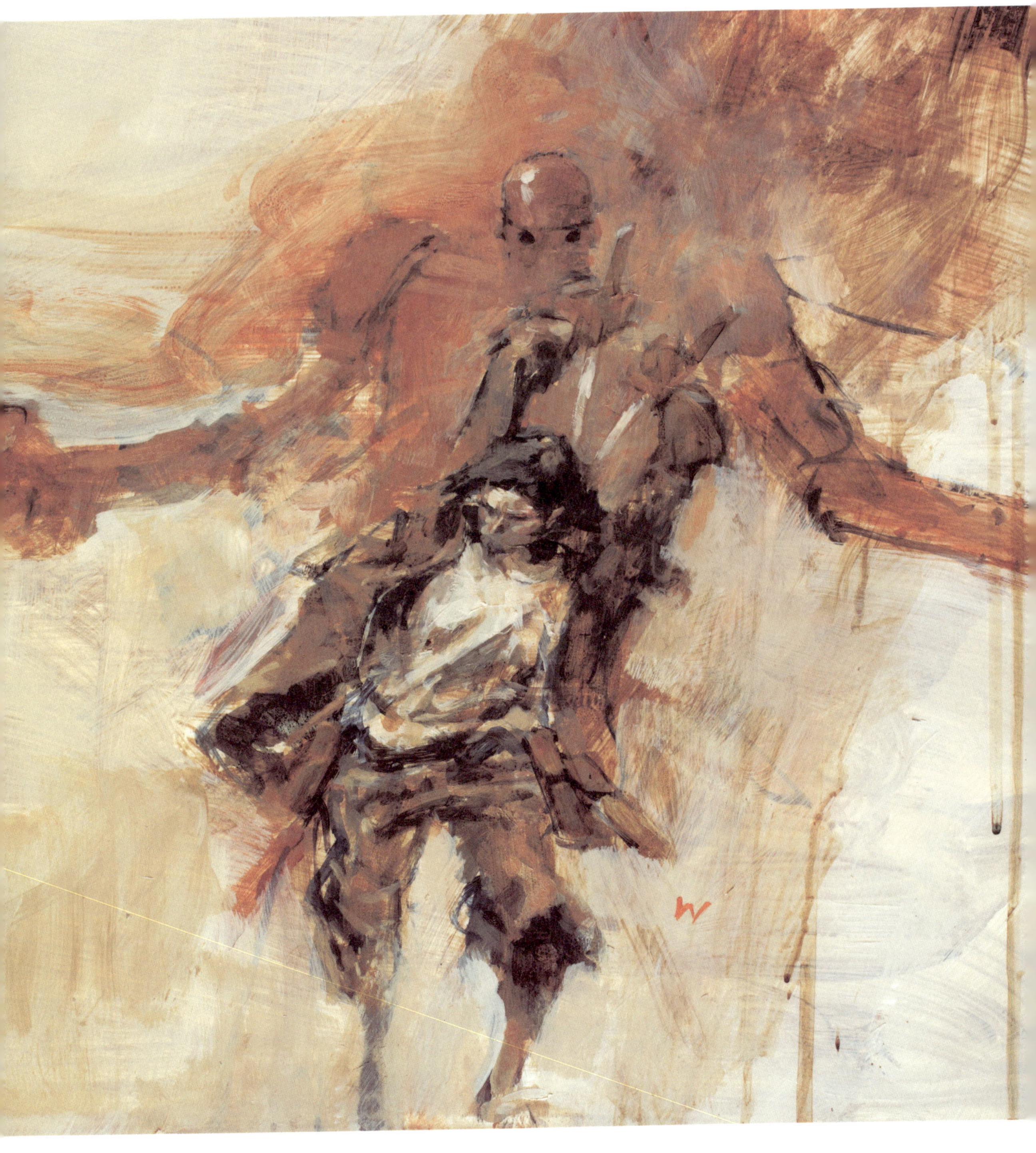

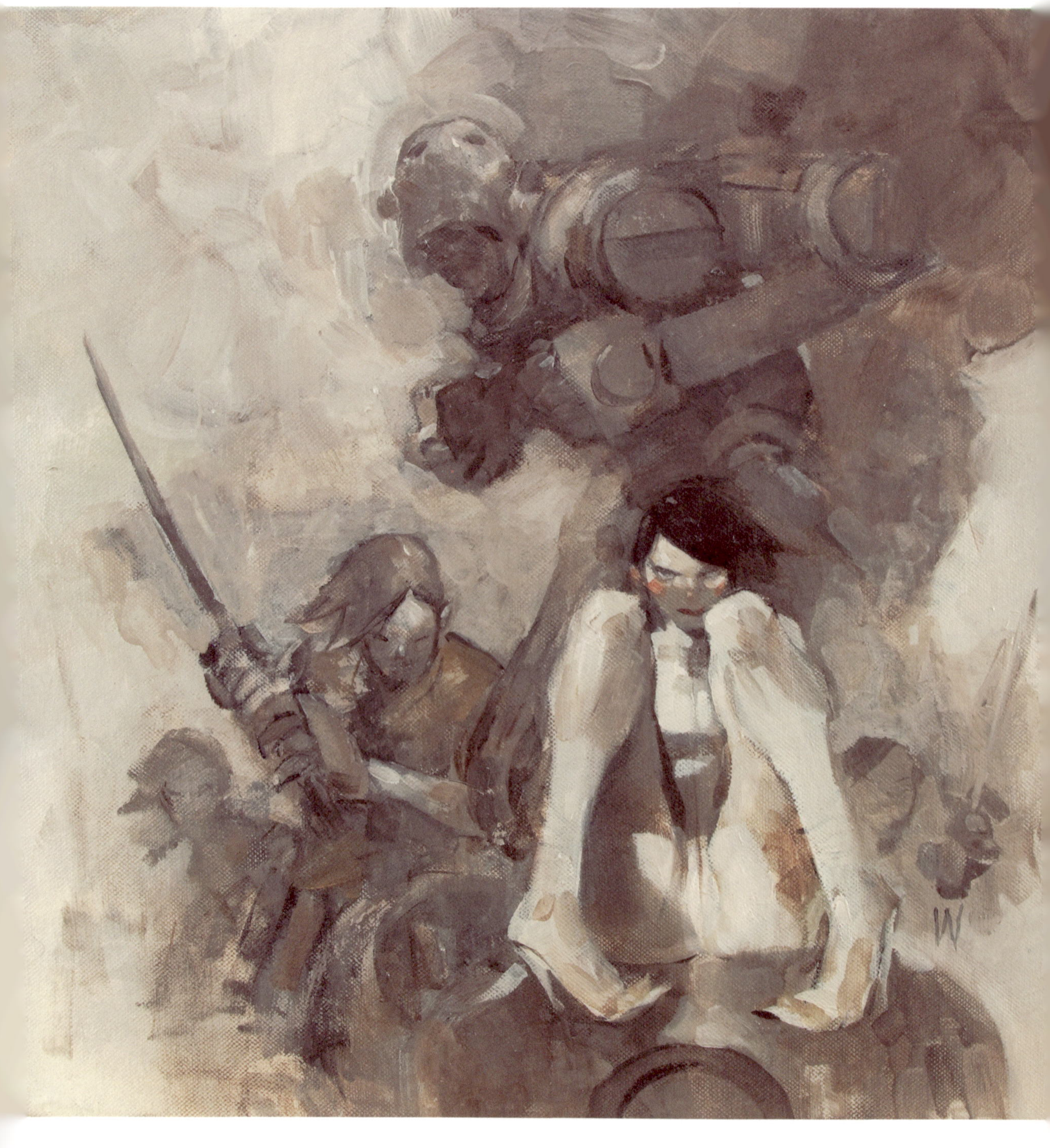

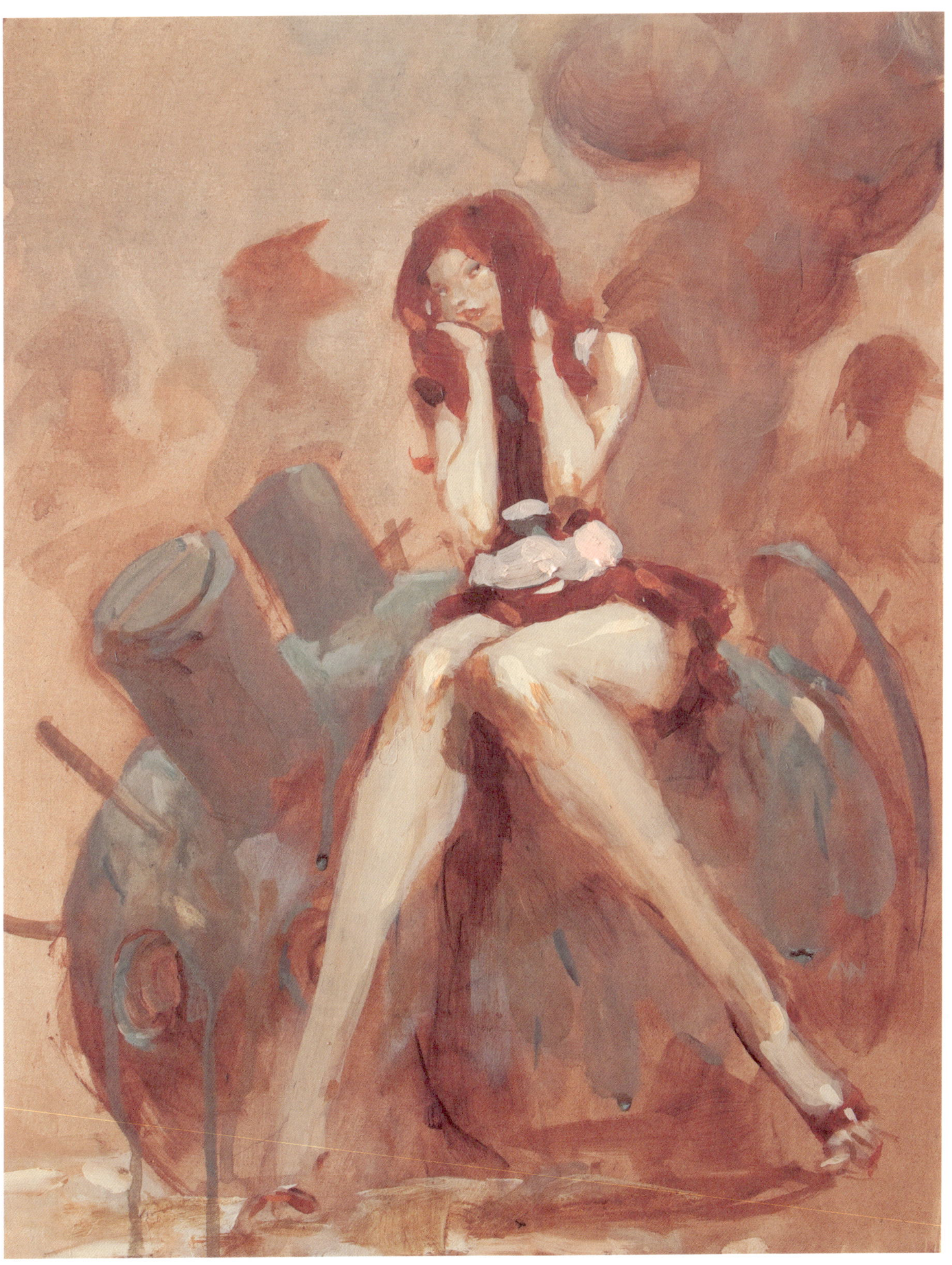

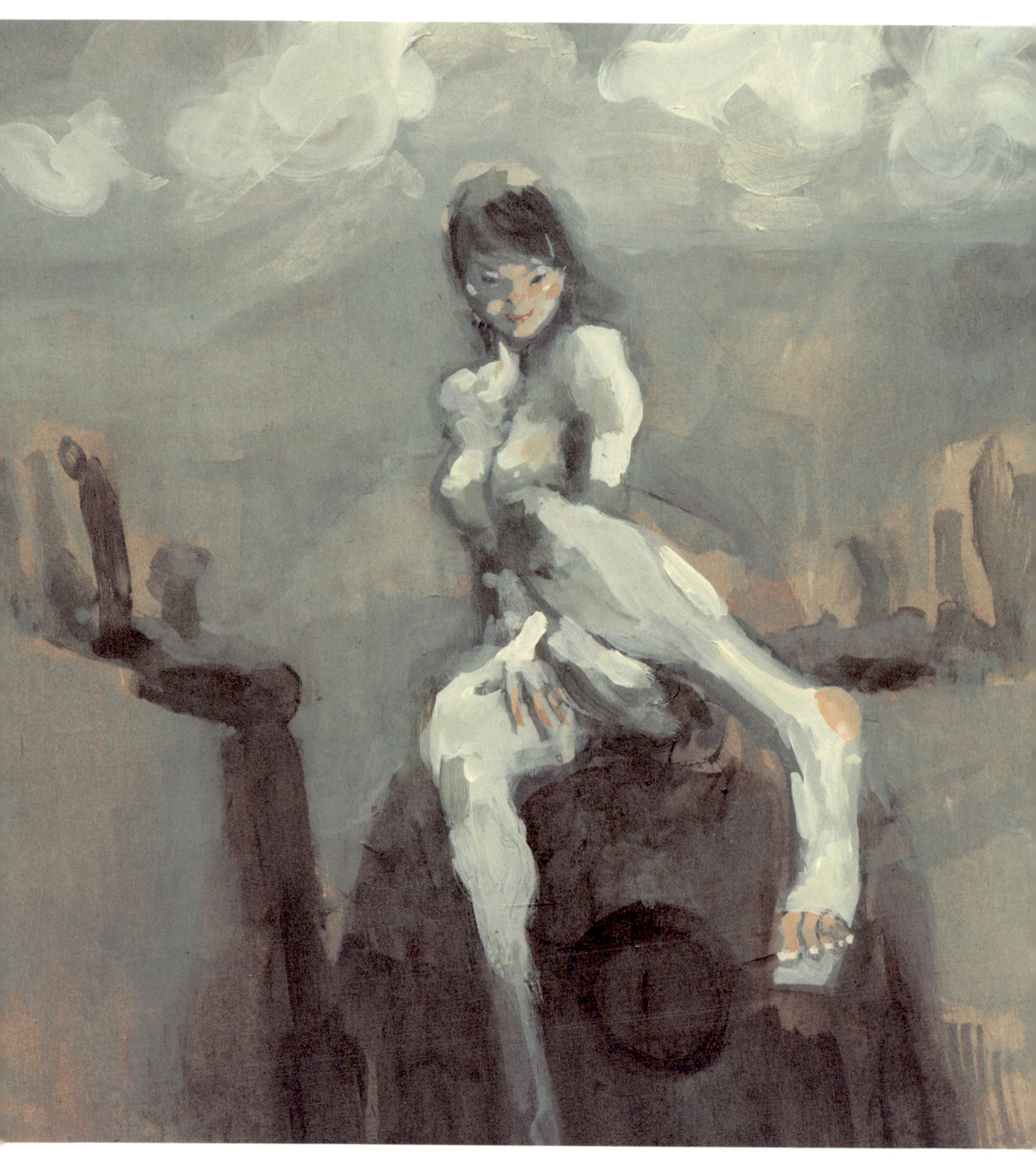

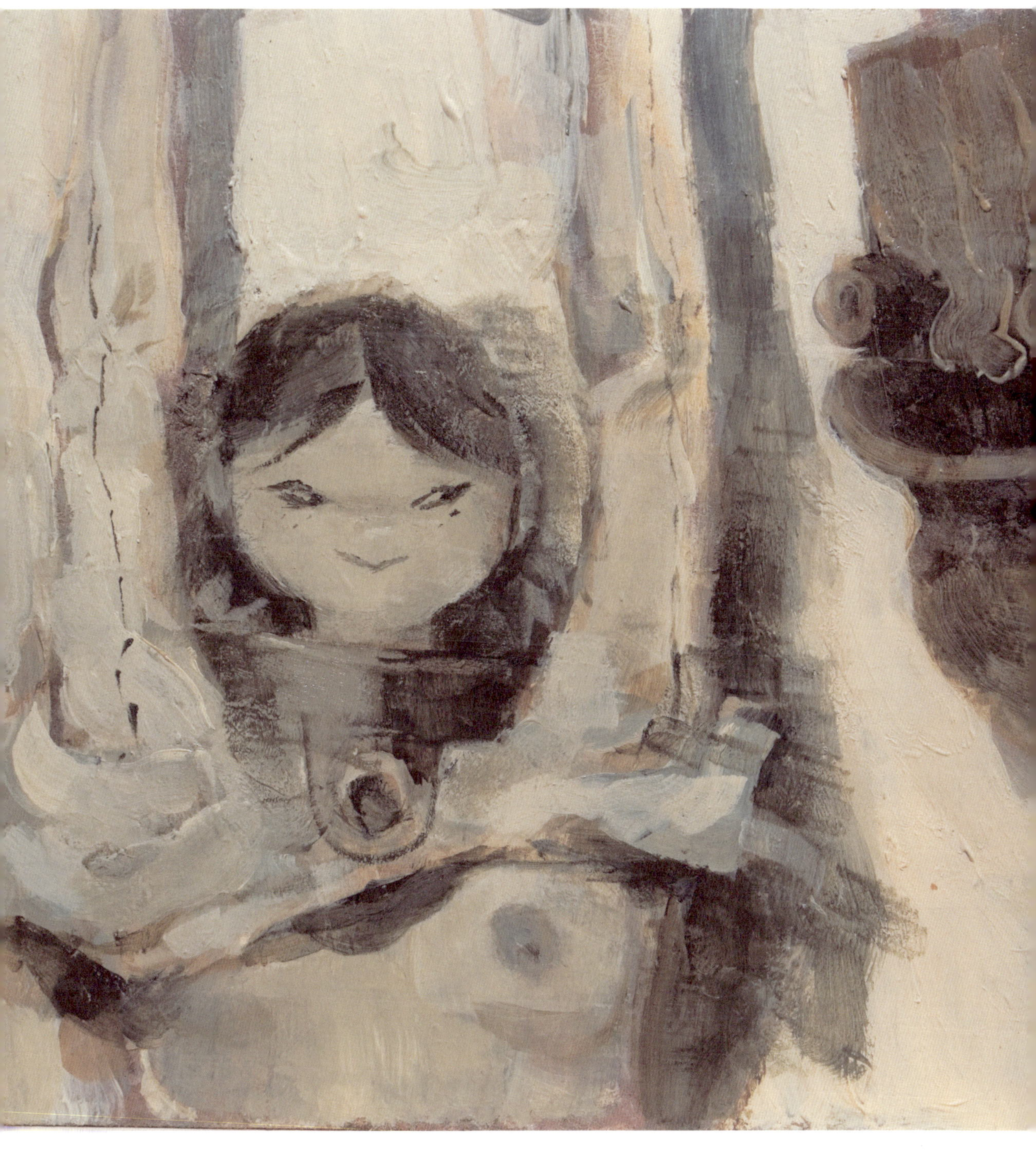

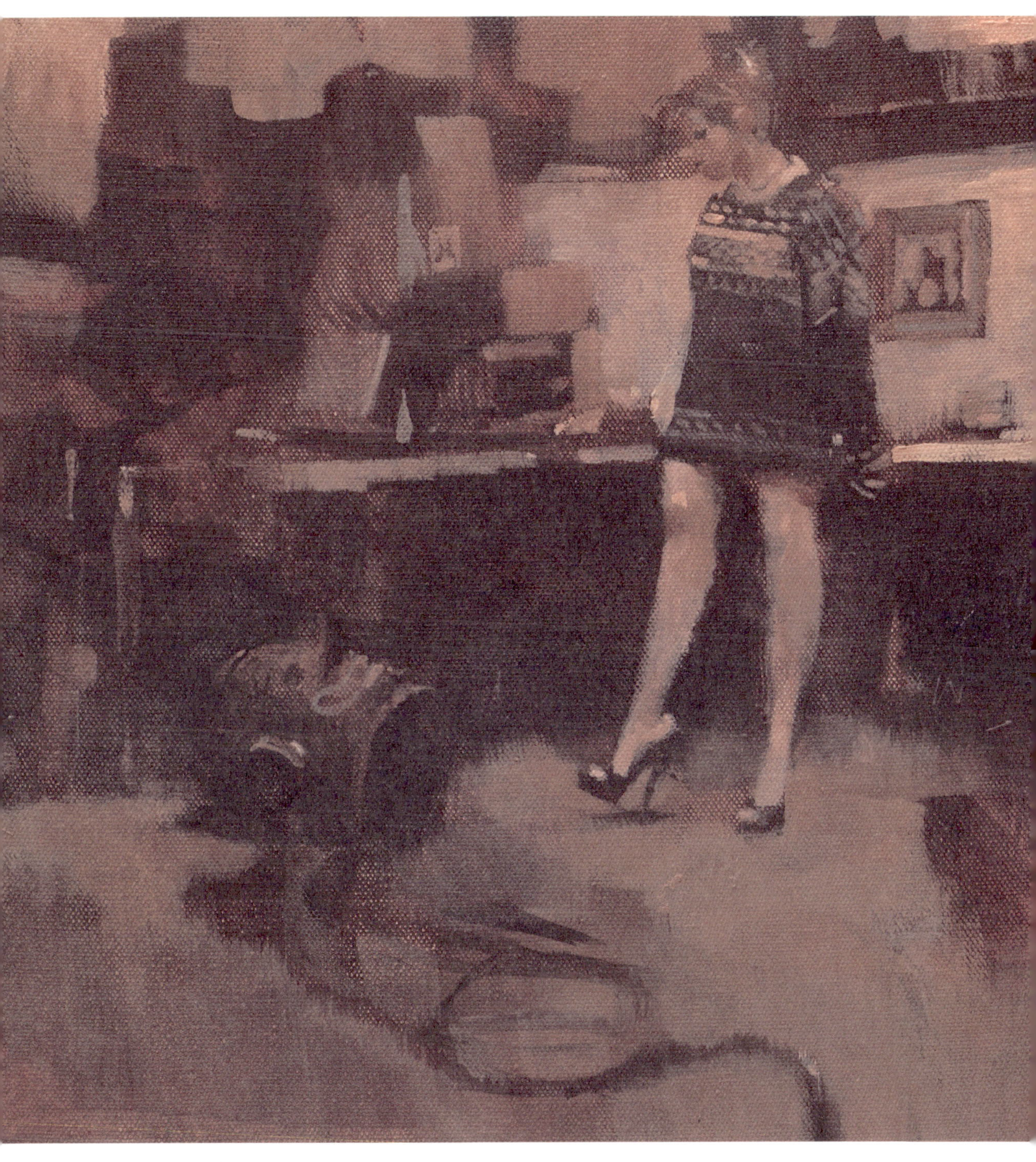

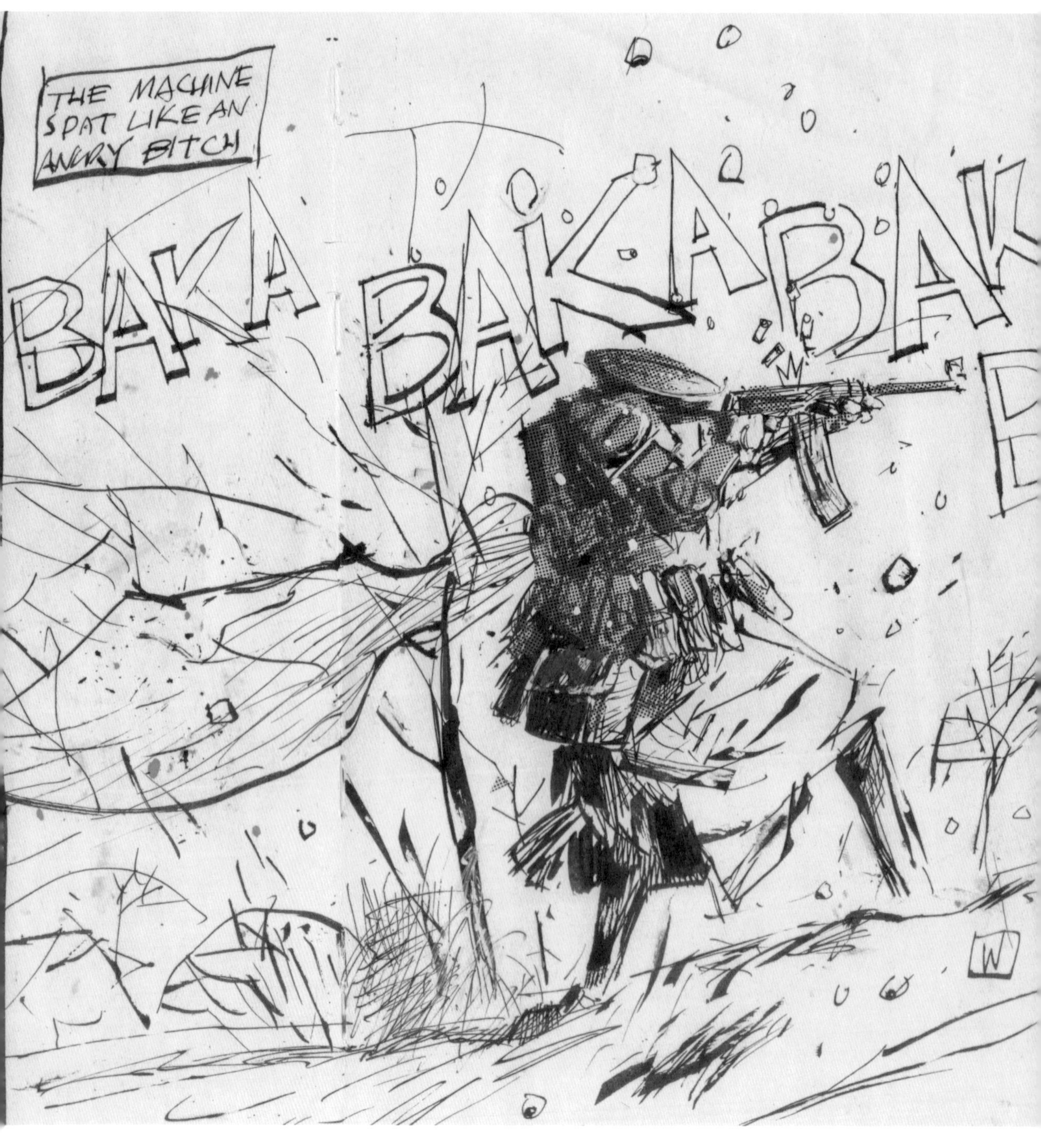

THE MACHINE SPAT LIKE AN ANGRY BITCH
BAKA BAKA BAKA BAK

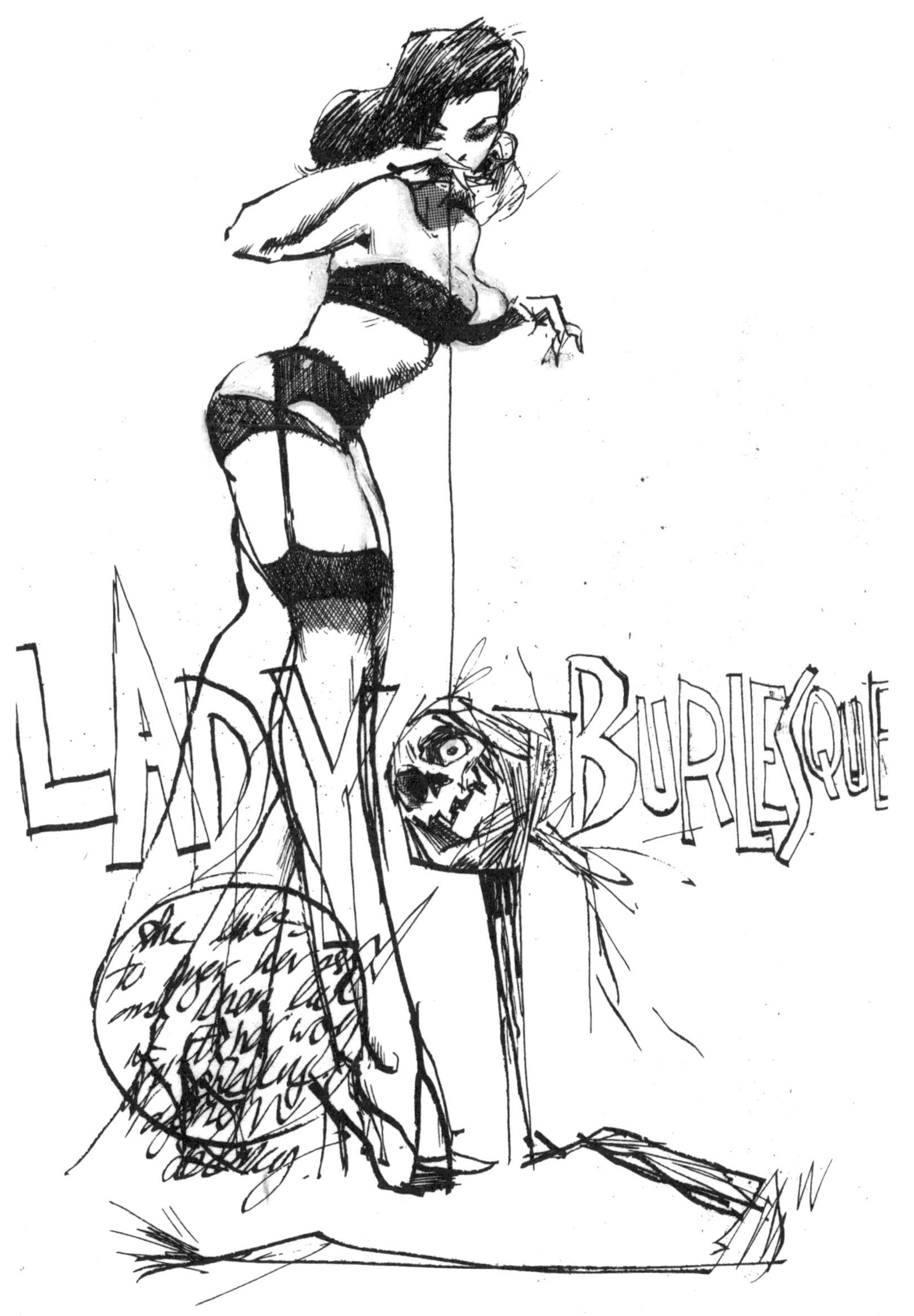

LADY BURLESQUE

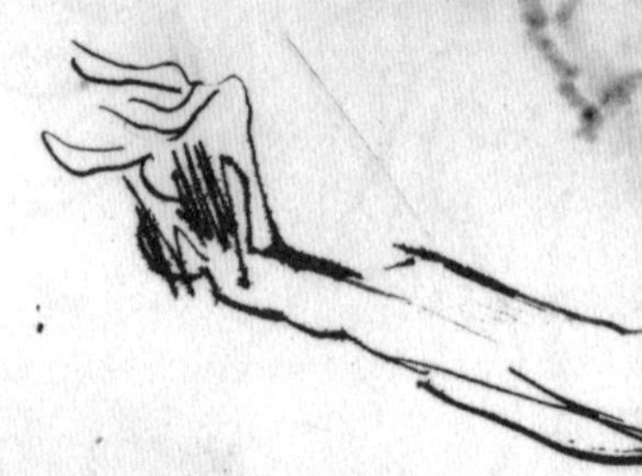

CAROL KNEW

REGARDLESS OF FAUX SECESSIONIST IM
IT WAS STILL A ...

ROBOT
FUCK
PARTY!

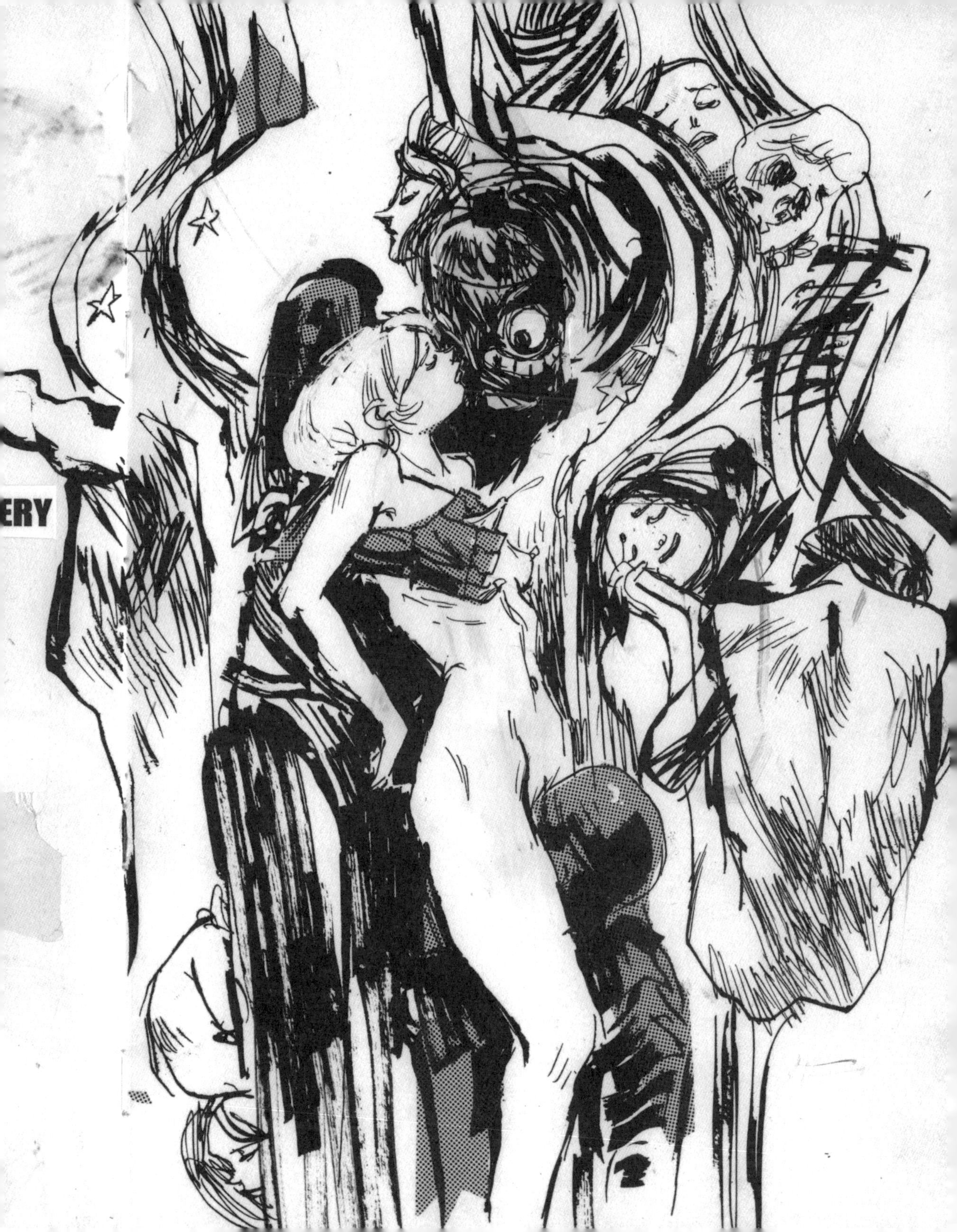
ERY

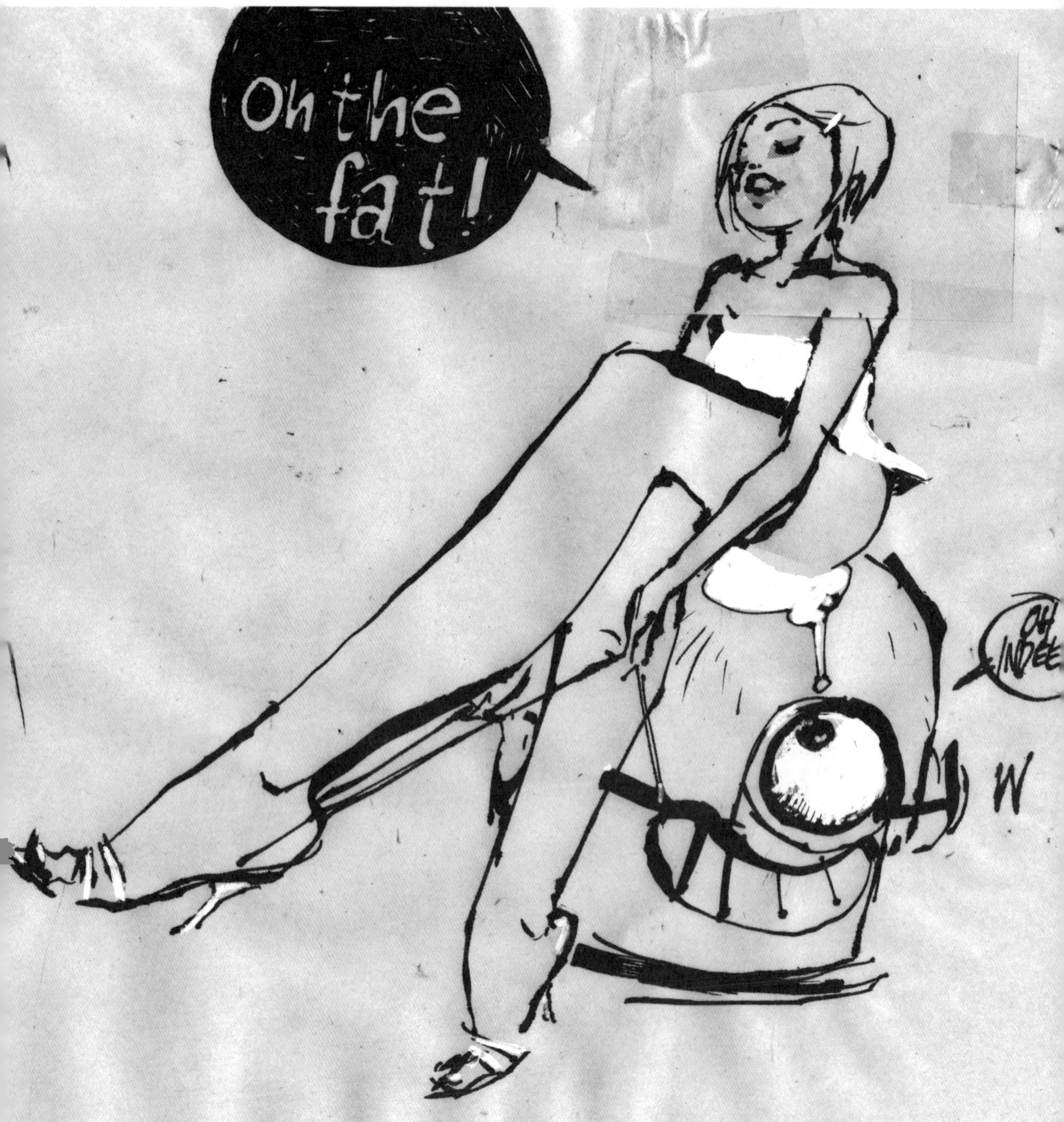

oh the
fat!
oh
indeed

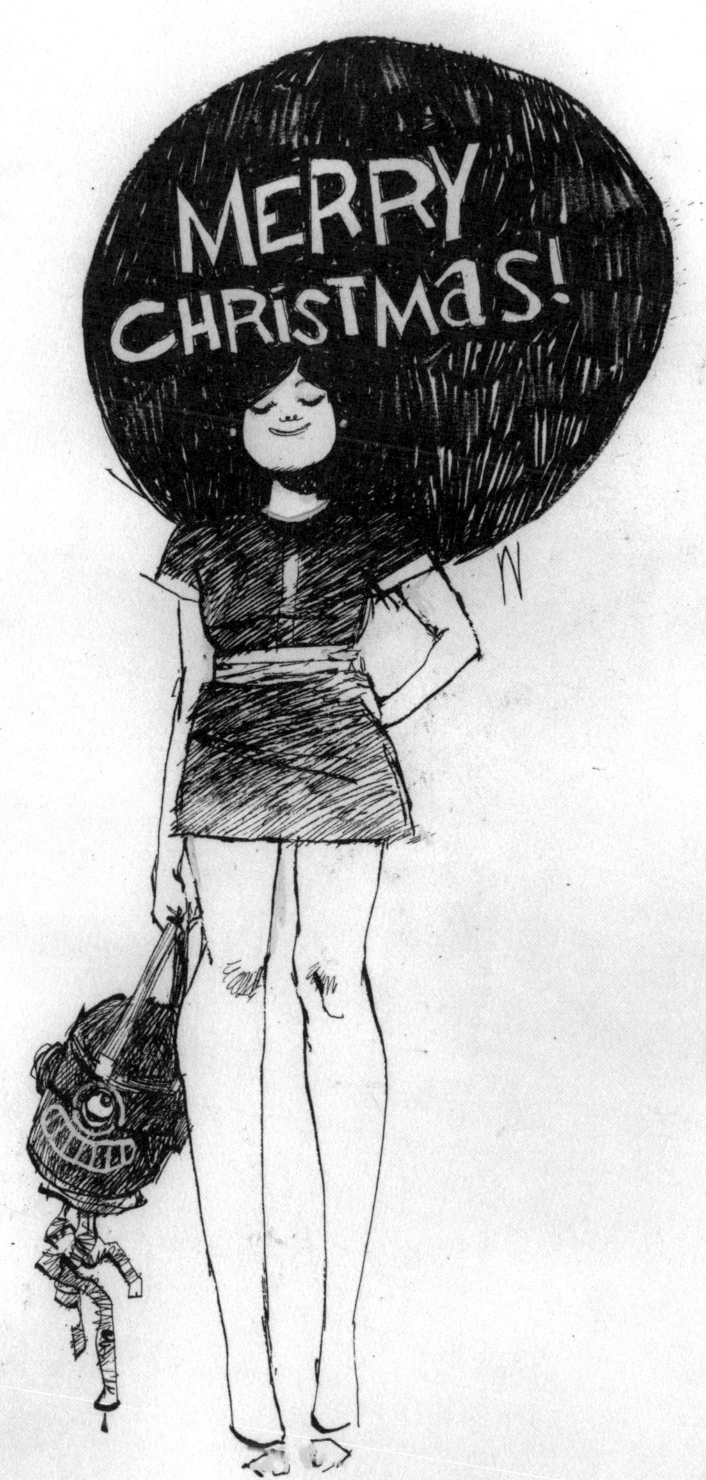

MERRY
CHRISTMAS!

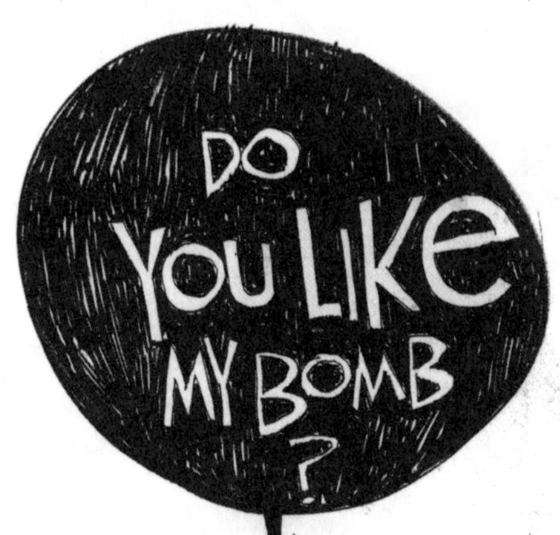

DO YOU LIKE MY BOMB?

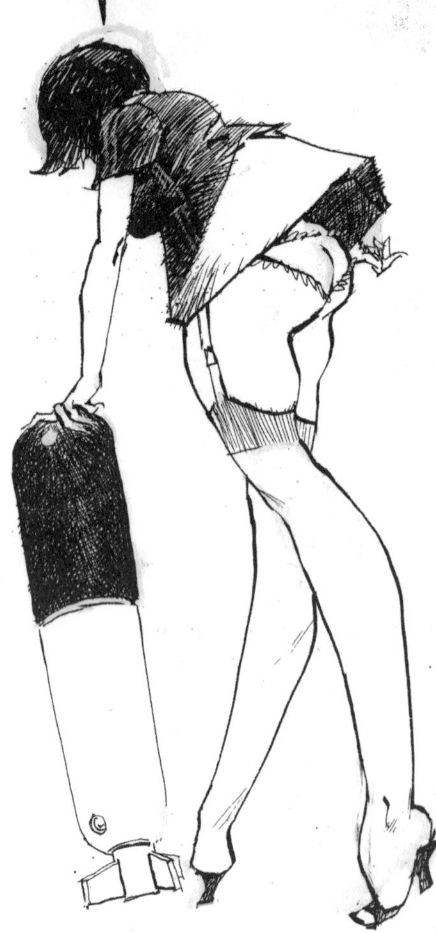

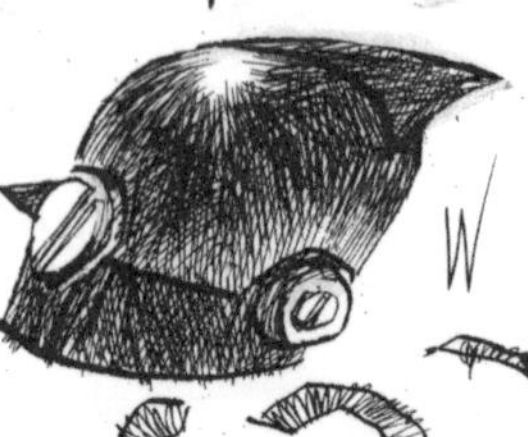

NO! BUT I LIKE YOUR.
*DEAR VIEWER YOU DECIDE...

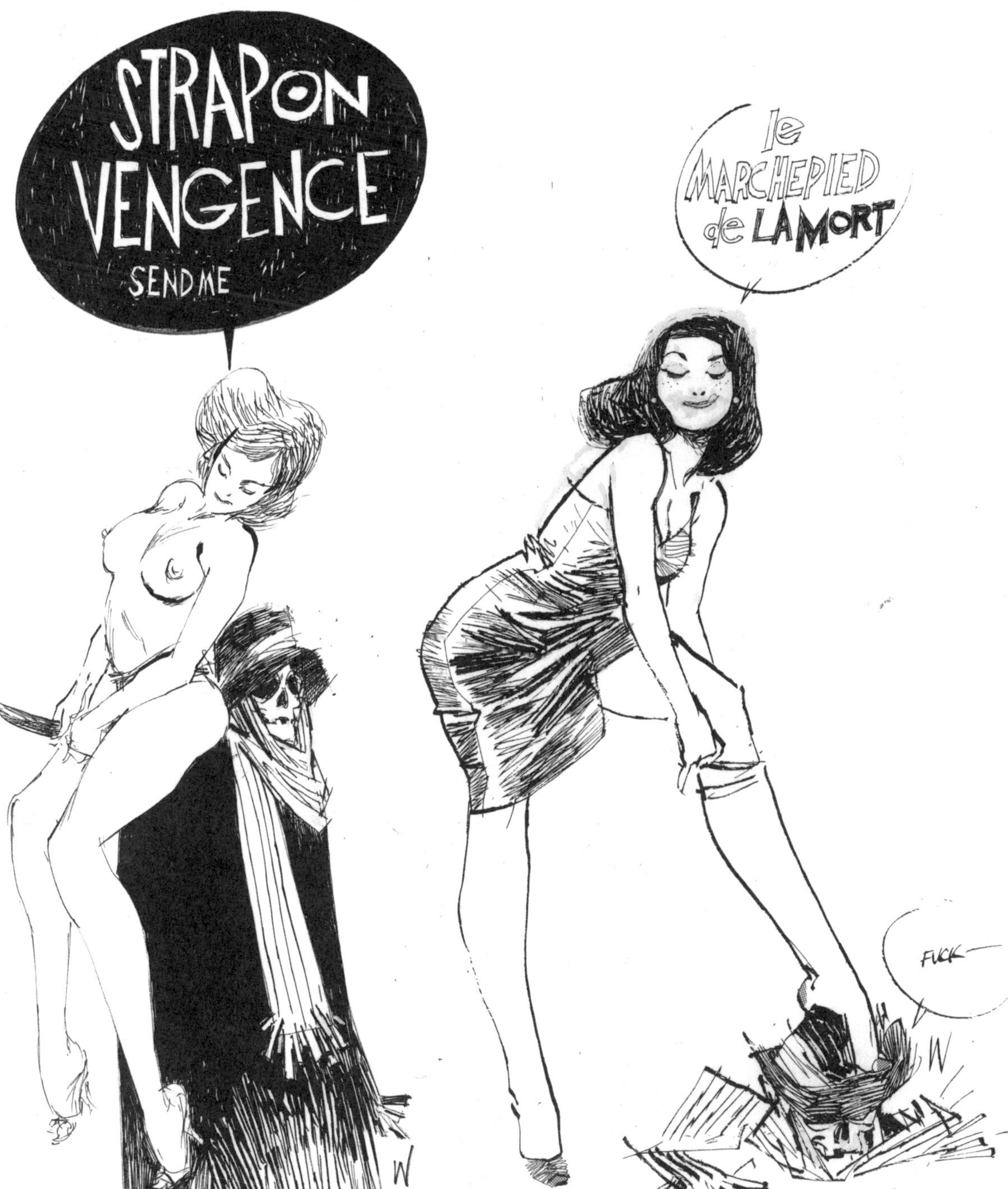

STRAP ON VENGENCE
SEND ME

le MARCHEPIED de LA MORT

FUCK

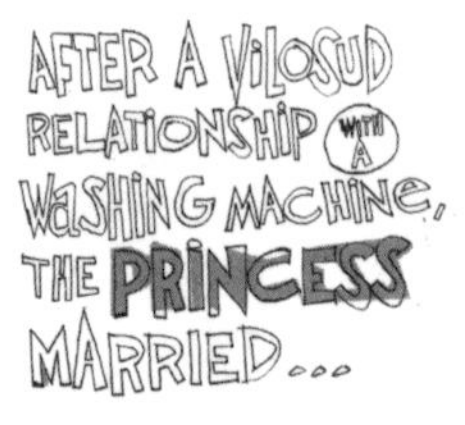

AFTER A VILOSUD RELATIONSHIP WITH A WASHING MACHINE, THE PRINCESS MARRIED...

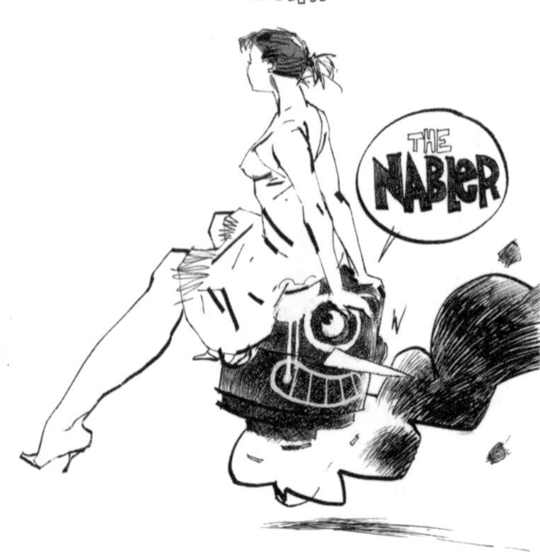

THE NABLER

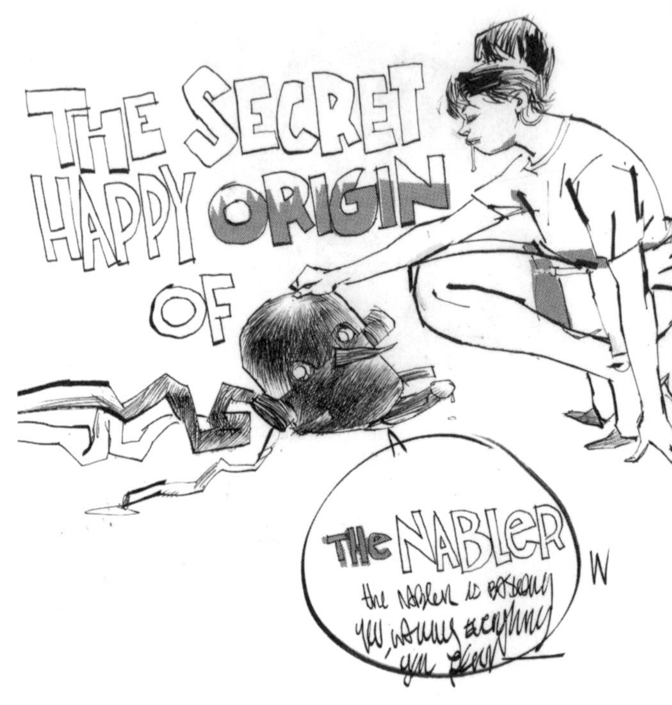

THE SECRET HAPPY ORIGIN OF
THE NABLER

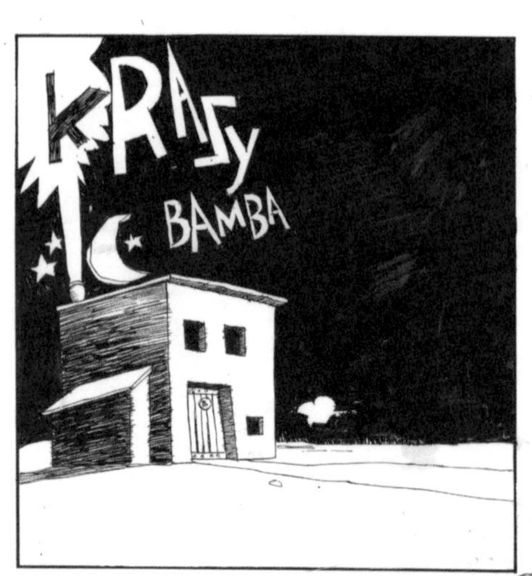

KRASY BAMBA

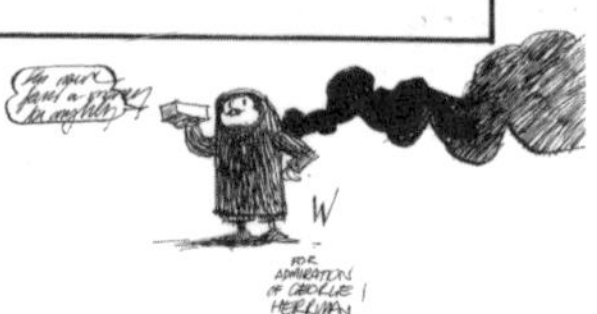

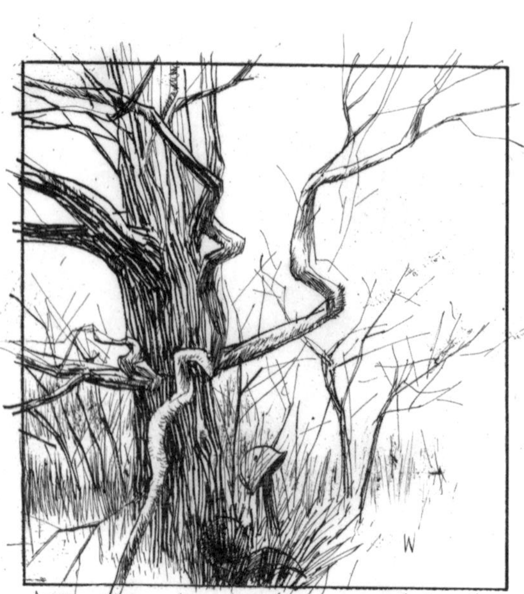

A TREE'S STORY-

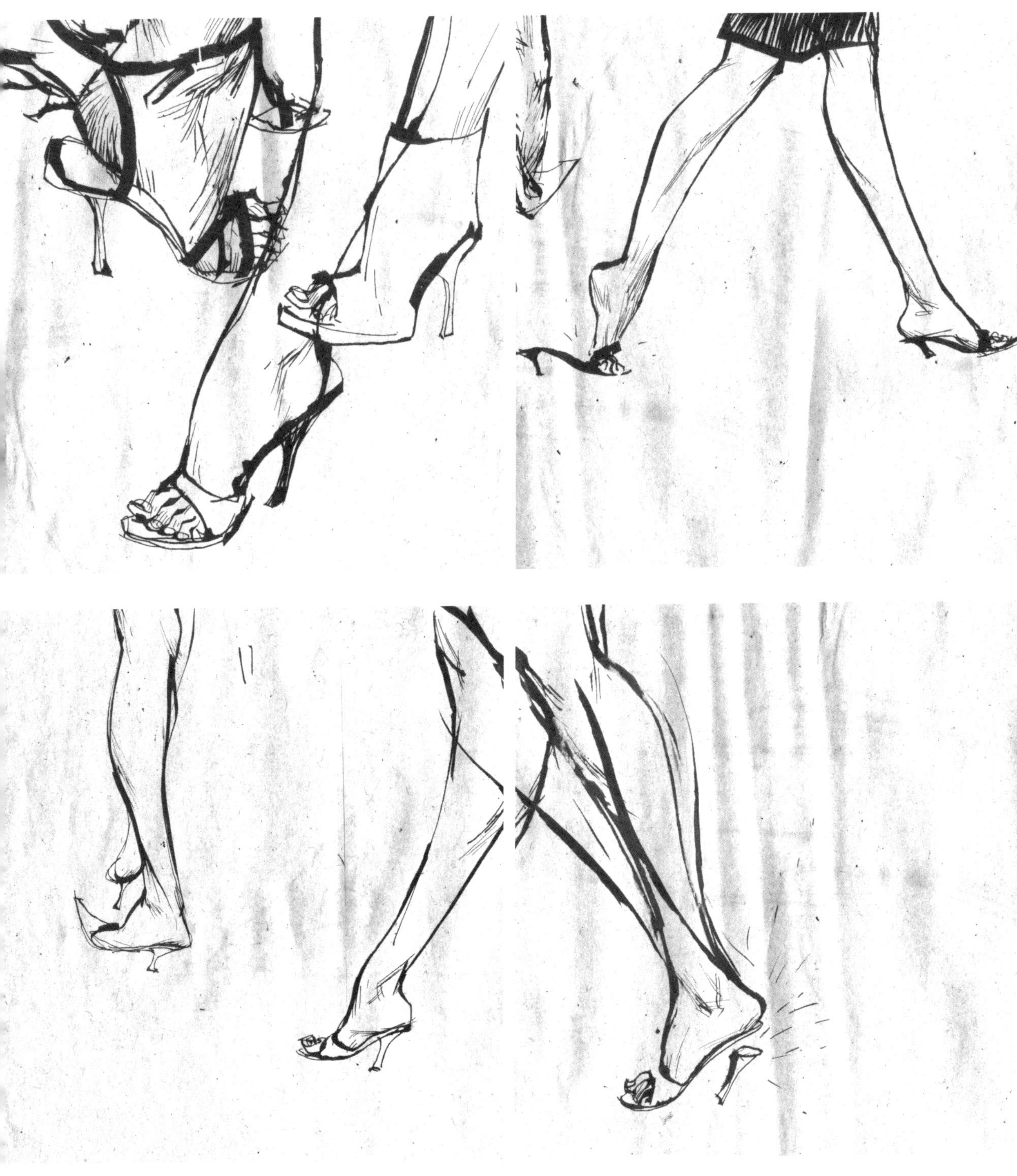

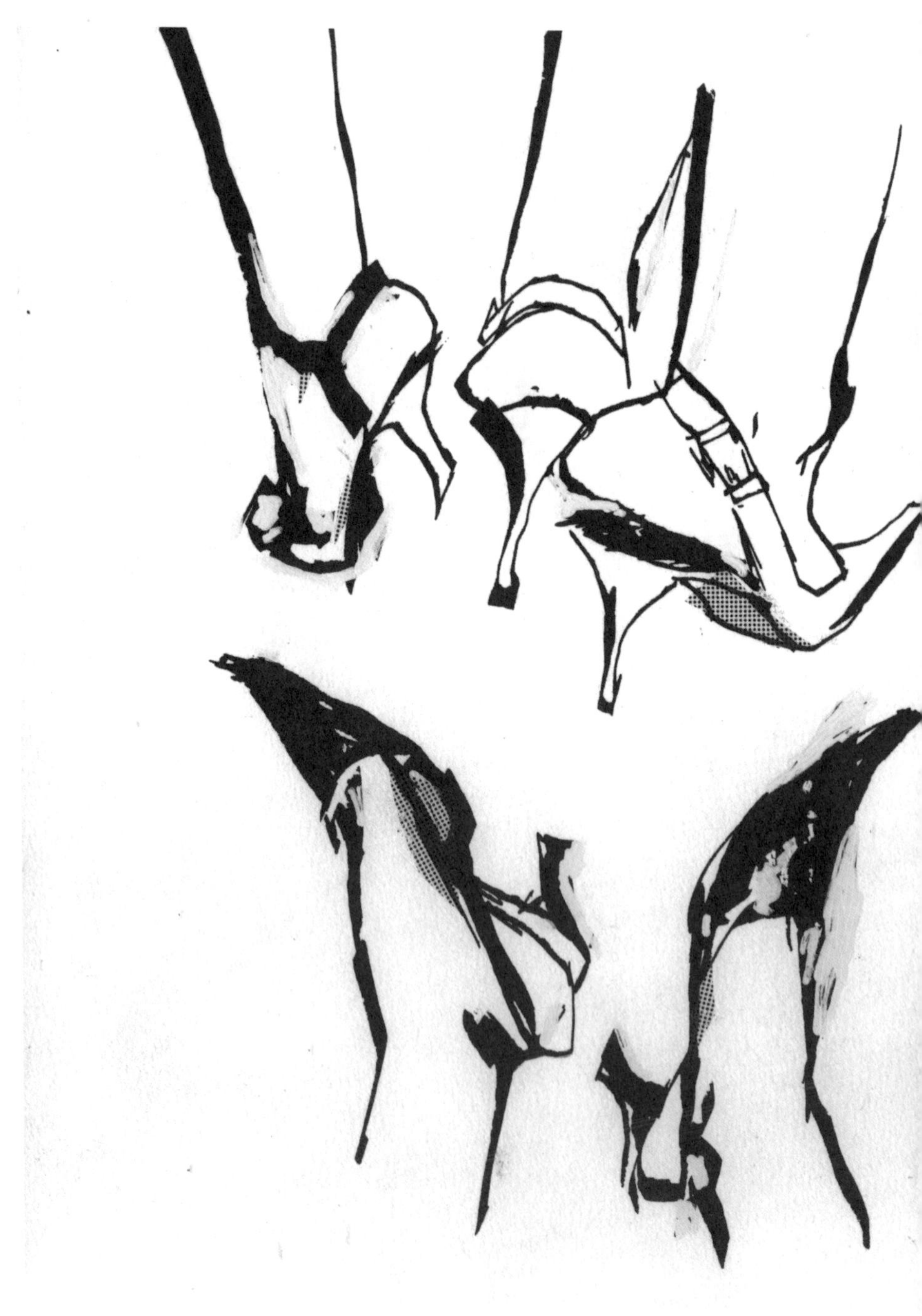

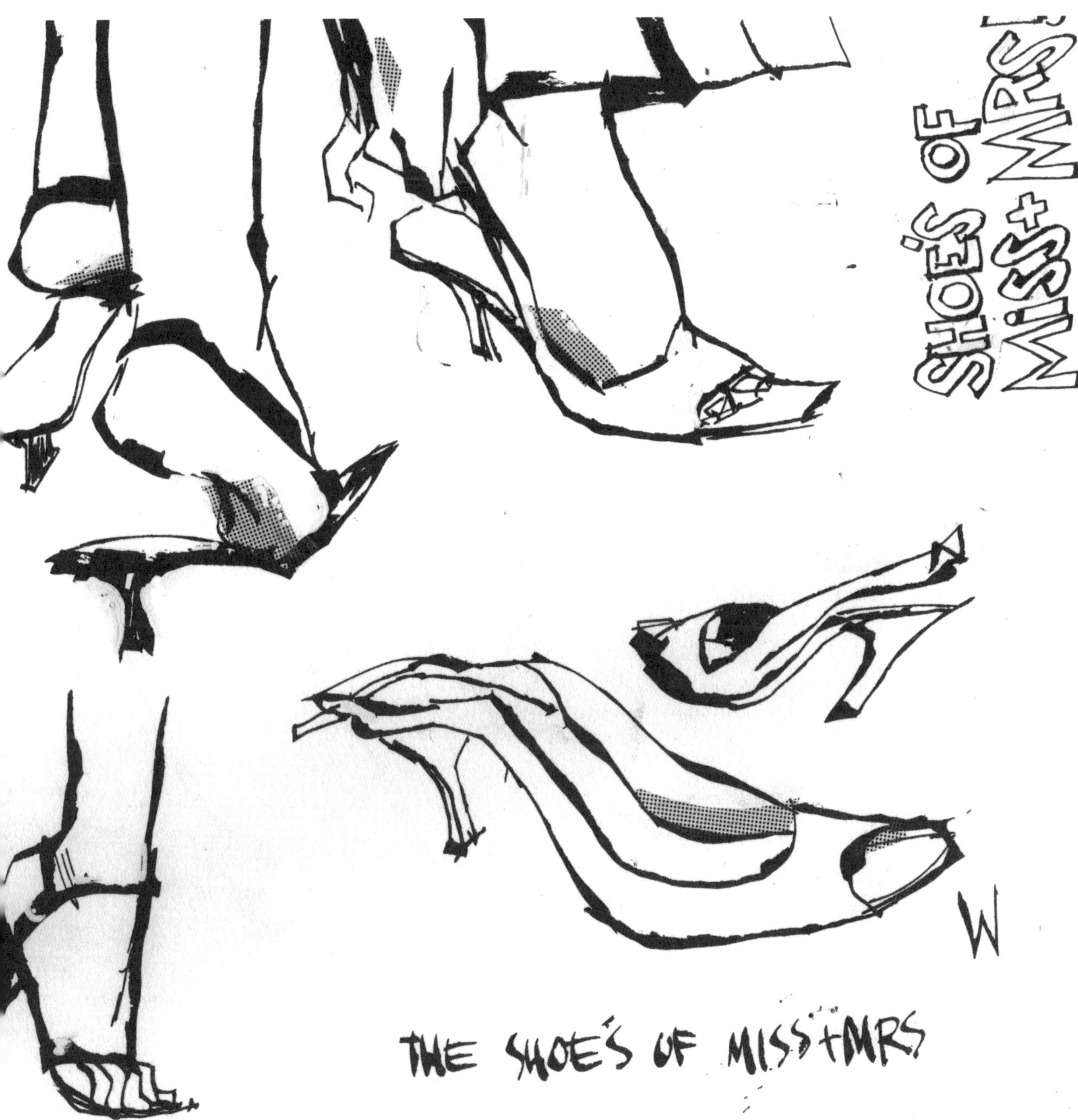

SHOE'S OF MISS + MRS
THE SHOE'S OF MISS + MRS

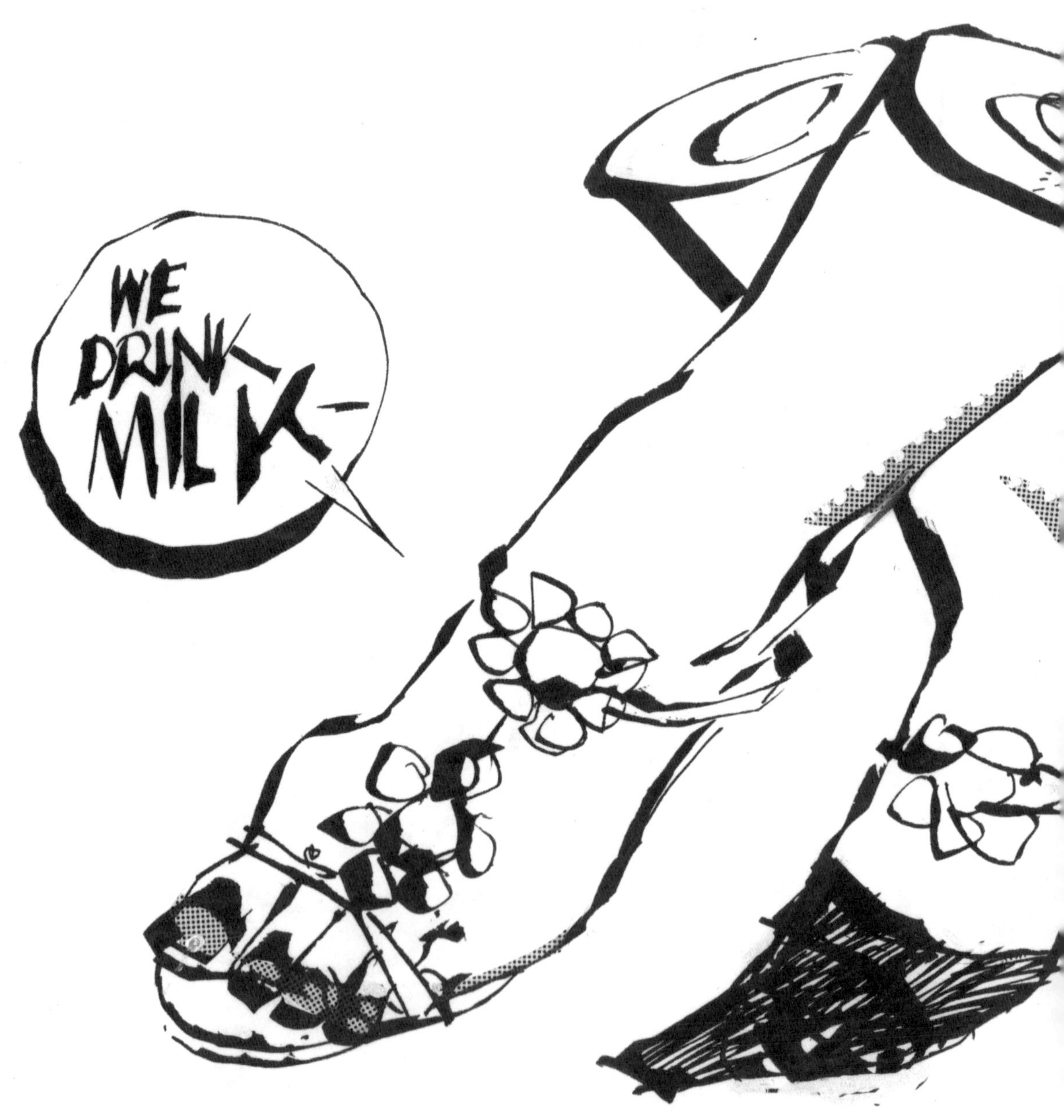

WE
DRINK
MILK

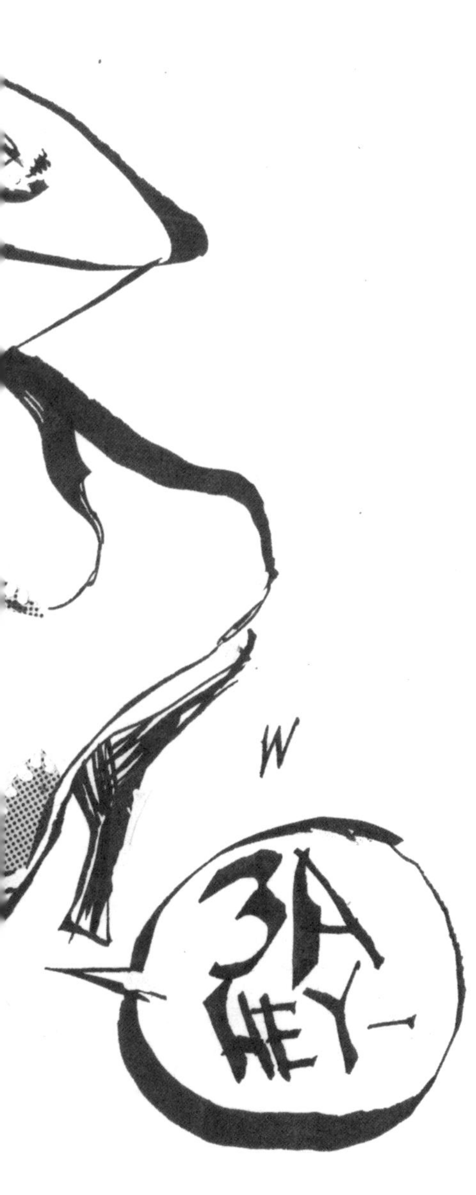

3A
CHEY-
W

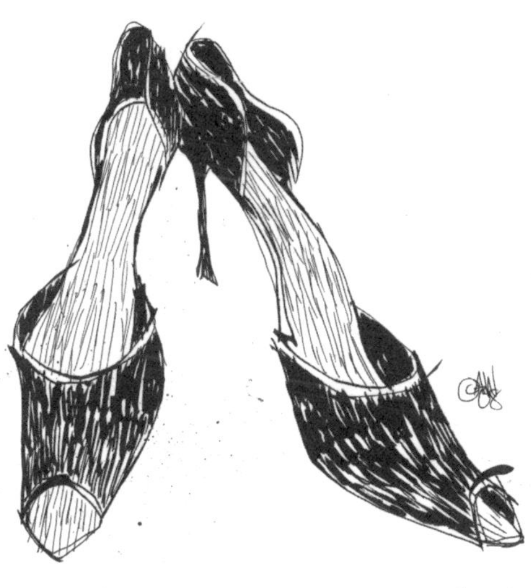

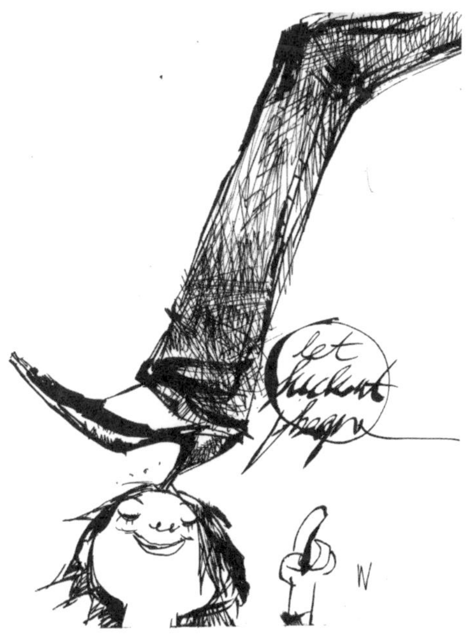

let
chuckout
begin
W

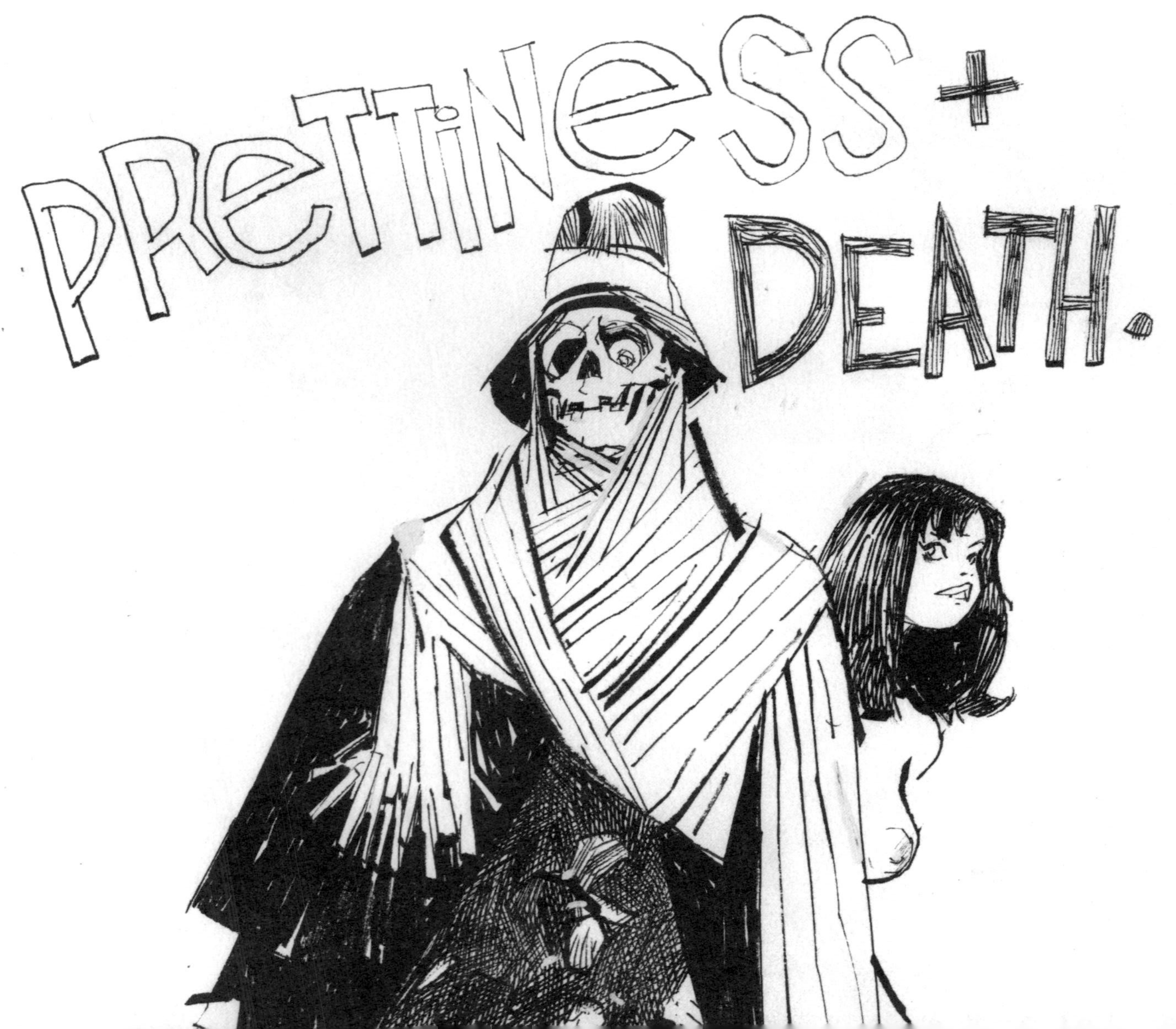

PRETTINESS + DEATH.

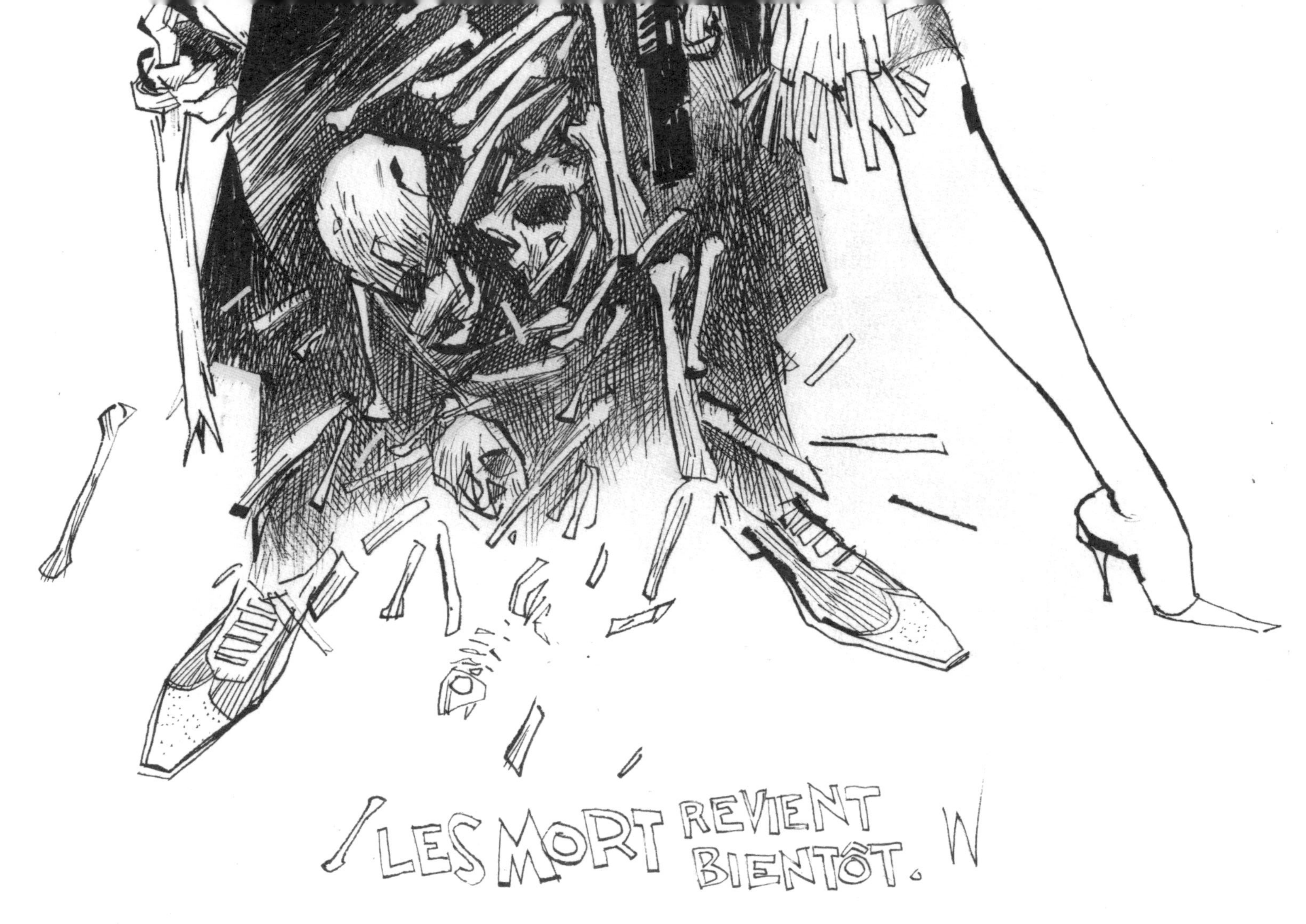

/ LES MORT REVIENT BIENTÔT. \

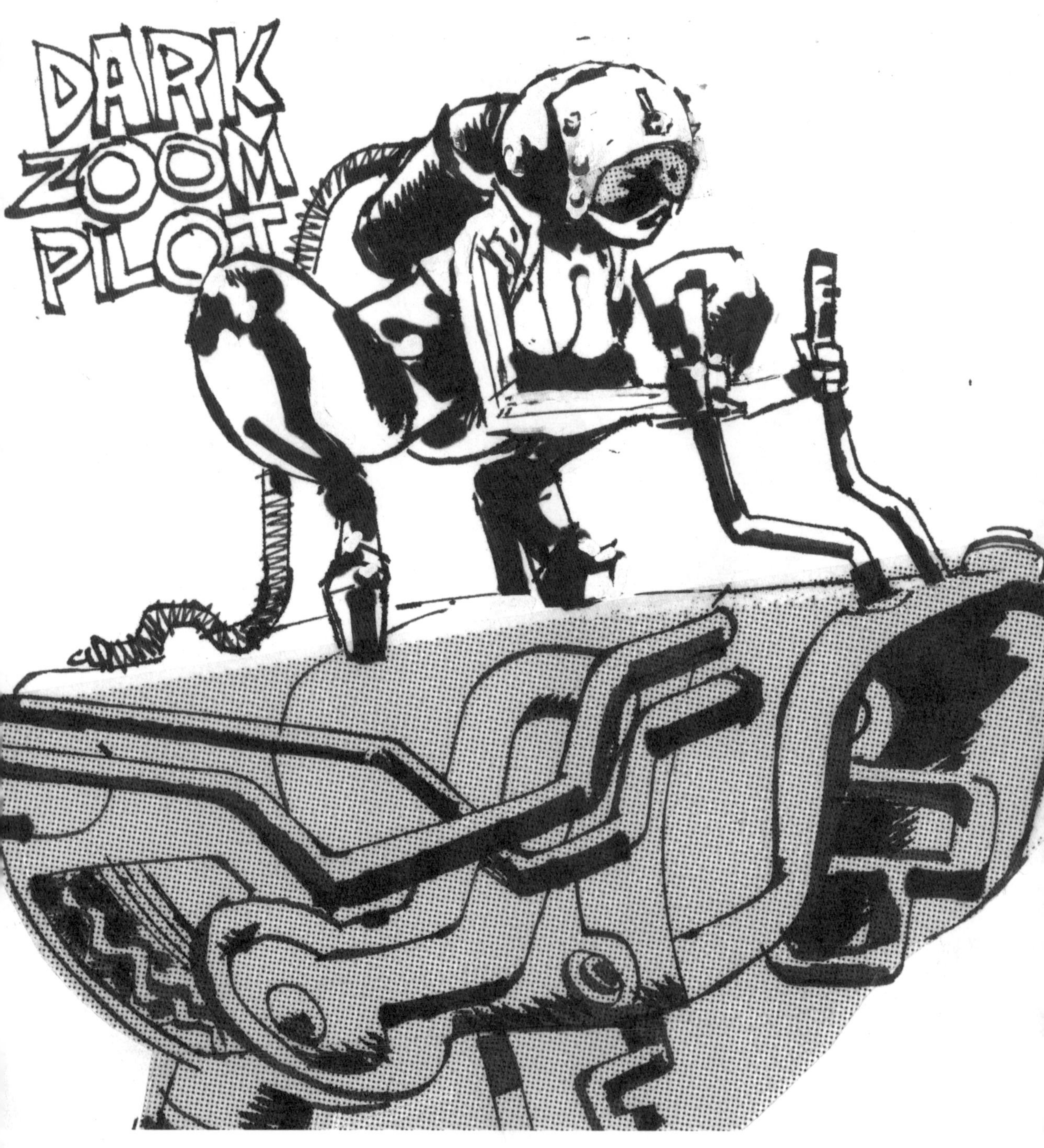

DARK
ZOOM
PILOT

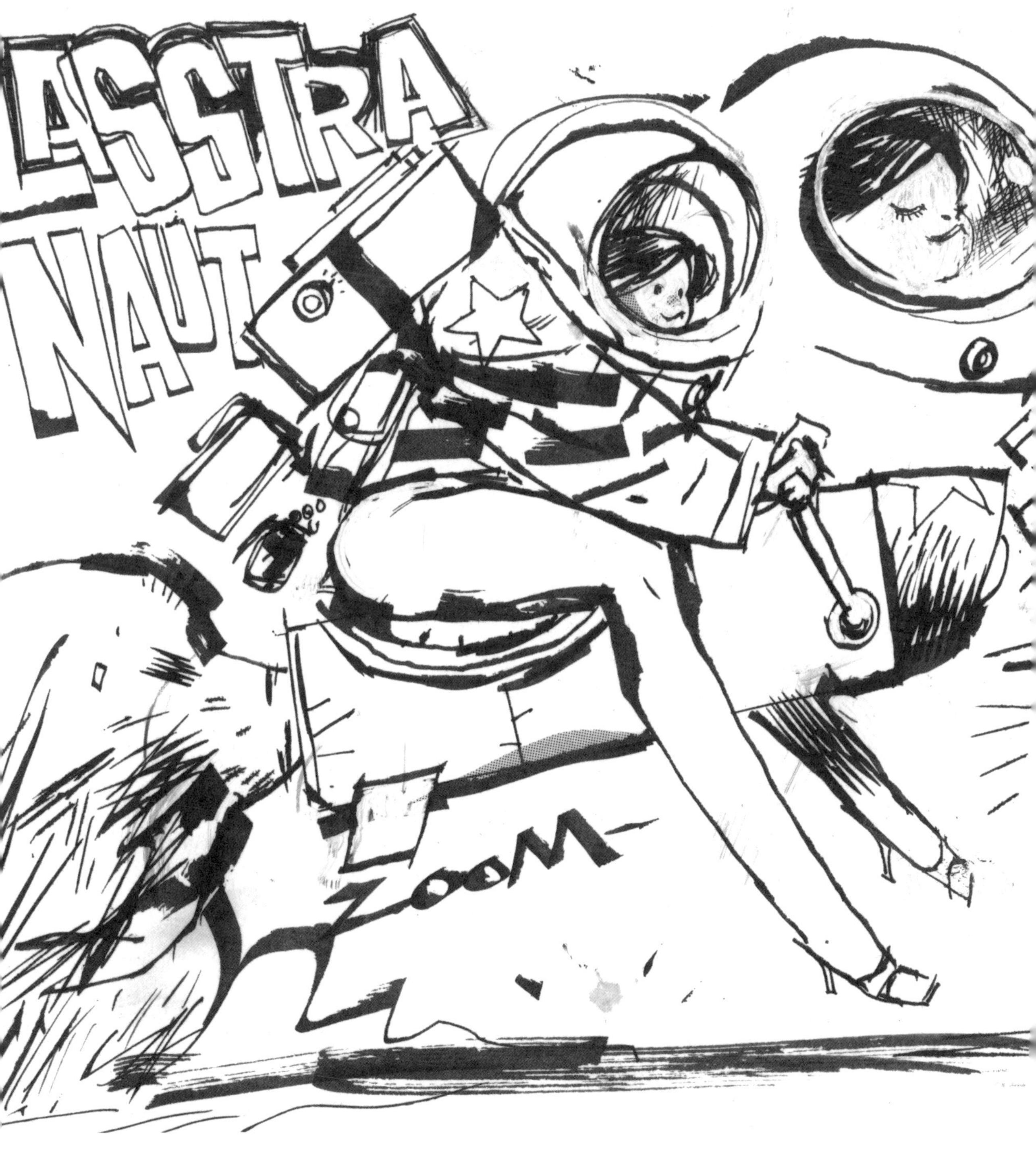

LASSTRA
NAUT
ZOOM

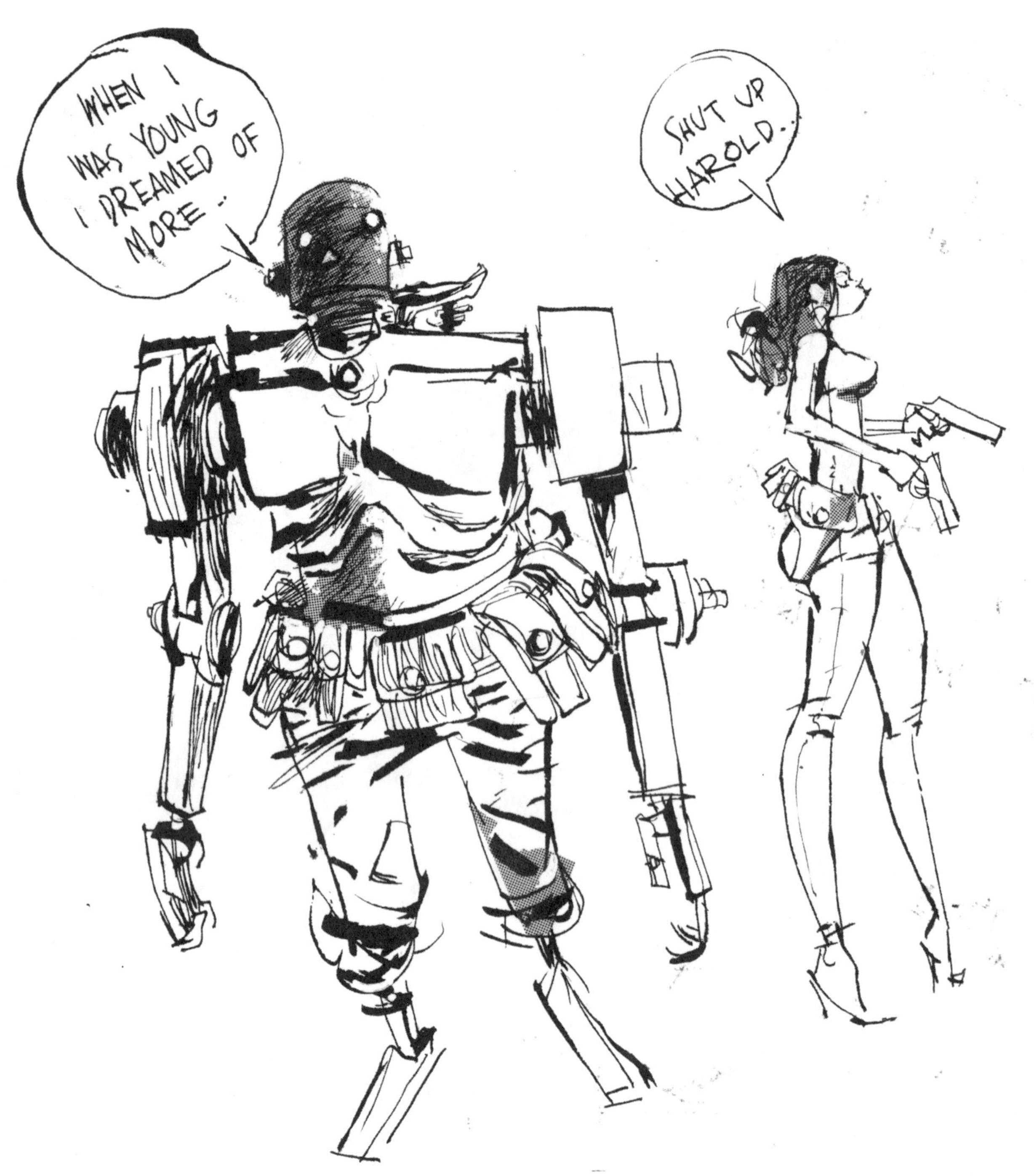

WHEN I WAS YOUNG I DREAMED OF MORE..
SHUT UP HAROLD..

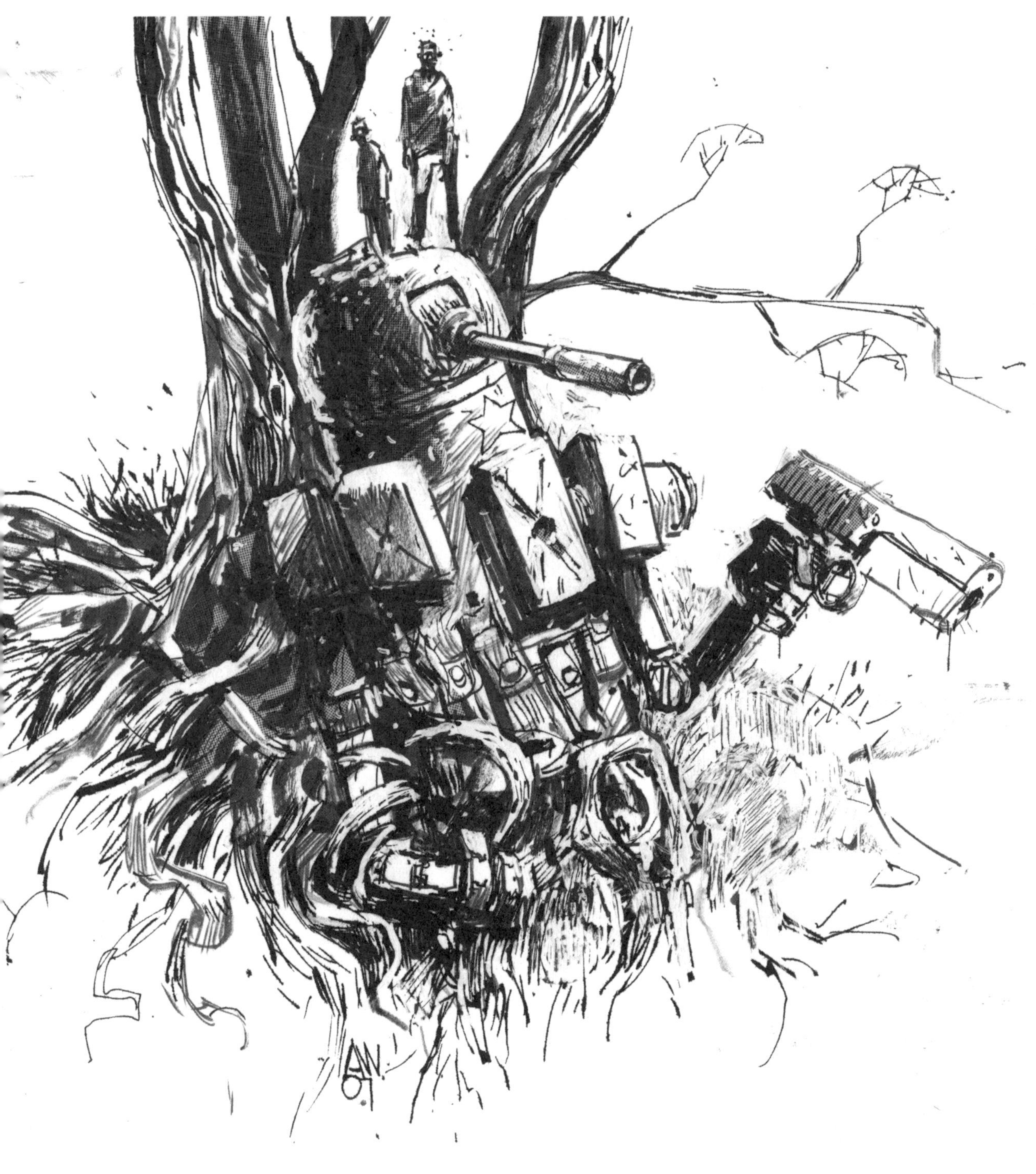

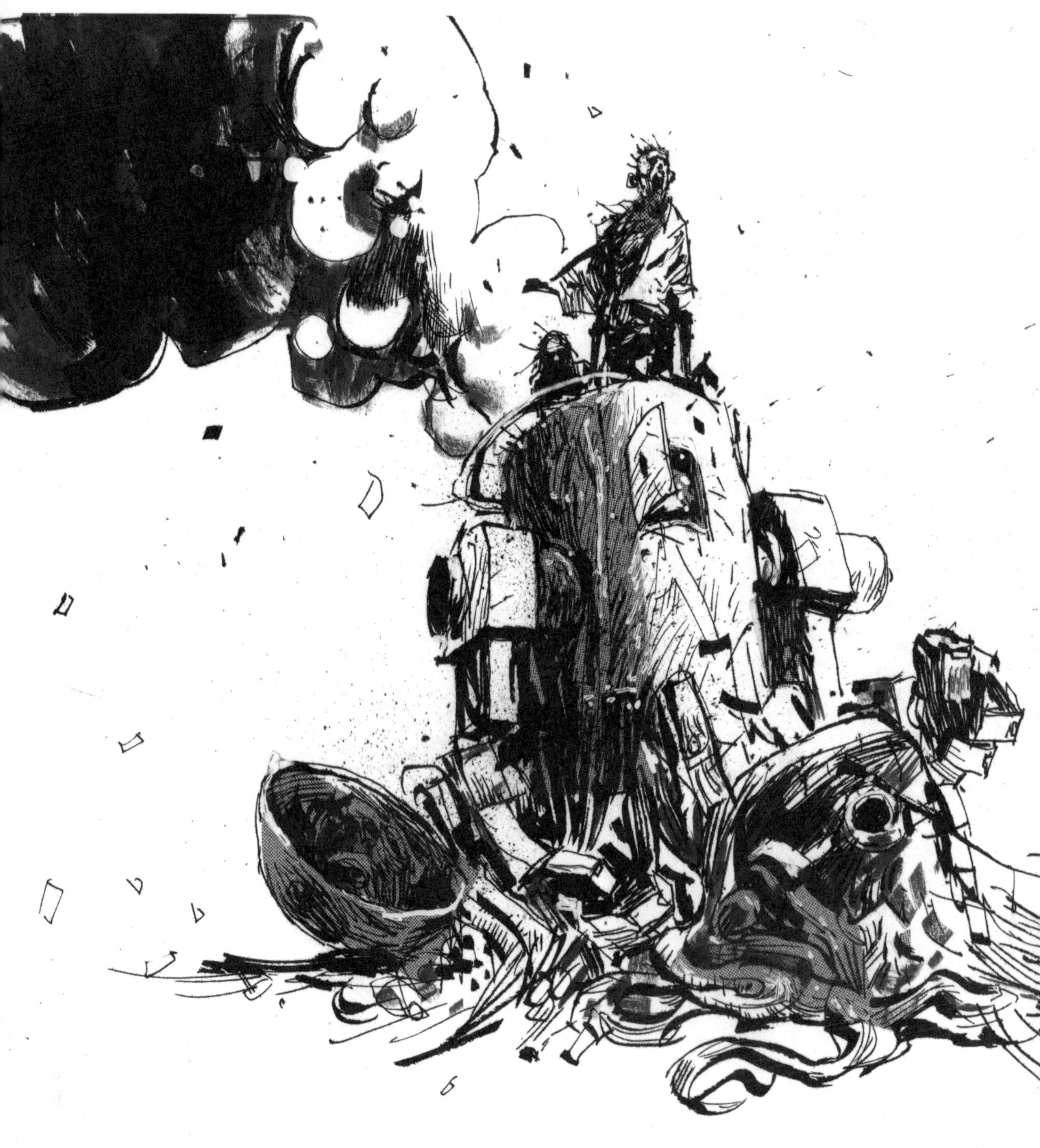

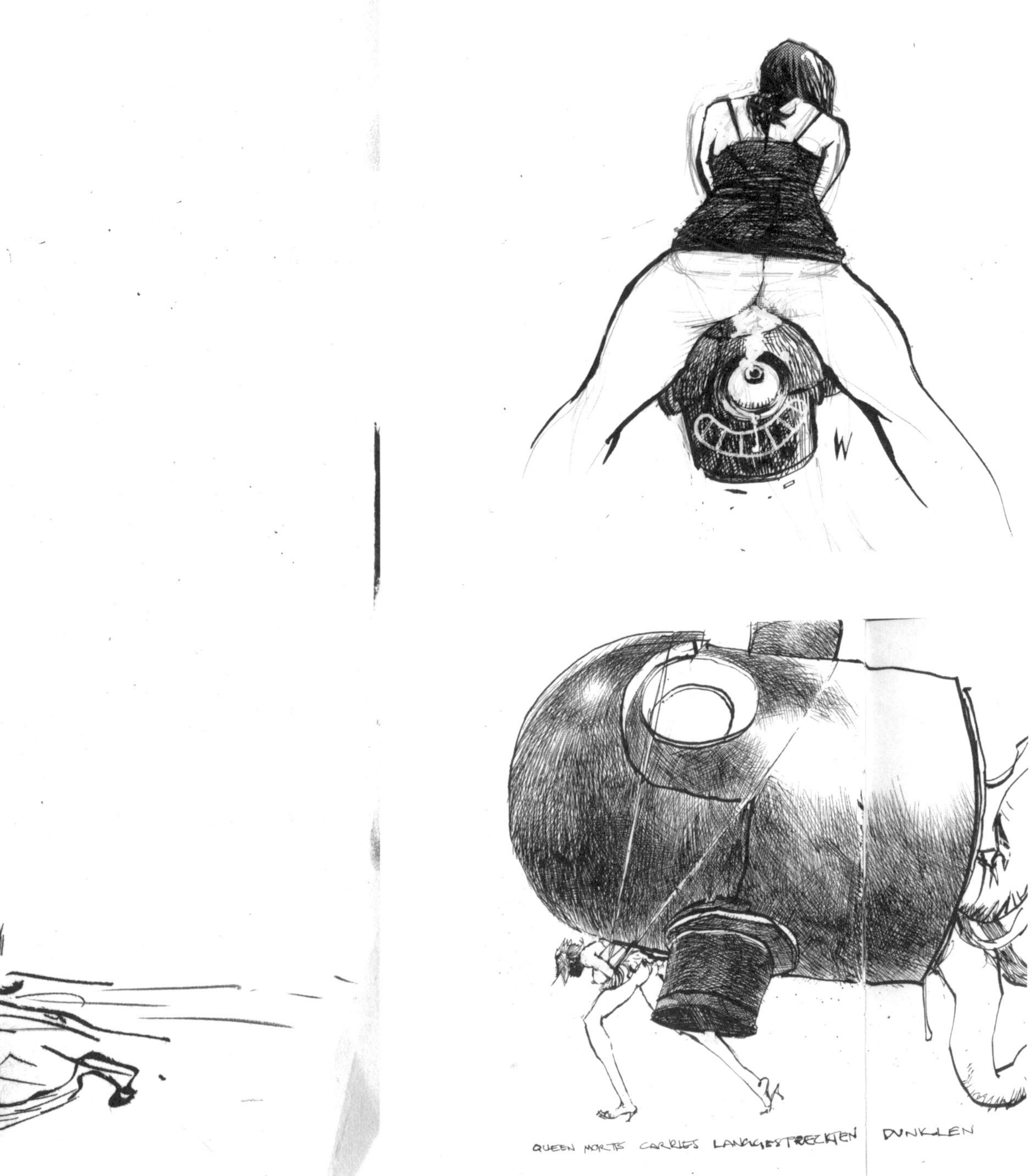
QUEEN MORTIS CARRIES LANGGESTRECKTEN DUNKLEN

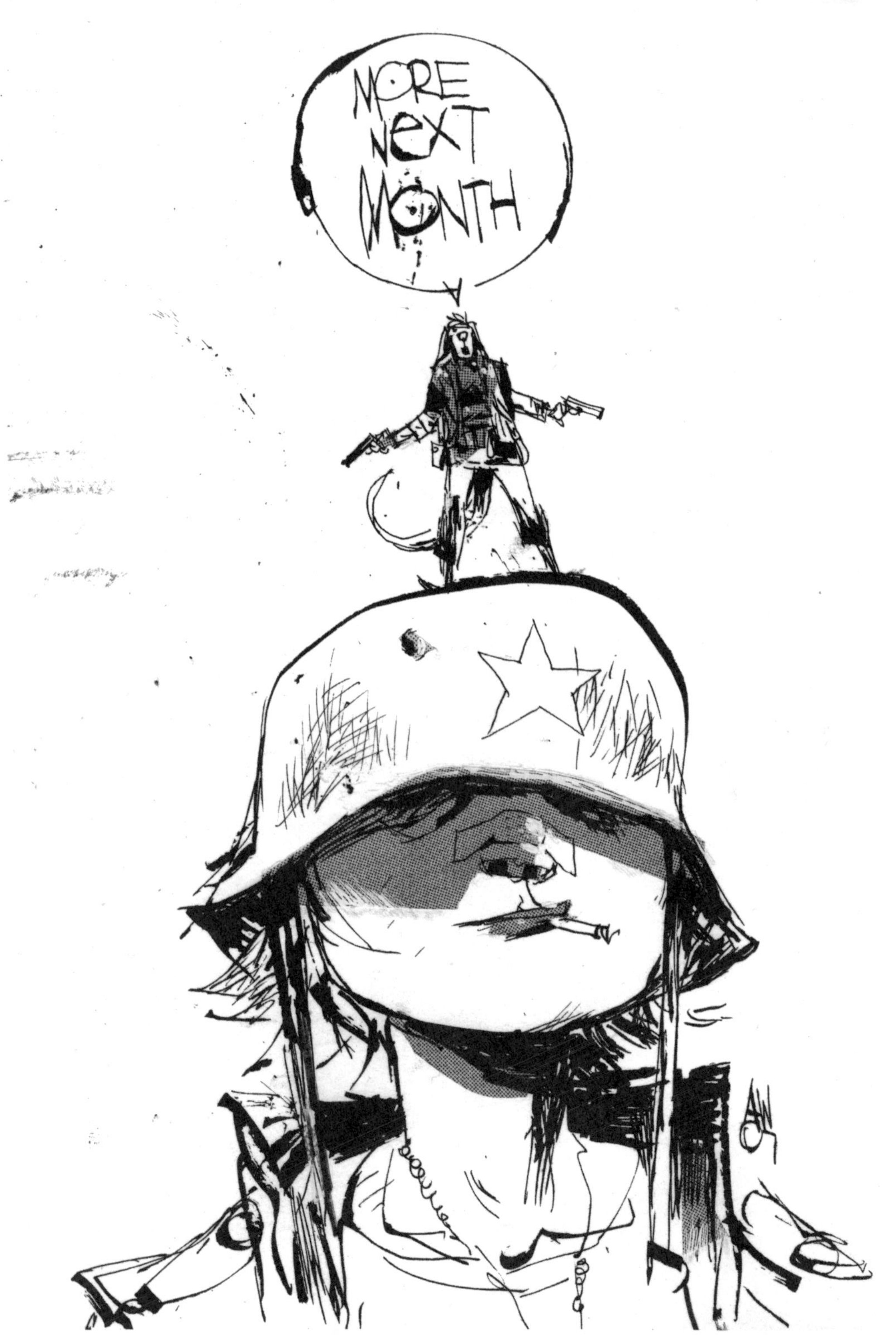

MORE
NEXT
MONTH

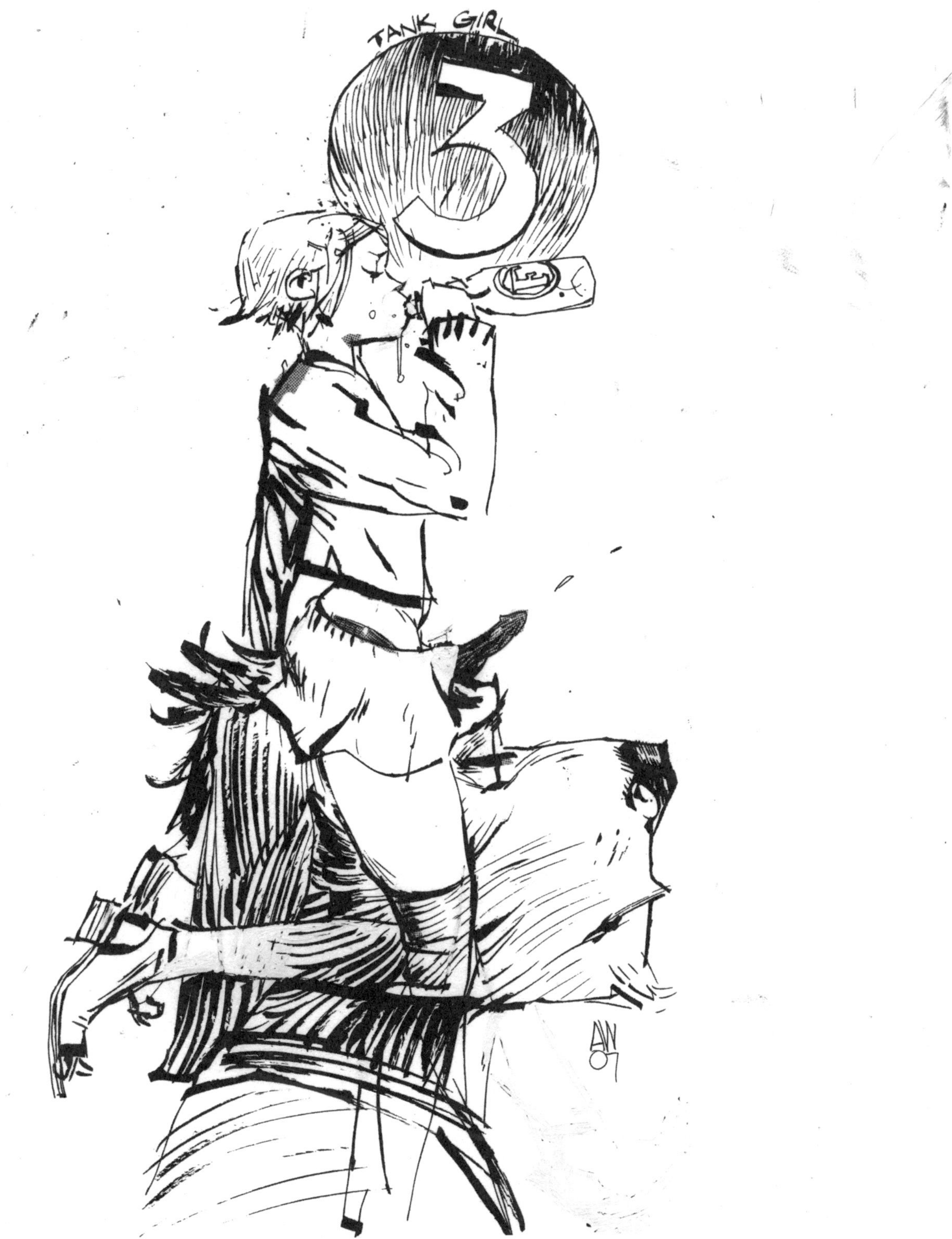
TANK GIRL
3

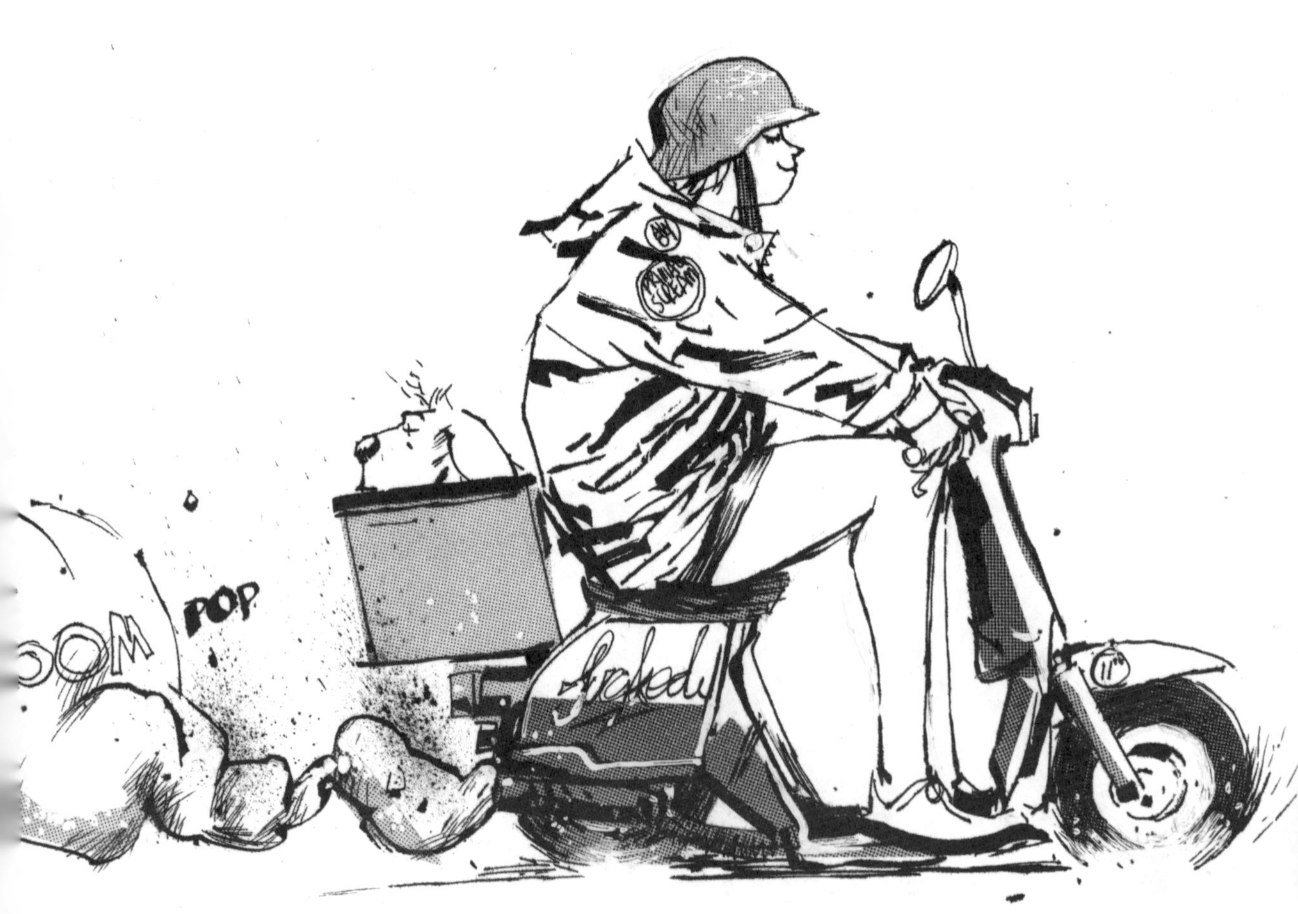
OOM
POP

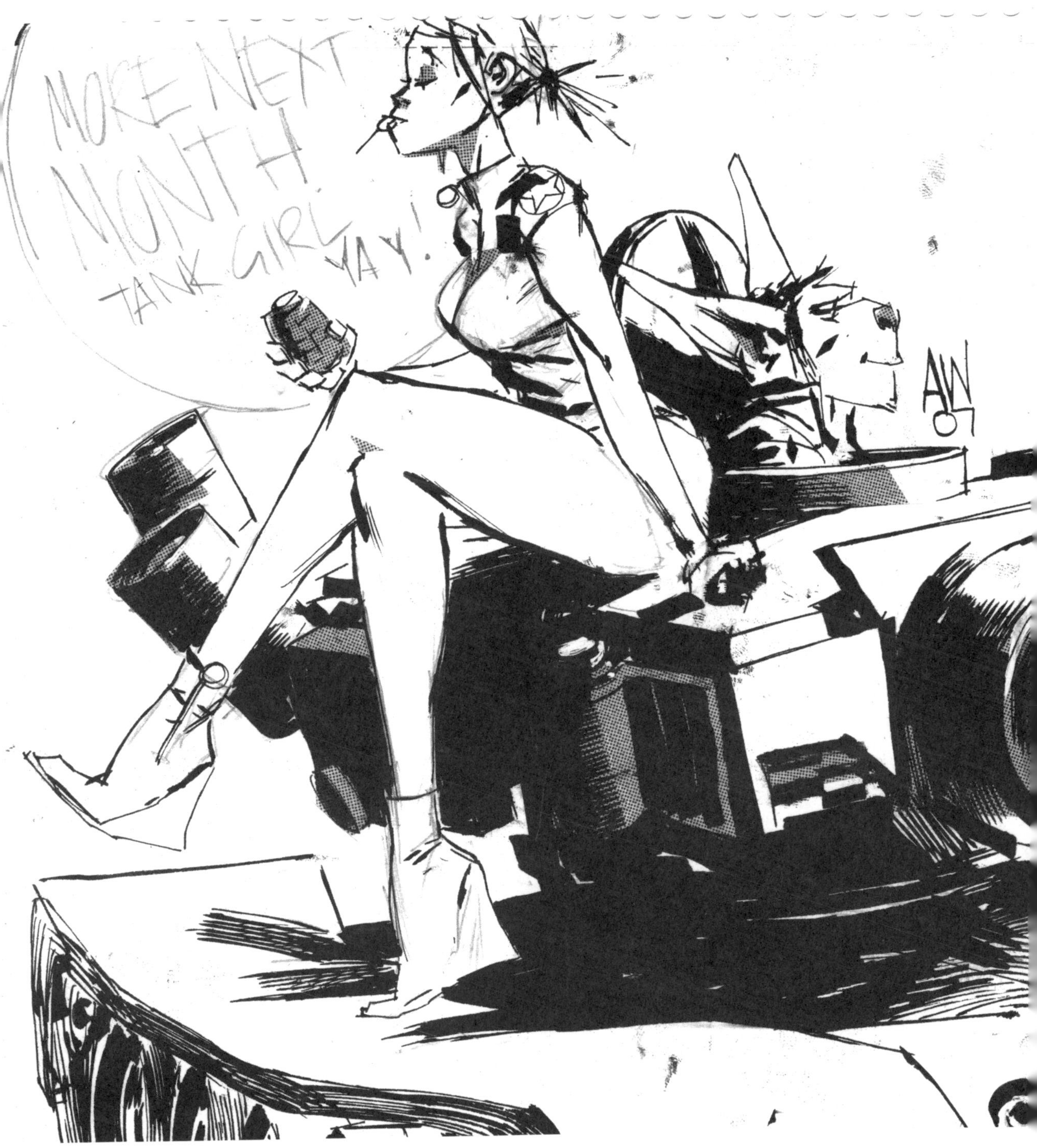

MORE NEXT MONTH.
TANK GIRL. YAY!

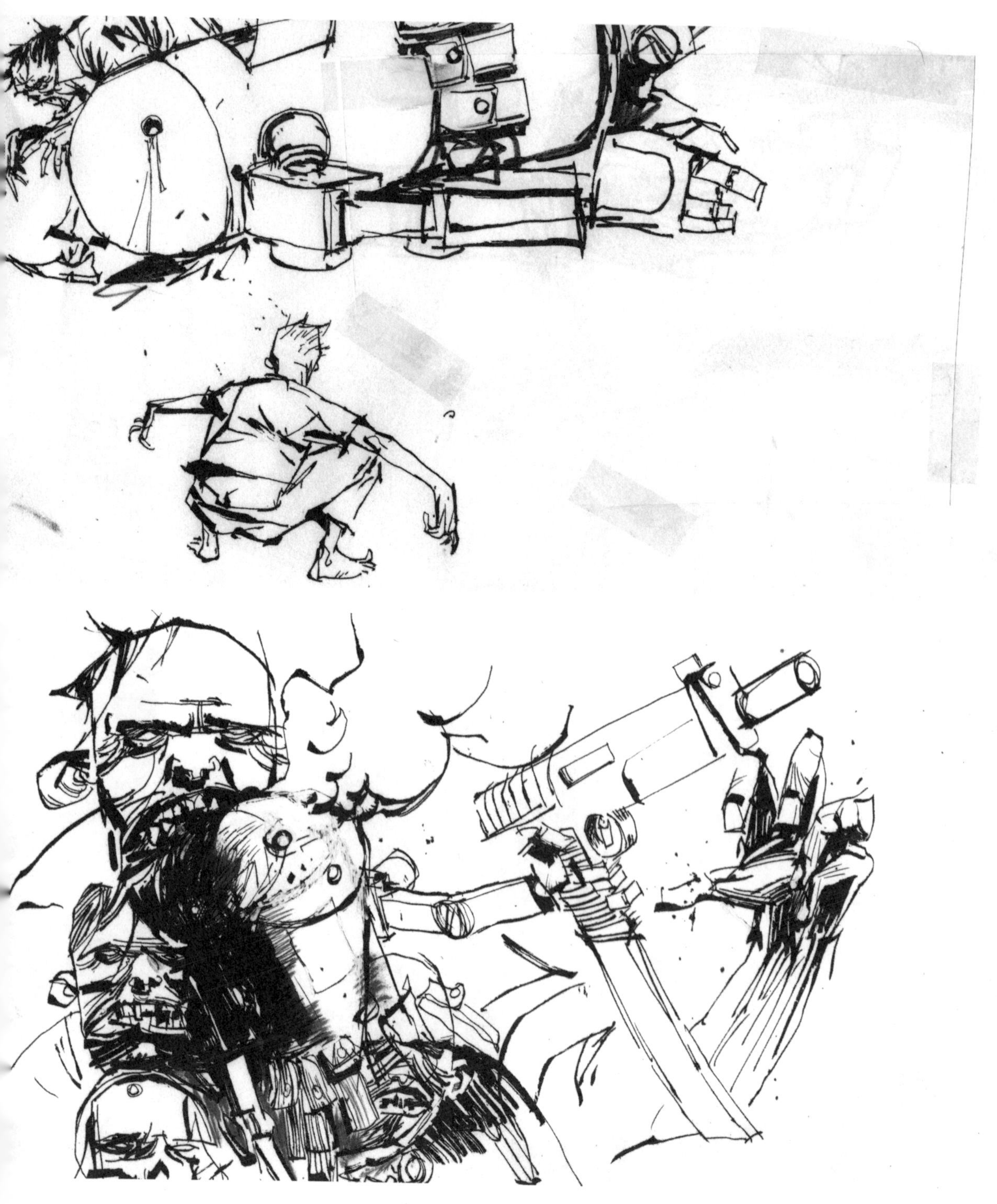

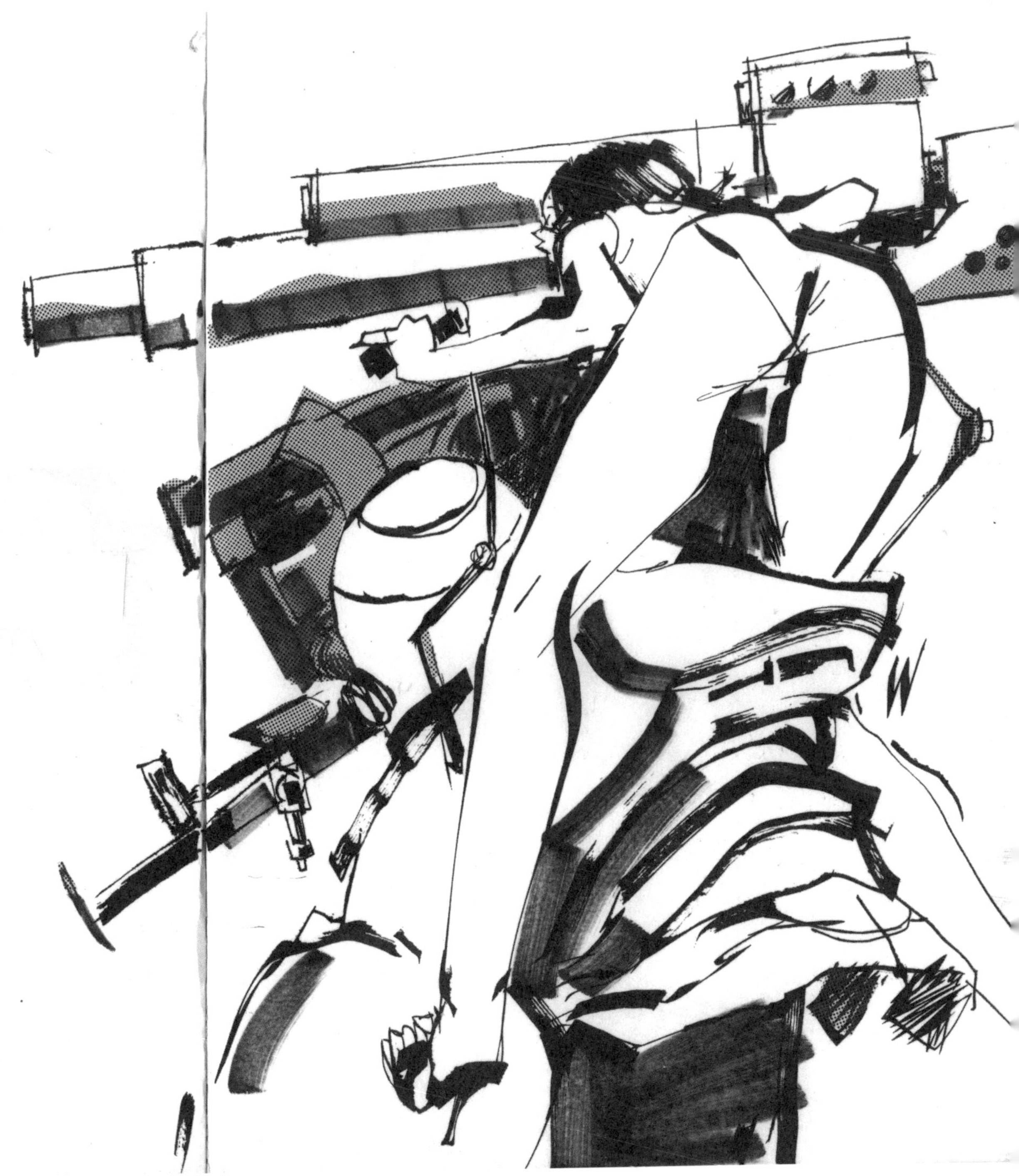

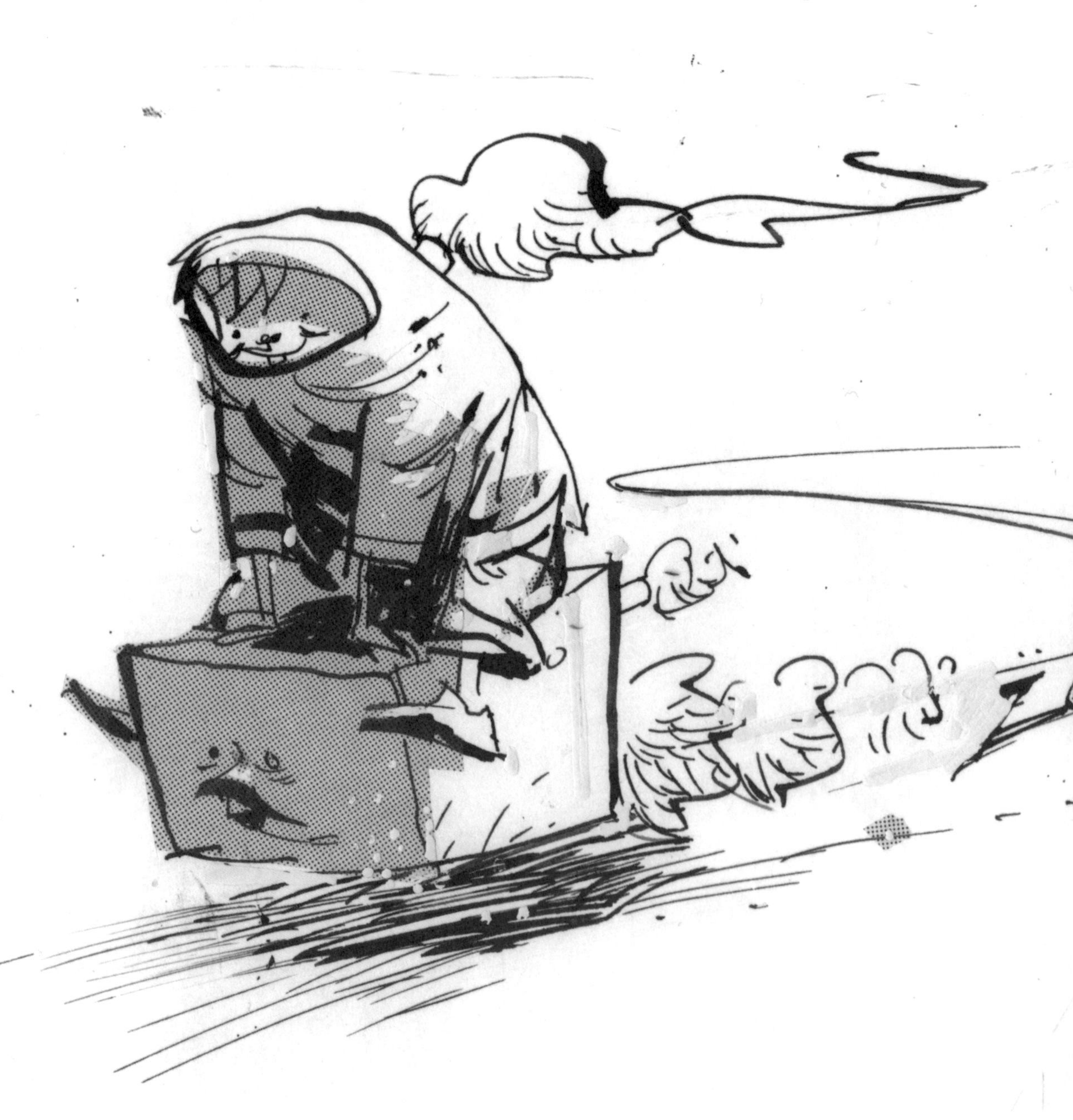

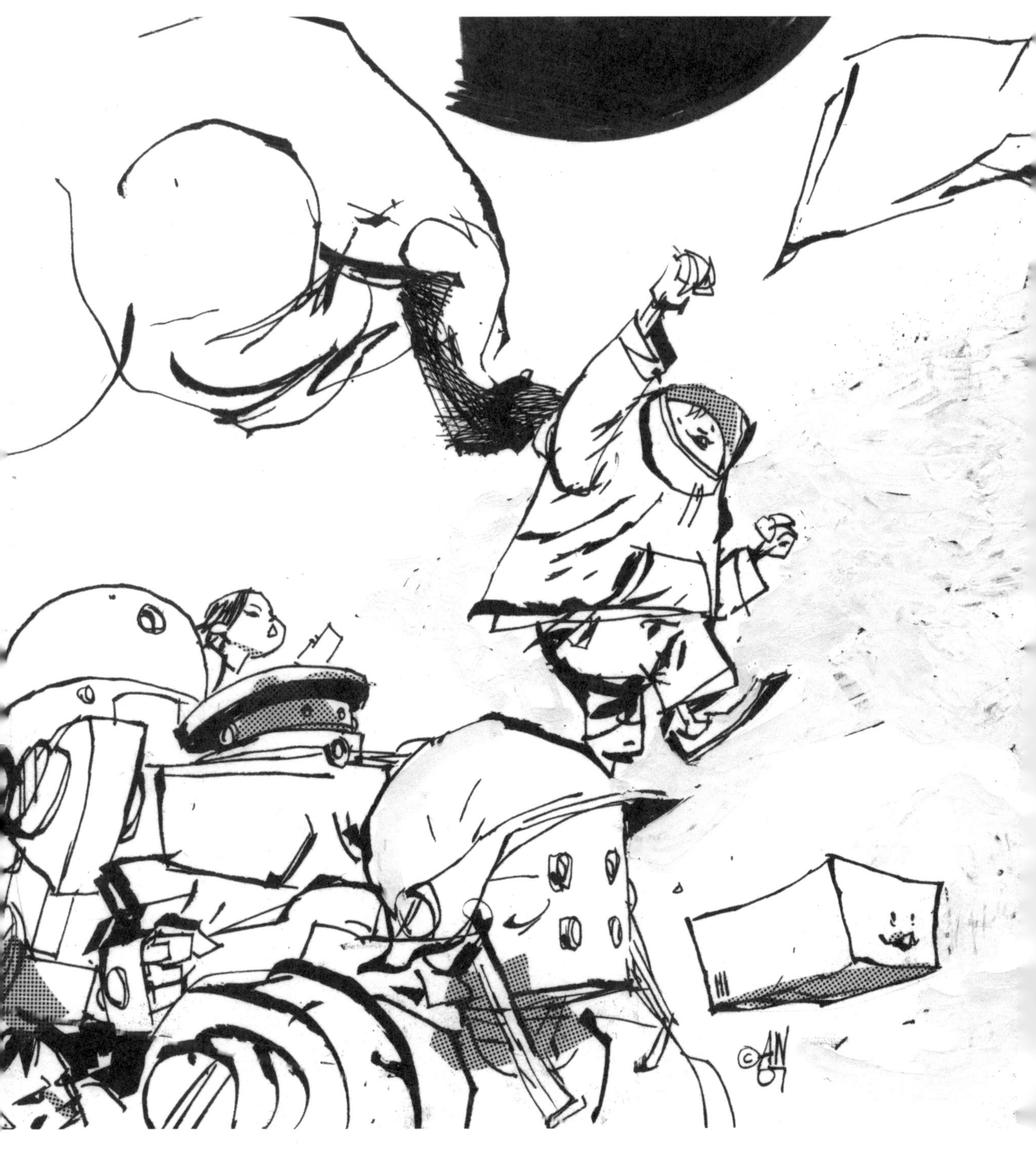

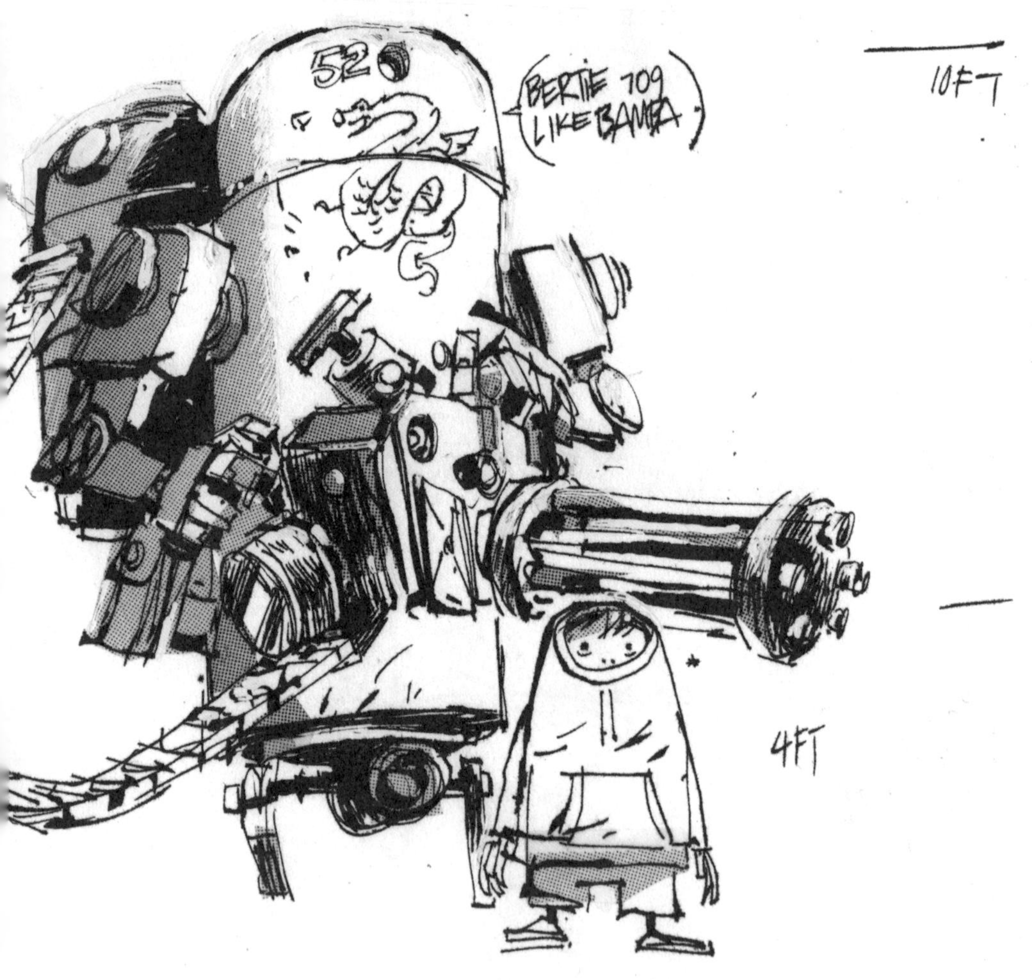

BAMBA and the BERTIE by ashley wood

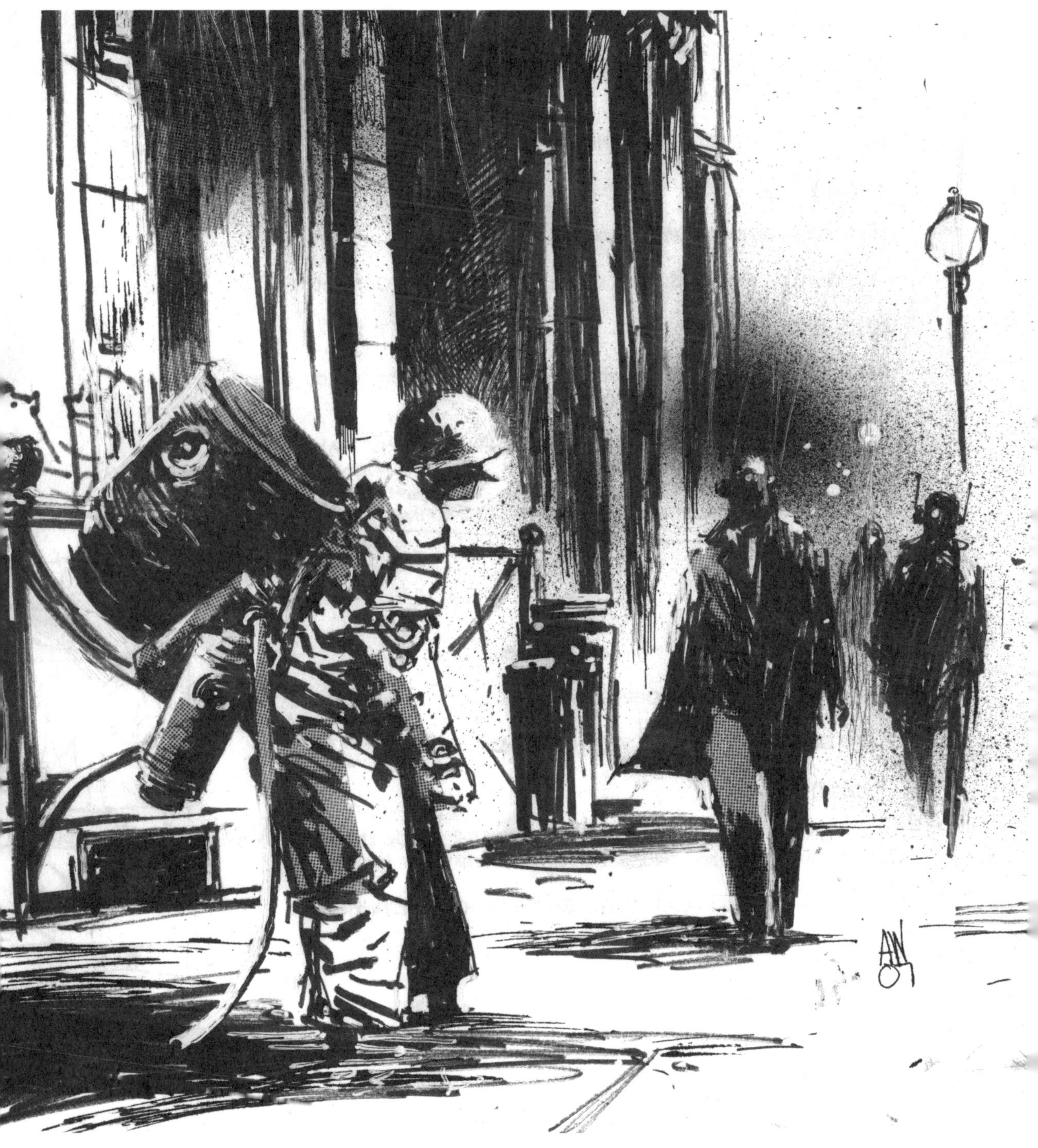

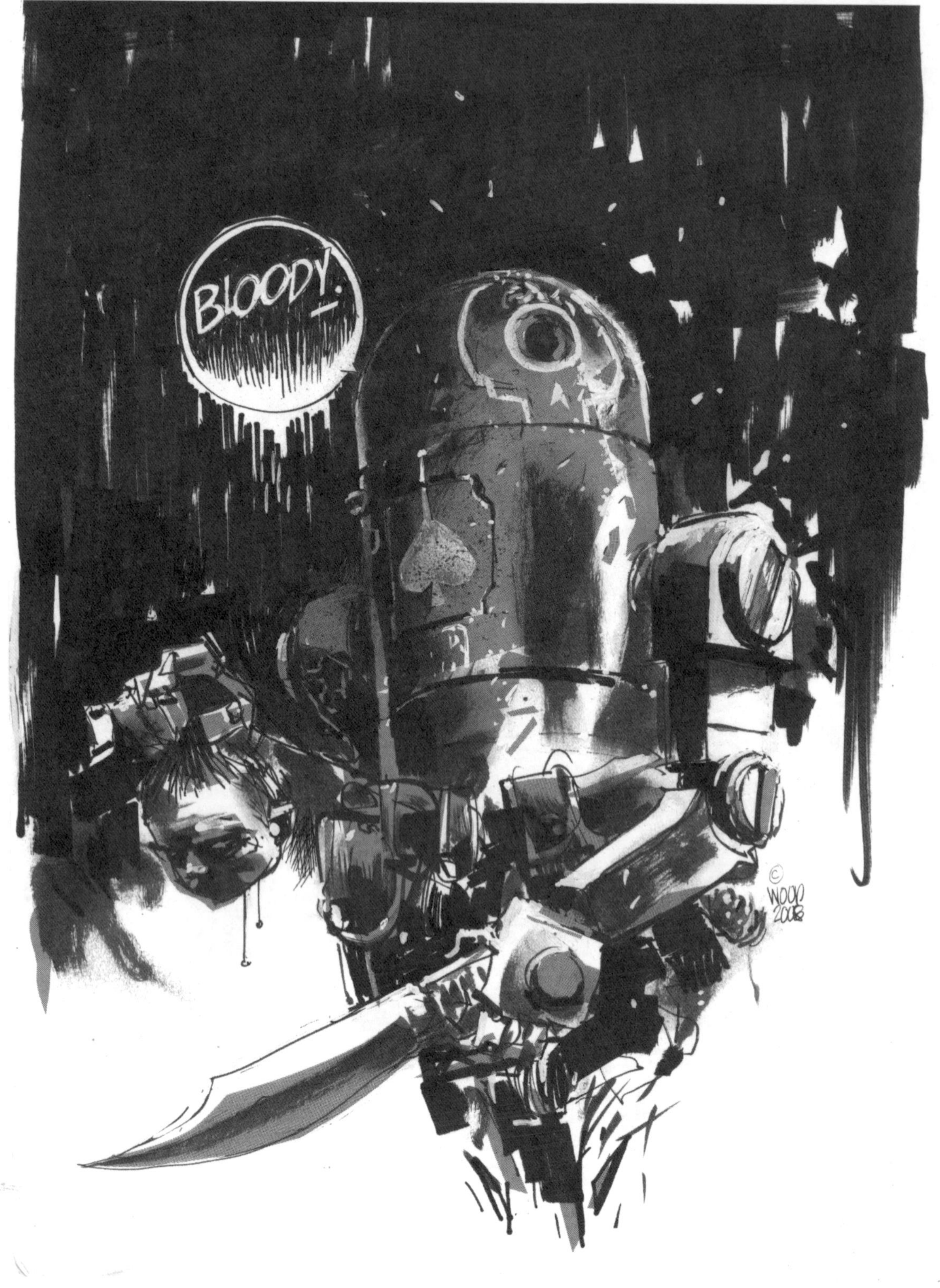

BLOODY.
WOOD
2008

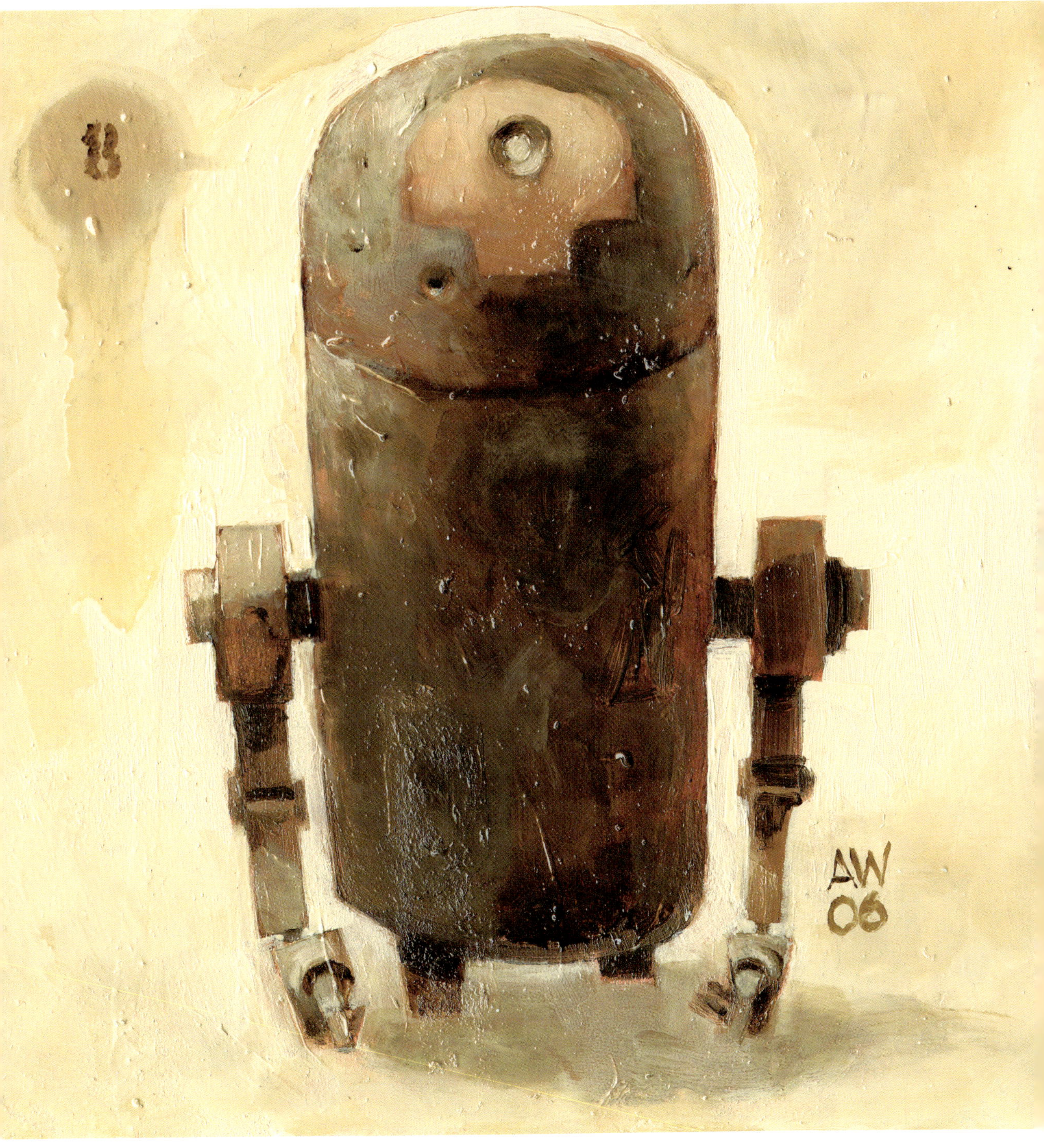
AW
06

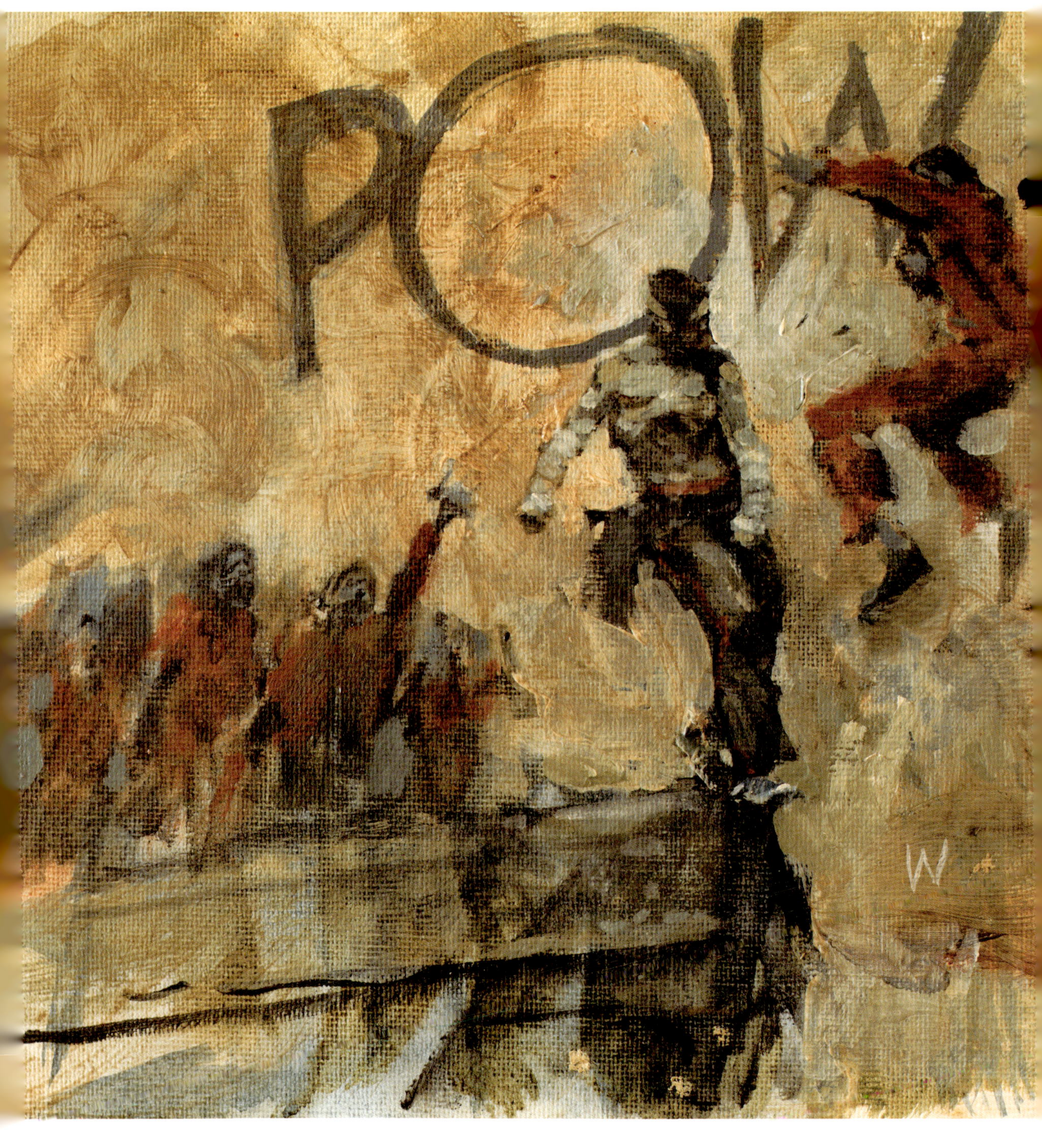
POW

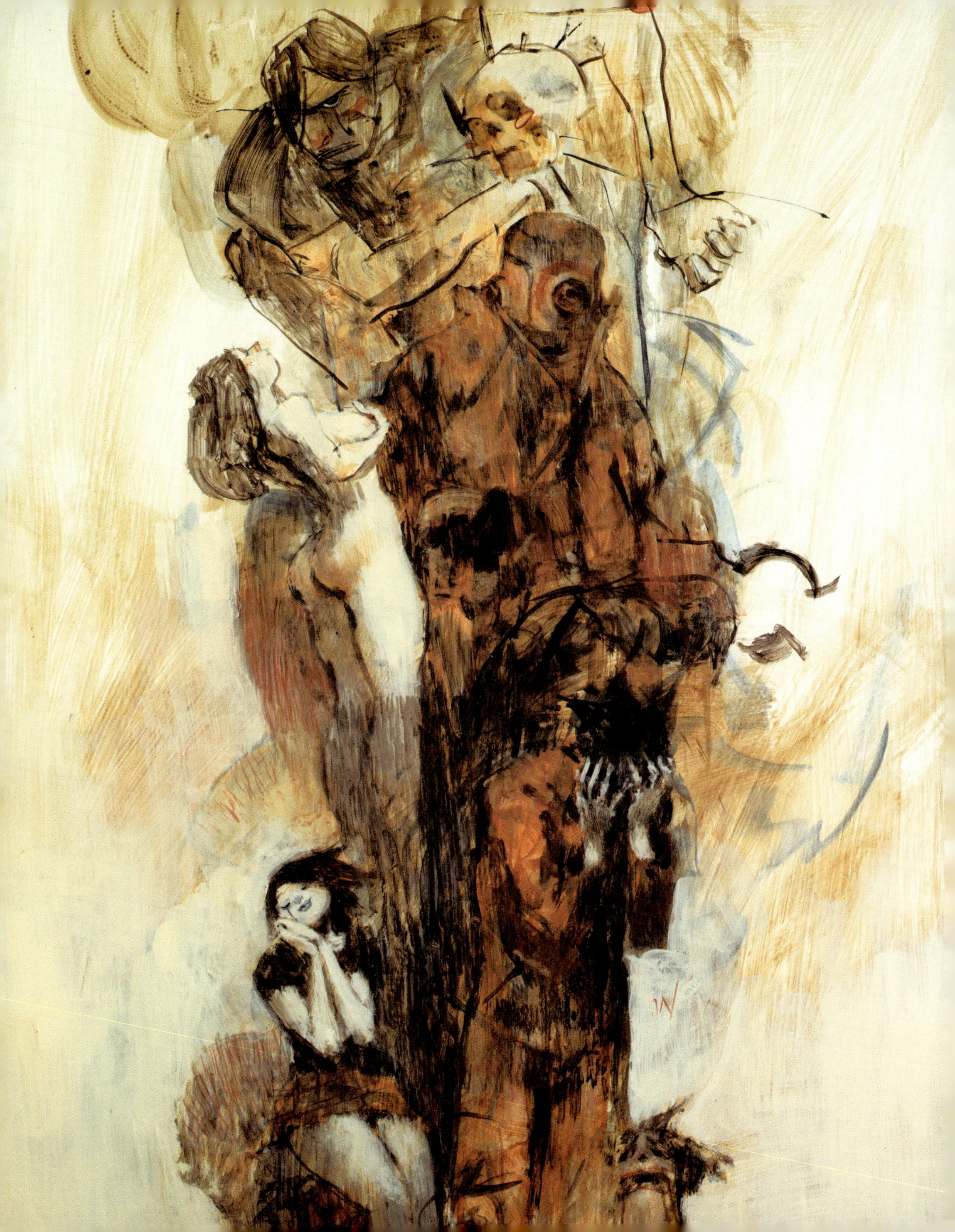

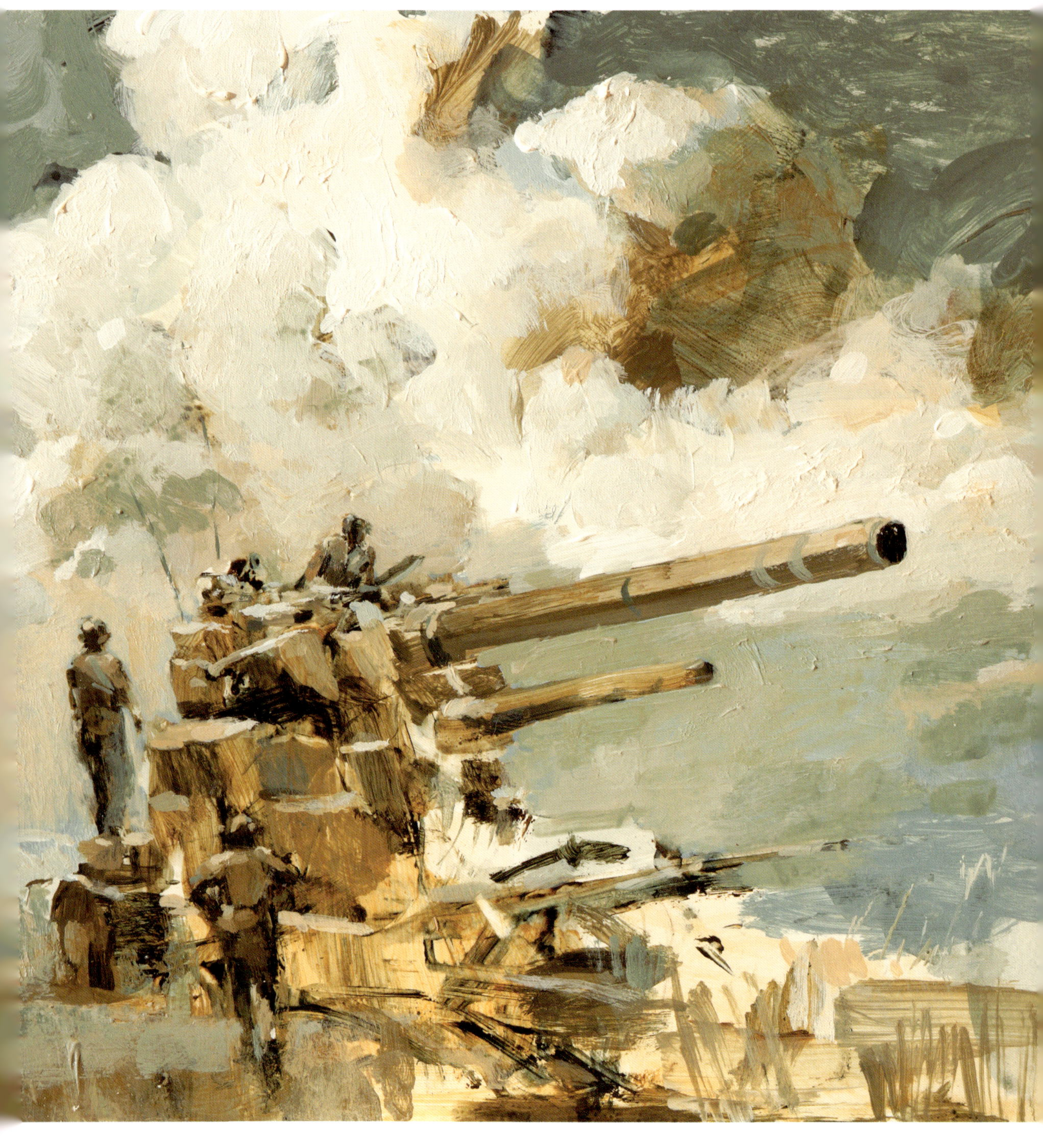

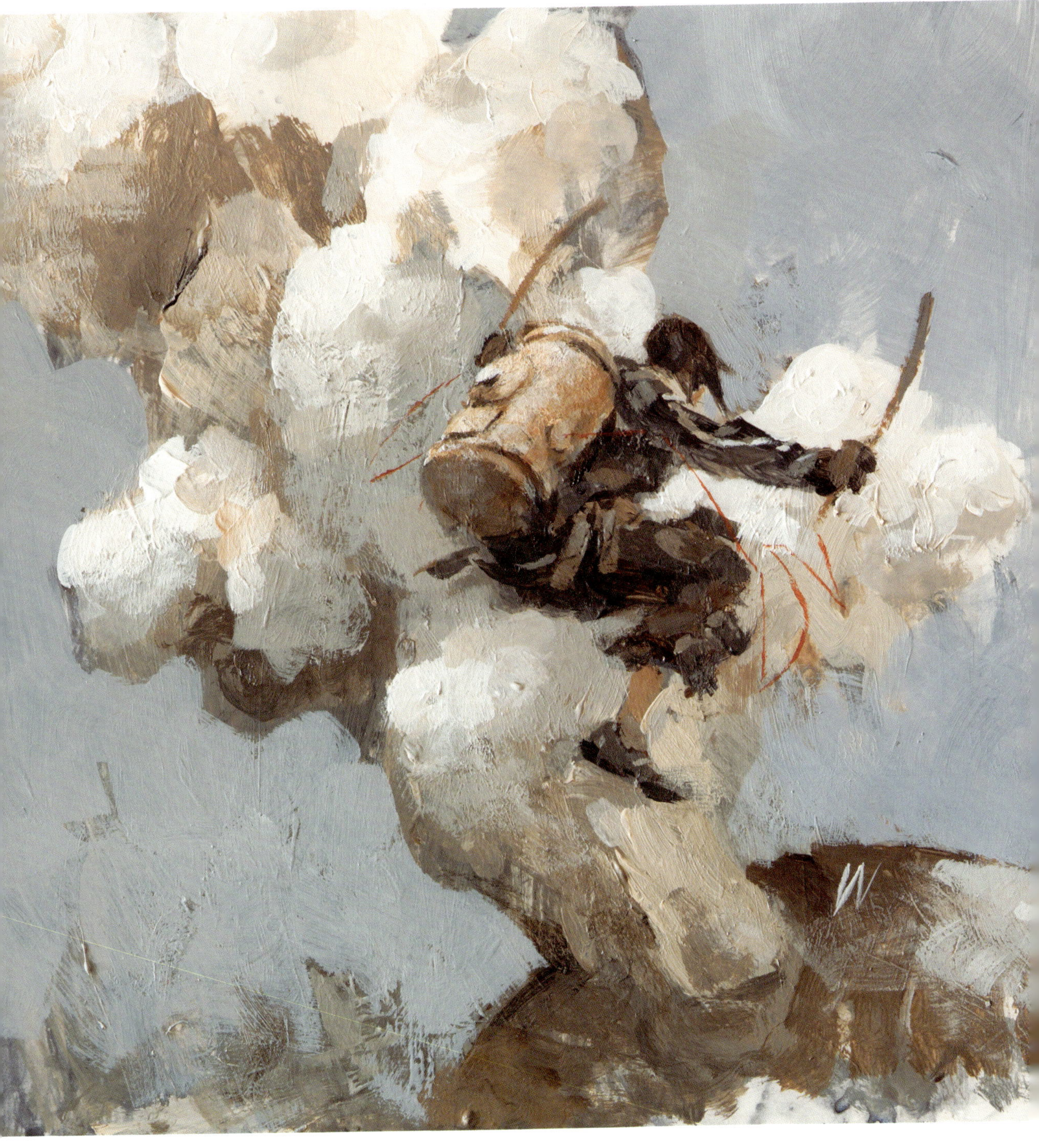

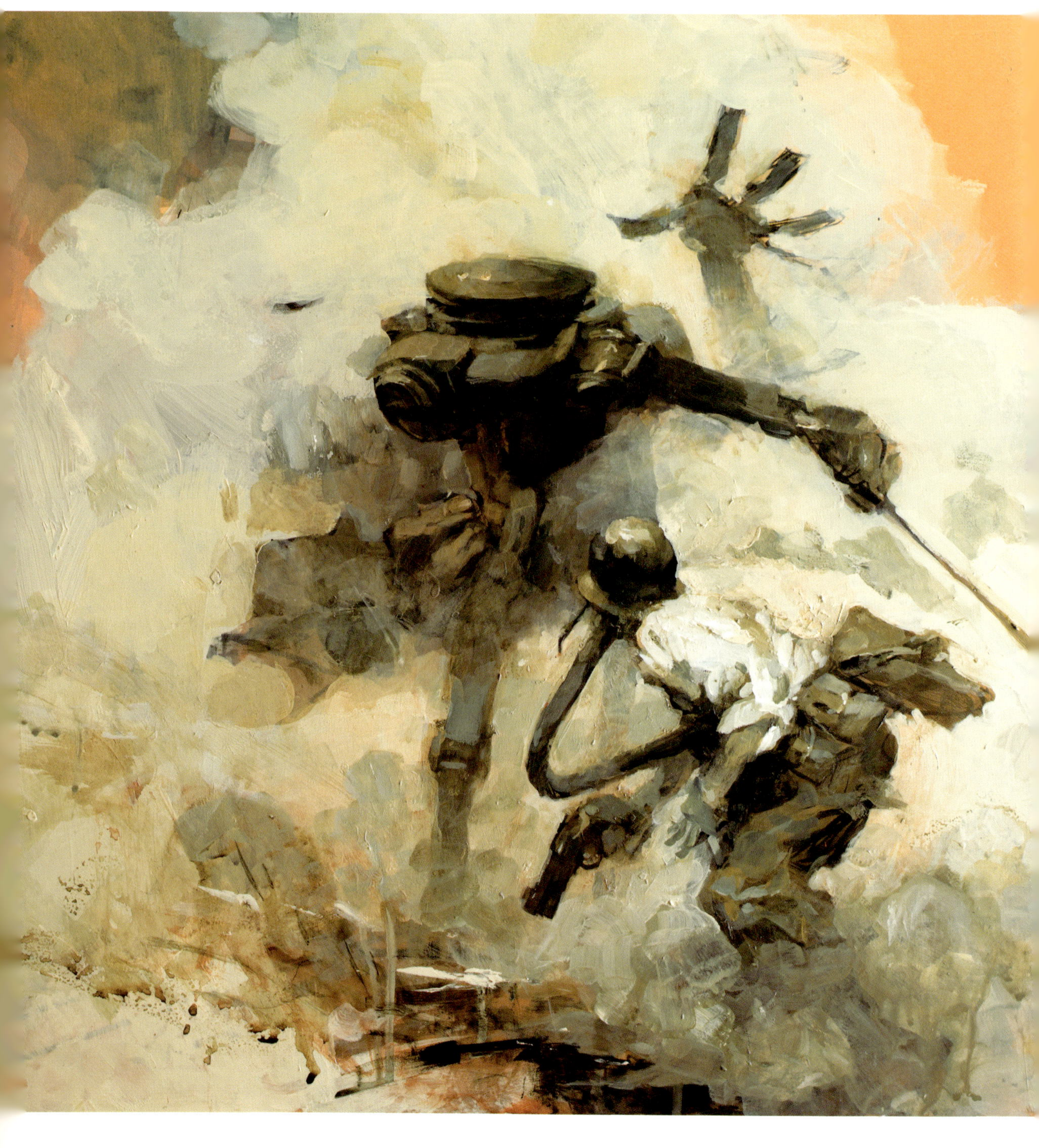

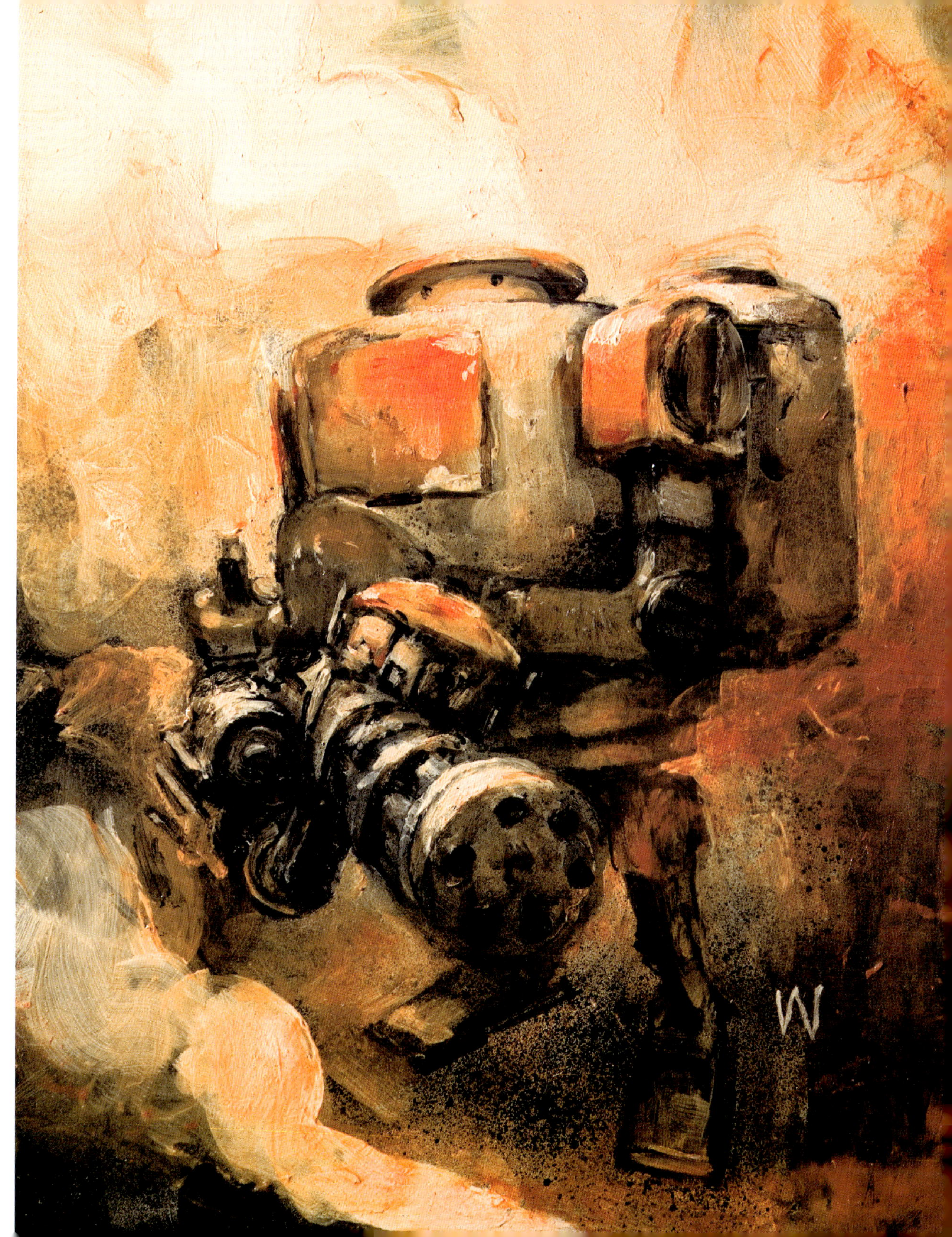

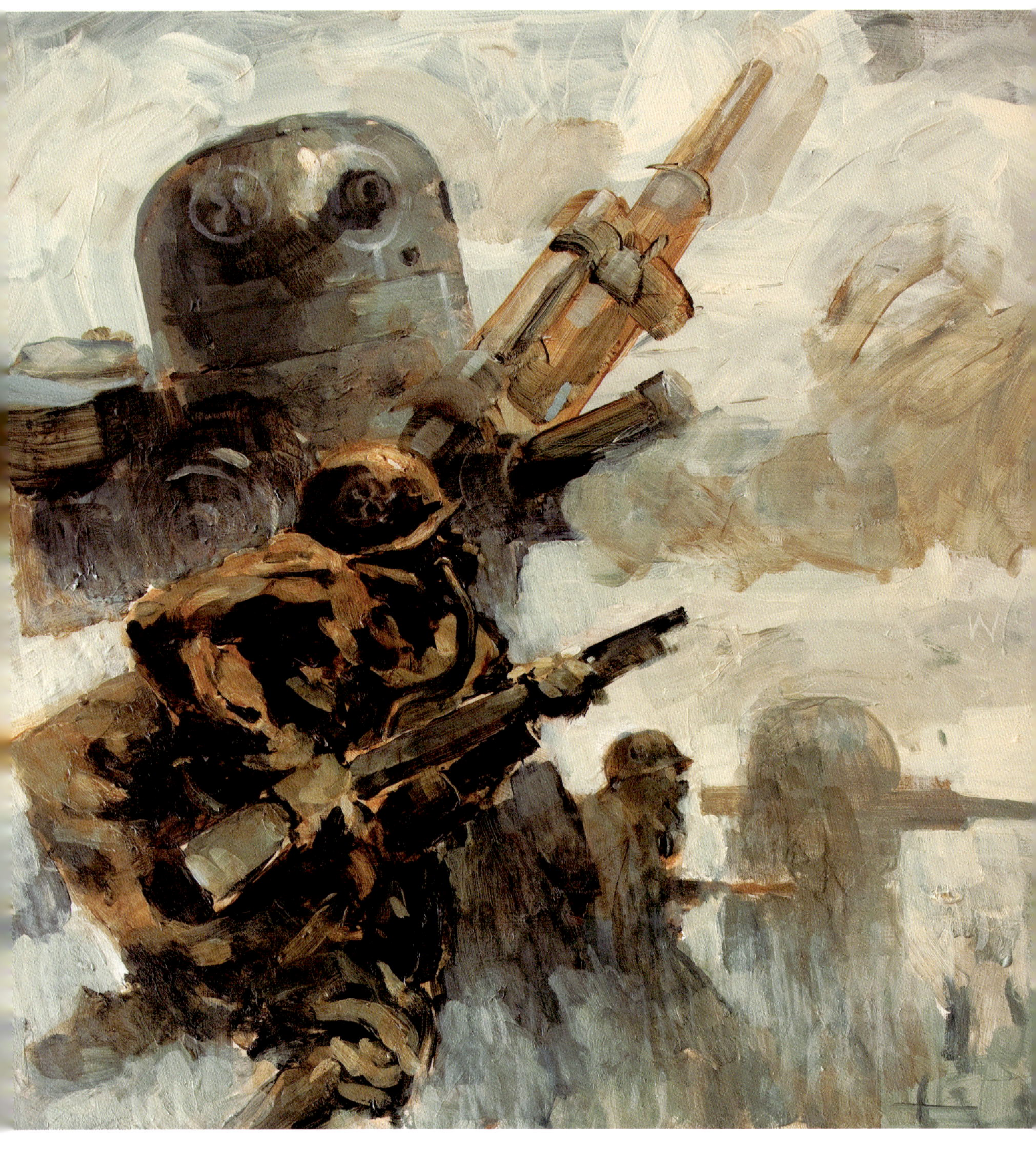

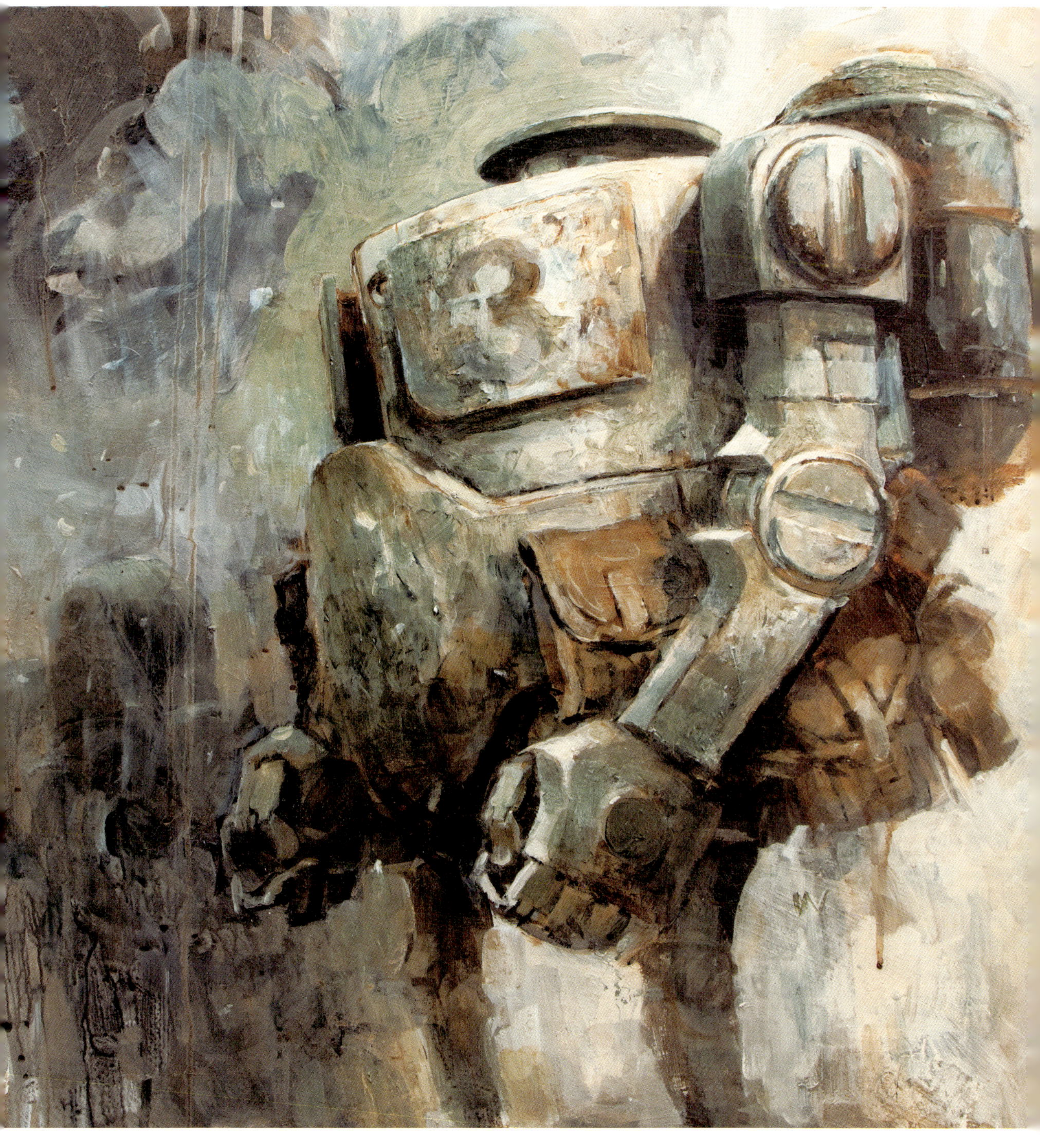

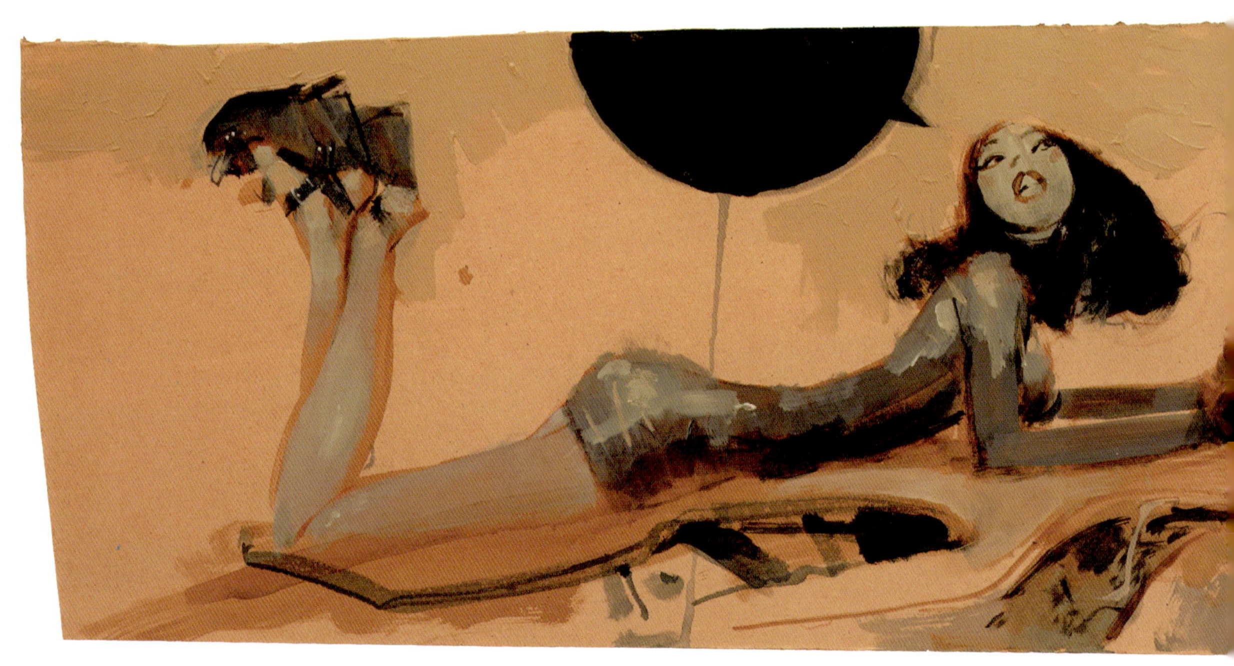

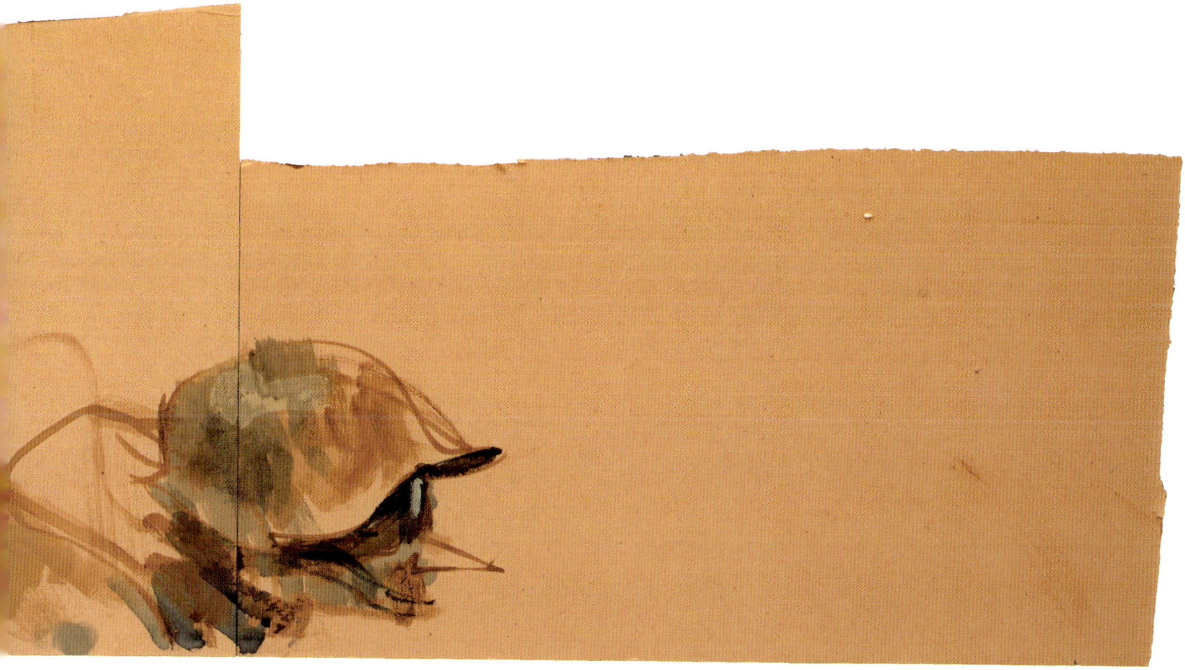

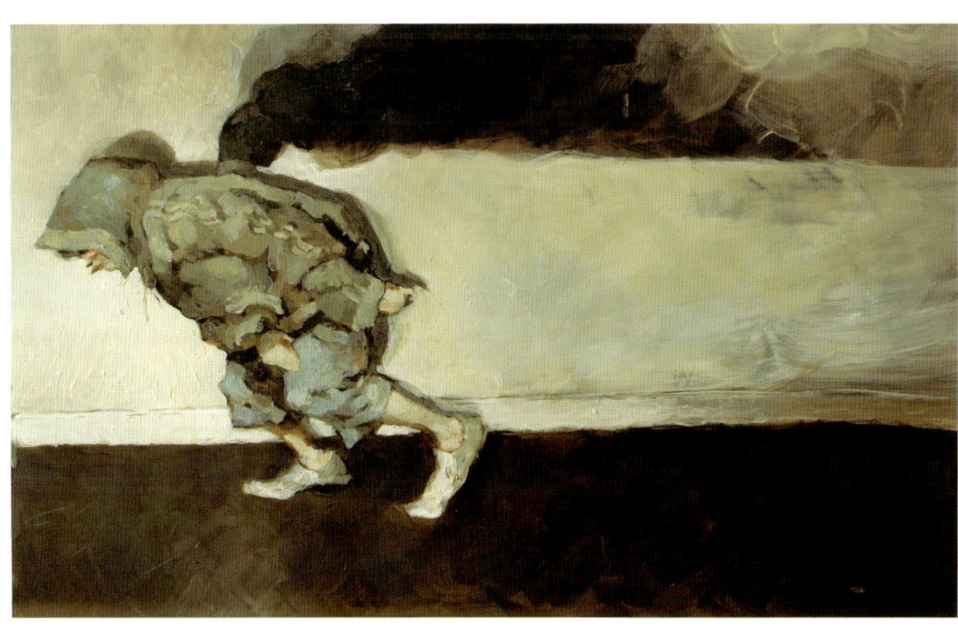

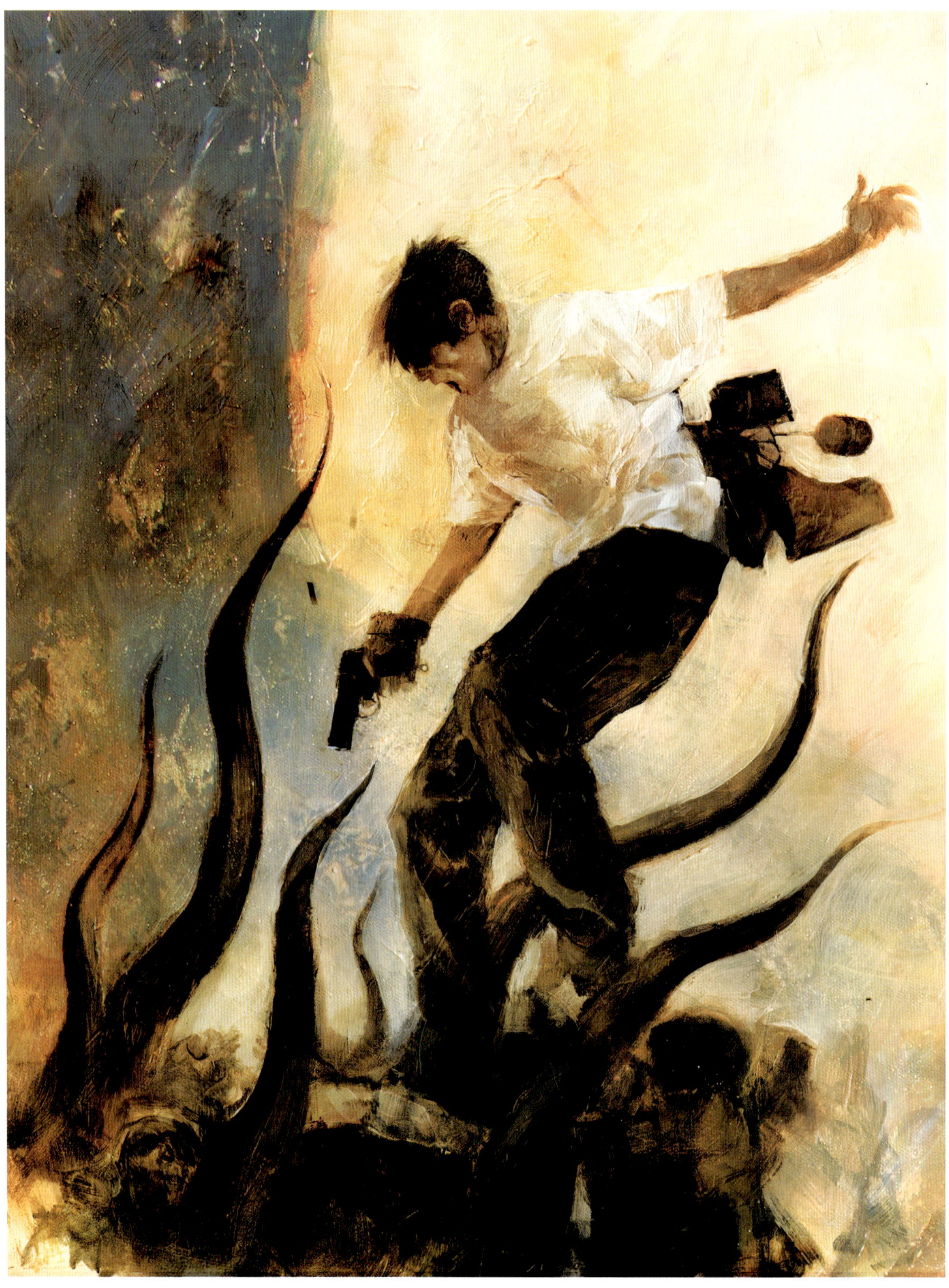

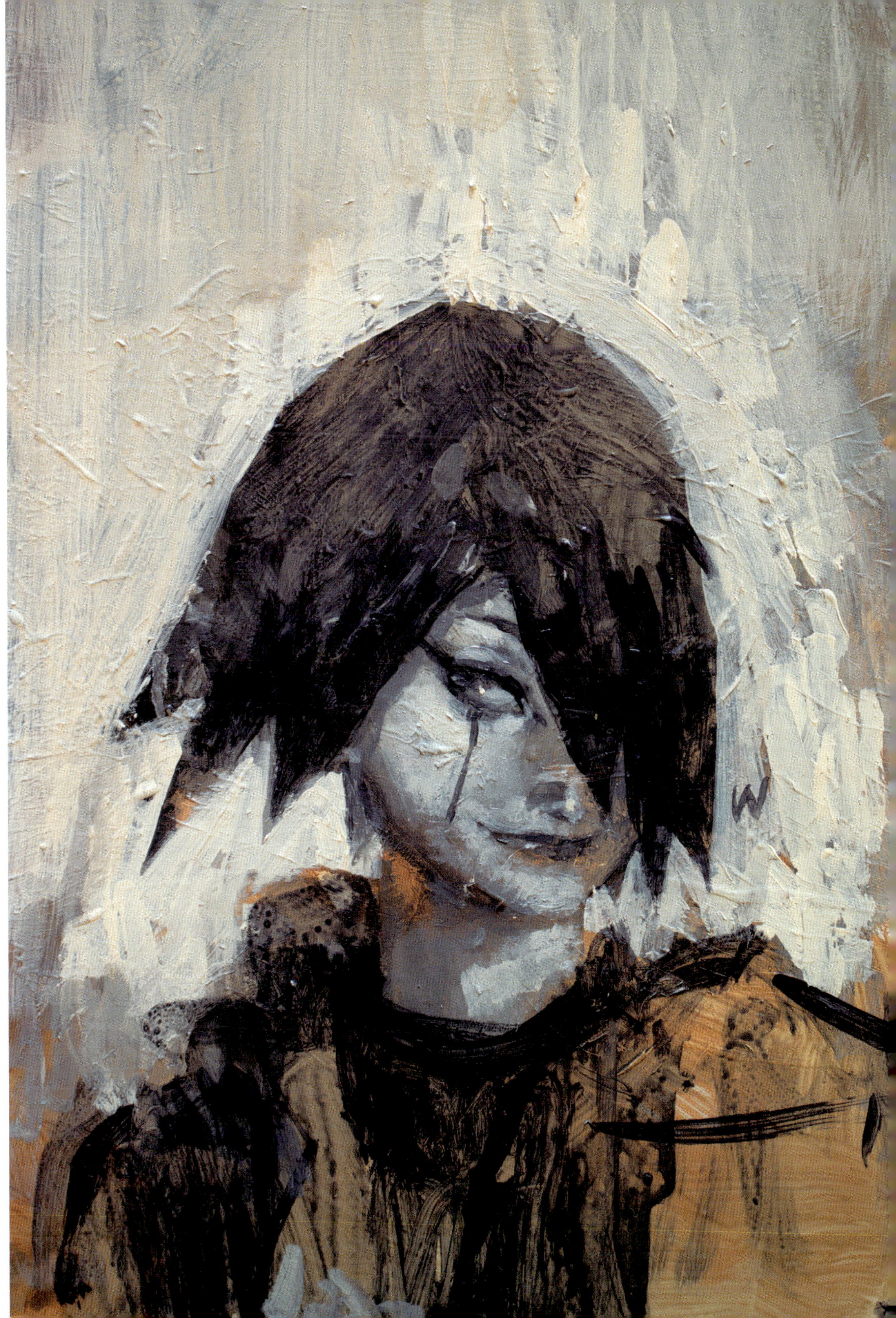

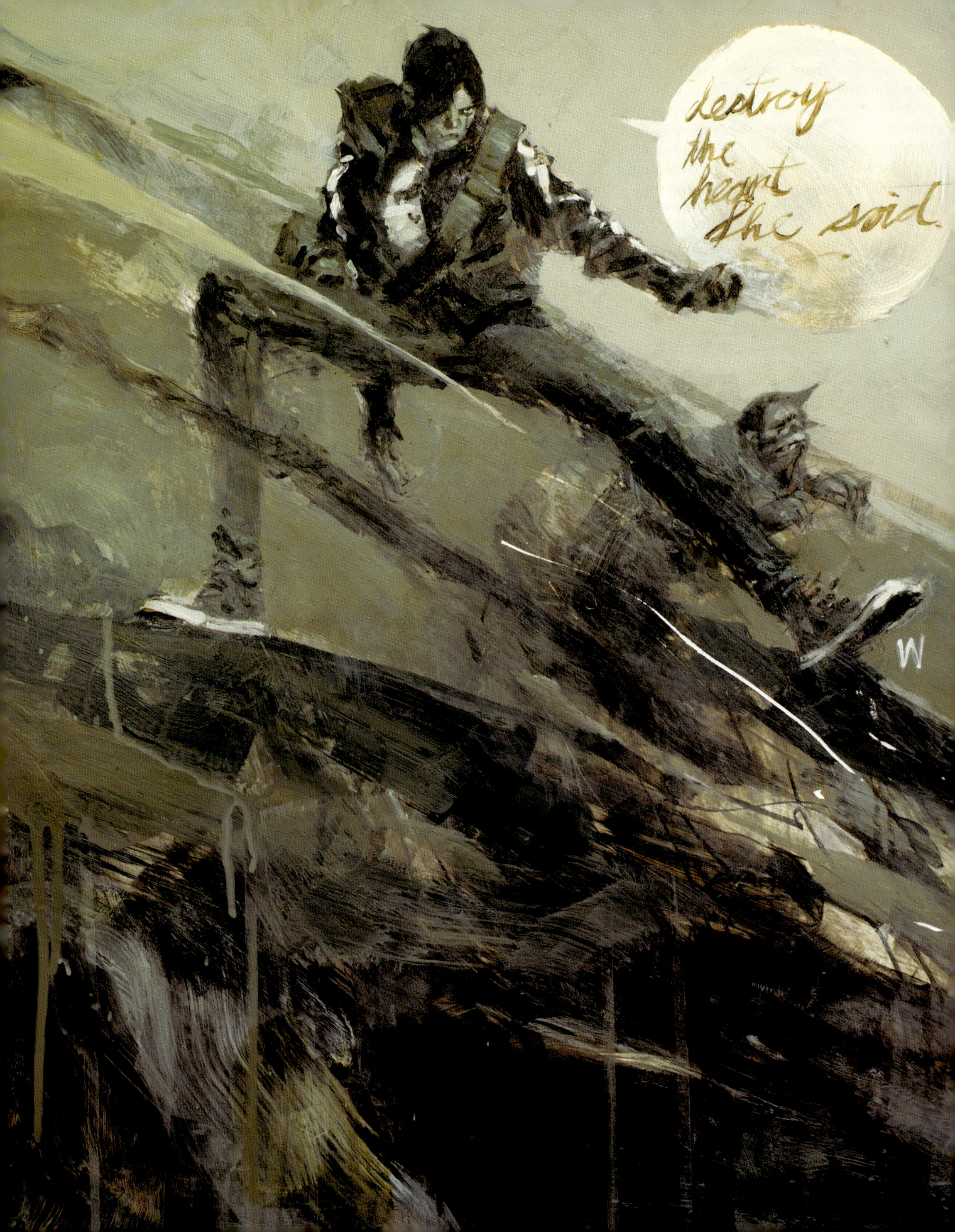

destroy
the
heart
she said.

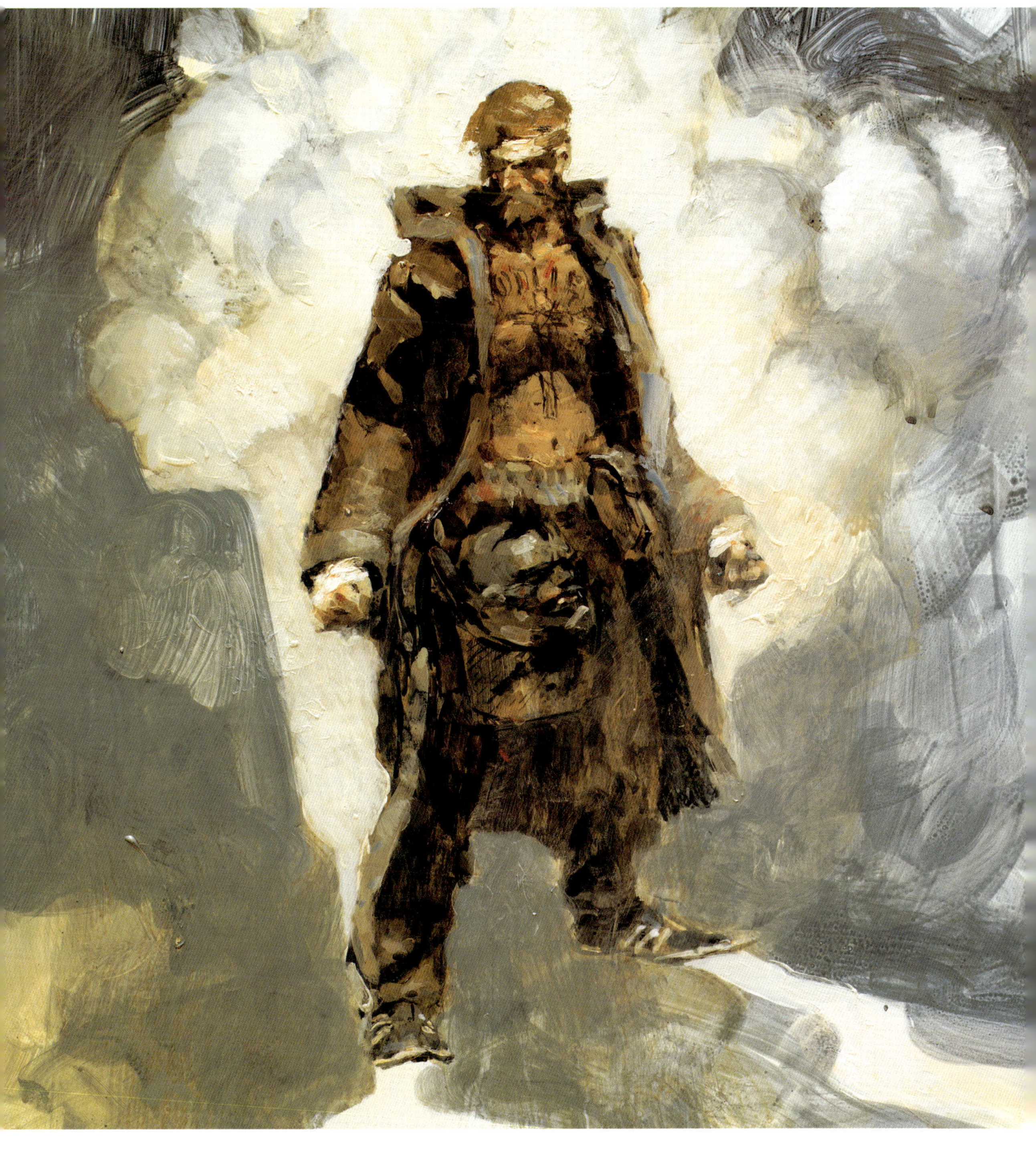

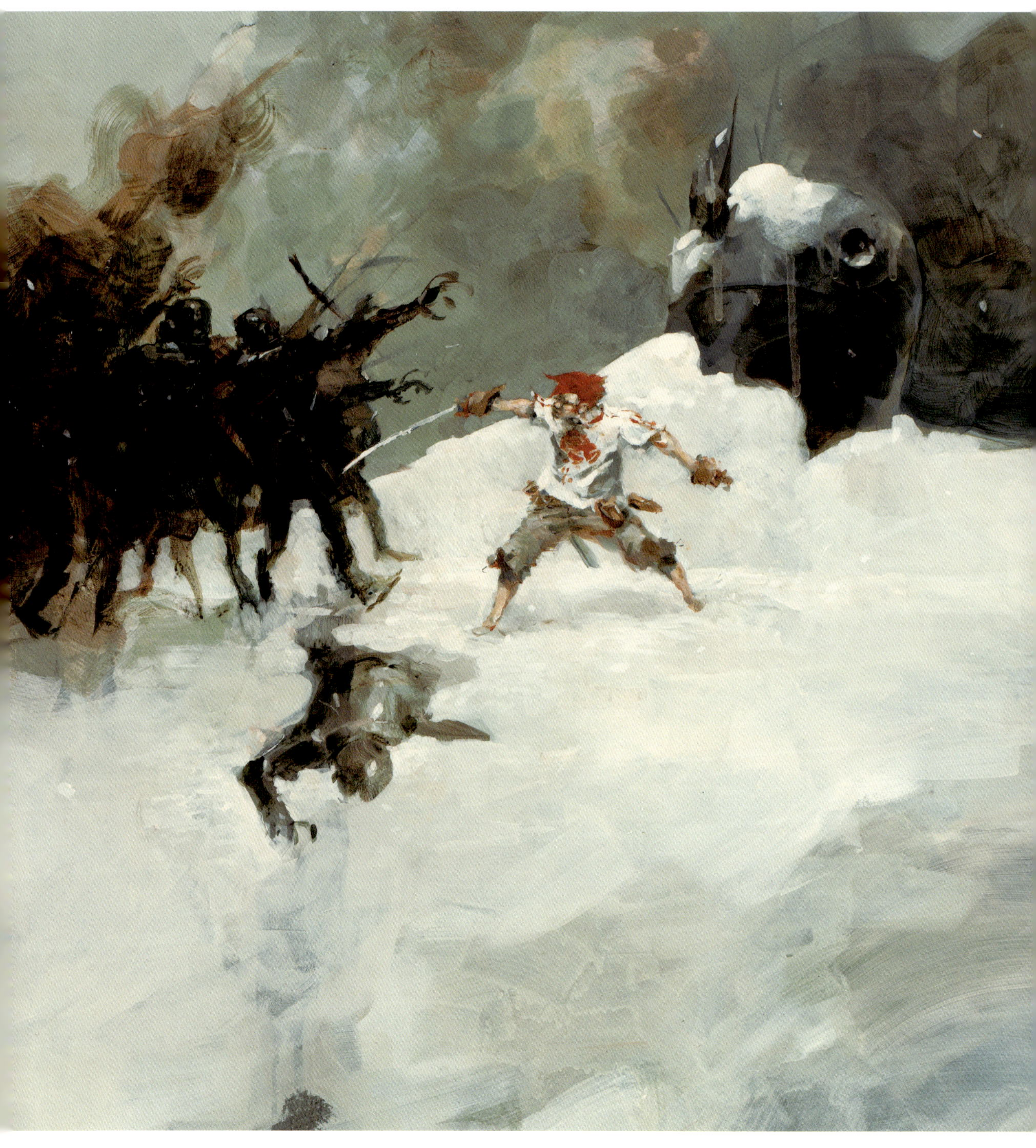

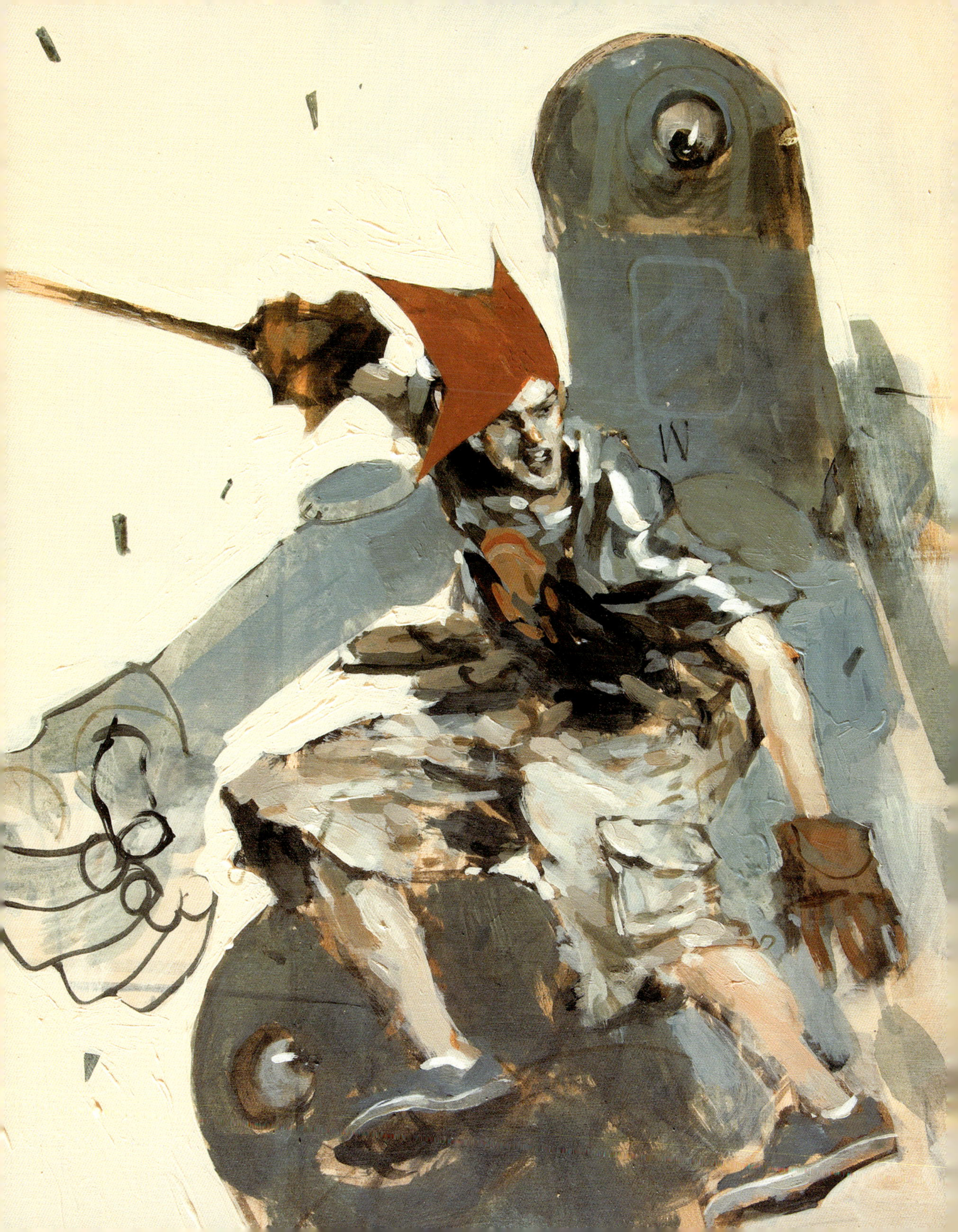

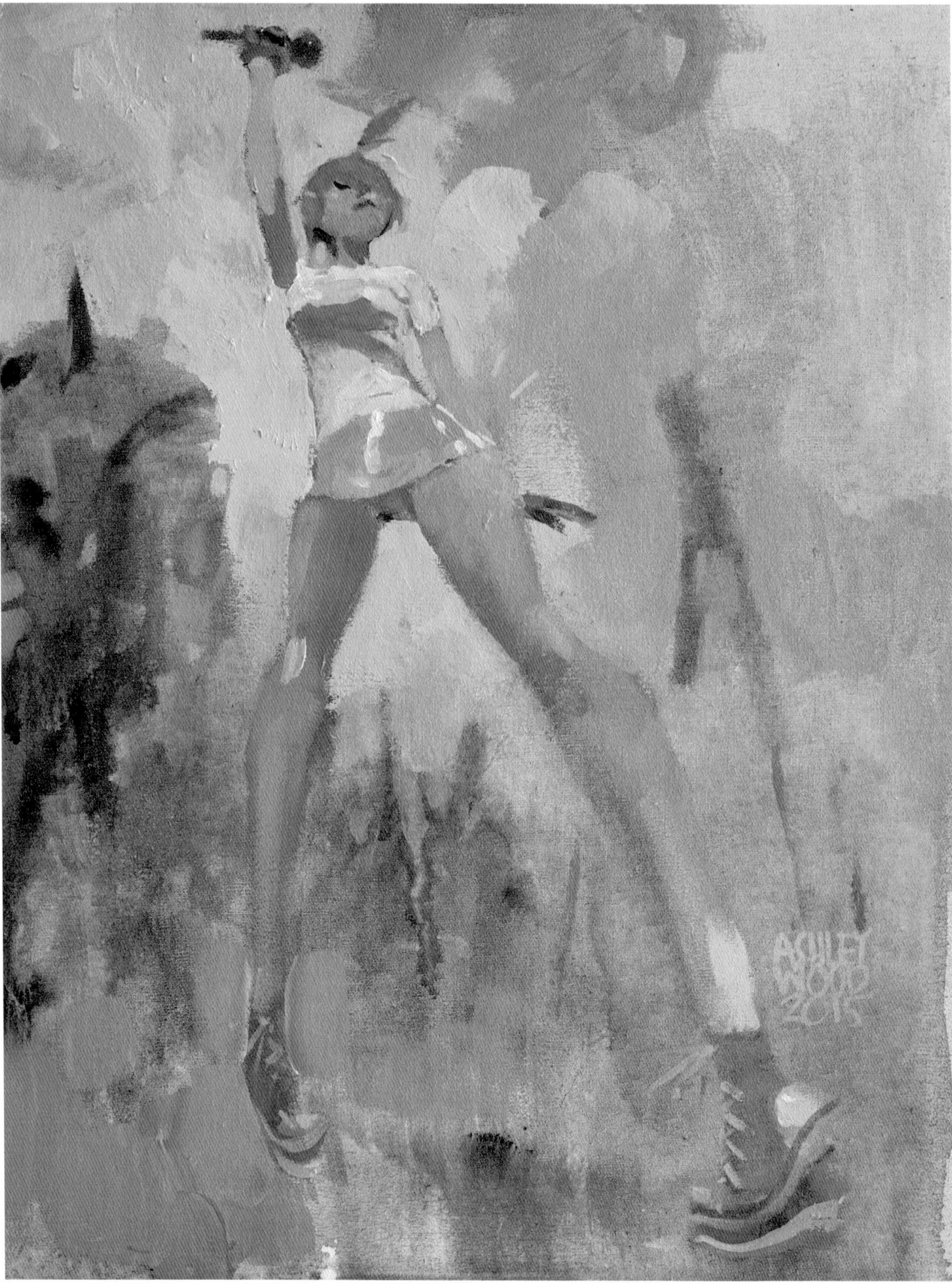

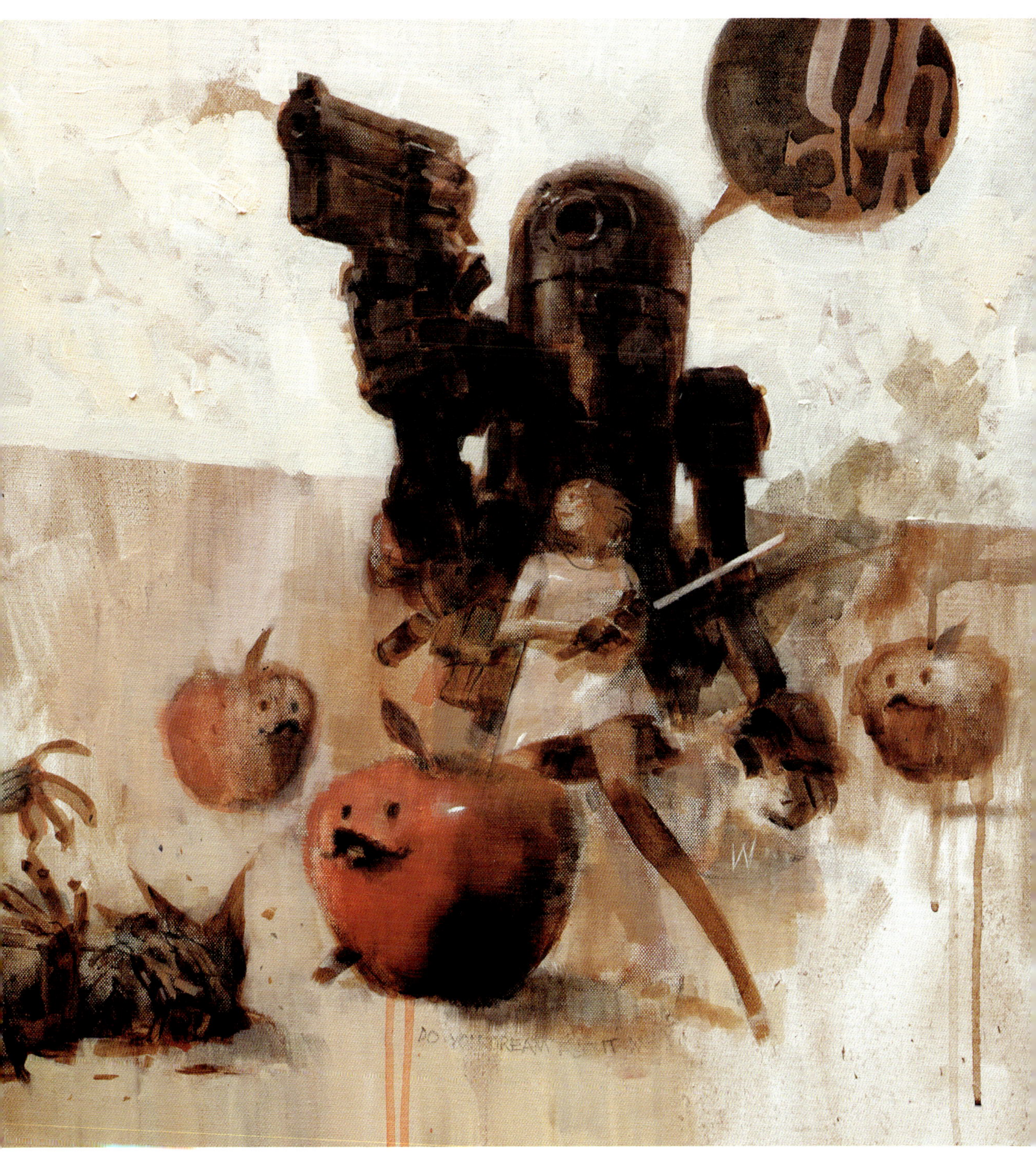
DO YOU DREAM

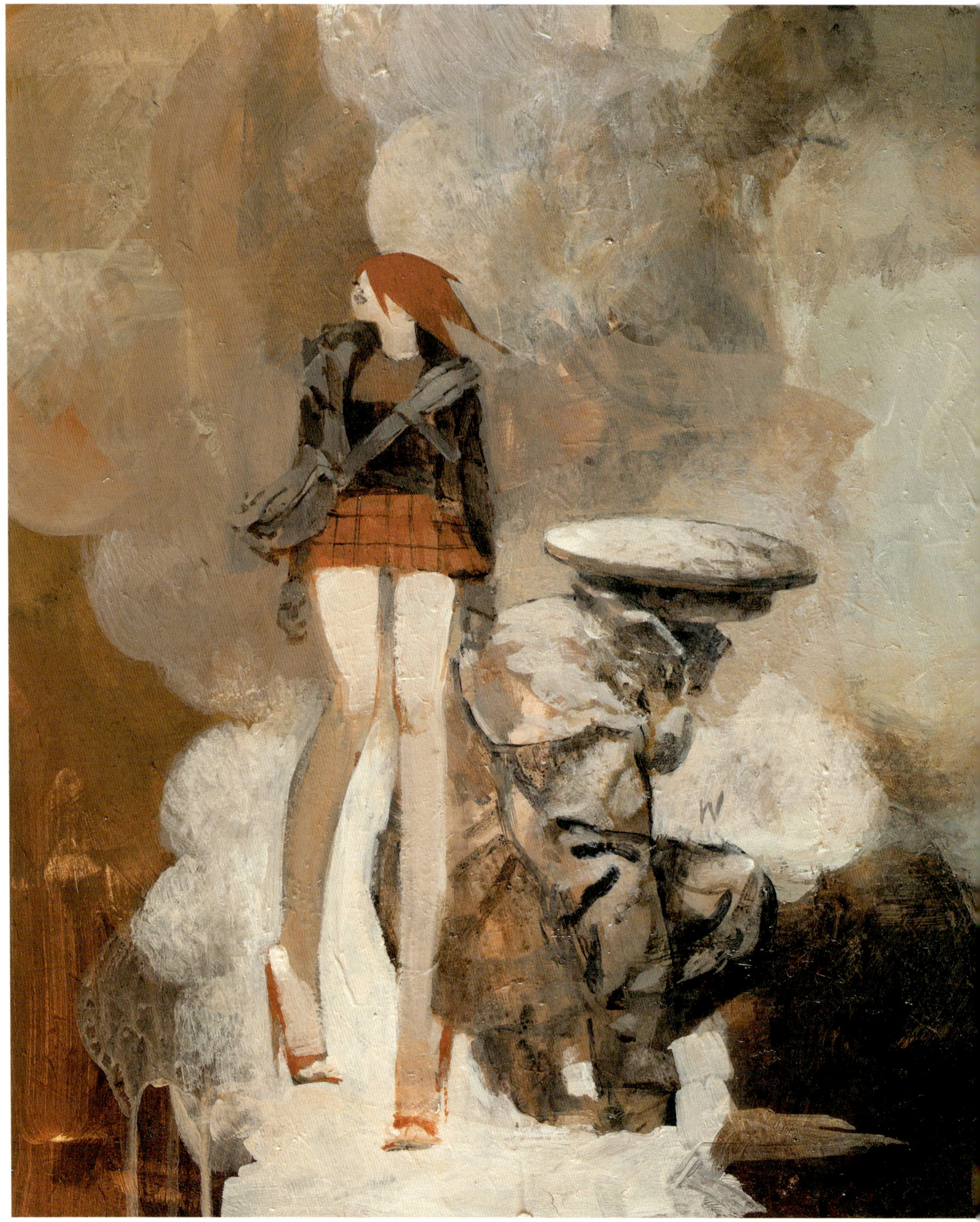

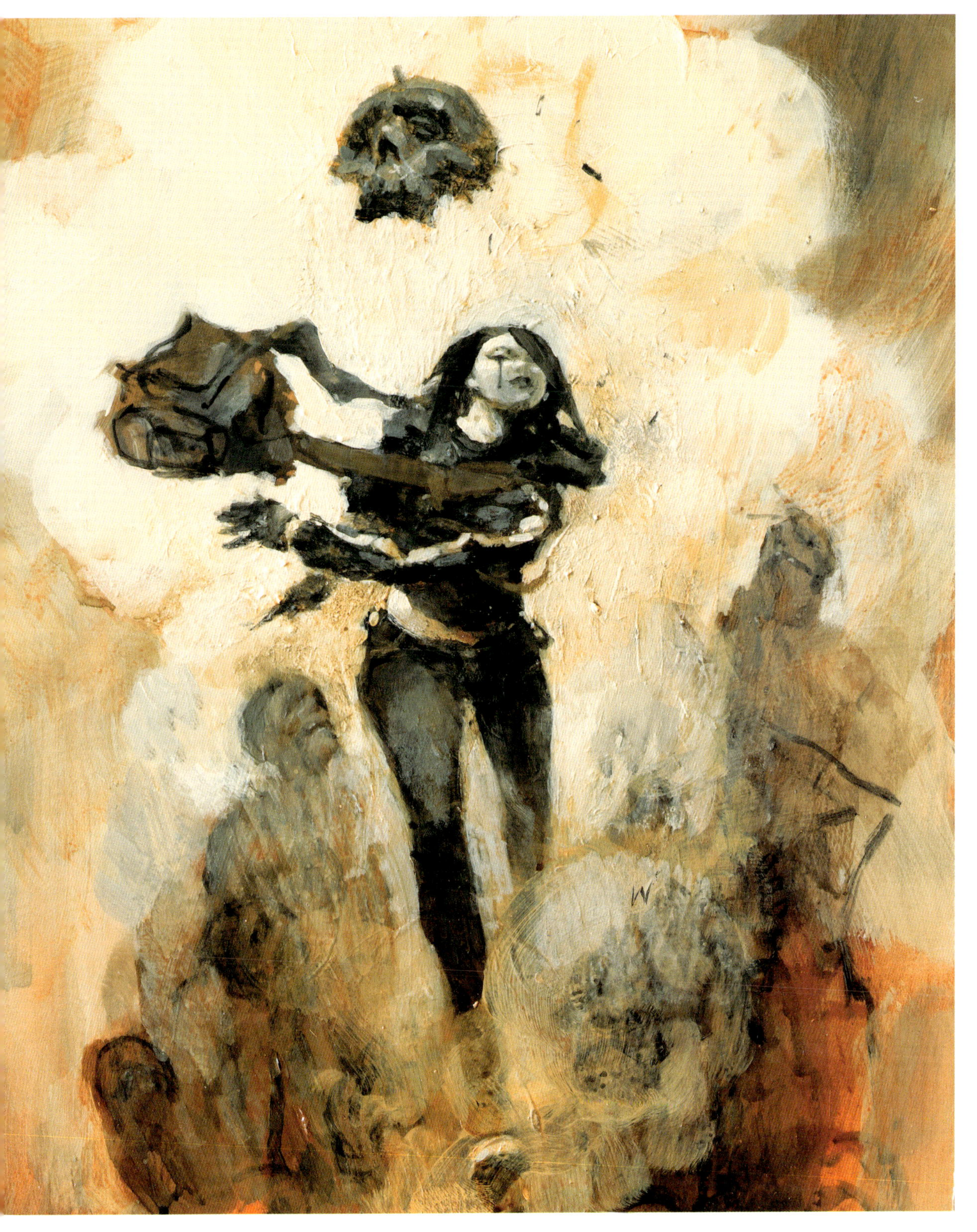

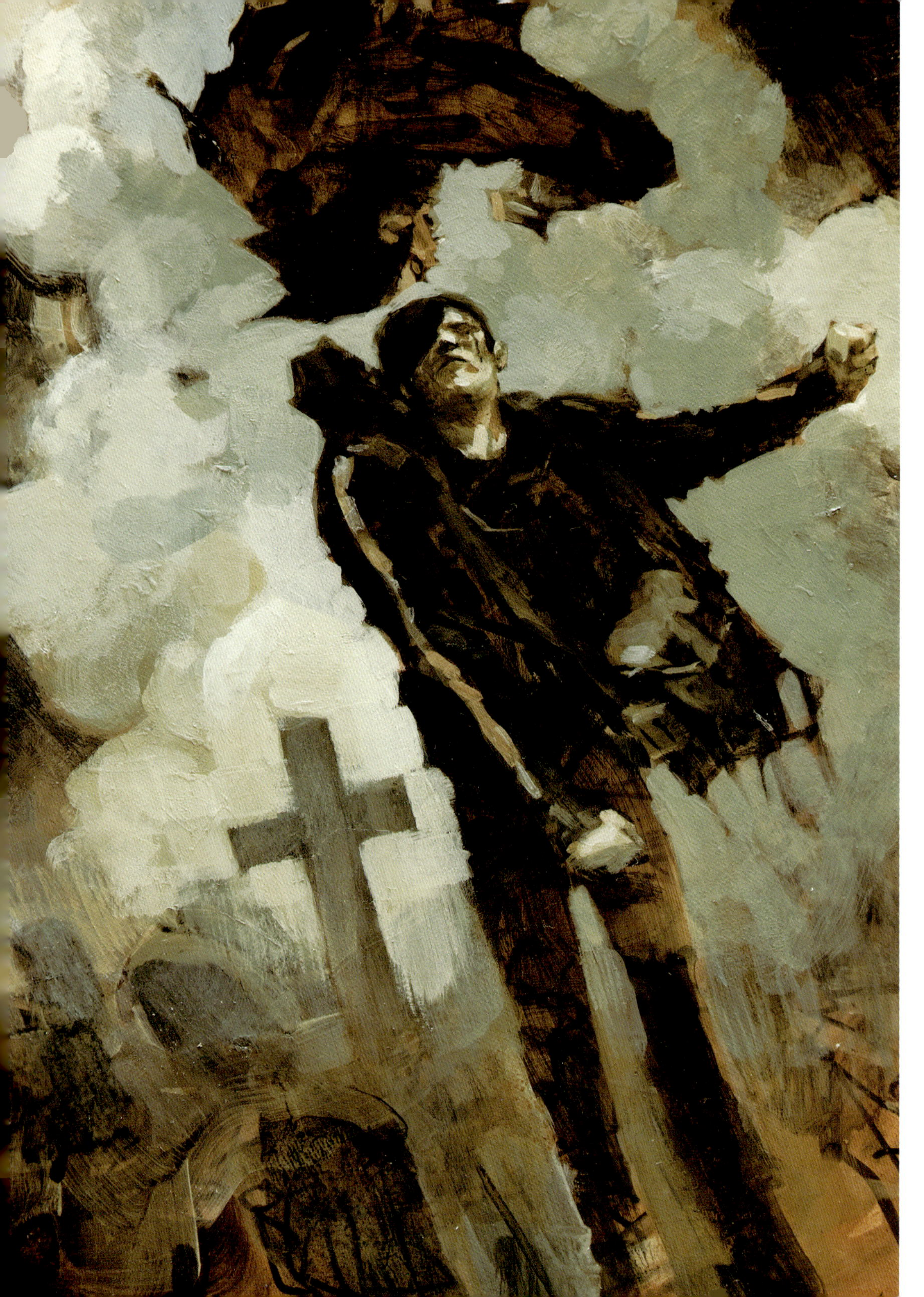

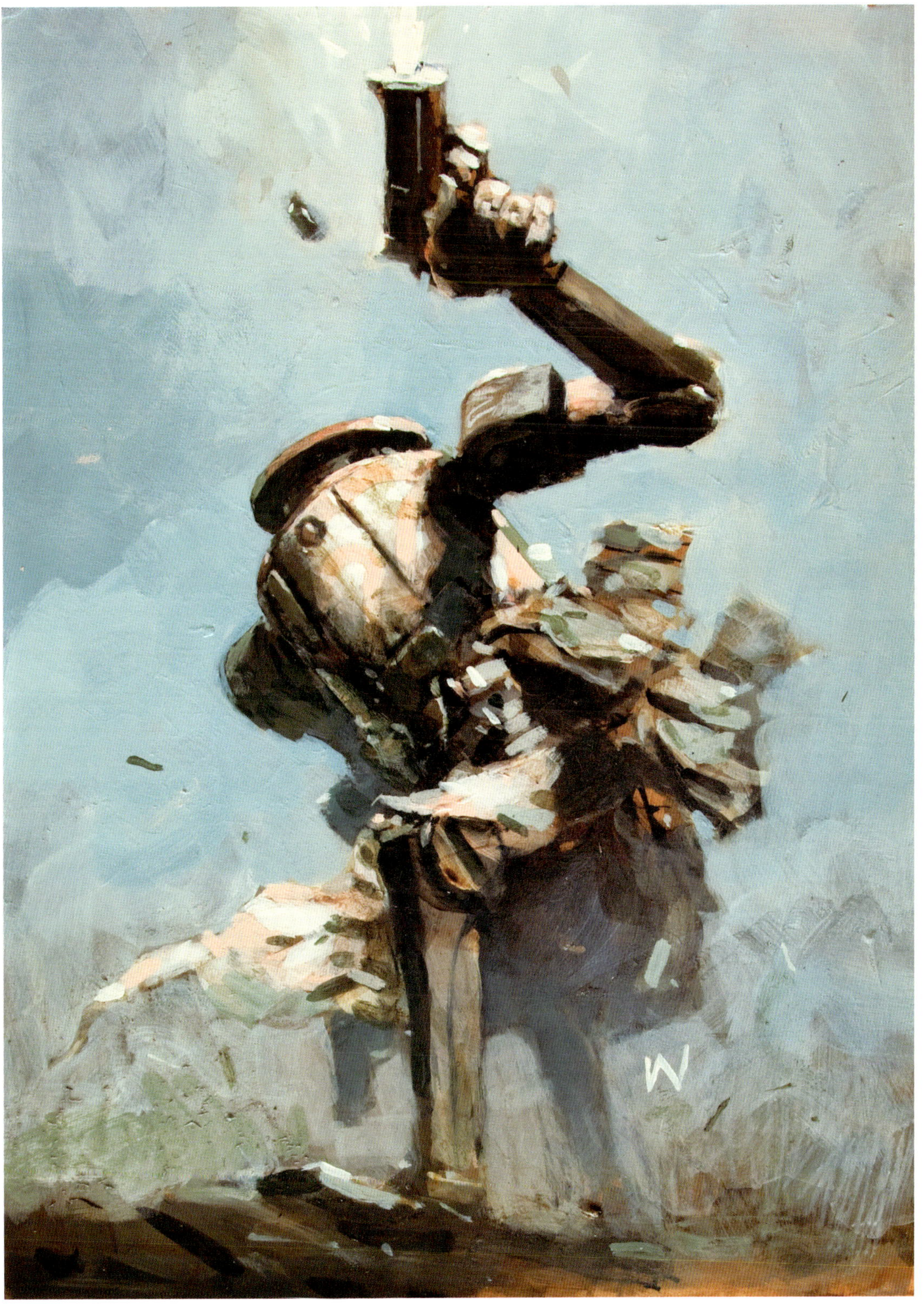

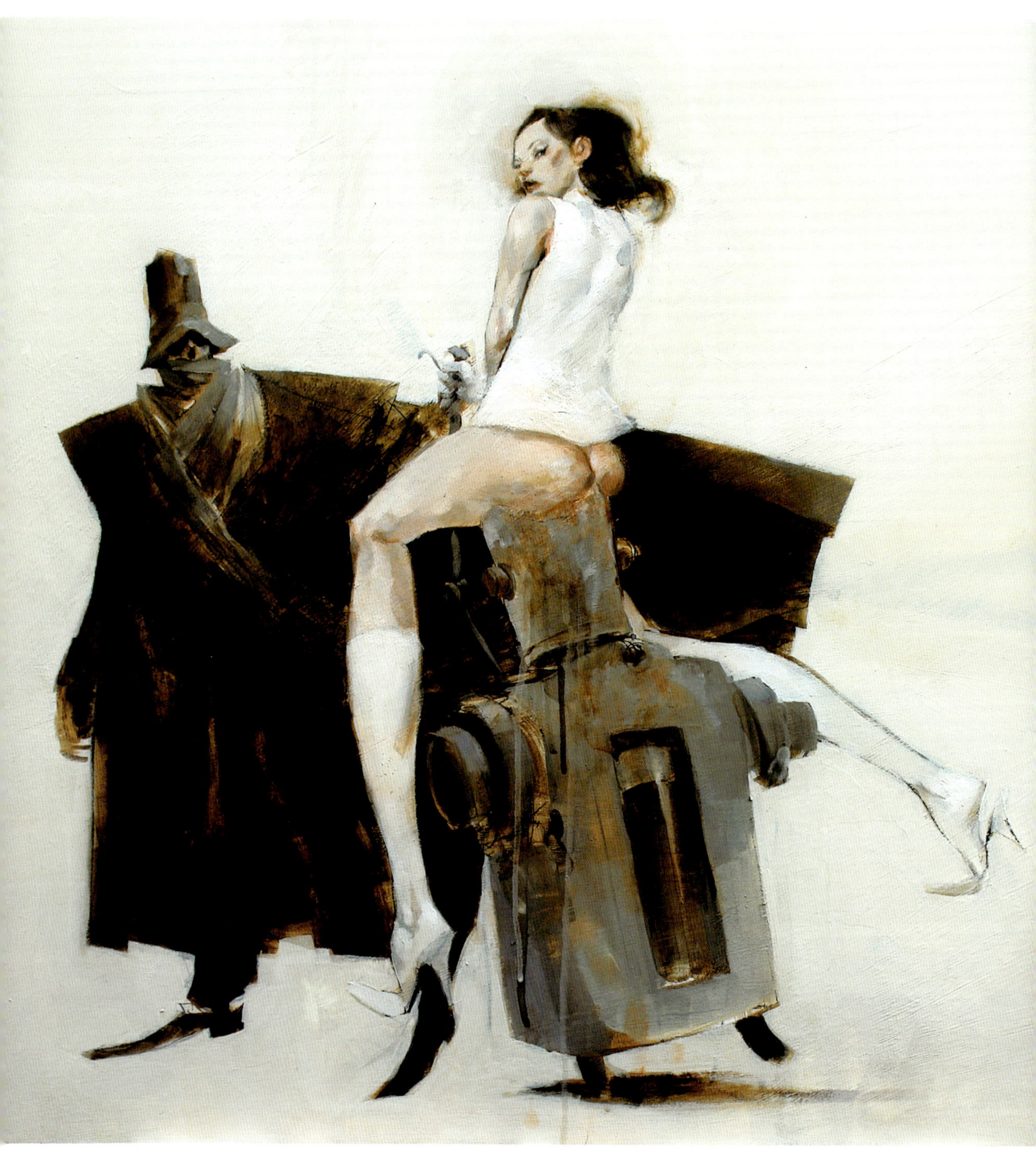

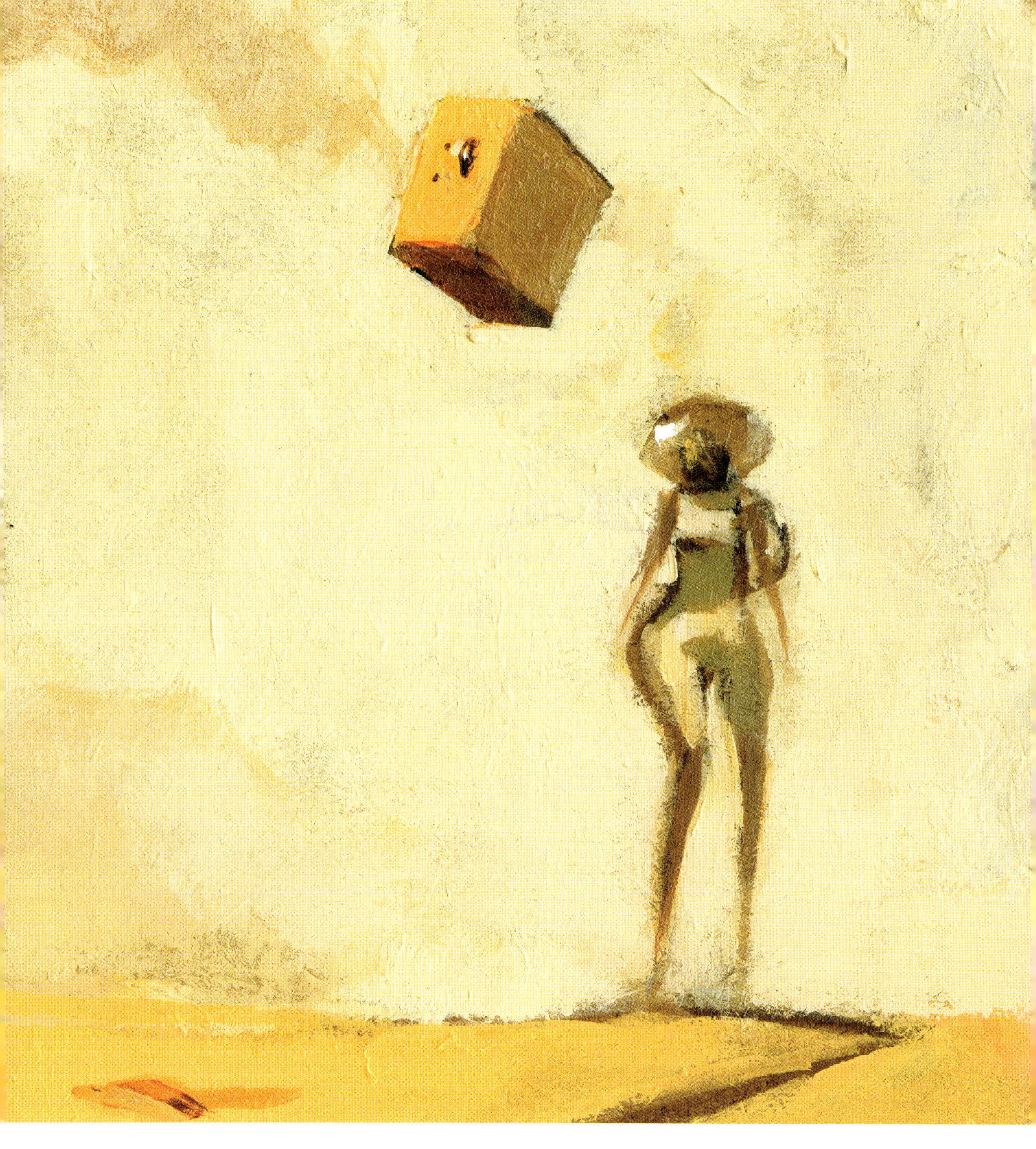

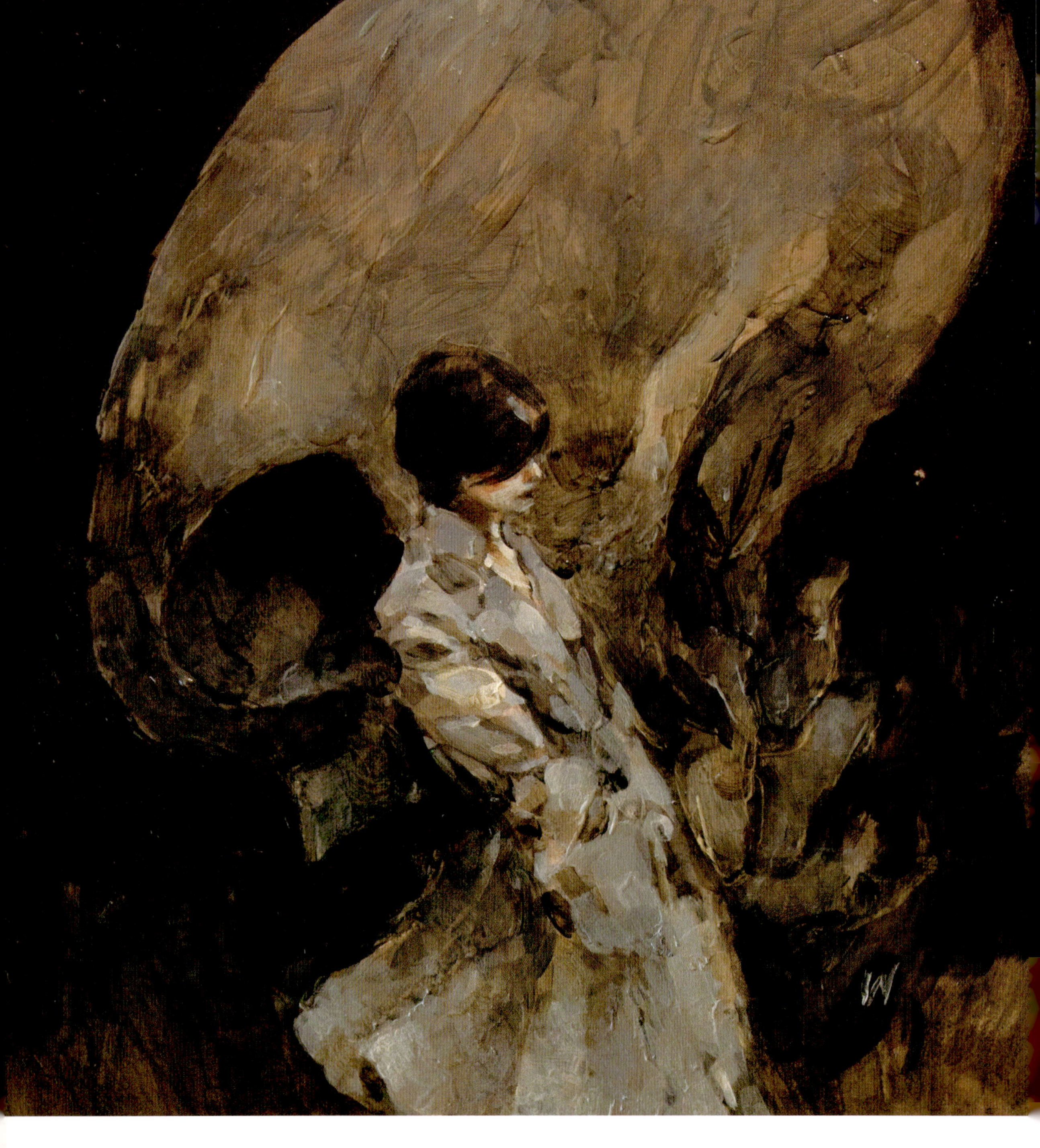

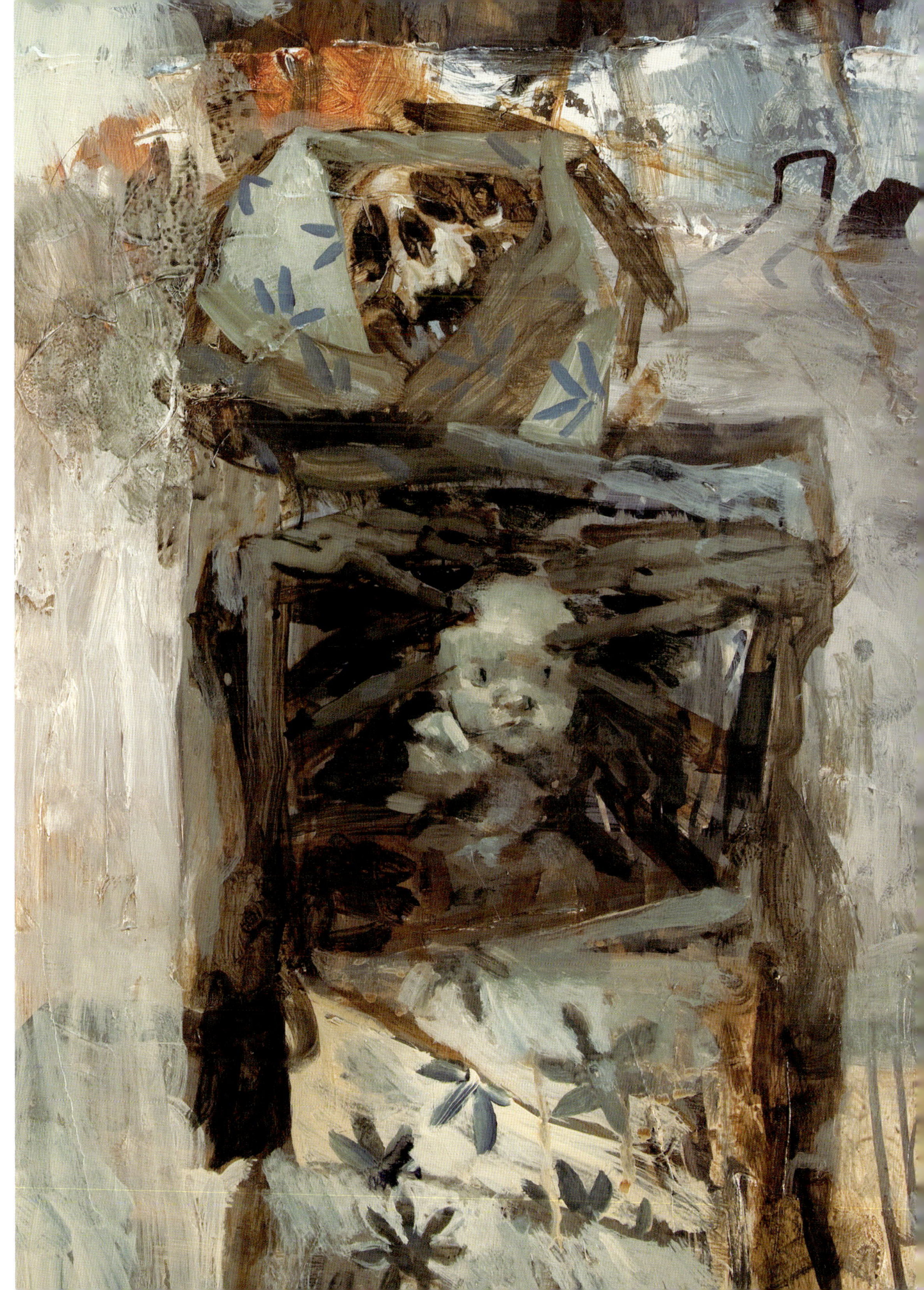

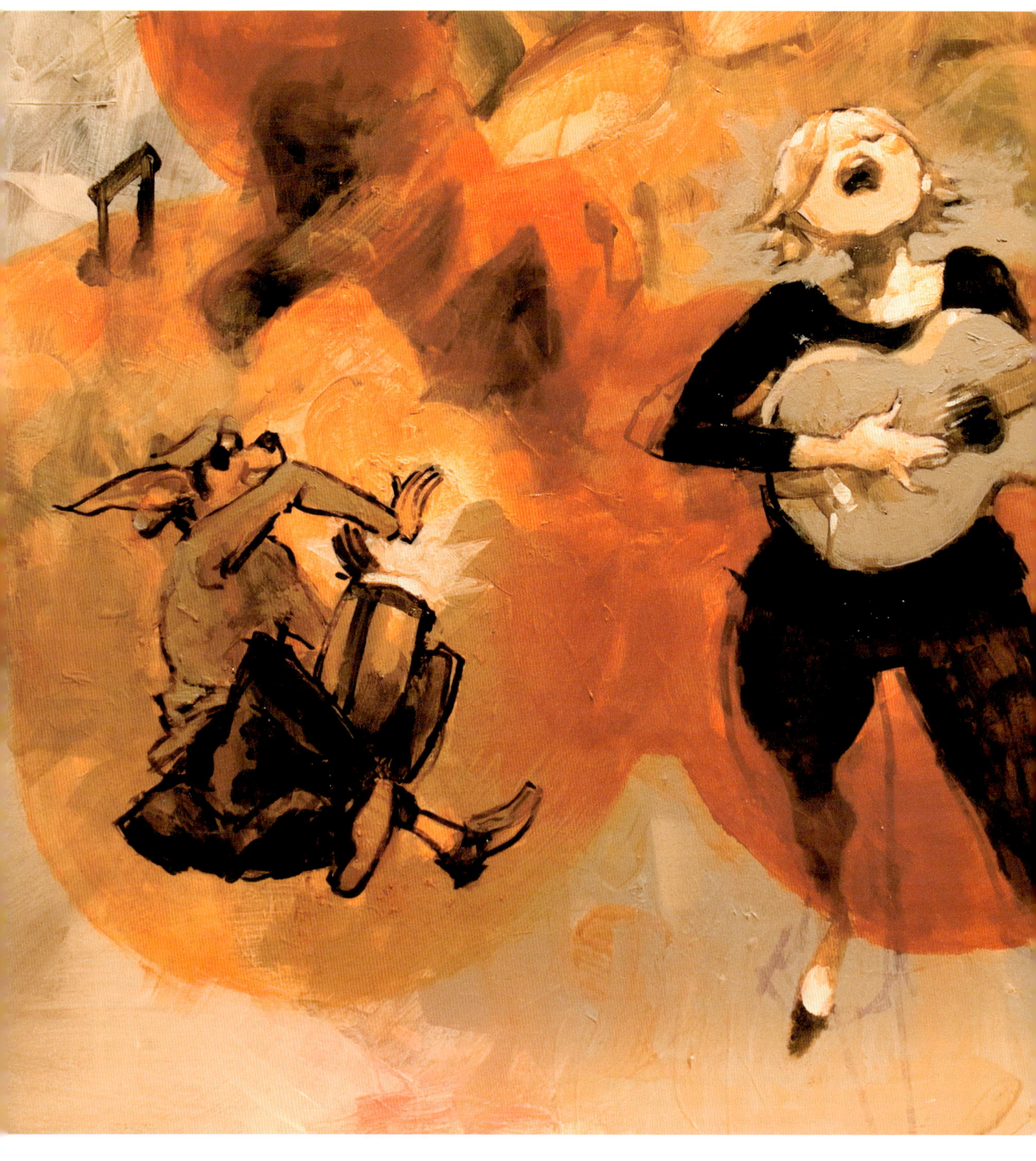

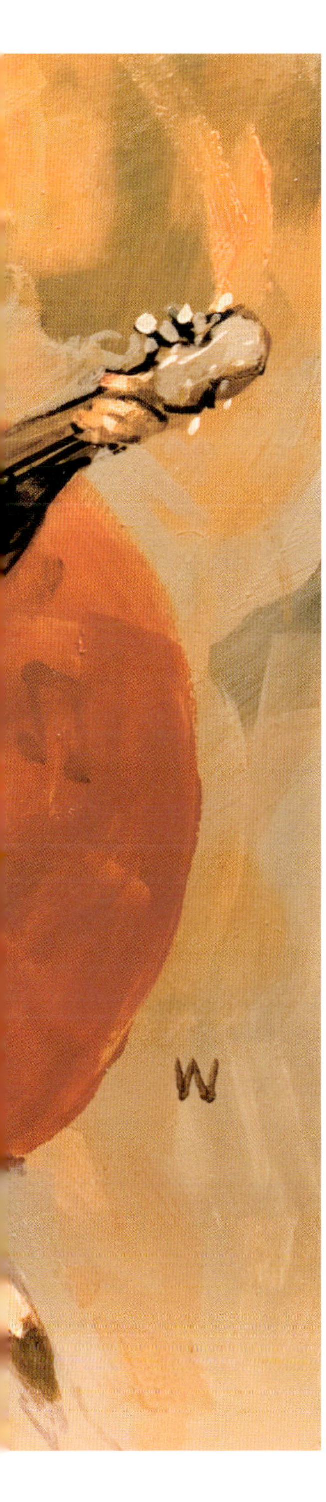

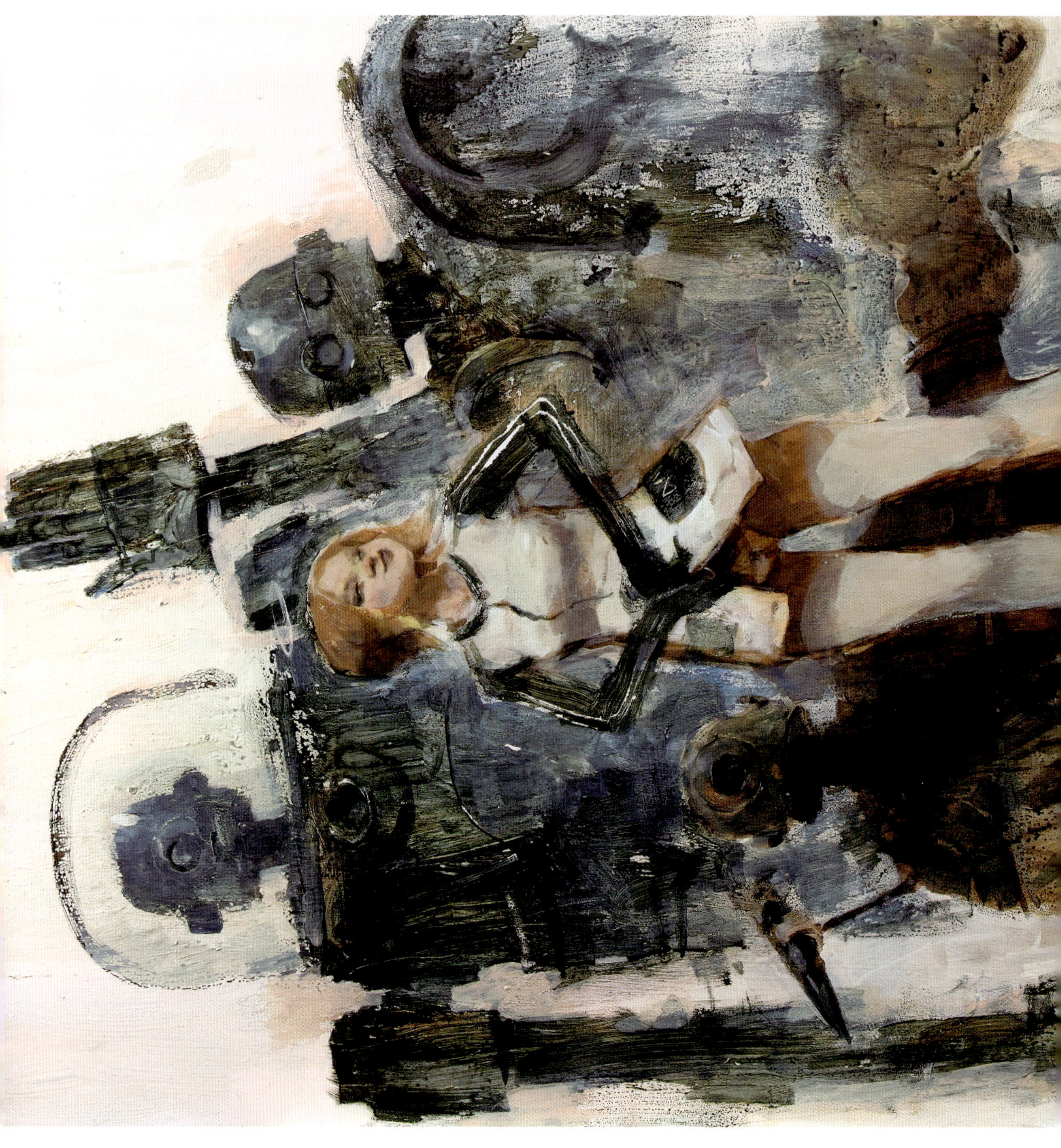

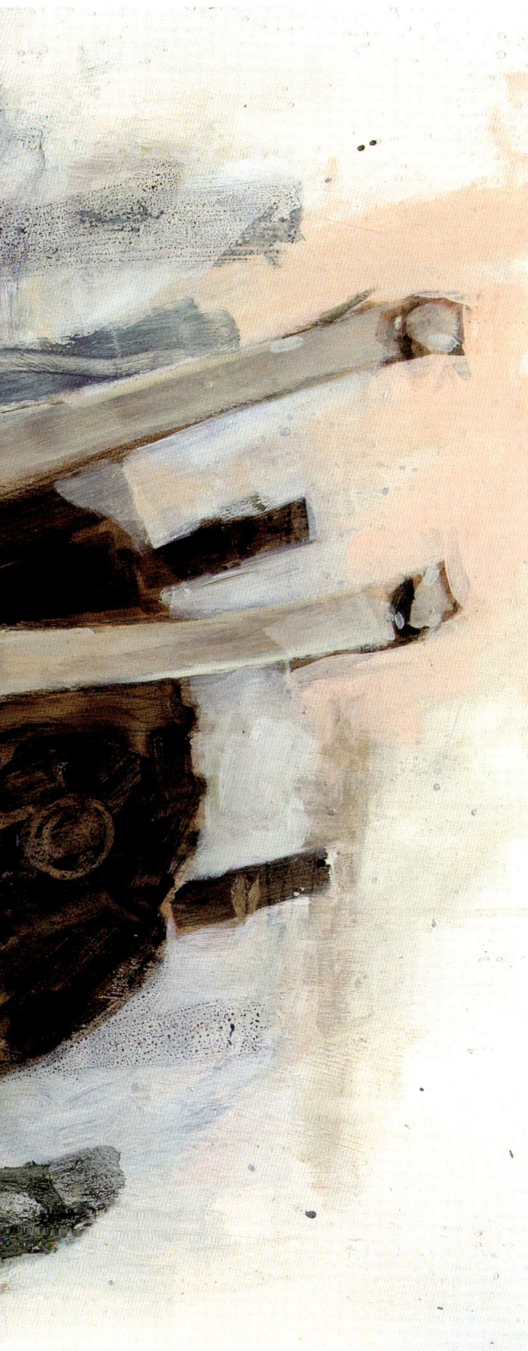

アッシュレイ・ウッド　画集
Zawa-zawa

2015年11月13日　初版第1刷発行
2024年1月6日　第6刷発行

著者　　　　　　　　　アッシュレイ・ウッド

翻訳・コーディネート　角家健太郎（three A）
デザイン　　　　　　　真々田絵（rocka graphica）

編集協力　　　　　　　田中里奈（ヒヨコ舎）
編集　　　　　　　　　大場義行

発行人　　　　　　　　三芳寛要
発行元　　　　　　　　株式会社パイインターナショナル
　　　　　　　　　　　〒170-0005 東京都豊島区南大塚2-32-4
　　　　　　　　　　　TEL 03-3944-3981　FAX 03-5395-4830
　　　　　　　　　　　sales@pie.co.jp

印刷・製本　　　　　　シナノ印刷株式会社

ザワザワ

Zawa-zawa
Treasured Art Works of Ashley Wood

PIE International Inc.
2-32-4 Minami-Otsuka, Toshima-ku, Tokyo 170-0005 JAPAN
sales@pie.co.jp

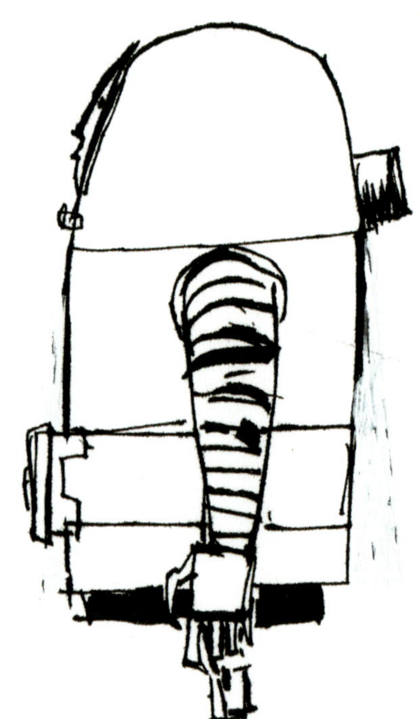